Modern Economics

PRINCIPLES, GOALS, AND TRADE-OFFS

M. Neil Browne
Bowling Green State University

Paul F. Haas
Bowling Green State University

Prentice-Hall, Inc., *Englewood Cliffs, New Jersey, 07632*

Library of Congress Cataloging-in-Publication Data

Browne, M. Neil, date.
Modern economics.

Includes index.
1. Economics. I. Haas, Paul F., date.
II. Title.
HB171.5.B724 1987 330 86-25256
ISBN 0-13-587940-X

To the flurry of motion called Nancy,
who refuses to accept that habit is a cruel tyrant, who bounds from experience to experience with astounding zeal, and who stretches locus of control to its outer limits.

M.N.B.

To Rosie, Greg, Karen, Christine, and Tim,
a family whose love and support provided the incentive to undertake this project.

P.F.H.

Editorial/production supervision and
interior design: Madelaine Cooke
Cover design: Lundgren Graphics, Ltd.
Cover photo: Stan Wakefield
Manufacturing buyer: Ed O'Dougherty

Printed in the United States of America

10 9 8 7 6 5 4 3 2 1

ISBN 0-13-587940-X 01

Prentice-Hall International (UK) Limited, *London*
Prentice-Hall of Australia Pty. Limited, *Sydney*
Prentice-Hall Canada Inc., *Toronto*
Prentice-Hall Hispanoamericana, S.A., *Mexico*
Prentice-Hall of India Private Limited, *New Delhi*
Prentice-Hall of Japan, Inc., *Tokyo*
Prentice-Hall of Southeast Asia Pte. Ltd., *Singapore*
Editora Prentice-Hall do Brasil, Ltda., *Rio de Janeiro*

Brief Contents

Contents

Preface

The one-semester introduction to economics course is a special opportunity. This course is especially important because it often provides the only contact most students will ever have with structured training in the principles of economics. Consequently, *Modern Economics* provides students with a foundation in economics that they can carry into the future. We are writing this book because we are dedicated to improving the level of economic literacy encouraged in the one-semester course. One-semester students deserve a book that will emphasize the relevance of economic concepts for their daily lives.

Modern Economics strives to teach students how to *use* what they will be learning. In this text we have consciously reduced the number of principles emphasized; we focus, instead, on only the primary economic principles. Our purpose is to improve students' critical reading and thinking abilities. We hope the result will be improved consumers of economic analysis.

Economics teachers face a dilemma. We recognize that for economics to be of lasting value to our students, we must emphasize ideas or principles that they can use decades after their economics courses. Furthermore, we pride ourselves in providing a tool kit that offers such promise. Students often feel more comfortable with a text that provides them with clear examples applying economics to current events. For this reason it is tempting to design a course around the immediate problems of the day. Yet such a strategy runs the risk of discounting the permanent significance of the principles of economics.

Our solution to the dilemma is described below. The thrust of our approach is to focus on only those economic issues and ideas that have staying power. Our illustrations and applications may be current, but the emphasis in the text will be on principles and problems that will probably be just as significant in the twenty-first century as they are now. As economics professors, we want to do more than just stimulate interest in economics. We would like the readers of *Modern Economics* to acquire skills and attitudes that will provide them with a richer understanding of their world.

LOGICAL AND THEMATIC ORGANIZATION

Modern Economics is divided into two major parts. The first consists of chapters that focus on a single economic goal, its advantages and disadvantages, the economic principles that enable students to understand how the goal is achieved, and international comparisons indicating how successful our economy has been in achieving the goal. The focus on economic goals helps explain *why* we study economics. Economics is useful; it helps us understand how to achieve our shared goals.

The meat of each of these chapters is the set of economic principles contained in the chapter. Our chapters consist primarily of the standard content taught by all economics teachers. These principles are taught within the framework of economic goals. Principles are included in a chapter when they enable students to understand how the goal is achieved. Thus, technical concepts are taught in terms of their function or use. Macroeconomics and microeconomics are integrated in this approach.

Particular economic goals have received special attention from professional economists. Hence, it is sometimes necessary to use multiple chapters to explain the process of reaching a particular goal. Because we share the belief of most instructors and students that short chapters are optimal, we wanted to avoid the type of lengthy chapter that would have been necessary to present adequately the goal of full employment and related economic principles. Thus, a goal such as full employment receives attention in several chapters.

The second major part of *Modern Economics* consists of a discussion of some of the major trade-offs that complicate economic decision making. In Part II the student is shown how individual goals can be attained. Part III describes the costs associated with achieving particular economic goals. Just as the goals discussed in Part II are permanently important, the trade-offs in Part III are ongoing problems that students will probably face during their lifetimes. For example, chapters in Part III examine the trade-off between efficiency and equity and the trade-off between full employment and price stability. Again, as in Part II, economic principles are taught in each trade-off chapter. By placing the basic ideas of economics in a useful context, students are able to see why they are being asked to learn specific principles.

ACTIVE LEARNING AND CRITICAL-THINKING APPROACH

An economics text is more than just an economics book; it can make an outstanding contribution to the student's general education. It can provide an opportunity for enlarging the learner's basic thinking and reading skills. Because we want the beginning economics course to have a liberal arts emphasis, we have designed our text to require its readers to interact with it in a spirit of critical inquiry.

Most professors are cognizant of the contribution that workbooks and supplementary readings books can make to the beginning course; yet they are understandably reluctant to require students to buy supplementary books. This text includes features that incorporate the review and application opportunities provided by supplements. These opportunities are structured so that application, integration, and evaluative skills are sharpened.

Specifically, after every few pages of text, a set of questions appears. These are not just the typical "can you repeat the text?" questions. Instead, the questions often push the learners to relate what they have just read to ideas encountered in earlier chapters. Other typical questions ask the student to form reasoned judgments about examples of economic analysis. The questions provide both a quick review of the material and rapid feedback about the extent of understanding. These questions are answered thoroughly at the end of each chapter. Then, to give students an opportunity to (1) summarize the entire chapter and (2) think critically about a more lengthy piece of economic analysis, each chapter concludes with two more self-test questions. One is answered at the end of the text; the second is left unanswered to coax readers to answer the question themselves.

In addition, self-test questions throughout the text encourage the student to read actively. Readers are encouraged to interact with the material, weigh it, use it, and digest it. The wide margins are included because we expect students to write notes to themselves as they read.

READABILITY

Regardless of the quality of a book's intentions, it will fail if it is not readable. Hence, we have self-consciously attempted to write the book so that it can and will be read. The style is conversational; key concepts are repeated for emphasis. Complex sentences have been minimized; paragraphs are brief.

We have made a special attempt to make the book coherent and orderly. As we move from topic to topic and chapter to chapter, we provide transitions to signal the logical development of the text. If the book makes sense as a whole, its readability will be enhanced.

The strengths of this book owe much to the perceptive comments of numerous reviewers. Special thanks are offered to James A. Aylsworth, Sheryl Berger, John Bockino, John H. Hoag, Linda L. Hudgins, Matt Mathis, Ellen O'Brien, Robert Schoeni, Jason L. Steinitz, Gary L. Stone, and Alejandro Velez.

1 Economic Decisions and You

A major part of the nightly news and a large number of newspaper headlines are about economics: INFLATION IS THREATENING; TREMENDOUS DEFICITS ARE PREDICTED; STEEL FIRMS ASK PRESIDENT FOR PROTECTION AGAINST IMPORTS. Do you regularly read, listen to, and understand such stories? Many people skip them, not because they think these issues are unimportant, but because they seem so complex and mysterious. Most of us recognize that economics is extremely important. Few of us feel we know enough to participate in discussions about economics.

The subject matter of economics is broad and difficult to describe in a few sentences. Yet there are common elements to the many topics that together make up the substance of modern economics. For one thing, you will notice immediately that economics discusses the material desires we have. It focuses almost exclusively on those aspects of human experience that money can buy. Beauty, innocence, kindness, and other nonmaterial values are largely ignored in the study of economics. Economists focus instead on one highly important facet of our lives—the struggle to satisfy our desires for goods and services.

A second common characteristic that unites economists working on diverse questions is the urge to economize. We economize when we achieve our goals with a minimum of cost. The desire to economize is so much a part of economics that it is frequently the primary standard an economist applies when she asks, "What is best for our economy?"

The logic supporting the attempt to economize is powerful. When we reduce the costs of meeting our material desires, we have more resources left to buy additional material goods. As you can see, economizing behavior and the materialistic emphasis of modern economics are closely related.

You will have a more complete definition of economics after you have studied the questions and principles contained in *Modern Economics*. Economics is a broad and varied discipline. It has made contributions in many areas of human behavior. Yet the focus of all these contributions has been on the discovery of methods of economizing to satisfy our desires for goods and services. There are several features of this text that will help you appreciate the wisdom economics provides.

This book will explain economics in a form that you can use. After learning the concepts of economics, you will be able to see why the economy takes particular jumps and dips. The more about economics you can absorb, the more uses you will see for economic literacy. When you complete this book, you will probably wonder how anyone can get by without an understanding of basic economics.

The objective of this guide to basic economics is to enable you to participate in the economic decisions that affect you. Our message is that economics is much too important to leave to experts. Economic principles are useful in helping you understand the newspaper and the news. They enable you to make reasoned judgments about the suggestions politicians make when they promise improved economic performance. On a more personal level, economics makes you aware of how jobs are created and why the wages for some jobs are so much higher than those for others.

Not only can you learn the basic ideas, you can learn to use those ideas. Economics is an active, daily part of your life. It is much more than a set of technical terms that you must memorize in school and then never consider again. Economic concepts are used over and over again. Because you want to have some informed input into the economic decisions that affect you, you need to understand these key concepts. Then you will be able to use economics as you listen, read, discuss, vote, and consume.

This book encourages you to use the basic principles of economics. It is full of opportunities for you to become involved as an active reader. By using the economic ideas you encounter, you will see how beneficial they are as you form opinions on economic questions. *Modern Economics* emphasizes the uses of economics. By showing you how rewarding economics can be, this book should convince you that economics is one special area of knowledge that you will be eager to explore in greater detail.

PRIMARY ECONOMIC DECISIONS

Resources The basic building blocks or factors of production with which we produce goods and services

Scarcity The gap between human wants and available resources

Allocation The choice of what will be produced, how much of each to produce, and how the production will occur

Very few, if any, of us will ever have all the things we want. Each of us has a huge unsatisfied craving for goods and services. Economics begins by recognizing that the planet on which we live does not have the *resources* (raw materials, labor, capital goods, and entrepreneurship) necessary to fulfill all our fantasies. Try to imagine for a moment what it would be like for everyone to have all the health, vacations, housing, transportation, food, and entertainment that you yourself desire. If you are like us, it's impossible to picture. Why? Because the world we experience is nothing like that picture!

Economists recognize that we must unfortunately live in a world of scarcity, a world in which we persistently want to consume more than what we are capable of producing. *Scarcity* refers to the gap between the total amount of goods and services people desire and the capacity of our resources to provide those goods and services. Whatever economic decisions we make, scarcity provides the context or starting point. If scarcity did not exist, there would be no reason for studying economics.

Scarcity requires us to make choices we would rather avoid. It isn't pleasant to deny people goods and services they want. Yet that situation is exactly what scarcity requires every country to do. Scarcity forces us to choose from among goods and services that we want. For example, you may want a better car, but your tuition is due. Collectively, we may want better highways, but limited congressional funds are also sought by those who want better schools, better health care, and a stronger national defense. Each country lacks enough resources to satisfy the material desires of its citizens. Consequently each country must make the same type of economic choices or decisions.

Economists have identified two basic decisions that scarcity forces each country to make: allocation and distribution. *Allocation* decisions are responses to questions about *what* goods and services we should produce, *how much* of each to produce, and *how* we should provide them. So when the United States government decides to purchase fifteen Pershing missiles and pays an American corporation to produce them, the government has made an allocation decision. When a family decides to spend $500 on a video cassette recorder, another allocational decision has been made.

The second type of economic decision determines who will get

Distribution The choice of who will receive what is produced

what is allocated. Decisions about *who* will get the goods and services provided in an economy are called *distribution* decisions. For instance, when a local government finances elementary schools, it is distributing educational services to those between the ages of five and twelve.

Scarcity causes allocation and distribution decisions to be unpopular. When a decision has been made to allocate resources for a particular purpose and to distribute them to a particular group, other groups with alternative purposes will be frustrated. Why? There are too few resources to meet all our material desires. Thus, producing cars and distributing them to residents of California has the effect of denying the use of those same raw materials, labor, and capital to those in New York who might prefer the expansion of New York wineries.

Thus, because of scarcity the impact of every allocational and distributional choice is complex. One group of property owners, employees, and consumers will succeed in having their desires fulfilled; others will be frustrated because these resources were not used as they would have preferred. Consequently, every such decision has its advocates and its foes. Those who object to specific economic decisions are those who have other uses in mind for the resources in question. There is no perfect economic decision in the sense that such a decision would increase the economic welfare of every citizen.

ECONOMIC GOALS

Economic Goals The objectives or purposes that guide or shape economic decisions

Any decision is an attempt to accomplish some purpose. Whoever makes allocation and distribution decisions in an economy is being guided by some idea about how the world can be improved. The objectives or purposes that guide decision makers in the economy are *economic goals*. These goals are shared by all economies. So important are these goals that all economies can be organized around the efforts of countries to achieve them. Part II of this text consists of a set of chapters, each of which defines an economic goal and then explains how economic principles can improve our ability to meet that goal.

The economic goals that a particular economy pursues tend to be identical to those pursued in other economies. For example, full employment is one of the stated objectives of every economy. Yet, as you already know, there is a great difference between the Chinese economy and the United States economy. If their goals are roughly the same, how can we explain these sharp differences?

Two factors distinguish one economy from another. First, countries disagree about the priorities assigned to various goals. Second, countries use different institutions to reach their goals. You may have almost a carbon-copy set of goals as your friend and still be very different in how you view the economy. The explanation may be in the weights you respectively attach to each goal. In other words, the *intensity* with which you aim for a goal determines the choices you will be willing to make to accomplish it. While full employment may be a goal of every economy, some countries pursue it more aggressively than others. A 4 percent unemployment rate in one economy may cause riots in the street; in another economy the same news would result in self-congratulation and optimistic smiles.

You might well be wondering why all economic goals cannot be attained. Why establish priorities? Why not move ahead at full steam toward every economic goal? Our earlier discussion of scarcity contains the answer. As you might expect, devoting resources to allocation and distribution decisions that will move us toward one economic goal often makes it more difficult to achieve other goals that we have. Thus, countries are typically forced to establish goal priorities.

Certain goal conflicts are especially common. They arise so frequently that they are always lurking in the background as goal priorities are being debated. Part III of this book consists of chapters that describe several typical goal conflicts. Economic principles or ideas that improve your understanding of a particular conflict will be discussed in each chapter.

MARKETS AND GOVERNMENTS

A second factor that distinguishes one country from another is the mechanism on which it relies to reach specific goals. Earlier in this chapter you learned that the existence of scarcity requires economies to make allocation and distribution decisions. These decisions cause conflict between groups. Each would like to see an increase in the number of resources flowing in directions it prefers. Disputes over the use of raw materials, people, equipment, and money are a natural consequence of scarcity.

Market
Process of exchange between buyers and sellers

Understandably, people would like to settle these conflicts over resources without annihilating one another. Throughout history two methods of at least temporarily resolving these conflicts have been used—markets and governments. A *market* is a process whereby individual sellers of goods and services bargain with those individuals who wish to buy those same goods and services. For instance, the retail market for Bruce Springsteen albums consists of those selling the albums and those wishing to buy them. How are disputes settled in markets?

Before we see how conflicts are settled in markets, let's make sure you see the conflict clearly. Sellers in a market would obviously prefer for consumers to pay their entire income for a single unit of what is being sold. From the consumers' perspective, the ideal price is free. That's a real conflict!

Given this conflict, why does a purchase take place? How can an exchange occur? The mechanism that propels the buyers and sellers toward agreement in a market is a change in the price. Clearly consumers do not want an item so much that they will pay their entire income for it. Not even the most avid Bruce Springsteen fan would be willing to pay that price. Just as obvious is the fact that no seller can afford to offer a good or service for free. Gradually, prices change until some agreement is reached by those sellers and buyers who still wish to exchange at the existing price. Those sellers unable to sell at this price and those buyers unable or unwilling to buy at the existing price will be disappointed. But the exchange price will be high enough to cover the seller's costs and low enough to attract some buyers.

Governments provide an alternative process for attaining economic goals. Through voting, negotiating, lobbying, and persuasion, a government receives signals that particular goals are preferred to others. These signals vary considerably, depending upon which groups are able to most effectively send them. For instance, suggestions by the United Automobile Workers concerning allocation and distribution decisions to be made by the government will rarely resemble those made by General Motors. However, once government makes such a decision, there is an unspoken agreement that we will tolerate it for now. We recognize that decisions made for a society will please some groups in the economy and distress others. Whatever decision government makes, it will be displeasing to large numbers of people. Yet, like a market, the government responds to the desires of particular groups.

Both markets and governments provide an avenue for achieving economic goals. Neither is perfect. After economic decisions have been made by markets and governments, certain groups will be happy and others will be angry. Notice that everything we do in terms of economic decisions is haunted by the impact of scarcity. Markets and governments cannot escape the negative impacts of the choices they make.

Most decisions in our economy are made by a combination of governmental and market efforts. An important example of this joint participation by markets and government in making economic decisions is choosing whether or not to attend college. The tuition, room and board costs, and fees are a price that you must pay if you attend college. You are the prospective buyer. A large number of colleges want to sell you their services. The decision has the appearance of a market decision. Ultimately, you decide whether or not to pay the price.

However, the price of tuition, room and board, and fees has been reduced by governmental action if you are attending a college that is subsidized by some level of government. Taxpayers are then financing a substantial share of the costs of the services students are receiving. When the municipal, state, or federal legislatures agree to pay a larger proportion of the full cost of college, the price to the student is reduced. More potential students will be able and willing to pay the new price.

The point being made by this discussion about the decision to attend college is that few economic decisions are pure market or pure governmental decisions. Instead they represent a combination of market and governmental approaches. Since different groups are helped or hurt, depending on the choice to rely primarily on government or on markets, the debate about the form of cooperation between the two is vigorous. The decision to emphasize market or governmental approaches to attaining economic goals is more than technical. As we will see throughout the book, the decision is very much related to values.

To highlight the role played by values in determining the priorities assigned to economic goals, the discussion of each goal in Part II contains international statistics relating the United States record to that of other countries. The cumulative effect of these statistics will be to show you the apparent goal priorities of different countries. You can better appreciate the dominant values in our own economy by studying our historical record against a backdrop provided by the performance of other economies.

The discussion of each goal in Part II also contains a description of the roles markets and government can play in achieving economic goals. One basic difference between these two conflict resolution processes is the extent to which economic decisions require consultation with others. Market decisions are personal; they require only the approval of the person making the choice. Government acts only after considering what will be politically acceptable. Thus, governmental decisions about allocation and distribution use a unit of analysis different from that used in markets. Governments' attempts to achieve economic goals are based on what the public *as a unit* will permit. Comparable attempts by markets are the result of thousands of *individual* decisions by buyers and sellers.

ECONOMIC DECISIONS AND ECONOMIC PRINCIPLES

The emphasis in this book is on the improvement of economic decisions. The path to that improvement consists of your learning a set of economic principles. You have already begun. We encountered the pervasive impact of scarcity in this initial chapter.

To learn these principles you will be asked to learn quite a few technical terms. Economics, like other areas of expertise, has a unique vocabulary. However, we have been very conscious of your needs. While we recognize that you do not plan to be a professional economist, we know you want to master the most important economic concepts. Each of the terms defined in this text is one that will improve your ability to read, listen, discuss, and vote more intelligently.

What is your responsibility when you encounter a new term in economics? If the new idea is to be of any future use to you at all, you must do more than highlight it with a felt-tipped pen. After you have learned the definition, ask yourself why you have been asked to learn this term. Jot down in the margin or in your notes the purpose or use of the term. For instance, "A *market* is one of the two primary devices we used to solve the conflicts caused by scarcity." By reminding yourself of the use of economic concepts, you are more likely to learn them.

ORGANIZATION OF THE BOOK

This book was written with a particular logic in mind. We want to share it with you so that you will understand how the chapters fit together. Knowing our organization should make the material flow more smoothly for you.

Chapter 2 consists of an introduction to the special way in which economists and other social scientists attempt to understand human behavior. Your awareness of the strengths and limits of social science analysis will increase your appreciation for the power of modern economics. Many of the concepts you will learn in Chapter 2 will also be beneficial to you in other social science courses.

Part II presents the economic goals that every society attempts to attain. The chapters in Part II follow a particular format. The goal is first defined. Then the ambiguity associated with the goal is explained. Next, the desirability of the goal is made clear. The bulk of each chapter will consist of the economic principles that guide market and governmental attempts to attain that goal. The discussion of each goal in Part II ends with a description of how the United States has done relative to other countries in terms of that goal.

Part II could have the effect of leaving you with the belief that each goal, if defined carefully, can be achieved. Economic decisions guided by an awareness of economic principles can move us toward any chosen economic goal. A problem arises, however. In the course of achieving one goal, we pay the cost of moving even further from achieving others. Thus, solutions to economic problems tend to create new problems. The search for a perfect policy with no costs or disadvantages appears hopeless in a world of scarcity.

Consequently, Part III provides you with a heightened sense of the role of trade-offs in economics. Earlier in this chapter, we mentioned that Part III would consist of certain standard goal conflicts. These conflicts, or trade-offs, help explain why economics is so exciting. The ongoing arguments about which trade-offs are desirable or worth the price stimulate efforts to discover new principles that will better identify the costs of an economic decision. Even more relevant to you, these arguments are ones in which you can participate.

Goal priorities are to a large degree value judgments. Reasonable people may well differ about which economic goals are more important than others. Because these decisions affect whether you will have a job, the prices you will pay, and the income you will earn, you cannot just leave them to professional economists.

2
Tools for Economic Reasoning

Economics, like other social sciences, tries to explain specific aspects of human behavior. Economists are curious about such questions as why some people work part-time while others work full-time, why the rate of inflation fluctuates, and why profits in particular industries are relatively high. Because the answers to such questions affect your future income, you probably share their curiosity.

As economists try to answer questions about the behavior of consumers, employers, or property owners, they often rely on certain concepts, or *tools*. In this chapter, several of the most fundamental economic tools will be discussed. The concepts presented here are so important that they are used by almost all economists whenever they comment on an economic problem. Economists may disagree about the emphasis to be placed on specific economic goals, and they frequently disagree about solutions; but they regularly agree about the usefulness of the tools in this chapter.

One pleasant side effect of your learning how to use these basic tools for economic reasoning will be your increased ability to understand psychologists, historians, sociologists, and political scientists. All these professionals use the tools discussed in this chapter. In a sense, these tools are not simply economic tools; they are concepts fundamental to most scientific reasoning.

MODELS: MAPS OF CAUSE-AND-EFFECT RELATIONSHIPS

Why should any of us care why our neighbors buy, sell, work, take vacations, save, or spend? Several possible reasons may pop into your mind. You might simply be curious. To try to explain why others behave the way they do may be as natural to many of us as breathing or eating. We want to know. Thus, we can benefit from some mental device that will help us *explain*.

Another possible reason for being concerned about the timing and extent of economic activity is our desire to *predict* the future. We feel more secure in a world where we can forecast today what will happen tomorrow or next year. For instance, if we can predict the amount of inflation that will occur next year, we can better decide whether to buy a personal computer immediately or wait until later.

Finally, if we know why an action occurs, we may be able to change or *improve* the behavior in question. Those of us who dream of a better world must first enlarge our understanding of why current behavior occurs. Perhaps we can alter behavior we do not like if we can figure out what caused the behavior in the first place. Efforts to improve our behavior depend on a mental picture of why particular actions are typical.

Suppose, for example, that you are unhappy that Congress has reduced the amount of financial aid available to college students. You may be able to explain why the cutbacks occurred if you become aware of the current federal budget crisis, the characteristics of most recipients of aid, and the goal priorities of people like those in the current administration. This explanation identifies factors that could restore federal aid to college students. For instance, the election of those with different economic goal priorities might produce more federal aid to college students. A plan for improvement would focus on changing the factors that we identified as causing the "undesirable" condition.

Model Simplified picture of a cause-and-effect relationship that links specific events to the behavior we are studying

Economists attempt to explain, predict, and improve economic behavior by using *models*. A model is a simplified picture or map of a cause-and-effect relationship. The essence of this map is a link, or association, between some behavior in which we are interested and some causal event or factor. For instance, if album prices fall whenever a new record store opens in your community, you can form a model that explains why album prices vary.

Notice that any such model will, at best, be generally true. Human behavior is so complex that no model can ever capture all the factors that are associated with it. If a model could be complete, it would no longer be a model. A particular model is adequate if it satisfies the purpose for which we are using the model. An explanatory model should be evaluated in terms of its explanatory power; a predictive model is as good as the accuracy of its forecasts.

SELF-TEST

1. Explain the following statement: Just because economists disagree about the need for tax increases does not mean that they disagree about the tools that should be used to settle the debate.
2. A roommate explains to you that our economy experiences prosperity whenever (1) Republicans are in office and (2) the American League team wins the World Series. What is the quality of the model your roommate is using?
3. Indicate the deficiencies in the following statement: Any model that attempts to explain changes in average wages must include a measure of the percentage of workers in unions; otherwise the model will not include all the factors that affect average wages.

OPPORTUNITY COST AND ECONOMIC MODELS

You recall from Chapter 1 that economists are always searching for economizing techniques. If we can discover some process that would reduce the cost of training new workers or of constructing new homes, then we can have more for less—a great economic achievement. Such achievements are worth seeking, but their number and magnitude are limited by a fundamental characteristic of economic behavior—the necessity of paying *opportunity costs.* The focus on scarcity in chapter 1 prepared you for understanding opportunity costs.

Opportunity Cost The value of the benefits lost from choosing a particular alternative

Why does opportunity cost limit economizing behavior? Why can't we make choices that have no opportunity costs associated with them? The answers to these two questions are the same. Almost all resources are available in much smaller quantities than would be required to meet all our desires for material goods and services. Hence, we can use our limited supplies of resources to satisfy one set of desires, but that choice denies the availability of those resources for creating alternative goods and services. A cost is being paid for the choice. The *lost value* of the next best alternative is the opportunity cost of our choice.

As an example of the required payment of opportunity cost, think about the choice that must be made about how to use our energy resources. Initially we must remember that these resources are sharply limited. At the same time we realize the many potential uses we have for these resources. We want fuel for our machinery, gasoline for transportation, electrical current for heating and air conditioning, oil for national defense, and many other things that require energy. Unless we expand the supply of energy resources or discover an economizing technique, an increased use of energy for one purpose requires reductions in our capability to meet alternative uses for energy.

When economic decisions of any kind are made, we must, as a consequence, pay opportunity costs. These payments are the inevitable result of any choice caused by the existence of scarcity. There is thus a logical connection linking (1) the existence of scarcity, (2) required allocative and distributional choices, and (3) the payment of resulting opportunity costs.

To make sure you understand the concept of opportunity cost, we can draw a visual representation of economic choice. The curve in Figure 2–1 is called a production possibilities, or an opportunity, cost curve. Each point on the curve represents a different allocative choice. Each point indicates the maximum output possible given the current supply of resources and existing technology. Points A and B each represent a particular allocative choice about how much steel and how many computer units to produce. This curve can be thought of as representing either the choices available to a company or those facing a society. Both firms and society are limited by their inabilities to acquire unlimited resources. Thus the potential choices that lie beyond the opportunity cost curve are not currently realistic. Points outside the production possibilities curve become relevant only when we improve the quantity or quality of our physical resources, skills, motivation, and innovation.

Figure 2–1
Opportunity Cost Curve

This graph represents several allocative possibilities. It permits us to measure the opportunity cost of more steel production in terms of reduced production of computer units.

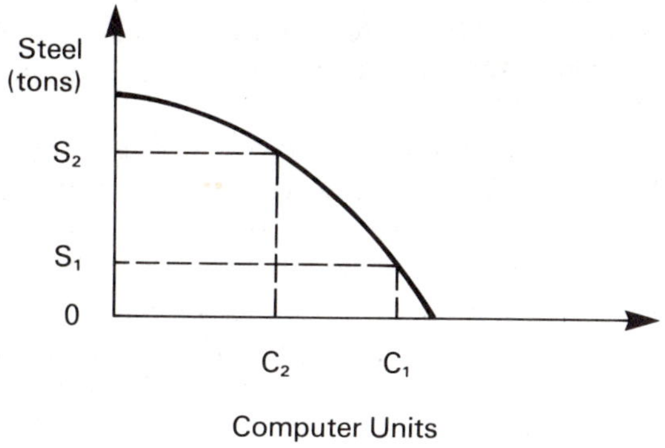

An opportunity cost curve can be drawn to represent the economic choices available to consumers or governments as well. For instance, consumers must choose between cars and houses; governments must decide how many missiles it will not build in order to expand the construction of housing units for the poor. Any such choice results in an opportunity cost that can be expressed in terms of lost benefits. Economic choices are rarely free.

SELF-TEST

4. Suppose someone tried to explain to you that opportunity cost is a gloomy idea dreamed up by those who want to explain failures in our economy. What response could you provide that would demonstrate that opportunity cost is real, not imaginary?
5. Why does it make sense for Figure 2–1 to be called an opportunity cost curve?
6. Provide a concrete example of a way to escape temporarily the limits imposed by a particular opportunity cost curve.

VARIABLES: INDEPENDENT AND DEPENDENT

Any model contains at least one relationship between an event or type of economic behavior and some other event or behavior. For instance, one model used by some economists asserts that there will be a change in the amount of money spent by you and your neighbors when the banking system changes the amount of money existing in the economy. Notice that both sets of behavior (amounts of spending and the amount of money in the economy) can vary in frequency and size. They are *variables* in the sense that they occur with different intensities or values, depending upon changes in other variables.

In a particular model, one variable begins or encourages a change in another variable. Suppose we discover that whenever a corporation's labor costs rise, the prices it charges also rise. Next we identify which variable is depending on the other. After examining several time periods and being certain that one variable is actually causing changes in the other, we conclude that labor costs tend to rise nine months before typical price increases. Thus increases in labor costs will cause the price to increase.

Independent Variable The variable that stimulates changes in a model

Dependent Variable The variable that changes its value in response to changes in the independent variable

When changes in one variable stimulate changes in a second variable, we call the initiator of change the *independent variable.* It is the variable that starts the process described by our model. In the two models described above the independent variables would be changes in the money supply and changes in labor costs. These models imply that when the respective independent variable changes its value, another variable changes in response. The responding variable is called the *dependent variable.* Changes in the dependent variable are what originally caused our interest in the model.

Models consist of relationships between independent and dependent variables. If economic behavior did not change or vary, models would be unnecessary. Remember that models are used to explain, predict, or improve human behavior. If that behavior did not vary, there would be little to explain, no need to predict, and no hope of improvement. One exciting aspect of economics is the incredible variation of human behavior that we must somehow put into a meaningful story. This variation causes many interesting relationships between independent and dependent variables.

You should be alert to a particular limitation of most economic variables or data. Economists, like other specialists, do not pay attention to all aspects of human behavior. Economics concerns itself primarily with the spending, producing, saving, and earning components of human behavior. This focus follows from the concern for material wants discussed in Chapter 1. By restricting our attention to these four elements of human behavior, economists hope that they can enlarge our understanding of those important sectors of our life. Imagine how confusing it would be to study all aspects of human behavior at once. Thus, economists focus on just a few important behavioral variables while recognizing that humans are much more complex than our models suggest.

Because economists are primarily fascinated with earning, spending, saving, and producing behavior, economic variables are typically expressed in monetary terms. Variables in economics usually are expressed in terms of dollars, yen, francs, and so on. This expression of economic behavior in monetary terms has at least two effects that you should remember as you study economic variables.

First, economists will sometimes express essentially nonmonetary behavior in monetary form so that such behavior can be included in an economic model. For example, an economist might represent the decision to marry in the form of a variable that estimates how much money each potential wife or husband will earn over the next thirty years. Such a variable may make sense or be silly, depending on the purpose of the model in which it is used.

A second effect of expressing economic variables in monetary terms creates the impression that behavior that is not in monetary terms is relatively unimportant. Honesty, humility, creativity, and insecurity are not monetary variables, but they have enormous effects on economic behavior. A variable does not lose its importance because it does not come packaged in monetary terms.

SELF-TEST

7. Explain why the models used by economists do not include all the independent variables that affect the behavior they are discussing.
8. Suppose that you are wondering why the price of eggs has risen so sharply in the past two years. You go back to the monthly record of egg prices and find that before the two major jumps in egg prices hundreds of chickens died of a mysterious disease. What model could explain what happened? What is the dependent variable? The independent variable?
9. Explain whether the model of marital choice suggested in the previous section might be a good predictive model or a good explanatory model.

REDUCING COMPLEXITY WITH *CETERIS PARIBUS*

You will recall from our earlier discussion of economic models that economic reasoning must adapt to a world of immense complexity. The number of variables that have some impact on a particular economic decision is huge. In other words, there are many independent variables which affect any dependent variable that represents some economic behavior.

Economists recognize that their models are incomplete imaginary pictures. Only certain independent variables are included in any model. When these independent variables change, the model claims that the economic behavior being studied (the dependent variable) will also change.

But what happens when an important independent variable not included in the model changes? To avoid the complexity of considering the impact of every conceivable independent variable, economists often ignore the impact of all independent variables not included in their models. Another way to express this effort to reduce complexity is to say that economists hold all independent variables constant, except the ones included in the model in question. The Latin term *ceteris paribus* is frequently used in economic reasoning to indicate that the economist is holding all independent variables constant, except the ones in the model.

Ceteris Paribus The assumption that no independent variable except the one specified has changed

An example of this effort to reduce complexity in economic reasoning is the attempt by economists to explain what causes individuals to increase the amount of money they save. One model of savings behavior suggests that individuals save more when their income rises. Such a model includes the limitation of *ceteris paribus.* Economists who use this model believe that the change in income is the dominant independent variable. Actually many things affect savings. A person's age, the amount of governmental aid available to the elderly, the future income a person expects, and many other independent variables all affect the amount a person saves.

Economic models can never be interpreted skillfully unless you remember that *ceteris paribus* has now been assumed. Recognizing the *ceteris paribus* assumption may stimulate you to think of significant independent variables that have a large effect on the dependent variable but were excluded from the model. When you realize that *ceteris paribus* is a limitation on economic models, you are not as likely to exaggerate their contribution to economic understanding.

ORGANIZING ECONOMIC DATA WITH SCHEDULES AND GRAPHS

Graphs of economic variables are often used to provide a visual picture of a model. Some people can understand economic relationships better when they have a graphic picture of the behavior. For that reason graphs are often used by economists to supplement their words. Because your objective is to understand the type of economic analysis used in newspapers and political speeches, you will need to have at least an elementary appreciation of graphic analysis. To the extent that the graphic analysis can be used to help organize your thoughts, this too will be useful to you later when you hear or read economic commentary.

Before we study the basics of graphic interpretation, we need to recognize the origin of the numbers that eventually appear on economic graphs. Economic models, as you already know, consist of relationships between dependent variables and independent variables. Variables, by definition, take different values over time as events and attitudes change them. Dependent variables change their values as the values of pertinent independent variables change. Remember, for instance, that many economists claim that the dependent variable "savings" changes as the independent variable "income" changes.

Schedule A list of values for an independent variable and the matching values of a dependent variable

Economists chart the movement of these variables with schedules. A *schedule* is a list of various values of an independent variable together with associated values of a dependent variable. Schedules of economic data are thus a way of organizing and presenting an economic model.

One of the most frequently used models in economics is the one relating the amounts of a good or service that consumers demand and the price charged for the goods. This model of demand can be represented by a demand schedule. This schedule (see Table 2–1) indicates how changes in the price of x affect the quantity of x that is demanded. The demand schedule for peaches indicates that as the price of peaches falls, *ceteris paribus,* the quantity of peaches demanded increases. The demand schedule is an orderly way to present this model.

A graph of the information in a schedule is an additional format for organizing the variables in a model. As we transform the schedule into a graph, we should make sure that you are familiar with some basic characteristics of any graph.

When we draw a graph we are associating the numbers or values of the variables with the points on two lines. One of the lines is horizontal (the x-axis) and the other is vertical (the y-axis). Where they meet is called the origin. Each row in a schedule can be represented by one point on the graph. For instance, point 1 in Figure 2–2 corresponds to the situation where the price of peaches is \$.99 per bushel and the quantity of peaches demanded is 500 bushels. Connecting the five points that correspond to the information in the demand schedule for peaches results in a demand curve for peaches. This graph indicates what quantity of peaches is demanded at each possible price.

The axes of the graph must be labeled. Otherwise the curve has no meaning. The labels consist of the dependent and independent

Table 2–1
Demand Schedule for Peaches
This schedule shows the effect on quantity demanded of changes in price.

Price of Peaches/Bushel	Quantity of Peaches Demanded
\$8.99	100 bu
6.99	200
4.99	300
2.99	400
.99	500

Figure 2–2
The Demand Curve
This curve demonstrates what happens to the quantity of peaches demanded when price changes.

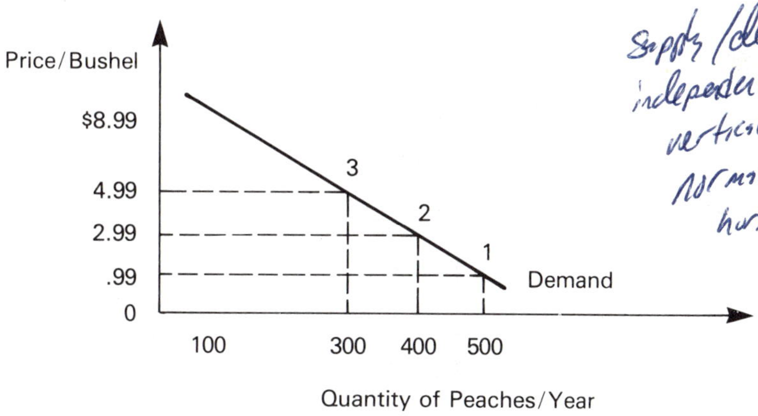

variables. In Figure 2–2 we placed the independent variable, price, on the vertical axis and the dependent variable, quantity of peaches demanded, on the horizontal axis. This particular placement is a habit economists have when they draw demand and supply curves. Ordinarily, however, the dependent variable will be on the vertical axis when we discuss any economic model *except* demand and supply.

SHIFTING A CURVE OR MOVING ALONG A CURVE?

Take another look at Figure 2–2. How could we slide from one point to another on that demand curve? We could get from point 3 to the situation described by any other point by changing the price from $4.99. In general, we move along a curve by changing the value of the independent variable in the model. As you may have already guessed, each curve is drawn *ceteris paribus*. The only variables that are being allowed to change are the variables whose names are on the two axes. Thus, movement from point 3 to point 2 indicates a change in the quantity of peaches demanded when the price changes from $4.99 to $2.99.

If we are curious about the effect of some other independent variable on the dependent variable we are studying, we must step beyond the boundaries of our model. The only independent variable we used in Figure 2–2 to explain changes in the quantities of peaches demanded was the price of peaches. However, we know that the quantity of peaches demanded is affected also by the price of oranges, growth in the income of consumers, and consumer preferences for

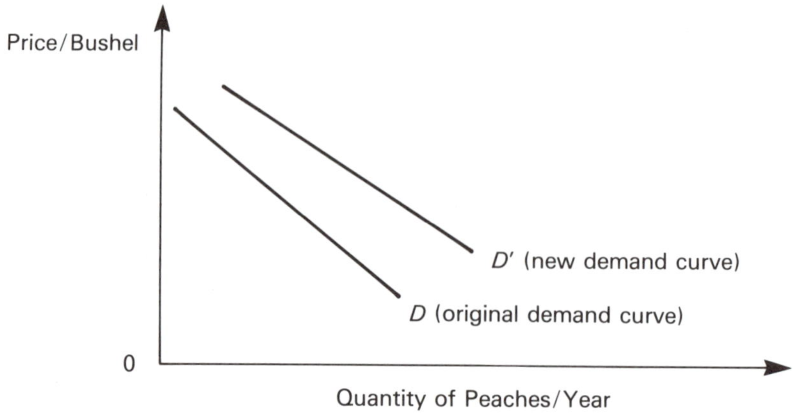

Figure 2–3
Shifting a Curve
This graph illustrates the impact of a change in an independent variable other than the price of peaches.

peaches. Each of these independent variables can stimulate a change in the quantity of peaches being demanded.

Changes in any relevant independent variable, except the one on the vertical axis, cause the entire schedule to change. At each price, the quantities demanded will be different from those in Table 2–1. The entire context in which consumers think about how many peaches they want at all possible prices is different. Changes in the price of oranges or some other independent variable would alter the way consumers think about the value of peaches. For example, when incomes rise, consumers are typically willing to buy more peaches at every possible price. The entire curve will shift when the *ceteris paribus* condition is not honored.

When the entire demand schedule changes, the demand curve shifts. None of the original points on the demand curve in Figure 2–2 is on the new demand curve for peaches. Figure 2–3 shows the effect of increased income on the original demand curve. The entire demand curve shifts. On the new demand curve, as on the old, a change in the price of peaches causes a movement along the demand curve.

The example using a demand curve for peaches illustrates a general rule. We move along a given curve when we change the value of the independent variable on the graph. We shift a curve when we change a relevant independent value that is not on the graph.

SELF-TEST

10. Draw a graph that would represent a model which claims that savings increases when consumers' income increases.

11. Indicate the worth of the following graph:

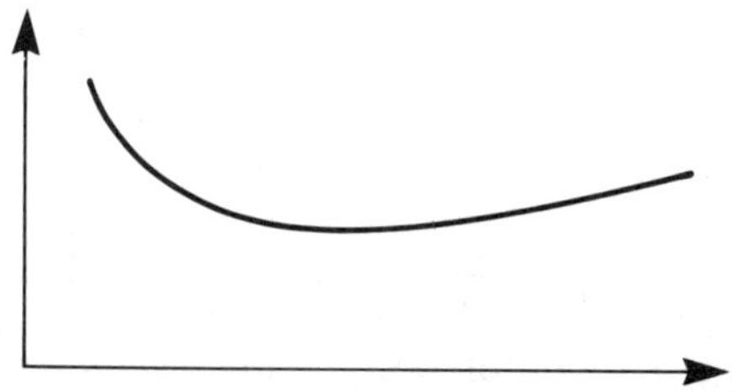

12. Evaluate the following comment on the distinction between movements along curves and shifts in curves: It hardly seems to matter whether a curve shifts or whether there is movement along a curve. The point of both is that something has happened to the dependent variable. Since that change is what we are primarily interested in, how we represent the change on a graph is not particularly informative.

Each section in Chapter 2 has provided you with a concept that should prove useful to you whenever you are reading or thinking about human behavior. Although the examples have been from economics, each idea or distinction plays an important role in other social sciences. The next time you identify the dependent and independent variables in the reasoning of a social scientist, you will recognize that in an economics class you get more than just economics. While we could have introduced each of these tools in the text as it became important or in an appendix, the significance of each concept in Chapter 2 is so great that we placed them in a chapter by themselves.

ACTIVE REVIEW

This section is a combination summary and review of Chapter 2. Its purpose is to provide you additional practice with the central concepts that make up this chapter. As you read each of the two mini-essays, keep a list of those concepts in front of you as a reminder of what you should be focusing on.

1. Many of us have the idea that United States companies can make more profit when they produce goods and services that are shoddy. The poor quality of many of the things we buy makes us wonder what is wrong with the production process. We have all encountered doctors who don't cure us and refrigerators that don't provide the energy efficiency we were promised. What exactly is going on?

Profit is a complicated concept. A firm can expand its profits by increasing the revenue it earns or by reducing the costs of production. The costs of production in modern firms are often dictated by the demands of organized labor or monopolistic suppliers of inputs. Thus the firm that wants more profits must focus on its revenue. The firm simply has more control over its sales than it does over its costs.

Now think about the effect on a firm's revenue of a bad reputation. If it is generally known that Rudy's Burgers sells sandwiches with little meat, what happens to Rudy's sales? They fall because consumers will not tolerate shoddy products for long. Rudy's profits will fall, *ceteris paribus*, right along with his sales.

Firms cannot take the risk of producing shoddy products. Consumers may not know what they are buying from a particular seller when they make the first purchase. However, they won't return again and again for a defective good or service.

a. What are the independent and dependent variables in the model used by the author of this essay?

b. Create a schedule and graph that would *disprove* the author's main point.

c. Why was it necessary for the author to indicate that diminished sales will cause profits to fall, *ceteris paribus?*

2. When the output of our economy falls at a rapid rate, we experience a depression. Wages and other incomes decline at a rapid clip. Naturally, no one wants another depression to occur. However, wishing that a depression will not happen does not provide adequate protection. Evidence is growing that a depression is on its way.

This evidence takes many forms. As Figure 2a illustrates, the

Figure 2a

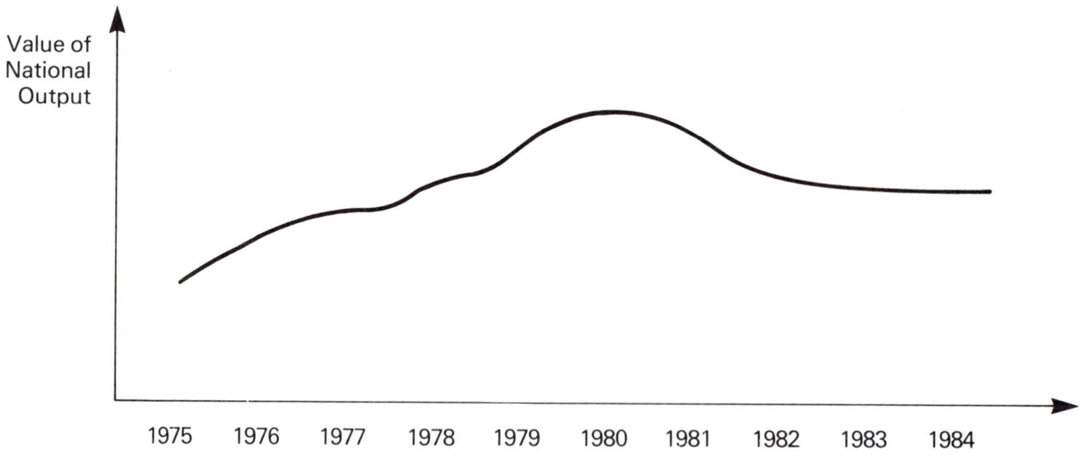

value of our output measured reached its peak in 1980 and is now declining. The recent decline in the value of our national output is not by itself convincing evidence of an eventual depression, but it does warn us that we may be in trouble.

The most powerful evidence that a depression will occur is the high unemployment rate. Output naturally falls when workers are out of jobs. When economics textbooks discussed unemployment in the 1960s, they were talking about unemployment rates between 3 and 4 percent. Now the same textbooks must explain the 7 to 12 percent unemployment rate of the 1980s. Evidently, our economy cannot provide jobs for large numbers of us. Output levels consequently decline. A depression may be near.

a. Create a graph that would illustrate the model of depression used by the author. Remember that the dependent variable in the model is the level of national output.

b. What variables could cause a shift in the curve you drew?

c. Identify a statement in the essay that makes sense only if "*ceteris paribus*" were added to it.

d. Evaluate this summary reaction to the essay:

The author makes a compelling case that a depression is coming.

ANSWERS TO ACTIVE REVIEW

1a. Profits are the dependent variable. Two dependent variables—costs and revenue—are discussed. However, the author contends that because costs are out of the firm's control, profits are directed primarily by the size of the firm's revenue.

1b. Both Schedule 2a and Graph 2a indicate that changes in profits are being caused by something other than changes in revenue. According to the data from Schedule 2a, when revenue rises, profits often fall rather than rise. Yet, the author contended that revenue must stay high to keep profits high.

Schedule 2a Comparison of the Profit and Revenue of Typical American Firms

Year	Profit	Revenue*
1960	16	130
1965	16	116
1970	40	160
1975	20	170
1980	10	172
1985	10	190

*Millions of dollars

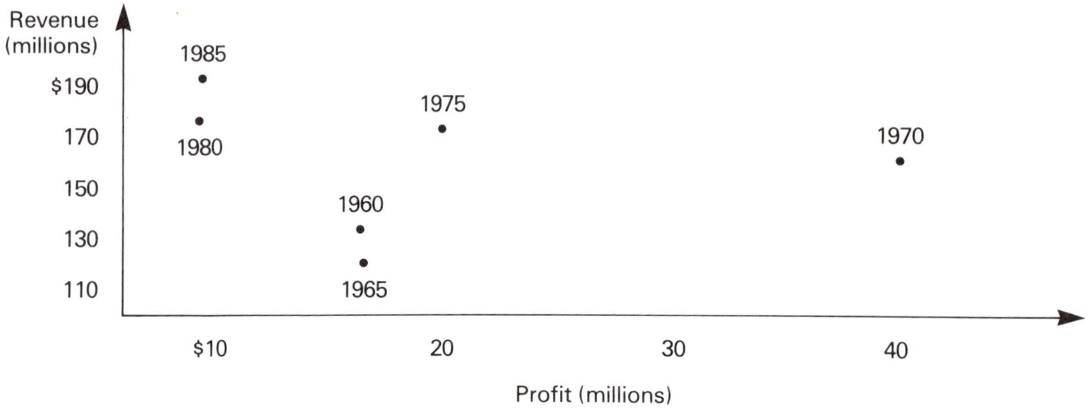

Graph 2a
Revenue and Profits of Typical American Firms

1c. Sales are not the only independent variable that affects profits. Hence it could be claimed that diminished sales would cause profits to decline only if the other independent variables were held constant. Suppose, for instance, that any factor affecting costs had been allowed to change such that costs fell. Now the impact on profits would be unclear. Diminished sales cause profits to fall; decreased costs cause them to rise.

ANSWERS TO SELF-TEST

1. Certain ideas or tools used by economists are so basic to the way an economist approaches a problem that they are almost universally used. Economists may, and often do, disagree about the worth of a particular model. What they agree about is the need to reduce complex human relationships into manageable patterns or maps. The resulting model will help us grasp what we could not see otherwise.

   A tax increase has many effects, so many that none of us can expect to know them all. Different models will highlight different impacts of a tax cut. Since these impacts will differ in terms of who the projected tax increases will benefit and harm, economists have difficulty agreeing about the need for a tax hike. However, they can agree that the device around which the debate should focus is a model suggesting the effects of tax increases on the economy.

2. The quality of a model depends on the purpose of the model. Suppose, for example, that your roommate is attempting to predict when prosperity can be expected in the future. Then, the model is as good or bad as the statistical correlation over time between the predicted event, prosperity, and the occurrence of the two events that the model

claims will occur together with prosperity. The point is that a model's value depends on its ability to satisfy the purpose for which it is being used.

3. No model will be complete in the sense desired by the person who made this statement. To expect a model to include every factor that has some impact on the economic activity being analyzed is unrealistic. Just as a map cannot record every path, bump, or creek, a model includes only those relationships that are particularly important. Whether or not the number of workers in unions at a particular time helps us understand changes in average wages should determine its inclusion in or omission from the model.

4. Whether or not opportunity cost is gloomy is not relevant to the question of whether it is real or fictional. Its reality is inescapable. Whenever a choice is limited by a fixed supply of a necessary input, an opportunity cost results. Attending a particular lecture requires you to pay an opportunity cost measured by the worth of the next best way you could have used your time. Time is limited, so you must pay a cost whenever you choose a particular use for it.

   Economic choices result in opportunity cost because resources or factors of production are limited in terms of both quantity and quality. A choice to provide more of one good or service ordinarily requires a reduction in an alternative good or service.

5. The points on the curve represent different allocative choices. To change our minds and move from one point to another require us to give up a certain amount of the other good or service on the graph. An opportunity cost has been paid.

6. To escape the limits of a given opportunity cost requires us to figure out some way to expand the production possibilities from which we may choose. One way to improve those possibilities is to improve the skills of our labor force. The impact of such an investment would be to expand the range of allocative decisions.

7. Any human action is complex. Economists focus only on certain factors that affect economic behavior. Reality in its complete form is too involved for economists to describe. Hence they study only those variables that seem to have major impacts on buying, saving, producing, and earning decisions. Such simplification has costs, or disadvantages. The result may be missing some important independent variables. Nevertheless, models that are incomplete pictures of reality are an inevitable element of economic reasoning.

8. The dependent variable is the price of eggs. Because we are trying to explain changes in the price of eggs, we are searching for some event that seems to initiate changes in the price of eggs. Our study of egg prices revealed that when chickens die in large numbers, egg prices rise. Thus, our model will be that egg prices depend on the number of chickens available to lay eggs. The number of these chickens is the independent variable.

9. If we want to predict whom people marry, the suggested model may be useful. *If* we examined the potential income of the persons that are being considered as potential spouses and discovered that those actually chosen are again and again the ones with the highest prospective income, we may have an excellent model. Its excellence stems from its ability to predict. When we forecast whom a particular person will marry, such a model can help us.

   However, if we want to understand the causes of a marital choice, that is, explain the choice, our predictive model may lose its appeal. When we hunt for causes, we are hoping to find those variables that are most essential to the behavior we are studying. The model we are using suggests a link between marriage and the probable income of alternative spouses. Does the evaluation of potential incomes tell us why one is chosen and everyone else is rejected? In a sense it does. The model alleges that estimated future income causes the selection of a particular mate. But suppose we question married people more and discover that what they were seeking above all else was a marital life in which there were few arguments. It would be an understandable (but erroneous) logical leap to assume that rich people argue less. A new independent variable with real explanatory power has been discovered. People marry those with whom they plan to argue least.

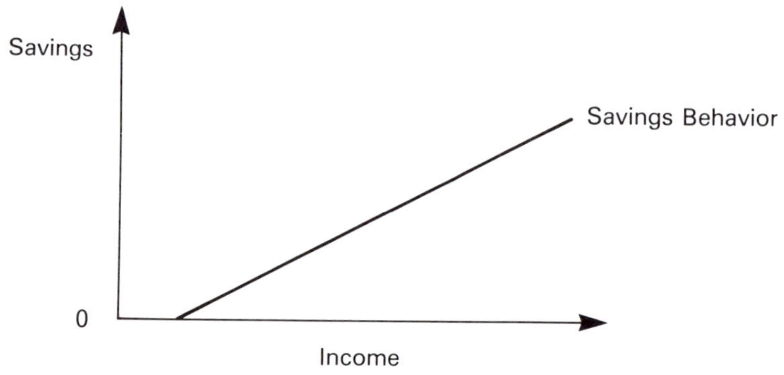

10. The independent variable, income, is placed on the horizontal axis; the dependent variable, savings, is located on the vertical axis. We do not have enough information to plot points, but we can draw a line indicating that both variables increase or decrease together. When income rises, savings increase; if income falls, savings decrease. Notice that we have placed the dependent variable on the vertical axis because this is not a demand or supply model.
11. This so-called graph is gibberish. There is no way we can make any meaning out of it. There are no labels on the axis. It is just a squirming line. Thus, we cannot decipher the variables the curve is charting.

12. It matters a great deal whether we represent a change in economic behavior in terms of a movement along a curve or as a shift in a curve. We want to know why the value of the dependent variable is different. If there is a movement along a curve, we check the vertical axis to find what variable initiated the change. If, instead, the entire curve has shifted, we know that some independent variable other than the one on the vertical axis has caused the change we are studying. This distinction is important because it indicates responsibility for the changing economic behavior.

3 The Importance of Economic Goals

7 goals

We are all curious about how the economy is doing. In addition, we are always concerned about the impact of new housing developments or defense contracts on our economy. To respond to our curiosity about what is happening in our economy, we need a set of performance indicators. We want to be able to measure advances and dips in our economic well-being. We require specific criteria by which we can chart the quality of our economic efforts.

Such performance measures are available. They provide the criteria by which we judge our economy. These measures are our best attempts to represent whether we are achieving our purpose in an economic sense. Performance indicators such as the unemployment rate and the Consumer Price Index (measuring the extent of inflation) enable us to record our achievements and failures. Our purpose as an economic community is to accomplish a set of goals. Each *economic goal* represents a desirable target that we wish to hit. The set of goals that an economy emphasizes provides an important picture of its aspirations and the opportunity costs it might be especially willing to pay. Later, in Part III, when you learn about a few of the more common opportunity costs that must be paid when a particular goal is chosen, you will be able to use that knowledge to determine the advantages and disadvantages of various combinations of goals.

BRIEF DESCRIPTIONS OF THE GOALS

In the language developed in Chapter 2, economic goals are the specific dependent variables we are trying to increase when we select particular economic policies. They justify policy proposals. A member of Congress suggesting that farmers should be subsidized when they produce sugar cane will phrase the advantages of his of her proposal in terms of its effects on economic goals.

To give you an impression of what these goals are, this section describes in simple terms the goals that will constitute the organizing structure for Part II in this text. The goals discussed will all be major ones. Your instructor may want to add more-specialized goals, but the goals discussed here will be the core of any economist's list of economic purposes. The remaining chapters in Part II will go into great detail about the meaning of and policies for achieving each goal. First, we want to give you a simple definition of each goal: efficiency, economic freedom, equity, environmental protection, economic growth, full employment, and price stability.

Efficiency

Efficiency
Maximizing the output of each resource

Efficiency avoids waste. The importance of avoiding waste can be seen by thinking again about the meaning of scarcity. Because resources are far too few to meet human wants even when these resources are used without waste, the inefficient use of such resources should be avoided whenever possible. Every inefficiency chews up potential goods and services. Whether we want more personal computers, microwave ovens, or therapy sessions, waste denies us potential consumption.

Another way to think about efficiency is to recall the opportunity cost curve in Chapter 1. Although the discussion in Chapter 1 focused on movements along the curve, all the points of possible production inside the curve are equally important. They all represent choices that will occur when waste or inefficiency forces us to make choices of output below the curve.

Efficiency is achieved when each resource is used in its most productive manner to produce those goods and services that consumers desire. Efficiency is typically accomplished by specialization and exchange. Certain resources are much more able than others to perform particular tasks. By exchanging one type of resources for another, those who organize production try to increase output while reducing their costs.

Economic Freedom

Economic Freedom The right of individuals to participate in an economy with minimal coercion from public or private sources

As with each of the other economic goals, it is hard to imagine anyone opposing *economic freedom*. On an abstract level we all oppose coercion or the lack of freedom. However, the complexity of economic freedom begins to become more evident when we ask, what are particular consumers, workers, property owners, or government officials free to do, or what specific problems are they free from. Consumers and sellers, for example, have some interests in common—they both want a purchase—as well as some interests that inevitably conflict—the size of the price. Freedom for one of these groups to pursue its objectives fully without restraint or guidance from any outside group may mean a reduction in the opportunity available to the other. For example, when there is only one producer of insulin, that seller has the freedom to set prices. However, diabetics would not have the freedom to choose among sellers.

In its most general sense, economic freedom refers to the opportunities a person has to achieve whatever economic objective he or she may choose. This goal reflects our desire for self-control. We believe that no one understands our needs as well as we do. Hence, we should be able to exercise economic freedom in pursuing those needs.

Equity

Equity A legitimate distribution of income and wealth

Equity is an important and potentially confusing economic goal. It has many synonyms—economic justice, greater equality, and fairness. *Equity* exists when the distribution or division of income and wealth is legitimate. When we say that a particular distribution is legitimate, you would be correct to wonder, in whose eyes? The answer is in the eyes of a consensus of voters. However, the fact that voters at any particular time have approved a particular distribution need not prevent any of us from arguing that a mistake was made and that a different distribution should be established the next time distributional policies are selected.

Equity is important because money plays such an important part in determining who has power in our society. Power may stem from leadership ability, occupation, or physical beauty, but it is certainly advanced and perpetuated by money. Thus, the contest over distributional shares is an unusually serious game. We are concerned about the rules of that game as well as the reasoning of those who wish to alter those rules in the name of equity.

Whenever you think about equity, visualize a distribution of income or wealth among various income, racial, gender, or occupational groups. If a system of affirmative action in the nursing industry reshapes the amount of income going to male and female personnel in the health industry, an impact on equity has occurred. When a legislative proposal attempts to limit inheritances to $5 million per recipient, the proposal is attempting to move us toward the proponent's concept of equity.

No particular distribution of income and wealth constitutes equity. Equity is a matter of dispute among reasonable people. Consequently, the goal of equity does not refer to one particular distribution that we can describe for you. The most legitimate distribution is a matter for you to determine for yourself.

Environmental Protection

Our environment has always presented us with problems. Fires, storms, insects, and floods have all interrupted our productive efforts at unpredictable times. However, many of the most pressing contemporary environmental problems are ones we have caused. Increasingly, we are becoming aware of the environmental deterioration caused by our efforts to manufacture, transport, and populate.

The health of workers, quality of air and water, and the level of toxic substances in our soil are all relevant to economic performance because they affect the future productivity of these resources. In addition to the beauty and serenity provided by our natural environment, people and natural resources are a source of future output. To carelessly reduce that flow of potential output is to rob future generations. Thus, the goal of *environmental protection* consists of controlling current use of resources so that their usefulness for future generations is not ignored. This goal is one we must constantly remind ourselves of because it is so easy to forget about those who will follow us when we make allocative choices.

Environmental Protection Preserving our our natural environment so that it can be used by future, as well as current, generations

Economic Growth

You recall from chapter 1 that economics focuses on the material welfare of the individuals who make up a country. We would like as a community to be able to produce more goods and services. Hence one of the tasks of any economy is to increase its ability to satisfy human wants. *Economic growth* is the increase in our capacity to provide more goods and services per person. Economic growth is an appealing goal because it can often postpone painful debates about

Economic Growth An increase in the economy's capacity to provide more goods and services for the average person

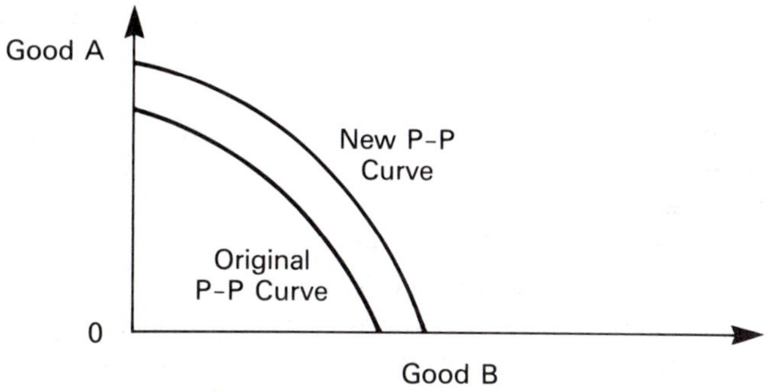

Figure 3–1
Economic Growth and the Production Possibilities (P-P) Curve
This change in the production possibilities curve indicates that economic growth has occurred.

equity. Economic growth promises to make it possible for everyone to have more. If the standard of living for everyone is increasing, we may not notice that some are advancing faster than others.

On a production possibilities curve, growth is represented by an outward shift of the entire curve. Figure 3–1 illustrates economic growth. On the new curve, it is possible for the economy to obtain more capital goods and more consumer goods than were possible prior to growth.

Full Employment

One of our most important resources is our labor force. Each of us is capable of many different outputs of varying size. However, many of us are not able to produce those outputs unless we are brought together with other resources and paid to make our contributions to output. In other words, someone must have a job for us.

Full Employment
Making jobs available for every person who wishes to work

Full employment consists of providing jobs for all human resources who are willing to contribute to production. Any person who wishes to work but who does not have a job represents a wasted resource. In addition, failure to have a job often has destructive impacts on a person's family and on the unemployed person's opinion of his or her own worth. A job is how many people define themselves, and full employment permits the broadest number of people to feel that they are meaningful participants in the community's efforts to meet our material needs.

Price Stability

Inflation harms our ability to make intelligent financial decisions. Individuals cannot decide in a rational manner how much to save and how much to spend, because they cannot anticipate what prices and incomes will be like in later periods. Businesspeople cannot decide whether to build or expand because they cannot predict either how much it will cost them to borrow in the future or how much they will be charging for their output in the future. Hence inflation prevents the kind of planning that is optimal in a smoothly running economy.

In another important respect inflation makes our lives difficult. Every price we pay is an income to someone else. Because inflation is a general rise in the prices we pay for various goods and services, it also has the effect of causing some incomes to rise at a much faster rate than others. Consequently inflation acts as a distributional device. It causes incomes to be something other than what they would have been in the absence of inflation. What is unfair about this distributional process is that it is covert. The distributional impact of inflation is shaped neither by the votes of our political representatives nor by the conscious choice of buyers and sellers to reward some more than others.

Price Stability Maintaining the general price level at a low and stable rate of inflation

For these two fundamental reasons—its inhibiting smooth financial transactions and its covert distributional impact—inflation is resisted by all economies. *Price stability* refers to our desire to keep inflation at a low and stable level. A zero rate of inflation is not especially desirable in a dynamic economy. Price increases can be an important signal that more resources are required in a particular market. However, inflation at a low and stable level does encourage greater investment and more confidence in the equity of our distribution of income.

SELF-TEST

1. Explain the following statement: The goal of full employment is just our way of focusing on a particular kind of efficiency.
2. Economic growth usually requires an increase in private investment. For our productive capacity to expand, we usually need new purchases of equipment and plant capacity. Why would price stability be one stimulus for economic growth?
3. What might be defective about the following argument? Pollution reduces the costs of producing output. Thus, environmental protection reduces our ability to meet the material needs of our citizens. If pollution were not restricted, more could be produced and more of our material needs would then be met.

POSITIVE AND NORMATIVE ECONOMIC ANALYSIS

It is now appropriate to combine two ideas you have learned. First, you know that economic goals represent a set of performance targets that economies want to achieve. Second, you remember from our discussion of scarcity in Chapter 1 that we lack the ability to meet all our economic goals. That inability is exactly why tough, unpleasant allocative and distributional choices must be made.

Scarcity should suggest to you that pursuing particular goals is never simple nor free. It is very difficult to achieve any single economic goal. Moreover, it is made even more difficult by the fact that pursuit of one goal often inhibits our movement toward another. This tension among goals is the subject matter of Part III.

Economists disagree about the priority to be assigned to particular goals. Whenever their analysis encourages a particular priority or goal, they are proposing what *should* exist. They are indicating what they would like the world to be like. When economists suggest that certain policies or a particular goal should be primary in our thinking, they are engaging in *normative analysis*.

Normative Analysis Assertions about what the economy should be like

Positive Analysis Assertions about the way the world is or about the logical results of an economic model

On the other hand, economists often make assertions that describe what the world is like at the moment or that describe what the logical consequences of a particular model are in fact. Economists refer to their descriptive claims as *positive analysis*. For example, the following statements are all examples of positive statements:

1. The current inflation rate is below the average inflation rate over the last ten years.
2. The competitive model creates pressures for firms to reduce waste.
3. One independent variable that affects the size of our national income is the quality of our labor force.

None of these statements represents an assertion about what the economist prefers to be true. Instead, these statements are descriptive claims.

It is particularly important when talking about economic goals that we keep the distinction between positive and normative statements in the forefront of our thinking. Because goal priorities represent implicit preferences for benefiting particular groups of people and harming others, you will want to be especially sensitive to normative statements. Do the values in those statements resemble your own?

SELF-TEST

4. Is the argument in question 3 an example of positive or normative analysis? How can you tell?
5. What initial question should you ask yourself if someone says that the economic goal of equity is more important than all others?
6. Why is every normative statement dependent on previous positive analysis? The question is very difficult, but ask yourself, how does anyone ever form the idea that he knows what is best for our economy? What are the building blocks on which the prescriptive statement is based?

THE MESSAGE FROM PART II

Because you are going to be spending so much time reading and thinking about the material in Part II, you deserve a preview of what you will learn. While you will be learning many specific bits of information that you will be able to use in the future, several major themes should stand out. Upon completion of Part II you should be able to answer the following questions:

1. What are the problems associated with *defining* each economic goal?
2. What *economic principles* are especially important in pursuing particular economic goals?
3. How can each economic goal be *achieved?*
4. What role is played by *markets* and *government* in meeting each economic goal?
5. How does the *United States' performance* compare with that of other countries with respect to each goal?

As you gain an understanding of economic thinking, you will recognize that it promises to be beneficial to you not only immediately but also long after you can remember the name of your course. The economic goals you will learn about are in rough form the same goals that people have been pursuing ever since we became aware of our ability to improve our material condition.

ACTIVE REVIEW

1. When we go to the grocery store, we waste an incredible amount of time trying to make choices about various products. Variety is terrific, but enough is enough. I recently counted forty-eight types of dry cereal and thirty-four brands of bar soap. Are there really that many unique forms of cereal and bar soap? Hardly!

   My time is especially valuable to me. In an important sense it is also valuable to the economy. Consequently I am urging producers to reexamine their habits. Sometimes less is more. Fewer artificial differences would make a consumer's role much simpler.

   a. What economic goal is the writer wishing us to pursue more vigorously?

   b. What economic goal would be frustrated had the writer have proposed a statute limiting the number of types of dry cereal?

   c. Is the analysis positive or normative, or is it a mixture of both?

2. The presidential budget proposal for the new year includes numerous budget cuts. All the cuts have their greatest impact on those in the lowest 40 percent of our income distribution. Subsidies for their housing, health care, and food all are cut sharply.

   The justification for these cuts focuses on the need to reduce the growth in federal budget deficits. These deficits threaten the low level of inflation that we have enjoyed recently. When government must borrow huge sums of money, the interest rate, like any other price in a similar situation, rises. Rising interst rates can reverberate throughout the economy. A chain reaction of inflation can result.

   a. What two economic goals are the focus of the analysis?

   b. Inflation has many effects on the economy. How does it affect the same 40 percent that the budget cuts harm directly?

   c. How might one justify the budget cuts by saying that those harmed in the short run will be the primary long-run beneficiaries of the cuts?

ANSWERS TO ACTIVE REVIEW

1a. The writer is concerned about waste, specifically the waste of time, and would like to be able to make selections at the grocery store more quickly. The vast array of choices available for many products has, the writer claims, gone beyond sensible variety.

The goal the author is championing is economic efficiency. By saving time, more time is available for productive activities. Think of an opportunity cost curve with time for going to the grocery store on one axis and time for everything else on the other axis. By moving along the curve, reducing the amount of time spent at grocery stores, more time is available to meet the material needs of both the writer and everyone else.

1b. We can figure out the goal that would be frustrated by asking who would oppose what is being proposed and why. Producers have created so many options because it is profitable to them. A law reducing the production choices available to businesses would reduce their economic freedom. The range of their choices would be reduced.

1c. The general purpose of the two paragraphs is to urge a change in the marketing habits of some United States businesses. Thus its intent is normative analysis. However, a number of positive statements provide the basis for the author's suggestion. For instance, notice how the link between resources and potential output is asserted as a rationale for the suggestion. Save a human resource's time, and potential output increases.

ANSWERS TO SELF-TEST

1. When an economy is efficient, it is using all of its resources to produce that output for which those resources are best suited. Workers are resources. When they are idle, they are not producing output. They are unhappy, and we lose their potential output. Thus, full employment is a special case of efficiency. Employing a worker is a path to greater efficiency for the economy.
2. The key to answering this question is to remember that investment decisions are disrupted by inflation. The potential investor is uncertain about the expected return that he or she must have to compensate for the fluctuating cost of borrowing money. Hence a low and stable amount of inflation will, *ceteris paribus,* encourage investors to act rather than wait. Their actions will typically stimulate economic growth.
3. The argument that reduced environmental protection is a stimulus to production is accurate as far as it goes. Its failure is in its shortsightedness. Reducing the costs of production now may increase production today, but what about future production? To the extent that pollution retards the quality of necessary resources, it weakens our capacity to meet the material needs of future generations.
4. On one level the argument appears to be an example of positive analysis. The author is simply stating an impact of environmental protection efforts. Yet, the argument does not stop after having described the impact. It urges a reduced quantity of resources devoted to protecting our environment. Thus, the argument is a normative one. As such, you would want to be especially demanding in requiring solid evidence and sound reasoning from the proponent of the prescriptive assertion.

5. Because you know there are many other important economic goals, you must wonder why equity is so much more important. What values must the person have that have resulted in the giving of lesser importance to alternative economic goals? Most important, do I, the reader, have value priorities consistent with what is being advocated?
6. An economist who engages in normative analysis is necessarily molding a conclusion on top of a set of beliefs about the way the current economy works. Any policy proposal is motivated by a dislike for the current reality. Hence normative analysis is ultimately dependent on positive economic analysis. Descriptive claims and logical consequences flowing from economic models provide the foundation for any claims about how our economy could improve.

4
Economic Efficiency: The Importance of Markets

Efficiency is something like love and peace—everyone is in favor of it. Just as no one will advocate hate and war, no one will argue for waste. It would appear at first glance that every economy would be efficient; yet significant amounts of inefficiency do exist in the United States and in other countries, just as hate and war both exist. This paradox leads us to the conclusion that efficiency is a complex concept.

Because many economists argue that an economy in which there is free exchange between buyers and sellers is essential to attain economic efficiency, we need to study this type of economy to appreciate the goal of efficiency. We will devote six chapters (4–9) to the discussion of how efficiency relates to a market economy. Although the definition of efficiency itself is not too difficult, the process of achieving efficiency is complex and often controversial. We will study each aspect of the process of achieving efficiency so that we can gain an understanding of how the goal of efficiency is attained.

WHAT IS EFFICIENCY?

In Chapter 1 we learned that the study of economics exists because we live in a world of scarcity. Our limited access to the factors of production (labor, capital, and natural resources) make it virtually impossible for us to fulfill all our wants and needs. We learned in Chapter 2 that whenever we increase our production of one good (for example, personal computers), we must sacrifice the production of some other good (for example, television sets). In other words, we experience opportunity costs. Because these trade-offs are inevitable, every economic system attempts to minimize these opportunity costs by becoming more efficient.

Technical Efficiency

Technical Efficiency Production of the maximum output from a specific combination of labor, capital, and natural resources

One way to achieve this efficiency is to produce every product with the minimum amount of resources, that is, we want to be *technically efficient*. For instance, if a shoe company that employs 50 workers can produce 200 pairs of shoes a day, it is more efficient than if 50 workers produced only 150 pairs of shoes per day, *ceteris paribus*. Each worker produces 4 pairs of shoes in the first case, whereas in the second case each worker produces only 3 pairs. In the second case, the company is employing the same number of workers but is getting 50 fewer pairs of shoes (200 − 150 = 50).

All economic systems desire to produce every good and service with technical efficiency. By achieving this level of efficiency, companies can maximize the level of production in an economy; that is, they move toward producing a combination of goods and services that is on the production-possibility curve.

In Figure 4–1 both points *A* and *B* are technically efficient in that

Figure 4–1
Production Possibilities Curve
This curve demonstrates the efficient production of combination *A* or *B* and the inefficient production of combination *C*.

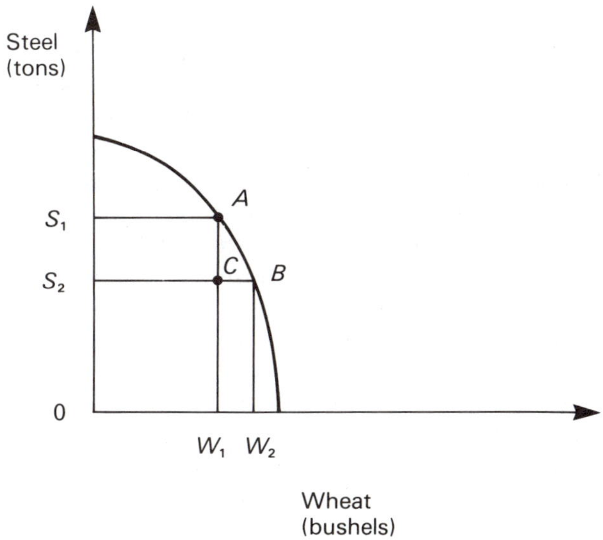

they represent maximum levels of output that can be produced by a given combination of capital, labor, and natural resources. If, however, an economy produced only combination *C*, then the economy would be producing inefficiently, because combination *C* produces a smaller combination of total output than either combination *A* or *B*. For example, if the economy would use its resources more efficiently, it could expand its output of steel from S_2 to S_1 or wheat from W_1 to W_2 without sacrificing any other output. In other words, as an economy moves from a less-efficient level of production (*C*) to a more-efficient level (either *A* or *B*), it experiences zero opportunity costs.

Economic Efficiency

Economic Efficiency Technically efficient production of the combination of goods and services that best satisfies the needs and wants of society

Technical efficiency tells us only how to produce a given combination of goods and services, but it does not give us any clue about what combination is preferred by consumers. Even if an economy does achieve technical efficiency, it may not have achieved its maximum level of *economic efficiency*. The economy must still ask what goods and services an economy should produce. For example, if we examine the production-possibility curve in Figure 4–1, we know that this economy is technically efficient in the production of both combination $A(S_1W_1)$ and combination $B(S_2W_2)$. However, we do not know whether the economy would prefer to consume combination *A* or combination *B*. To answer that question we must understand economic efficiency.

When an economy is faced with scarcity, it must answer the questions, What should we produce? How much should we produce of each? How should we produce those goods and services? and For whom are the goods and services produced? Technical efficiency helps us to answer the "how" questions, but economic efficiency is needed to answer the "what," "how much," and "for whom" questions.

An economy must decide what it wants to consume and then combine its factors of production to achieve the maximum combination of the goods and services it desires. For example, in Figure 4–1 some country named Capital-land may prefer S_1 quantity of steel and W_1 quantity of wheat (point *A*) because it wishes to expand its construction of new factories, and it does not have a very large population to feed. If Capital-land can actually produce combination *A*, then the economy of Capital-land has achieved economic efficiency, because it is efficiently producing the combination most desired by the citizens and consumers.

Whereas a second country, named Consumer-land, prefers wheat to steel and wishes to consume only S_2 quantity of steel and a larger quantity of wheat, W_2. Consumer-land has already established a large number of factories and is more concerned about feeding its large population. If Consumer-land actually produces combination *B*, it has also achieved economic efficiency, because Consumer-land is efficiently producing its most desired combination of goods and services.

Economic efficiency answers the "what" question by determining the combination of goods and services that consumers wish to purchase. Economic efficiency also answers the "how much" question by examining the interaction between what consumers wish to purchase and the ability to produce the product (technical efficiency).

Thus, one significant aspect of economic efficiency is the recognition that an economy can be technically efficient without being economically efficient. In other words, even though goods and services may be produced with a high degree of technical efficiency, there is no guarantee that consumers wish to purchase that particular combination of goods and services. Economic efficiency requires that producers determine the combination of goods and services consumers are willing to purchase and then produce that combination with technical efficiency. We will examine this concept of economic efficiency in great detail in the next five chapters.

SELF-TEST

1. If an economy moves from one position on a production-possibility curve to another, will the economy be less technically efficient?
2. Can an economy achieve economic efficiency without attaining technical efficiency? Explain.
3. Evaluate the following statement: Technical efficiency is more important than economic efficiency because technical efficiency emphasizes maximum output from a given level of input.

WHY SHOULD EFFICIENCY BE A GOAL?

With a little reflection on the definitions of technical and economic efficiency the importance of efficiency as a goal becomes readily apparent. The limited availability of economic resources means that our economy will not be able to produce enough goods and services to satisfy the desires of everyone. Consumers will always want more than an economy is capable of providing. To minimize the complications caused by this scarcity, countries should attempt to produce goods and services as efficiently as possible.

As we saw in the previous example of shoe production, a country that manages to produce 200 pairs of shoes a day with 50 workers achieves a higher standard of living than an economy that must use 50 workers to produce 150 pairs of shoes a day, *ceteris paribus*. Why?

Let's assume that both countries can produce two products, shoes and coats. In the first case if the economy decides that it needed only 150 pairs of shoes, then some of the factors of production that were used to produce shoes could be transferred to the production of coats. However, in the case of the second country 50 laborers are needed to manufacture 150 pairs of shoes. There are no extra workers to produce coats. If the second country wishes to increase its production of coats, it can do so only by decreasing its production of shoes (opportunity cost). Thus, this country cannot have a standard of living as high as the one that requires fewer workers to manufacture shoes.

When a country achieves economic efficiency, it has achieved its highest standard of living possible with the available labor, capital, and natural resources, and the current technology. Because scarce resources make it impossible for consumers to satisfy all of their desires to consume, economic efficiency allows us to move as close to the optimal level of consumption as is currently possible.

HOW CAN EFFICIENCY BE ACHIEVED?

Economic efficiency is achieved when businesses produce with technical efficiency the goods and services that consumers wish to purchase. But how can we establish an economic system that will permit consumers to express their desires and businesses to offer their products? One way to accomplish this interaction is to develop a *market* where buyers and sellers meet and exchange goods, much as is still done today in farmers' markets and at shopping malls and garage sales. In fact, this type of market or exchange system is the foundation for the United States economy.

Market Place or situation where buyers and sellers interact and exchange goods and services

The economic system upon which the United States economy is based is called *capitalism*, which in very simple terms means that buyers and sellers are free to bargain and exchange goods and services in markets. If a group of individuals wish to manufacture a new space-age toy, they are free to do so. In capitalism there are relatively few laws that restrict the activity of business. However, consumers are also free to consume whatever products they wish as long as consumers can afford to pay for them. When buyers and sellers agree

Capitalism An economic system in which economic decision making occurs in markets

upon price, exchanges will occur. This exchange process has many parts to it, and we will have to examine each to gain a full appreciation for the goal of efficiency.

How Do Markets Work?

All of us are probably familiar with garage sales and farmers' markets, and we certainly are familiar with supermarkets and shopping malls. Each of these examples is a market that has important characteristics that will help us understand how this exchange process improves efficiency. In the case of a shopping mall we can find the following characteristics:

1. There are *many buyers and sellers*. As a consumer you have many choices. If you are shopping for shoes, there will be several stores selling similarly styled shoes. As a buyer you can exercise your choice by purchasing the style you wish at the lowest price. But also, the seller knows that there are many buyers who have widely different tastes for shoes. Consequently, the seller will attempt to anticipate the styles people wish to purchase and offer those shoes for sale.
2. Companies must be *free to enter or exit a market*. If shoe sales are very good and shoe stores are earning high incomes, then we should expect additional stores to begin selling shoes. When additional stores begin selling shoes, customers have more choices, and that will pressure sellers to reduce their prices. If shoe sales are very poor and stores are losing money, then the stores should be free to close their shops and cease sales. This entry or exit is a response to consumer buying patterns.
3. Consumers and sellers must have *good knowledge and understanding of the market*. When you are shopping for shoes, you must do some comparison shopping, and you need to appreciate that some shoes have more quality even though their styles are similar. Without knowledge and understanding, consumers can not take proper advantage of the variety of shoes and prices that are offered. In a similar manner the sellers must be aware of the types of shoes that are selling well throughout the mall. If the sellers do not gather this information, they are unlikely to offer a successful line of shoes.

When these three characteristics interact, the economy will experience some rather astounding results. Because there are many buyers and sellers, customers have a great deal of choice. As a consequence sellers will attempt to offer the types of shoes we most prefer to wear. When one or more sellers succeeds by selling a large number of shoes, they earn more income (profit), *ceteris paribus*. Other sellers will recognize this success and will begin selling similar shoes because they, too, want to increase their sales. But as more stores present similar shoes, the consumer will have a wider range of stores and shoes to choose from and will purchase the shoes from the stores that sell them at the lowest prices.

When shoe sellers realize that they all will experience pressure to keep the prices of their shoes low (at least, keep the prices from rising too quickly), they must search for ways to keep the cost of manufacturing shoes from rising; that is, *the companies must become more efficient*. At the same time, the companies will be researching ways to provide consumers with different and better shoes. Consequently we find that these three characteristics create constant pressures to keep costs down, prices down, and attempts to develop new products up; in other words, a market works to provide us with economic efficiency.

SELF-TEST

4. There is only one laundry in an area. How will the efficiency of that market be affected by this limitation on consumer choice?
5. Evaluate the saying, "You pay for what you get." That is, explain what conditions must exist for this saying to make sense.

Role of Incentives and Freedom

Caveat Emptor A Latin phrase emphasizing that in a market economy consumers are responsible for what they purchase

A market economy emphasizes the role of individuals both as consumers and as producers. A market economy gives individuals the right to choose the goods and services they wish to consume, but it also gives them the responsibility to be smart consumers (*caveat emptor*, meaning "buyer beware"). If we wish a market system to function properly, individuals must accept the responsibility of being rational consumers who will, at the very least, study a market by comparison shopping before making a purchase.

Companies realize that consumers have extensive freedoms to purchase whatever goods and services they can afford. Companies also realize that consumers are generally looking for new, different, and better products to consume. Consumers' freedom to choose whatever products or services they find appealing provides a huge incentive for firms to search for better and more-efficient ways to provide consumers with products that meet their interests. This incentive extends not only to more-efficient production of existing goods and services but also to the introduction of new goods and services.

Because companies have the freedom to determine the goods and services they wish to produce, companies will research the interests and desires of consumers. If some companies can identify particular consumer interests, they have great incentives to produce those products to meet those consumer desires. When they are successful in anticipating consumer demand, companies will earn a higher level of income and will become more profitable.

Consumer Sovereignty The power of consumers to decide what goods and services get produced, how many of each are produced, and who produces them

As firms are successful in putting new products on the market, consumers have the incentive to shop for the "best buy." That is, consumers can exercise their *consumer sovereignty* to purchase the quality of products they wish at the lowest possible price. If the incentives and freedoms function effectively, a sophisticated system of checks and balances emerges. Consumers have the freedom to choose the goods and services they wish to consume and the incentive to purchase those products at the lowest possible prices. Sellers, on the other hand, have the freedom to offer consumers a wide variety of goods and services and the incentive to sell those goods and services at the highest possible prices.

If the three basic characteristics of a market exist (many buyers and sellers, easy entry and exit, and good knowledge), the eventual result will be a price that satisfies those buyers and sellers who wish to participate in the market. In addition, the companies will have to produce their goods and services as efficiently as possible. The details of this process will be discussed in the following three chapters.

ACTIVE REVIEW

1. Examine the following production-possibility curve (Figure 4a).
   a. Identify the point(s) of technical efficiency and explain why you have made your choice.
   b. Is either combination *B* or *C* superior to combination *A*? Explain why.
   c. How will the people of this economy know when they have achieved economic efficiency?

Figure 4a

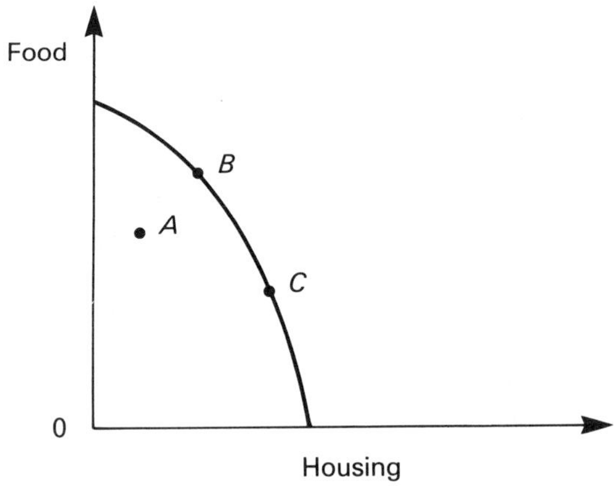

2. Many economists argue that a market economy is necessary to achieve economic efficiency. They claim that the interaction of consumer sovereignty and the freedom of businesses to produce whatever goods and services they wish will compel these businesses to produce efficiently.
   a. Describe how the characteristics of a market interact to cause businesses to produce efficiently.
   b. If new businesses are impeded from entering a profitable market, what will happen to efficiency? Why?
   c. If consumers do not exercise their responsibility to search for the "best buy," will economic efficiency be reduced? Why?

ANSWERS TO ACTIVE REVIEW

1a. By definition *every* point that lies on the production-possibility curve is technically efficient. Thus, in Figure 4a both points *B* and *C* are technically efficient. If the society wishes to produce the combination of food and housing signified by point *B*, we know that point *B* is the maximum output we can achieve given the available supply of labor, capital, and natural resources. The same reasoning applies to point *C*.

1b. Both combinations signified by *B* and *C* are superior to combination *A* because both *B* and *C* are using the same factors of production that are available for the production of combination *A*. Because *A* represents a smaller amount of the combination of food and housing than that of either *B* or *C*, combination *A* must represent an inefficient use of resources. For example, combination *A* may represent 10 units of food and 2 units of housing, whereas combination *B* may represent 12 units of food and 4 units of housing.

1c. A production-possibility curve identifies a series of combinations of outputs that are all technically efficient, but the curve itself does not tell us which combination is most desired by the consumers. To achieve economic efficiency a society must integrate its knowledge of technical efficiency with an understanding about *what* consumers wish to purchase. Without measuring what consumers desire, there is no way to decide whether *B* or *C* is a superior combination. Once the dimension of consumer's desire is added, we can then choose whether combination *B* or *C* achieves economic efficiency.

ANSWERS TO SELF-TEST

1. No! By definition all the points on the production-possibility curve are technically efficient. The production-possibility curve demonstrates the maximum combination of two goods that can be produced given the available supply of labor, capital, and natural resources.
2. No! Economic efficiency is attained when we are able to produce with technical efficiency the combination of goods and services that consumers want most to purchase. If production were technically inefficient, consumers would always have less output to consume than would be possible if the economy were producing with technical efficiency. Although businesses could produce a desirable combination of goods and services while being technically inefficient, businesses can always improve the amount of output and, therefore, the standard of living by becoming technically efficient.
3. Technical efficiency is a very important concept, because a company that is technically efficient eliminates waste. Economic efficiency, however, is more important, because it includes the concept of technical efficiency. To be economically efficient a company must produce what buyers wish to consume with technical efficiency. That is, if an economy was technically efficient at producing rear-wheel-drive automobiles, but consumers wanted front-wheel-drive automobiles rather than rear-wheel-drive autos, the production of rear-wheel-drive autos would actually be wasteful.
4. Many sellers is one of the important characteristics of a market that produces efficiently. When many sellers exist, consumers can choose the seller from whom they wish to purchase their products. Because consumers have this wide range of choices, they tend to purchase the products that are sold at the lowest prices. This desire to purchase at the lowest price encourages businesses to find ways to lower their costs (become more technically efficient). These lower costs eventually allow prices to fall. If only one laundry exists in an area, the pressures

to reduce price and costs are no longer present. It is probable that the one laundry will be less efficient than if that same laundry had to compete with several other laundries in the area.

5. The saying "You pay for what you get" assumes that the price of a product accurately reflects its quality. If the basic competitive characteristics of many buyers and sellers, easy entry and exit, and good product knowledge exist, then the saying does make sense. If, however, competitive characteristics are not complete, then the price may be higher than the cost of production and not accurately reflect the quality of the product.

5
Supply and Its Importance to the Goal of Efficiency

In the general market model discussed in Chapter 4 we learned that companies experienced competitive pressure to produce goods and services efficiently, but we were not given any detail about how that pressure actually occurs. Chapter 4 did define technical efficiency as the production of a specific quantity of goods or services with the least amount of factors of production. We now need to determine how companies attempt to achieve this technical efficiency. Chapter 5 will expand upon the definition of technical efficiency to develop the concept of supply and all its cost components. Eventually we will introduce the concept of demand to explain how demand and supply interact to achieve economic efficiency.

SUPPLY: WHAT IS IT?

Supply Amount of product or service that a company is willing and able to offer for sale at various prices, *ceteris paribus*

In the world of an economist, *supply* has a very specific meaning. Instead of identifying just the quantity of goods and services that companies have available for sale or have already sold, economists want to know how much a company is willing and able to sell at various prices.

The concept of supply can be illustrated most effectively through example. Let's assume that Jean Dunn owns a doughnut shop. Before she can bake and sell any doughnuts Jean must have a stove, the proper cooking utensils, the right ingredients, and some laborers to bake the doughnuts. To supply doughnuts (that is, to offer doughnuts for sale) she must incur certain costs of production. In examining these costs she can determine the price below which it is unprofitable to sell any doughnuts, and she can also determine how high the price must rise to encourage her to offer increasingly larger amounts of doughnuts.

Upon reviewing the costs associated with doughnut making Jean learns that when consumers are willing to pay higher prices for doughnuts, she can increase the number of doughnuts she is willing to sell (see Table 5–1). The information from this *supply schedule* provides us with the seller's estimate of how many units of production he or she is willing to offer for sale at each price in a series of prices. For example, if consumers are willing to pay $.40 per doughnut, the doughnut company is willing to supply 350 doughnuts for a total value of sales of $140 (350 × $.40 = $140). If, however, consumers only wish to pay $.20 per doughnut, then the doughnut company will offer only 100 doughnuts for sale per day.

Supply Schedule A list that identifies the quantity of a good or service that can be produced at various prices

Can you explain why the seller must increase the price of doughnuts if production increases? At first glance you might guess that as a company increases production its costs would fall. But according to the doughnut example, just the opposite occurs. Increasing opportunity cost is the reason higher prices are necessary to encourage higher levels of production. In other words, as we increase the output of one product, we will sacrifice increasingly larger amounts of other products, *ceteris paribus*. Remember the production-probability curve in Chapters 2 and 4 indicated that when production of one product increased, the amount of the other product decreased in ever-increasing amounts. This principle is demonstrated in the *supply curve.*

Supply Curve A graphic representation of the information in a supply schedule

If we read Figure 5–1 properly, we see that this doughnut maker is willing to sell 100 doughnuts per day at $.20 per doughnut, but she is also willing to sell 350 doughnuts per day if customers are willing to pay $.40 per doughnut. Neither the graph nor the supply

Table 5–1
Supply Schedule

Price/Doughnut	Quantity/Day
$.10	0
.20	**100**
.30	250
.40	**350**
.50	425
.60	475

Figure 5–1
Supply Curve for Doughnuts

This diagram demonstrates that a company will increase its production if it can receive higher prices to pay for the higher costs of production.

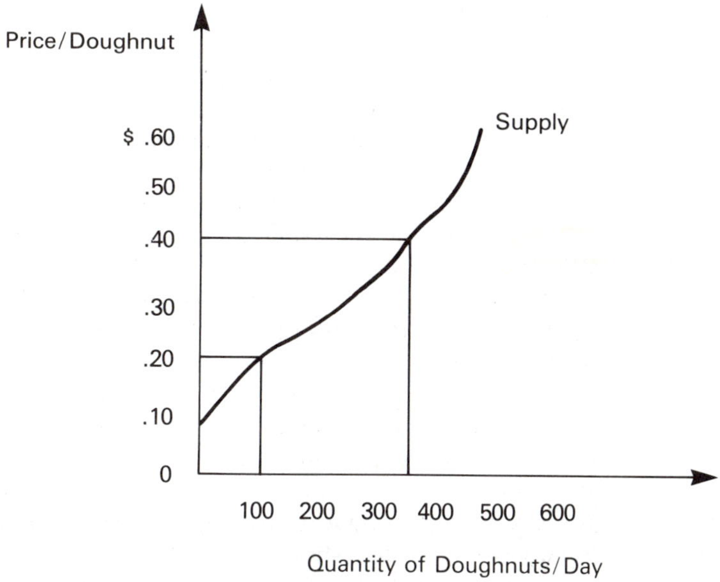

schedule, however, explains why the seller needs higher prices to entice the production of more doughnuts. To understand why supply behaves in this manner we need to understand the nature of production.

SELF-TEST

1. Assume that you are a seller of bicycles. Explain the conditions under which you would be equally satisfied if you sold 5 bicycles per day or 25 bicycles per day.

PRODUCTION AND PRODUCTIVITY

The willingness and ability of a company to supply any product (doughnuts in this case) depend upon the company's ability to combine the factors of production (labor, capital, and natural resources) to produce the goods and services effectively. Whenever production occurs, it does so within the constraints of the available plant and equipment. For example, in the production of doughnuts, each seller has a store with certain size of oven and a certain number of cooking utensils that fit properly into the oven. As Jean Dunn considers changing the number of doughnuts she wishes to sell each day, she must remember that she will make those alterations by changing both the quantity of ingredients that she needs to bake the doughnuts as well as the number of people working for her. But in the short run, Jean cannot change the size of her store or the oven.

Short Run A period of time during which certain factors of production cannot be increased or decreased

It is important to note that economists define the *short run* as that period of time in which a company is unable to alter the size of its capital. They do not identify the short run as a specific period of time because the short run would differ in different industries.

Because virtually all production takes place under the constraints of the short run, the supply concept is usually analyzed under short-run conditions. The consequence of this constraint is that changes in production must occur in the established plant with existing equipment. In the specific case of the doughnut shop, if the owner wishes to increase output in the short run, she must work longer hours, hire more workers, and purchase more ingredients. Because Jean cannot increase the size of her shop, she will experience a decrease in *productivity* (rate of production) as the production of doughnuts increases.

Productivity The rate of change in output as one factor of production is increased, *ceteris paribus*

In Table 5–2 we see the production of doughnuts expanding as the number of workers increases (200 units of production with one workers to 825 doughnuts with five workers). But upon closer examination of the data, we find that the addition of each new worker does not have the same effect on total production. The first worker bakes 200 doughnuts per day, whereas the second worker raises production to 425, an increase of 225 doughnuts. Assuming that the two employees have the same doughnut-making skills, why would the second worker be more productive than the first one?

To understand this result we must understand the relationship between productivity and the short run. Because production requires

Table 5–2
Doughnut Production

Number of Workers	Quantity of Doughnuts Total Production (TP) per day	Additional Production of Doughnuts Marginal Product (MP)	
0	0		
1	200	200	increasing marginal returns
2	425	225	
3	600	175	diminishing marginal returns
4	750	150	
5	825	75	
6	825	0	

a combination of all factors of production (labor, capital, and natural resources), the particular mix of the factors will influence productivity. In the short run we know that the amount of capital (plant and equipment) cannot be altered. Thus, any increase in output will result from an increase in the amount of labor and materials working with a fixed amount of capital.

When a company is employing a very small number of workers (for example, one employee), it probably is using its capital equipment very inefficiently. If, for example, the doughnut company doubles its employment from one to two employees, the production of doughnuts is likely to expand by more than double the previous amount (200 doughnuts to 425 doughnuts). But as the doughnut company continues to employ more workers, output will continue to increase but at a diminishing rate. The larger number of workers causes increasing problems with coordination and scheduling. We can see this change in productivity by observing the change in the *marginal product* as a company increases the number of workers it hires while keeping the size of its plant constant.

Marginal Product
Change in total production that results when there is a change in the variable resources (often labor) without changing the fixed resource (often capital)

In Table 5–2 we see that an increase from one to two workers more than doubles total product. That is, the marginal product for the second worker is 225 doughnuts (425 − 200 = 225 doughnuts). This significant increase in production makes sense because the bakery probably is designed to hire substantially more than one doughnut maker. This example demonstrates that when only one worker is employed, the bakery is not using its equipment very effectively. As employment increases, the bakery will initially experience a dramatic increase in output because the workers can become more specialized, which will permit a more efficient utilization of resources.

We cannot, however, expect this dramatic gain in productivity to continue. In Table 5–2 the marginal product of the fourth employee is only 150 doughnuts. Although 150 doughnuts is a clear increase in the number of doughnuts, the marginal product is not as large as that from the second employee because the short-run constraint imposed by the size of the bakery results in diminishing marginal output. Each additional worker will tend to add fewer doughnuts to the total output of doughnuts as the company moves closer to its point of maximum production.

Figure 5–2 illustrates this relationship by showing total production of doughnuts rising to 825 units as employment increases to five workers. After the second worker is hired, total production increases at a diminishing rate because the marginal product declines when the third through sixth workers are hired (Figure 5–3). In fact, in this

Figure 5–2
Total Production

This diagram demonstrates that total production tends to rise, although at slower and slower rates, as more labor is hired.

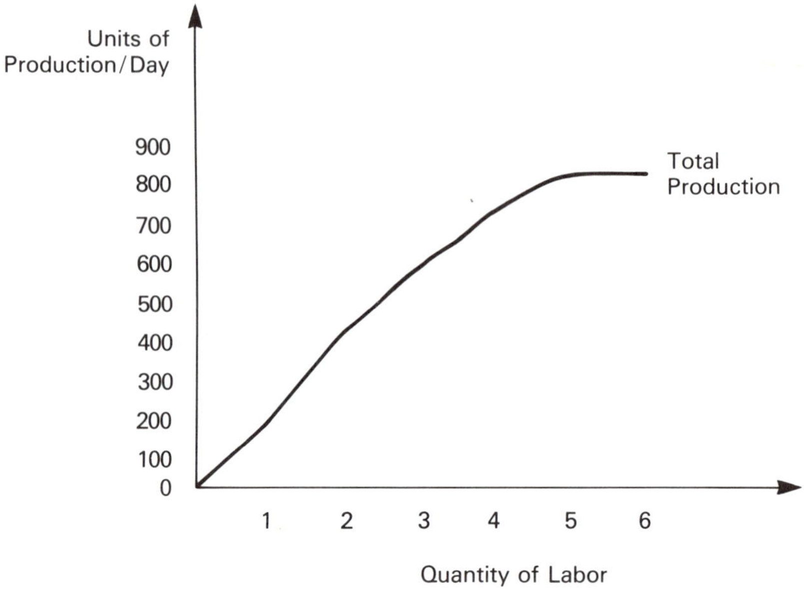

example, the sixth worker has zero productivity; that is, total production did not increase with the hiring of the sixth worker.

In more general terms, marginal product may increase as we hire our first few units of labor, but typically the marginal product will decrease as we continue to employ more workers. When businesses

Figure 5–3
Marginal Production

This diagram shows that as long as marginal production is greater than zero, total production in Figure 5–2 will continue to rise.

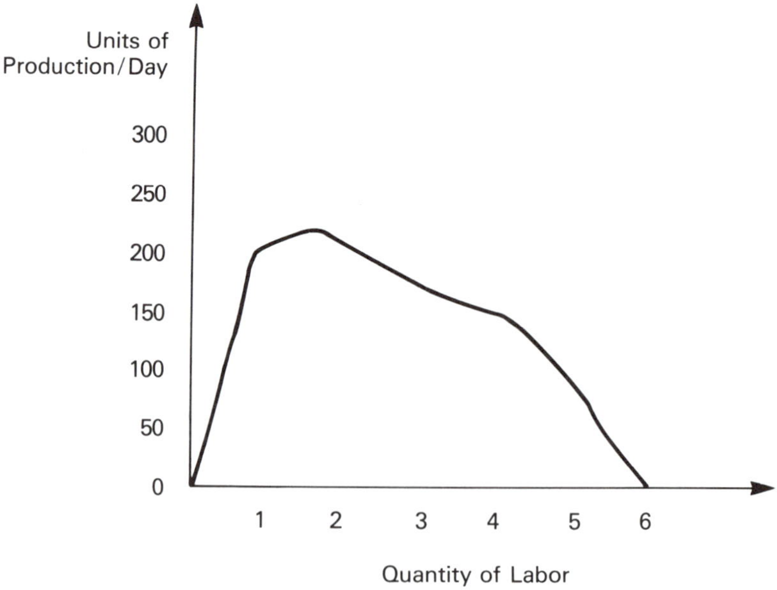

The Law of Diminishing Returns Additional employment of one factor of production (usually labor) will increase total production at a decreasing rate, *ceteris paribus*

expand production without increasing the size of their plant, these businesses will experience the *Law of Diminishing Returns*. In other words, although we pay each worker the same wage, and each worker has the same basic skills, each additional worker tends to produce fewer and fewer products. Consequently, the labor costs of producing each additional product will rise.

SELF-TEST

2. Explain the economic meaning of *short run*.
3. What is the relationship between the concept of short run and the Law of Diminishing Returns?
4. If you owned the doughnut shop that we have discussed in this chapter, what, if anything, might you do to increase the productivity (marginal product) of your workers?

THE LINK BETWEEN PRODUCTIVITY AND COSTS

Everyone in business strives to be efficient. To achieve this goal they must compare production in terms of physical unit (number of doughnuts) with the cost of producing each unit. This comparison can be demonstrated by continuing our doughnut example and introducing the cost of labor. In Table 5–3 we have added labor costs so that columns 1–3 identify the changes in production caused by changes in the number of employees; column 4 identifies the wage that is paid to each worker; and column 5 shows the marginal labor costs associated with the increased production of doughnuts.

Table 5–3 Doughnut Production and Costs

Number of Workers (1)	Total Production of Doughnuts (2)	Marginal Production of Doughnuts[a] (3)	Labor Cost of Each Worker (4)	Marginal Labor Costs[b] (5)
0	0		0	
1	**200**	**200**	**$20**	**$.10**
2	**425**	**225**	**20**	**.09**
3	600	175	20	.11
4	750	150	20	.13
5	825	75	20	.27

[a]Change in column 2
[b]4 ÷ 3

A close examination of Table 5–3 reveals an important relationship between productivity and costs. Column 3 illustrates that marginal production (productivity) initially rises and then falls as the number of employees increases. Column 4 shows that as the owner hires additional bakers, typical hiring practices leads her to pay each worker the same wage. In this case the workers are paid $20 a day.

However, because the marginal product of the bakers changes as the bakery hires more workers, the labor costs associated with the production of each doughnut changes. More specifically, as the marginal product of labor increases, the *marginal labor costs* will decrease. For example, as employment increases from one to two workers, marginal product increases from 200 to 225 doughnuts, and marginal labor costs decrease from $.10 to $.09. But as employment increases from three to four workers, the marginal product decreases from 175 to 150 doughnuts and marginal labor costs increase from $.11 to $.13.

Marginal Labor Costs The labor costs associated with producing one additional unit of output, *ceteris paribus*

By examining the data in Table 5–3 we can identify that productivity and costs tend to move in opposite directions. Because of the constraints caused by the short run, sellers know that productivity and costs change over different levels of output. Furthermore, sellers know that they need to examine those different levels of output to locate the specific level at which the company can produce most efficiently.

SELF-TEST

5. If you owned a business and paid each worker wages of $50 per day, why would your short-run marginal labor costs tend to increase as you hire additional workers?

TYPES OF COSTS AND THEIR RELATIONSHIP TO EFFICIENCY

Fixed Costs

Fixed Costs The costs of production that do not change as the level of output changes

In the short run, a company experiences two types of costs: *fixed costs* (*FC*) and *variable costs* (*VC*). Before a company can begin production it must acquire a production facility with which to produce its goods and services. In the doughnut example, the doughnut shop must have an oven before it can even consider baking its first doughnut. Once this acquisition is made, the bakery will have to pay the rent associated with the building, regardless of how many doughnuts the company actually bakes. For example, if the rent is $50 per day, that rent must be paid regardless of whether the doughnut shop bakes 10,000 doughnuts per day or 10 doughnuts per day. The $50 per day rent is fixed for the life of the lease, or in other words, the rent is fixed in the short run.

Variable Costs

Variable Costs The costs of production that change as the level of production changes

In addition to the fixed costs, however, a company must incur other costs that are directly related to the level of productive activity. As output increases, total outlay on labor, materials, and energy must also increase, because more of these factors must be used. In the doughnut example, the owner must hire labor, and purchase such items as flour, sugar, yeast, oil, and utilities. As production increases, the owner must purchase more of these factors. The costs directly associated with production are called *variable costs*.

The relationships among the different types of costs are important in helping us understand how companies attempt to be efficient. These relationships are technical but necessary. If you follow the examples closely, you should be able to comprehend both the relationships and their importance.

Let's continue our doughnut example by assuming that the owner wants to determine her costs of baking one through eight batches of 200 doughnuts. To get a clear picture of her operation she examines her costs by looking at both total and average costs (average cost (AC) equals total cost (TC) divided by the quantity (Q) baked: AC = TC/Q.) The data in Table 5–4 clearly identify that fixed costs (FC) remain constant at $50, regardless of the level of output produced; for example, the FC of one batch of doughnuts is $50, and the FC of seven batches of doughnuts is also $50.

On the other hand, variable costs (VC) change as the level of output changes. Because the doughnut shop is operating in the short run (that is, with a given amount of fixed costs), productivity initially rises and then falls (Law of Diminishing Returns). Variable costs respond to the changes in productivity by rising more slowly at first, then rising more rapidly as the level of output increases.

To get a good sense of how these costs interrelate, let's examine what happens to costs if the owner decides to bake six batches of doughnuts. Because TC = FC + VC, we find that when six batches are baked, TC = $300; FC = $50; and VC = $250. If the owner wants to know the average, or per unit, cost of each batch, she must divide the total by the number of batches baked, six in this particular case.

Table 5–4
Costs of Baking Doughnuts—Shop 1

Batches of Doughnuts	Fixed Cost (FC)	Variable Cost (VC)	Total Cost (TC)	Marginal Cost (MC)	Average Fixed Costs (AFC)	Average Variable Costs VC/Q (AVC)	Average Total Costs TC/Q (ATC)
1	$50	$ 30	$ 80	$ 30	$50.00	$30.00	$80.00
2	50	55	105	25	25.00	27.50	52.50
3	50	85	135	30	16.67	28.33	45.00
4	**50**	**125**	**175**	**40**	**12.50**	**31.25**	**43.75**
5	50	180	230	55	10.00	36.00	46.00
6	**50**	**250**	**300**	**70**	**8.33**	**41.67**	**50.00**
7	50	340	390	90	7.14	48.57	55.71
8	50	460	510	120	6.25	57.50	63.75

Because ATC = AFC + AVC, we find that ATC = $50; AFC = $8.33; and AVC = $41.67 (see Table 5–4).

If the owner decides to bake only four batches of doughnuts, she will get different cost data. Fixed cost will still equal $50, but variable cost will be only $125. Total cost for four batches will be $175. If we examine the average cost, we will find that the baking is more efficient when done in four batches rather than six. ATC for four batches falls to $43.75 and AVC falls to $31.25. Even though AFC rises to $12.50, ATC for four batches is less than ATC for six batches, indicating the greater technical efficiency at four batches. These relationships are illustrated in Figures 5–4 and 5–5.

Figure 5–4
Total Cost = Fixed Cost + Variable Cost

This diagram illustrates the relationship between fixed costs, variable costs, and total costs.

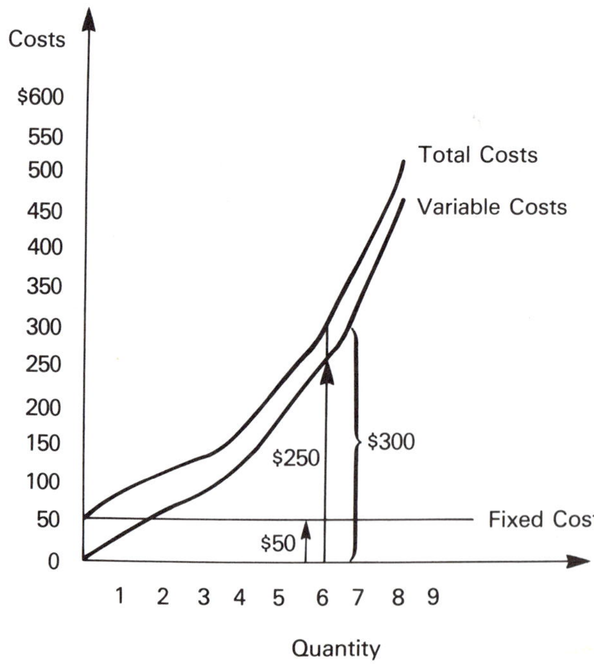

Figure 5–5 Average Total Costs = Average Fixed Cost + Average Variable Cost

This diagram illustrates the relationship between average fixed costs, average variable costs, average total costs, and marginal costs.

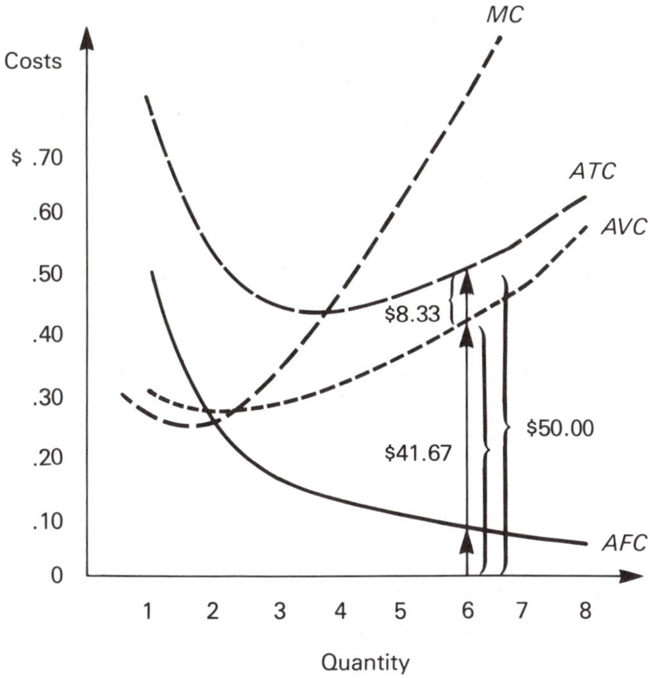

In Figure 5–4 the $50 fixed cost becomes a straight line because fixed cost remains the same regardless of whether two batches of doughnuts or six batches are baked. Variable costs and total cost curves will have the same shape because they are both influenced by the marginal productivity of labor (or other factors of production).

Figure 5–5 converts these same relationships to averages. Because all costs are now divided by the units of production, average fixed cost is a continuously declining curve. Average variable costs and average total costs reflect the changes in productivity by initially falling and then rising. The vertical difference between AVC and ATC is the value of AFC at each level of output.

Marginal Costs

Marginal Costs The change in total or variable costs as the level of output changes. Marginal cost is the added cost resulting from producing one more unit, *ceteris paribus*

At this stage you may be asking why do the variable costs change as output changes. You can see the numbers in Table 5–4 change, but you still may not be sure why they must change. The reason for the changes in variable costs stems from the concept of *marginal costs*.

If we return to our discussion about productivity (see Table 5–2), specifically marginal productivity, we recall that the marginal product of labor (or any factor) will generally rise as we hire the first few units of labor (or other factor), but the marginal product eventually declines as we increase the number of workers employed (Law of Diminishing Returns). When we introduced the cost of hiring labor to that analysis (see Table 5–3), we saw that the marginal labor costs initially fell but then rose as the doughnut shop increased its employment and production; thus, productivity and marginal labor costs move in opposite directions.

Because labor is a significant component of variable costs, it is safe to conclude that marginal labor costs will influence marginal costs. If we assume that labor is the only variable cost, then marginal labor cost equals marginal costs. In Table 5–4 we see that marginal costs behave very much like marginal labor costs. That is, marginal costs of producing doughnuts decrease from $30 to $25 as output increases from one to two batches of doughnuts. However, marginal costs rise as the doughnut shop increases production beyond two batches. The marginal cost of the third batch is $30; the fourth batch, $40; and the seventh batch, $90.

Marginal cost is important because it determines the shape of average total costs and average variable costs. In Figure 5–5 we see that when marginal costs lie below the average variable costs, the average variable cost curve falls. When the marginal cost curve rises above the average variable cost curve, the average variable cost curve must rise. The same relationship will hold true for marginal costs and average total costs. Because of this relationship we find that marginal costs will intersect average variable costs and average total costs curves at their lowest points.

The costs behave in this manner because of the definitional relationship between marginal and average concepts. For example, let's assume that you have a GPA of 3.0 at the end of your sophomore year. This GPA says that you have earned an average of B in all your courses to this date. Furthermore, let's assume that you earn a 3.5 for your courses in the first semester of your junior year. What will happen to your GPA? Because your 3.5 (the marginal grade average) is higher than your 3.0 accumulative GPA, your new accumulated GPA must rise about 3.0. If your grades for the first semester of your junior year fall to 2.8, then your accumulative GPA must fall below 3.00. Marginal and average costs behave in exactly the same manner as marginal and average grades.

SELF-TEST

6. Explain why the average cost curve tends to be U-shaped.
7. Explain why the average variable cost curve will be at its lowest (most efficient) point when the marginal cost curve intersects it.

8. Construct an example of average and marginal data to demonstrate the relationship between average variable costs and marginal costs.

COSTS AND EFFICIENCY

Now that we have examined several types of costs, it seems appropriate to ask how a company might use this information. It is not surprising that a company needs to know its costs of production, but it may not be immediately apparent that costs change as the level of output changes. Because costs do change as output changes, a company needs to identify the level of output that results in the lowest costs of production.

We can identify technical efficiency by determining the level of output that a company can produce at least average total cost. The relationship between ATC and MC gives us that information. When marginal costs equal average total cost, then the company has reached its level of maximum technical efficiency, at least in the short run.

Long-Run Costs

So far the emphasis in this chapter has been upon short-run productivity and costs, that is, the ability of a company to produce its output under the constraint of a given plant size. Yet, a company may wish to change its plant size. Before a company takes this action, however, it would generally do some planning to estimate what would happen to costs if the company were to operate with different plant sizes. More specifically, the company would examine its *long-run* costs.

Long Run A period of time that permits a company to vary its plant size. The long run assumes that all costs are variable

If we return to our doughnut shop, we know that the shop has reached its lowest costs when it bakes four batches of doughnuts for an average total cost of \$43.75 (Table 5–4). Yet, the shop owner may be curious about what would happen to costs if the size of the shop were expanded. The long-run concept provides a mechanism for making these estimates.

Table 5–5 examines the costs of baking doughnuts if the owner were to double the size of the plant (that is, double the fixed costs). Initially, this decision may not seem very attractive, because fixed costs have increased from \$50 to \$100 per day. As a consequence of this increase the average total cost of two batches of doughnuts increases from \$52.50 (Table 5–4) to \$87.50 (Table 5–5). But if we ex-

Table 5–5
Costs of Baking Doughnuts—Shop 2

Output	Fixed Costs	Variable Costs	Total Costs	Marginal Costs	Average Fixed Costs	Average Variable Costs	Average Total Costs
1	$100	$ 50	$150	$50	$100.00	$50.00	$150.00
2	100	75	175	25	50.00	37.50	87.50
3	100	90	190	15	33.33	30.00	63.33
4	100	100	200	10	25.00	25.00	50.00
5	**100**	**125**	**225**	**25**	**20.00**	**25.00**	**45.00**
6	**100**	**170**	**270**	**45**	**16.67**	**28.33**	**45.00**
7	100	230	330	60	14.29	32.86	47.11
8	100	310	410	80	12.50	38.75	51.25

amine the data a little more closely, we find that if the owner builds the larger shop, the average total costs of batches 4 through 8 are lower if they are baked in the larger shop than if they are baked in the smaller one. In fact, if the owner decides to bake six batches of doughnuts, the average total cost in the larger plant will be $45.00 (Table 5–5), whereas the average total cost for six batches in the smaller plant is $50.00 (Table 5–4).

This change in the relationship of costs to the level of output is seen clearly in Figure 5–6. Because shop 2 has higher fixed costs, the average total costs are significantly higher for the first few units of production. But as the output expands to four or more units, the importance of average fixed costs declines, and the more-efficient use of the variable resources reduces the average total costs. In the case of shop 2, the most efficient level of output is six batches of doughnuts.

ECONOMIES OF SCALE

Economies of Scale Reductions in the minimum average total costs that result from an increase in the size (scale) of the plant and equipment

Another way of explaining the above phenomenon is to point out that the doughnut maker achieved some *economies of scale* by doubling the size of the productive capacity.

After examining this data can you tell whether shop 1 is more efficient than shop 2? Do you have a tendency to say yes? If so, you must be careful, because we have asked you a slightly unfair question. To determine the most efficient shop we must know how many batches of doughnuts the owner wishes to bake. If he or she wishes to bake only one to four batches of doughnuts per day, then it would be smarter to operate shop 1, because the average total costs for four or fewer batches are lower in shop 1 than in shop 2. (In Figure 5–6c, ATC_1 lies below ATC_2 for output levels 1 through 4.)

Figure 5–6
Cost Relationships for Shops with Different Productive Capacities

These diagrams demonstrate what happens to average total costs as the size of the plant is changed.

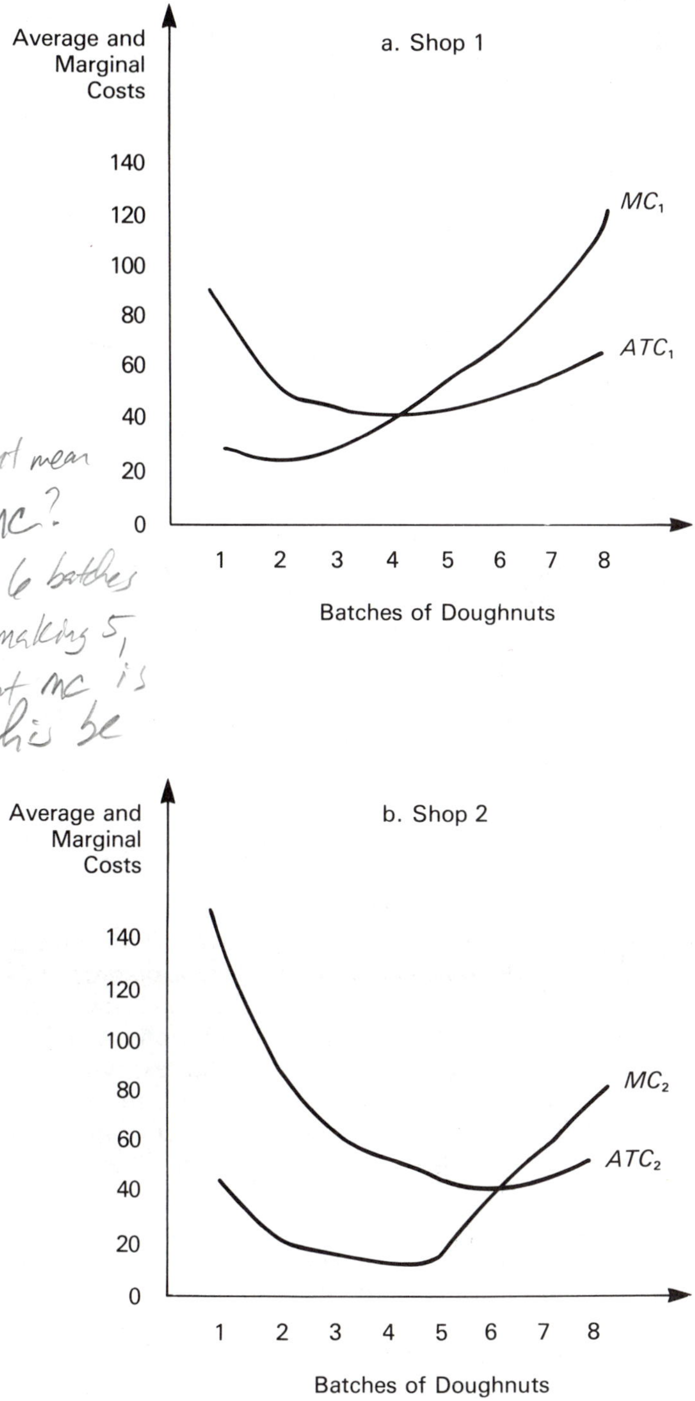

Figure 5–6
(Continued)

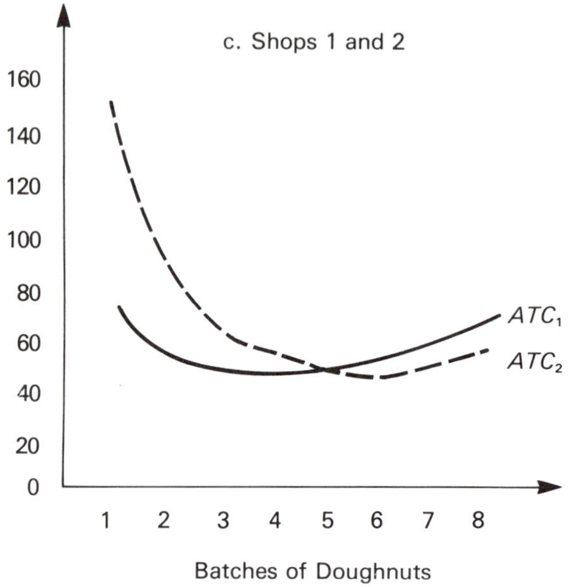

If, however, the owner expects to bake five or more batches of doughnuts daily, then he or she would want to use shop 2, because the larger shop is clearly more efficient at producing the larger level of outputs. Shop 2 has achieved some economics of scale. (In Figure 5–6c, ATC_2 lies below ATC_1 for output levels 5 through 8.) Thus, the owner can make significantly better economic decisions by examining long-run costs and choosing the plant that produces the desired level of output most efficiently.

As the example of the doughnut bakery demonstrates, businesses need to understand productivity and costs to determine their most technically efficient levels of output. First of all, businesses must realize that when production is increased in the short run (time period when one factor of production is held constant), the marginal product of labor (and other resources) will tend to decrease. The decreasing marginal product will cause marginal costs to increase and give the average total cost curve a U-shape.

Businesses will find their technically efficient level of output by finding that level of output where marginal costs intersect average total costs. If companies decide that their most efficient level of output has a higher cost than that of other sellers, then those companies must alter their plant size or incorporate some new technology. The actual level of output that companies will choose to produce will depend upon how much consumers wish to purchase. We will examine aspects of the issue in the next chapter.

ACTIVE REVIEW

1. Assume that you are an owner of a small business and you must decide whether you should expand output. To make the decision that will give you the most efficient output, you must answer the following questions.
   a. If you hire one or two additional units of labor (assume the Law of Diminishing Returns), will your marginal labor costs increase or decrease? Explain why.
   b. You are currently producing a level of output that is less than your most efficient level of output. If you hire an additional one or two workers, are your average total costs likely to increase or decrease? Explain why.
   c. Given your answers to the first two questions, would you expand your production? Why?
2. After you have answered the above questions, you realize that you have made a short run cost decision.
   a. What information do you need to make a long-run cost decision?
   b. What do you predict will happen to your average total costs if you expand the size of your company? Can you explain why?
   c. After studying your long-run cost information, you determine that doubling your plant size will enable you to achieve your most efficient long-run costs. What additional information do you need before you decide to expand the size of your business?

ANSWERS TO ACTIVE REVIEW

1a. Your marginal labor costs will increase because the marginal product of labor will decrease. If we assume that the Law of Diminishing Returns is in effect, then each additional unit of labor that you hire will increase production by a decreasing amount. Since you pay each unit of labor the same, the actual labor costs associated with each extra unit of production must increase.

1b. Your average total costs are likely to decrease. Although marginal labor costs are increasing, as the answer to question 1a indicates, you must also consider your fixed costs. If you are currently producing at an inefficient level of output, then you are probably producing an output below the efficient capacity of your company. If you increase production, your average fixed cost will fall significantly. The upward pressure of marginal costs will be offset by the more efficient use of your plant until marginal cost equals your average total cost, then your average total costs will begin to increase.

1c. You really cannot answer this question. You would like to expand production because the increased output would help you become more efficient. Nevertheless, you do not want to increase your output unless you know that consumers want to buy those products from you. Thus, you will increase your production only if you expect to sell that output. In other words, you will expand output only if you expect to become more economically efficient.

ANSWERS TO SELF-TEST

1. According to the concept of a supply curve, we know that a company is willing to increase the number of items it is willing to sell if the price of the product increases. The reason a company requires higher prices for increased output is that a company will experience increasing opportunity cost as its production increases; that is, as we increase the output of one product, we will sacrifice increasingly larger amounts of other products. In the case of bicycles you will be equally satisfied selling 5 bicycles or 25 bicycles if the price you receive for each of the 25 bicycles was sufficiently higher than the price for 5 bicycles to compensate adequately for the increased costs of production. Because of diminishing marginal productivity the marginal costs of extra units of production will rise. This higher cost of production mandates that the producer receive a higher price for the product.
2. Short run is that period of time in which a company is unable to expand the size of its plant. That is, a company is producing in the short run when it can change its level of output only by changing the amount of labor and materials. It cannot change the size of its plant in the short run.
3. The short run defines that period of time when a company cannot increase the size of its capital (for example, plant). The Law of Diminishing Returns states that increases in one factor of production will increase output at a decreasing rate, *ceteris paribus*. Because the amount of capital is held constant in the short run, the output produced from hiring more units of labor will increase at a decreasing rate.
4. Any particular marginal product relationship depends upon the existing combination of the factors of production. If you wished to increase the marginal productivity of your workers, you would have to alter one or some of the factors of production. For example, you could improve the equipment that you use to bake the doughnuts (that is improve your capital). You could train your workers so that they become more highly skilled bakers. You could also provide increased working incentives.

5. When considering how the hiring of additional labor will actually increase the costs of producing a product, we must recall the Law of Diminishing Returns and the tendency for the marginal product of labor to decline as more units of labor are hired. If you hired three extra workers at $50 per day and their marginal products were 30, 20, and 10 units, respectively, then each successive worker adds fewer units of production. Because wages remain the same, the marginal labor costs will increase from $1.67 ($50/30 units) to $2.50 ($50/20 units) to $5.00 ($50/10 units).
6. When a company is producing at a relatively low level of output, it typically is using its plant (capital) at a very low level of efficiency. As the company expands its level of output, the company uses it capital resources more efficiently, and the average total costs tend to fall. At the same time, however, marginal costs tend to increase. When average total costs and marginal costs intersect, the average total cost curve is at its minimum point. If the company attempts to produce a level of output beyond this point, the average total cost curve will rise, because the upward pressure of the rising marginal costs will be greater than the downward pressure from the falling average fixed costs. As a result the average total costs will tend to be U-shaped.
7. The marginal cost curve determines the shape of the average cost curve. When marginal costs lie below average variable costs, AVC must fall. When marginal costs rise above average variable costs, AVC must rise. Because the marginal cost curve tends to be a rising curve, the average cost curve will fall until AVC intersects MC. When marginal costs rise above average variable costs, AVC must increase. Therefore, AVC must be at its minimum point when it is intersected by MC.
8. There are many ways to demonstrate this principle. Let us examine the weight of students. Specifically, we want to know how each additional student will affect the average weight (Table 5a).

Table 5a

Student	Marginal Weight (Individual Weight)	Cumulative Weight	Average Weight
1	140 lbs.	140 lbs.	140 lbs.
2	120	260	130
3	70	330	110
4	70	400	100
5	150	550	110
6	250	800	133.3
7	220	1,020	145.7

Figure 5a

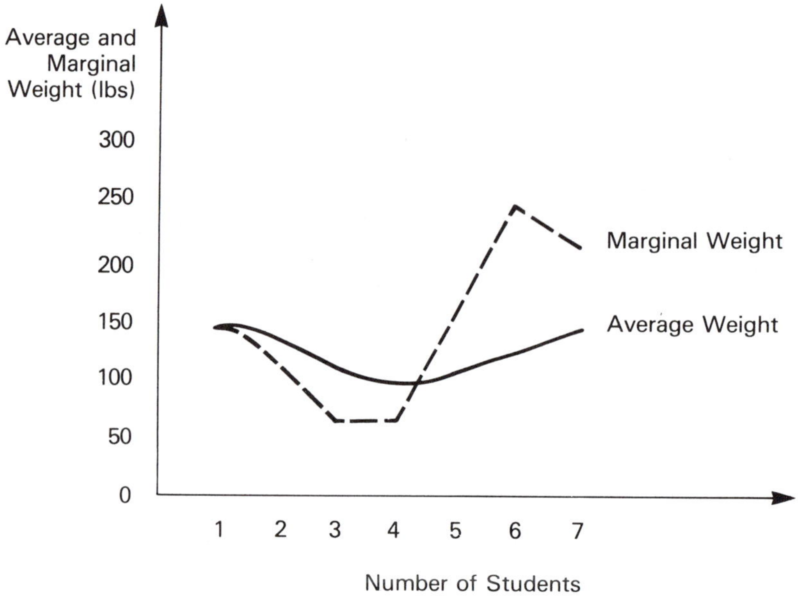

In Figure 5a, as long as the marginal weight (individual weight) is below the average weight, the average weight falls. But when the marginal weight rises above the average rate, the average weight rises.

6
Demand and Its Importance to Efficiency

The previous chapter emphasized how a company would strive to become technically efficient. But from the perspective of the entire economy, the goal is to become economically efficient. That is, companies must attempt to determine what consumers desire to purchase and then proceed to produce those goods and services with technical efficiency. The purpose of this chapter is to determine how consumers express their desire to consume certain goods and services and how companies respond to those desires. In Chapter 7 we will combine the features of demand and supply to complete our understanding of the market process and how it aids us in our pursuit of the goal of economic efficiency.

THE NATURE OF DEMAND

Typically, when we think about what we would like to consume, we say that we would like a steak dinner, a new sweater, a television set, a stereo, and many other items. Yet if we ask whether you actually possess or ever will possess all these items, most of you will respond no. Thus, your desire to consume certain goods and services is by itself not a very good indicator to businesses of whether you will actually make a purchase. Businesses need to know not only whether consumers *desire* to purchase certain goods and services but also

Demand Measure of consumer willingness and ability to purchase a good or service at each price, *ceteris paribus*

whether consumers have the *ability* to pay for these purchases. Producers thus measure *demand* by consumers' willingness and ability to pay for a good or service.

The demand for a good or service not only tells us that consumers have a desire for certain goods but also provides us with a measure of the intensity of that desire. An individual may want both a steak dinner and a sweater, but he or she may purchase only one of the items because he or she lacks the income (ability) to make both purchases. In essence, demand tells us how many units of a good or service consumers will purchase if the good or service is offered for sale at different prices, *ceteris paribus*.

In general, demand is an easily understood concept because people will typically purchase more of a product if its price is lower than expected. It is important to note, however, that we are changing perspectives. When we studied costs, we examined those concepts from the point of view of sellers and their costs of producing products. Now we want to think about the behavior of buyers. You must now think about what motivates people to consume.

Let us return to the doughnut example. Instead of thinking about how much it will cost to bake the doughnuts, you now need to think about your consumption pattern. If you were offered some fresh doughnuts at $.05 a doughnut, how many would you purchase? If the price were $.50 a doughnut, would you purchase the same number?

Most likely you would be willing to purchase a larger number of doughnuts at $.05 than you would at $.50. There are many possible reasons for your behavior, but one obvious reason is that you have only so much money to spend, and the impact on your budget of a dozen $.05 doughnuts is considerably less than that of a dozen of $.50 doughnuts.

As consumers, our goal is to maximize the satisfaction* that we gain from purchasing a variety of goods and services. If we simply made purchases upon impulse, we would often find ourselves with goods and services that provide us with relatively little satisfaction, while we are unable to purchase products that have a much higher degree of importance to us. Consequently, consumers develop a type of rating system that helps them make choices consistent with their tastes.

For most goods and services we gain a higher level of additional satisfaction from the first few items that we consume than we receive

*Economists refer to the satisfaction received from consuming a good or service as utility.

from the consumption of the last few items. For example, if you are interested in purchasing a winter coat, would a second coat be as important to you as the first one? In most cases, the answer will be no. The first coat will provide you warmth and protection from the cold. Regardless of its style, the first coat must give you substantial additional satisfaction because you have been able to change from a situation that provides you no winter protection to a situation in which you do have a coat with its warmth and protection from the cold.

If you were to receive a second coat, you might also receive considerable satisfaction because you can be more stylish or you can use the coats for different occasions, but it is unlikely that you can receive the same additional satisfaction as you did from the first coat. Your desire to keep warm has already been met by the availability of the first coat. In other words, your degree of additional satisfaction has declined. In more technical terms as you consume additional units of a product, you approach a point of saturation. Each additional unit tends to add a diminishing amount of satisfaction. Economists often refer to this concept as the *Law of Diminishing Marginal Satisfaction*.

The Law of Diminishing Marginal Satisfaction A general relationship that states that consumers will gain less additional gratification from the consumption of successive units of a good or service, *ceteris paribus*

If we apply this law to the concept of demand, we find that sellers must reduce the price of products when they wish to increase sales, *ceteris paribus*. In the case of doughnuts we may find that a local community may be willing to purchase 200 doughnuts a day if the price of doughnuts is set at $.50 per doughnut. But if the price is set at $.10 a doughnut, the community may be willing to purchase 2,000 doughnuts. At the higher prices the doughnuts are eaten sparingly, while at lower prices the purchasers do not mind if some of the doughnuts go stale and are either given to the birds or thrown away.

Demand Schedule Amount of a product that consumers are willing and able to purchase at different prices, *ceteris paribus*

Demand Curve A graphic representation of the information in a demand schedule

This demand relationship can be demonstrated by a *demand schedule* (Table 6–1) and a *demand curve* (Figure 6–1). The demand for doughnuts appears to be normal in that as the price falls, the amount of doughnuts that the community is willing to consume increases. If the price of doughnuts is set at $.45, the community will tend to purchase 350 doughnuts per day. But if the price is dropped to $.30, the amount of doughnuts purchased will tend to increase to 1,000 doughnuts per day.

Both the demand schedule and the demand curve emphasize the point that demand does not indicate one particular level of sales, but rather demand identifies a series of quantities that people are willing and able to purchase when they are offered different prices. Consumers will increase the quantity of doughnuts they are willing and

Table 6–1
Demand Schedule for Doughnuts

Price	Daily Demand Schedule Quantity Purchased Daily
.50	200
.45	**350**
.40	500
.35	700
.30	**1,000**
.20	1,400
.10	2,000

Figure 6–1
Demand Curve for Doughnuts

This diagram illustrates that consumers will tend to purchase larger quantities of a good as prices fall, *ceteris paribus.*

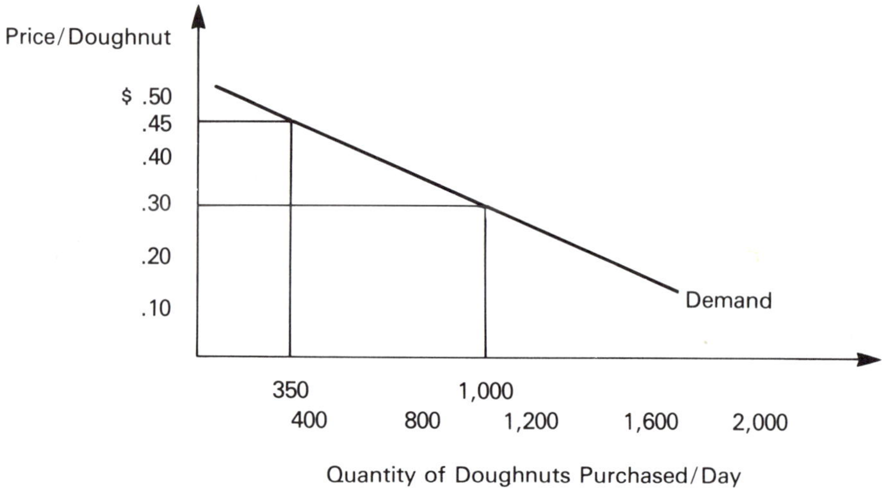

Change in Quantity Demanded A movement along a demand curve caused by a change in price

able to purchase when the price drops. In this example, price is an independent variable and quantity is a dependent variable. The demand curve demonstrates that the *quantity demanded* changes when the independent variable price changes. That is, when the quantity that consumers are willing and able to purchase changes as a result of a price change, there will be a movement along the existing demand curve, *not a change* or *shift* in the demand curve.

SELF-TEST

1. Let us assume that you are interested in purchasing some blue jeans, and you tell your friends that you are considering buying one or two pairs of jeans. Given the definition of demand, explain how you can demand two different quantities of jeans.

2. A demand curve illustrates that people will attempt to purchase more goods or services as their prices fall. Explain why businesses must drop their prices to encourage consumers to purchase more goods and services.

DETERMINANTS OF DEMAND

We have defined demand as consumers' willingness and ability to purchase a good or service, *ceteris paribus,* and we have identified the demand for a particular product as a schedule of price and quantity relationships, but other than price, we have not discussed any factors that influence the nature of demand. If you pause for a moment and consider why a community might be willing to purchase 500 doughnuts at $.40, you will focus on such factors as the income of the community, number of buyers, the general taste or preference for doughnuts, price of related goods, and expected future prices.

Suppose that the surgeon general of the United States just announced that the high fat and sugar content in doughnuts has been identified as a direct cause of heart disease. What do you think would happen to the demand for doughnuts? If you said the demand for doughnuts would fall, you would be correct (see Table 6–2). At every price consumers will tend to desire fewer doughnuts. The decline in the willingness to purchase doughnuts has not been caused by an increase in the price of doughnuts. Instead, a *change in demand* has been stimulated by a clear change in consumers' preference for doughnuts.

A Change in Demand
An alteration in the willingness or ability to purchase a good or service caused by a change in some independent variable other than price

Whenever any determinant of demand except price changes, the entire demand relationship between price and quantity will change (Figure 6–2). For instance, if the income of consumers increases, the demand curve is likely to increase, that is, shift to the right. If the

Table 6–2
Daily Demand Schedule for Doughnuts

Price	Pre-Surgeon General's Report Quantity per Day	Post-Surgeon General's Report Quantity per Day
.50	200	100
.45	350	225
.40	**500**	**325**
.35	700	425
.30	1,000	700
.20	**1,400**	**1,000**
.10	2,000	1,300

Figure 6–2
Demand Curve

This diagram illustrates that the demand curve will shift when some factor other than price changes.

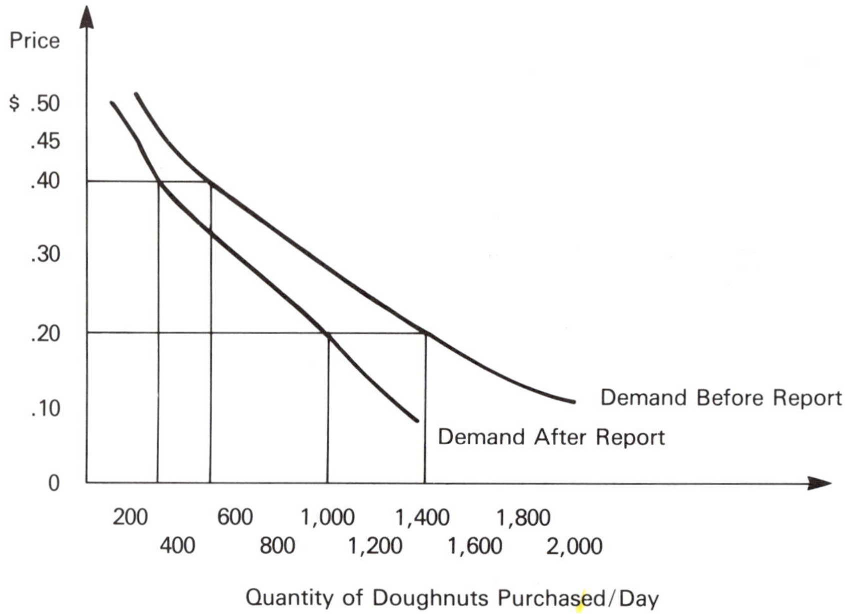

prices of substitute products (pecan rolls and danishes) fall, then the demand for doughnuts is likely to fall (shift to the left). But if the price of a complementary good (coffee) falls, the demand for doughnuts is likely to increase. Can you explain why each of these changes makes sense?

The distinction between a change in demand (shift in the demand curve) and a change in the quantity demanded (movement along the demand curve) is important because failure to recognize this distinction will cause considerable confusion about the causes of a market change. For example, if before the surgeon general's report the price of doughnuts falls from $.40 to $.20, we expect the sale of doughnuts to increase from 500 to 1,400 per day. This increase however, has occurred as a result of a price decrease, not as a result of a change in one of the other determinants of demand (see Figure 6–3).

Total Revenue The price of a product or service times the total number of units sold ($TR = P \times Q$)

When demand increases (demand curve shifts to the right, as in Figure 6–4), the opportunities to sell larger quantities at each price or to charge higher prices for each quantity exists. When companies exercise these opportunities, they increase their *total revenue.* When sales increase as a result of a movement along a demand curve (Figure 6–3), prices have fallen. When sales increase as a result of a price decline, we are no longer certain about whether total revenue will increase.

Figure 6–3
Changes in Quantity Demanded

This diagram demonstrates that a decrease in price will increase the quantity demanded, *ceteris paribus*. Sales increase to 1,400 from 500 as a result of prices falling to $.20 from $.40.

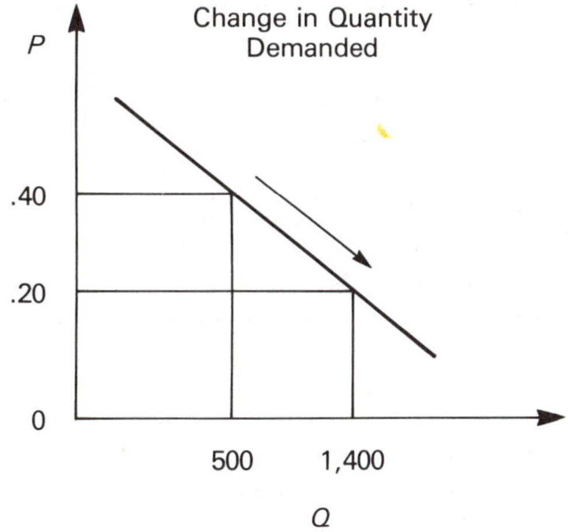

If sellers do not remember that prices have fallen, they may erroneously think that consumers are now willing to purchase 1,400 doughnuts at $.40. But as Figure 6–3 clearly illustrates, consumers will purchase 1,400 doughnuts only if the price drops to $.20 a doughnut. Total revenue would increase substantially if there were an actual shift in the demand curve (Figure 6–4), and consumers were willing to purchase 1,400 doughnuts at $.40 each. By studying the concept of elasticity in the next section, we can predict what will happen to total revenue when prices change, *ceteris paribus*.

Figure 6–4
Change in Demand

This diagram demonstrates that quantity demanded will increase at every price without a price decrease. Sales increase to 1,400 from 500 while the price remains at $.40.

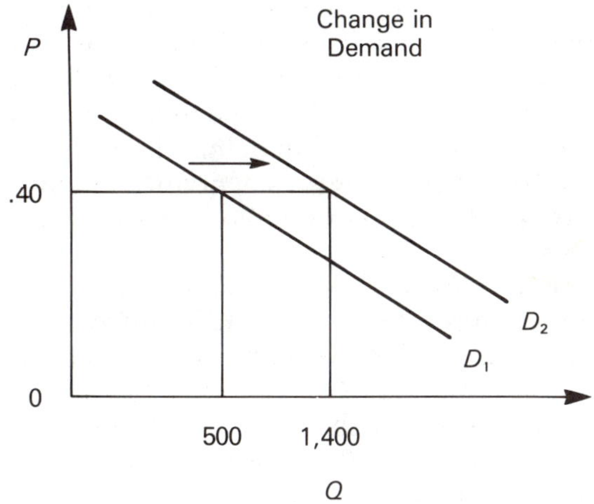

SELF-TEST

3. Assume that you are a travel agent. You learn that next month train fares will fall by 20 percent. What do you expect will happen to the demand for seats on airplanes? Explain why.
4. Economists emphasize the distinction between a change in demand and a change in the quantity demanded. Explain the distinction and its importance.

PRICE ELASTICITY OF DEMAND

Have you ever heard someone argue that if a company were to drop its price, it could make more money because sales would increase? At first glance that comment sounds reasonable. Because a demand curve slopes downward to the right, we know that the quantity of sales will tend to increase as the price falls. We do not know, however, whether the increase in sales will be large enough to cause an increase in total revenue. To ascertain whether a change in price will result in an increase in total revenue we need to understand the concept of *price elasticity of demand.*

Price Elasticity of Demand The degree of responsiveness of the dependent variable, quantity, to changes in the independent variable, price

Elastic Demand The condition where the relative change in quantity of sales will be larger than the relative change in price

Inelastic Demand The condition where the relative change in the quantity of sales will be smaller than the relative change in price

The responsiveness of consumers to price changes will depend upon several factors: (1) the availability of substitutes, (2) the necessity of a product or service, and (3) importance of the item in the consumers' budgets. If a product has many substitutes (any one brand of toothpaste is substitutable for any other brand of toothpaste), then the quantity that consumers are inclined to purchase will be very sensitive to changes in its price. For example, if the price of one brand of toothpaste rises, consumers will tend to decrease significantly their purchases of that brand (decrease in quantity demanded) and switch to another brand (increase in demand for the substitute brands). This high degree of responsiveness of quantity demanded to price changes results in our saying that demand for the first brand of toothpaste is *elastic.*

Demand will tend to be elastic if the product has many substitutes (for example, one brand of shampoo), is a luxury (for example, fur coat), or if its price is high relative to a consumer's income (for example, automobile). On the other hand, a product tends to have an *inelastic demand* if the product has few substitutes (for example, wheat), is a necessity (for example, insulin), and its price is small relative to a consumer's income (for example, salt). In each of these examples consumers tend to alter only slightly the amounts they consume as the price changes.

The concept of elasticity is an important tool for determining where a company should set its price. If a company knows that the demand for its product is relatively elastic, then that company should decrease its price if it wishes to increase the total revenue gained from sales. For example, if a company decreases its price from $100 to $90 (a 10 percent decrease) and its sales increase from 200 units to 240 units (20 percent increase), then total revenue will increase from $20,000 to $21,600. The reason for this increase in total revenue is that the loss in revenue from the lower price on each sale is more than recovered by the substantial increase in sales.

If the demand were inelastic, just the opposite would occur. For example, if a company decreases its price from $20 to $18 (10 percent decrease) and sales increased from 500 units to 540 units (8 percent increase), then total revenue will actually fall from $10,000 to $9,720.

SELF-TEST

5. Identify a product that you believe has an elastic demand. Explain your choice. Identify a product that has an inelastic demand. Explain your choice.
6. Why might a business be interested in the concept of price elasticity?

MARKETS: THE INTERACTION OF DEMAND AND SUPPLY

In Chapter 5 we learned that a company can find its most efficient level of output by examining the relationship between marginal costs and average total costs. But we could not identify the level of output a company should produce because we did not know the strength of consumer demand. Likewise, this chapter has taught us how to examine the demand of the consumers, but we have not been able to specify price because we have not related this demand to the costs of production (supply).

In a market economy we determine the price and quantity of a product by examining the interaction of demand and supply. The nature of demand informs us that consumers will increase the quantity of goods they are willing to purchase when they are offered lower prices. In contrast, companies are willing to sell more goods when they are offered higher prices. Graphically, we see that these two forces of demand and supply work in opposite directions in Figure 6–5. When the demand and supply curves intersect, the market is said to be in *equilibrium.*

Market Equilibrium

Equilibrium Price The level of output where the quantity demanded is equal to the quantity supplied

Shortage Quantity demanded exceeds the quantity supplied at a given price

The *equilibrium price* is an important concept because it helps us understand the dynamics of a market. For example, if the price of T-shirts were to drop from $10 to $8, consumers would like to purchase 600 T-shirts (*B*, Figure 6–5). When the price is $8, however, the suppliers are only willing to produce 400 T-shirts (*C*, Figure 6–5). That is, if the price for T-shirts is set at $8, the quantity demanded (600 T-shirts) will be greater than the quantity supplied (400 T-shirts), resulting in a *shortage* of T-shirts of the price of $8.

How will companies react to this shortage? If consumers wish to purchase more T-shirts (*B*) than suppliers have available (*C*), then some shops will sell out of the T-shirts, and these sellers will have to close their shops until more T-shirts are available. As long as the price remains at $8, sellers will continue to experience the short-run problem of selling out before meeting the demands of the consumers.

Because sellers do not want unsatisfied customers, they will attempt to reduce the shortage by allowing the price to rise until it is located where the quantity demanded is equal to the quantity sup-

Figure 6–5 Demand and Supply Curves for T-shirts

This diagram illustrates how the forces of demand and supply interact to establish an equilibrium price after a shortage.

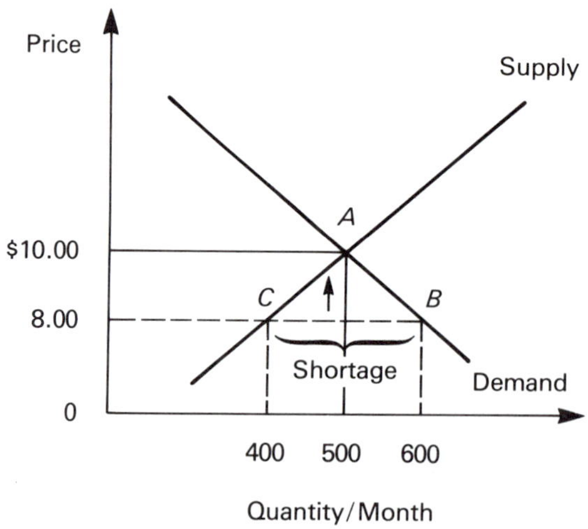

Figure 6–6
Demand and Supply Curves for T-shirts
This diagram illustrates how the forces of demand and supply interact to establish an equilibrium price after a surplus.

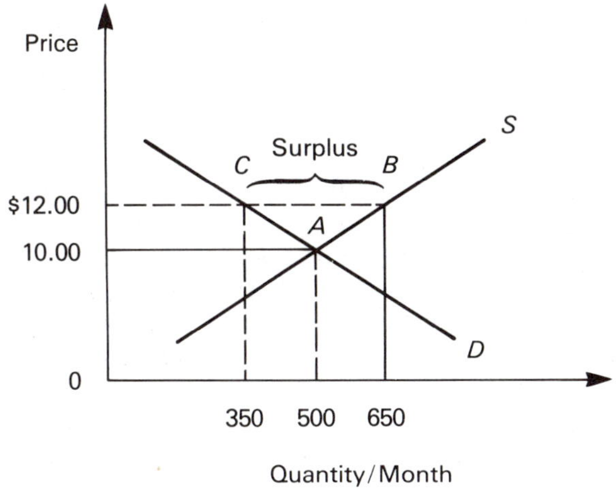

plied (*A*). In this example of T-shirts, the price will rise to $10. As the price rises, two phenomena are at work: (1) the number of T-shirts demanded will decrease (there will be a leftward movement *along* the demand curve because some consumers will not want to purchase T-shirts at a price above $8); and (2) the number of T-shirts supplied will increase (there will be a rightward movement *along* the supply curve because sellers will provide additional T-shirts at the higher price). The shortage will disappear when the price reaches $10 because consumers are willing to purchase 500 T-shirts and suppliers are willing to sell 500 T-shirts at that price.

Surplus Quantity demanded is less than the quantity supplied at a given price

If the price of T-shirts was set at $12, we would experience a *surplus* of T-shirts because suppliers wish to sell 650 T-shirts (*B*) but consumers want to buy only 350 (*C*) (Figure 6–6). At this higher price, sellers will have T-shirts left over. Consequently, their inventories will grow. Because companies want to sell T-shirts rather than keep them in stock, sellers will begin to drop the price. As the price falls, the quantity demand will increase and quantity supplied will decrease until the two quantities will be equal at a price of $10 and a quantity of 500 T-shirts (*A*).

Changing Equilibriums

Suppose all the schools in your community passed dress codes that forbid the wearing of T-shirts to school. What would happen to the equilibrium price and quantity? First of all, can you predict what will happen to either the demand curve or the supply curve? At least initially, the supply of T-shirts probably will not change, but the demand for T-shirts will most likely fall. Can you explain why? Because students are not permitted to wear the T-shirts to school, students are likely to purchase fewer T-shirts (Figure 6–7) and consequently increase their purchases of other types of clothing.

Once the demand curve shifts to the left (decreases), a surplus in T-shirts is created. The original demand curve is no longer relevant. In fact, readers of the diagram should act as if the original demand curve has disappeared. With the new demand curve we find that consumers are willing to purchase only 400 T-shirts at $10 (*A*). But because supply has not changed, sellers are still willing to sell 500 T-shirts. As in the previous example, a surplus will cause prices to fall toward a new equilibrium price at which consumers are willing to purchase and suppliers are willing to sell 450 T-shirts for $9 (*C*).

Any time there is a change in demand or supply (that is, a shift in the curves) a surplus or a shortage will be created. The companies will then adjust to the surplus or shortage and arrive at a new equilibrium price. This new equilibrium price satisfies both the consumers and producers remaining in the market. Consumers are able to purchase their desired quantity at the equilibrium price, and suppliers are willing to sell that same quantity because they are able to pay all their costs at the equilibrium price.

The dynamics of a market are critical to the goal of efficiency. We learned in Chapter 5 that companies could achieve technical efficiency producing that level of output that minimizes average total costs ($AC = MC$). In this chapter we studied the concept of demand

Figure 6–7
Changes in Equilibrium

This diagram demonstrates that a downward shift in demand will cause a new and lower equilibrium price.

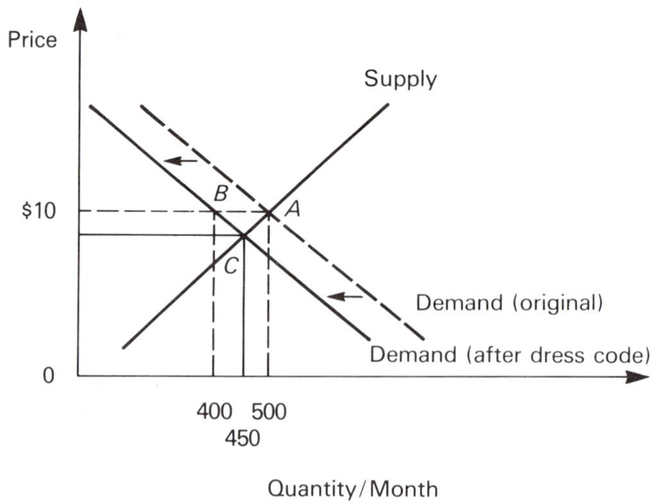

and how it interacts with supply to set a market price. Through this interaction of demand and supply we move toward achieving economic efficiency. In other words, we move toward our goal of producing with technical efficiency those goods and services consumers demand.

In Chapter 7 we will explain when forces of supply and demand work to achieve the goal of economic efficiency. We will discover that some very definite characteristics must exist for a market to force companies to produce efficiently.

ACTIVE REVIEW

1. You have a business that sells bicycles and you find that you cannot keep one particular style of bike in stock. Consumers want to purchase more bikes than you have available for sale.
   a. Explain your situation with the use of demand and supply concepts.
   b. Can you solve your problem in the short run by increasing your production (that is, by increasing your supply) of bikes? Explain.
   c. How will the forces of demand and supply correct the problem of an inadequate number of bikes? Whom will this market solution satisfy?
2. Assume that you own an apple orchard and that you sell your apples for $2 per pound. At this price you realize that the quantity demanded is less than your quantity supplied.
   a. Illustrate this relationship on Figure 6a.

Figure 6a

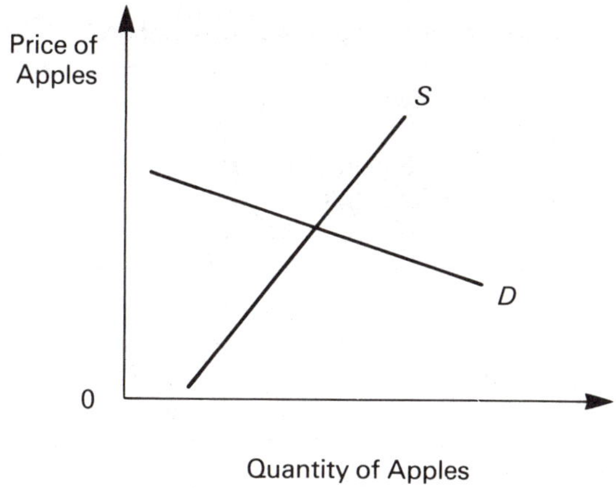

b. To reach an equilibrium price, will the price of apples rise or fall? Why?

c. Explain why the demand for apples is likely to be price elastic or inelastic.

d. Given the price movement you have described in question 2b and the degree of elasticity described in question 2c, will your revenues rise or fall as a result of the price change? Explain.

ANSWERS TO ACTIVE REVIEW

1a. At your current price the quantity demanded for bicycles is greater than the quantity supplied. In other words, you are experiencing a shortage (see Figure 6b).

Figure 6b

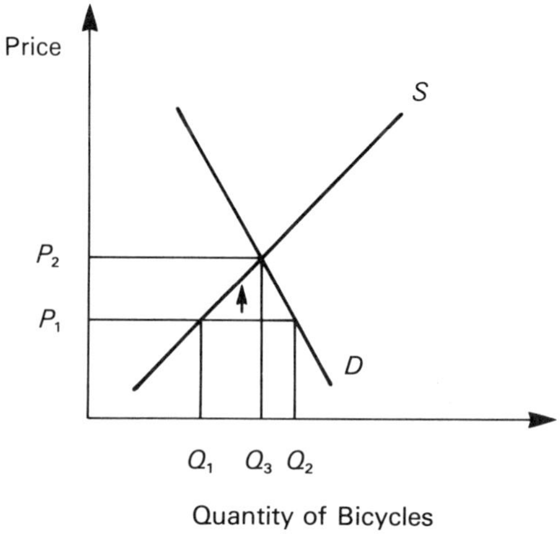

1b. You cannot solve the shortage problem by increasing supply because in the short run you cannot shift your supply. To increase supply you must increase the use of all factors of production, including capital. An increase in capital is a long-run economic activity. Consequently, in the short run the only way that you can increase the quantity of bikes that you are willing and able to sell is to increase the price of bicycles (P_2). That is, you will increase the quantity supplied (Q_3) (movement along the supply curve), but you cannot increase (shift) the supply in the short run.

1c. The forces of demand and supply will correct the problem of a shortage by causing the price of bikes to rise. When the quantity demanded for bicycles is greater than the quantity supplied, we know that the price of bicycles is too low. As the price begins to rise, the quantity demanded will decrease and the quantity supplied will increase until the quantity demanded and the quantity supplied are equal at one specific price, the equilibrium price.

We claim that buyers and sellers are equally satisfied with this price. All the consumers who wish to purchase a bike at that price can do so, and all the companies that wish to sell bikes at that price can sell as many bikes as they care to produce. Some consumers will be eliminated from the market because they either do not want to pay the higher price or cannot afford to pay the equilibrium price. Of course, the consumers who are eliminated from the market are unhappy. Nevertheless, according to this equilibrium analysis, the buyers who drop out of the bicycle market are free to use the money they would have spent on bikes on any alternative products they choose.

ANSWERS TO SELF-TEST

1. The concept of demand tells us how much consumers are willing and able to purchase at different prices, assuming that other determinants of demand remain constant. In your case you may be willing and able to purchase one pair of jeans if the price of jeans is $30 a pair. But if the price of jeans is $25, you may be willing and able to purchase two pairs.
2. Consumer demand is determined by the degree of satisfaction that we gain from additional purchases. According to the Law of Diminishing Marginal Satisfaction, consumers do not get as much additional satisfaction from the last item purchased as they did from the previously purchased item. That is, the first television set purchased by a family will provide greater satisfaction than will the second television set. To the extent that prices indicate the degree of marginal satisfaction that consumers expect from a purchase, consumers are likely to pay a higher price for a good or service when their purchases are few, but they are unwilling to pay that same price for larger quantities because they will not gain the same degree of marginal satisfaction from the additional items purchased.
3. To the extent that traveling on planes and trains are substitutes, a decrease in train fares will cause an increase in the quantity demanded for train travel. As more people choose to travel on trains, fewer people will purchase plane tickets. The airlines will experience a decrease in demand (see Figure 6c).
4. A change in the quantity demanded is caused by a change in the independent variable of price. The concept of demand states that change in price will cause changes in the quantity demanded, *ceteris paribus*. In the example in question 3, the quantity demanded of train tickets increased because the price of train tickets fell. A change in

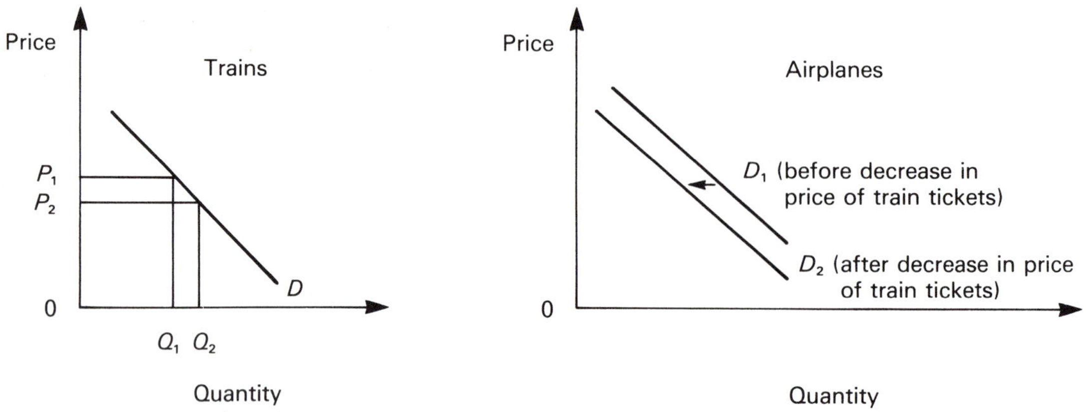

Figure 6c

demand is caused by a change in some determinant of demand other than price. In the airline example the demand for airline tickets decreased because the price of train tickets decreased.

This distinction is important because it can influence the company's ability to earn profits. If there is a decrease in the quantity demanded, the seller knows that the decrease was caused by an increase in price. Thus, the loss in sales may be partially or fully offset by the increase in price. But when a company experiences a decrease in demand, the company will sell fewer products at the same price. The company will lose revenue by an amount equivalent to the loss in sales.

5. A product will tend to have an elastic demand if it has many substitutes, is a luxury, or is expensive relative to your income. The following products will tend to have elastic demands:

   a. one particular brand of sweaters—many substitutes

   b. microwave oven—luxury

   c. yacht—expensive

   A product will tend to have an inelastic demand if it is a necessity, has few substitutes, and is inexpensive relative to your income. The following products will tend to have inelastic demands:

   a. electricity—necessity

   b. cigarettes—few substitutes

   c. bread—relatively low priced

6. Businesses are interested in the concept of price elasticity because it provides owners important information about how revenues will change as prices change. For example, if the demand for a particular product tends to be elastic (higher education, for instance), then the sellers know that a decrease in the price (tuition) will sufficiently increase

the number of students attending a university such that total revenues will actually increase.

If, however, a demand happens to be more inelastic, then a price decrease will cause a decrease in total revenue because quantity demanded will not expand enough to compensate for the price decrease.

7
Efficiency and the Competitive Market

Throughout the preceding three chapters we have been developing the importance of the goal of efficiency and how the concepts of demand and supply relate to that goal. As these three chapters have indicated, there are many steps involved in achieving the goal of efficiency. In addition to the importance of demand and supply, we must study how *competitive markets* tend to cause companies to be efficient. We need to understand that markets tend to cause efficiency only when they operate with competitive characteristics.

A Competitive Market Free and knowledgeable exchange among many buyers and sellers

In Chapter 4 we defined three characteristics of a competitive market: (1) many buyers and sellers, (2) freedom to enter and exit a market, and (3) knowledge and understanding of the goods and services and their prices. These characteristics are very important because they ensure that a market will achieve the goal of economic efficiency, that is, the producing of the goods and services that best match consumer preferences. The purpose of this chapter is to demonstrate how this process works.

COMPETITION AND AN INDIVIDUAL COMPANY

The three competitive characteristics cause competitive companies to behave in some well-defined ways that have some definite advantages for both the consumers and the community. First of all, the existence of many sellers of a similar product puts each competitive company into a price-taker situation. That is, no individual company has any control over the price it receives for its product. The prices are determined by the interaction of the demand for and supply of a product in the total market.

For example, in a wheat market we can determine the demand for wheat by measuring how much wheat buyers are willing to purchase at a series of prices. We can also determine supply by estimating the costs associated with producing different quantities of wheat. Because all wheat is basically the same, consumers are not concerned about who actually produces the wheat. Instead consumers will search for the best buy, meaning the lowest price. Farmers, on the other hand, are concerned about how much they will be paid to produce the wheat. If the price of wheat rises, they will produce more wheat.

Because consumers cannot distinguish among sellers, one seller cannot gain any price advantages on the other sellers. In other words, farmer A cannot charge a higher price by claiming that her wheat is better than that of farmer B. Consequently, when competitive conditions exist, the price of wheat (or any product) is determined by the interaction of the market demand and supply. Neither the individual seller nor the individual buyer has the ability to alter price.

Because all wheat is essentially the same, one price will emerge as the price at which all wheat will be sold. In the example demonstrated in Figure 7–1, the equilibrium price is $3 per bushel, meaning that every farmer who wishes to sell wheat can sell all that he or she wishes at $3. The example indicates that all farmers will sell 900 million bushels of wheat at $3 a bushel.

Because the market is so vast and sellers are so numerous, each

Figure 7–1
Market Demand for and Supply of Wheat

This diagram demonstrates the price and quantity that result from the interaction of demand and supply in a competitive market.

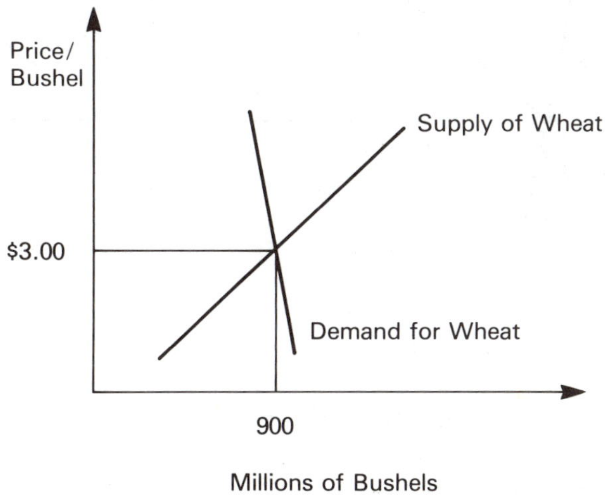

farmer contributes an insignificant amount of wheat to the total supply. If one farmer decided to cease production of wheat, the market supply curve would not reflect any significant decrease. Likewise, if any one farmer decided to double or triple the size of his or her harvest, there would not be any significant increase in the market supply of wheat. In other words, individual farmers have no ability to influence the price of wheat. They are price-takers because they must accept the market equilibrium price set by the interaction of the market demand for and supply of wheat.

In the wheat market example above, any individual farmer must accept the price of $3.00 per bushel. Why? If a farmer decides to increase his or her price of wheat to $3.10 a bushel, the farmer will not sell any wheat. Can you explain why? The competitive characteristics of many sellers of a similar product provide consumers with multiple options for purchasing as much wheat as they wish at $3.00 a bushel. There is no reason for anyone to pay a price higher than $3.00.

For much the same reason a farmer will not offer to sell wheat for a price below $3 a bushel. Because the output of any one farmer is so small relative to the total, each farmer can sell all the wheat he or she can produce at the existing market price. Because of this opportunity, the farmers cannot increase sales by lowering price. In essence, the demand curve facing the individual becomes a horizontal line or a perfectly elastic demand curve.

The information presented in Figure 7–2 identifies the important

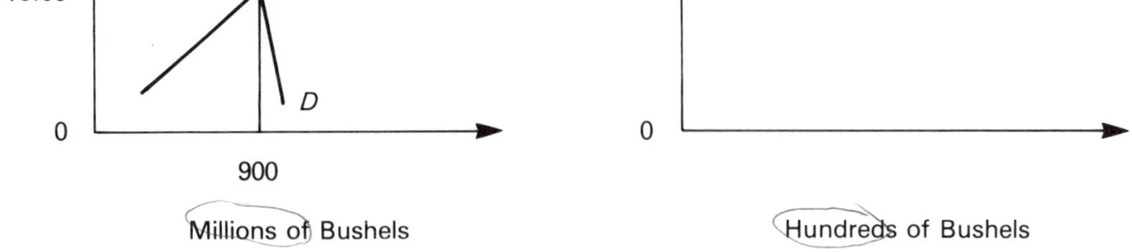

Figure 7–2
Determination of the Competitive Price

These diagrams illustrate that the equilibrium price in a competitive market becomes the demand curve of consumers for the product of an individual seller.

relationship between the equilibrium market price and the demand curve of an individual company. Once a market equilibrium price is determined by the interaction of the market demand and supply curves, that price ($3 in the example in Figure 7–2) becomes the demand curve for individual sellers. Because this demand curve is perfectly horizontal, it may appear as if any seller can sell an unlimited amount. But that appearance is incorrect for two reasons:

1. If a seller could expand sales to an unlimited amount, that seller would no longer be one of many small sellers. In fact, that one seller would dominate the market and competition would disappear.
2. The size of the seller's output is limited by its productive capabilities. These limits are identified by the units on the quantity axis. In Figure 7–2 the market demand for and supply of wheat are measured in terms of *millions* of bushels, whereas the demand for the wheat of an individual farmer is measured in terms of *hundreds* of bushels.

If a market experiences any changes in demand or supply, there will be a change in the price that can be charged by the individual company. If, for example, wheat farmers experience a poor harvest as a result of a summer drought, the supply of wheat will decrease, shifting the market supply curve to the left. This decrease in supply will cause a shortage of wheat at $3.00 a bushel. Consequently, the price of wheat will have to rise, causing the demand curve for the

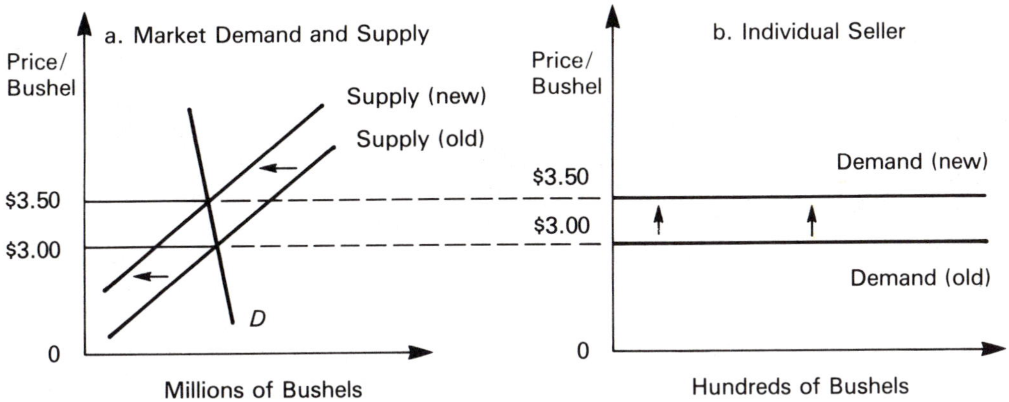

Figure 7–3
Change in the Competitive Price

This diagram illustrates how a change in the relationship between market demand and supply will cause a change in the price (demand curve) for the individual seller.

wheat crop of an individual competitive seller to rise to $3.50 (see Figure 7–3). As changes occur in the market supply of wheat, the demand for the wheat of the individual farmers will change. The changes, in turn, have important influences on the efficiency and profitability of the individual firm.

SELF-TEST

1. Under conditions of competition individual companies are identified as price-takers. Explain why these companies are price-takers.
2. Assume that you are one of many sellers of lettuce. Identify two reasons why demand for your lettuce may shift downward. What impact will these shifts have on the price of your lettuce? Why?

COMPETITION AND PROFIT

The actual amount of output that a competitive company is willing to produce depends upon the relationship between the demand for the product and the individual company's costs of production. Although a horizontal demand curve indicates that an individual company can sell an indefinite amount of goods without lowering its price, we can identify the amount of output that a company will actually produce by examining a company's cost of production for each level of output (see Figure 7–4).

Companies are always searching for output levels that will give them more profit. Whenever revenues exceed economic costs, the firm has earned an *economic profit*. The desire for economic profits is a fundamental motivator for those who start and own businesses.

Economic Profit
Total revenue minus total economic costs

When the market price is $3 per bushel, the individual farmer is able to earn an economic profit. How can we tell? In Figure 7–4 we see that the individual company experiences $P = AC$ at both output levels of Q_a and Q_d. Thus, if the company produces either Q_a or Q_d amounts of wheat, the farmer will break even; that is, the farmer will experience total revenue equal to total cost and will not earn any economic profit. Remember, total revenue is price times quantity and total cost is average cost times quantity.

If, however, the farmer chooses to produce any level of output between Q_a and Q_d, he or she can earn an economic profit because at

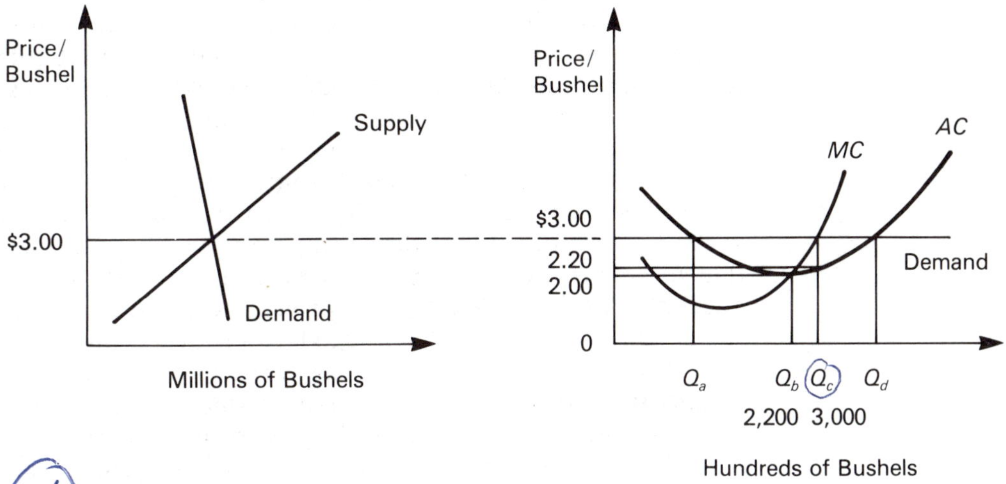

Figure 7–4
Profit Maximizing Level of Output
This diagram shows that output Q_c maximizes profits for the individual seller.

any level of output between Q_a and Q_d the price or average revenue is greater than average cost. For example, the total revenue received from selling Q_c amount of wheat equals the price ($3.00) times the quantity (3,000 units), or $9,000. The total costs incurred from producing Q_c of wheat equals the average costs ($2.20) times the quantity (3,000 units), or $6,600. Thus, the economic profit equals total revenue minus total costs ($9,000 − $6,600), or $2,400.

The farmer must now determine the level of output that will actually maximize profits. If you had to make the farmer's decision, which level of output would you choose? It should be clear that you would not choose Q_a or Q_d because we have already indicated that a farm breaks even at each of these levels of output.

What about output Q_b? According to our discussion in Chapter 5 output Q_b identifies the most technically efficient level of output for this farmer. (Remember the relationship that states that marginal costs will intersect average costs at the lowest or most efficient point on the average cost curve.) There does seem to be some rationale for the expectation that a company will be most profitable when it is most efficient. In a competitive market output Q_b represents the level of sales at which the difference between price and average cost is maximized.

Yet, we need to be very careful about this type of reasoning. To determine the accuracy of this line of reasoning, we should check the data. At output Q_b total revenue is \$6,600 (\$3 × 2,200 units) and total cost is \$4,400 (\$2 × 2,200 units). Total profit is equal to total revenue minus total costs (\$6,600 − 4,400), or \$2,200, which is less than the profit of \$2,400 that could be earned if output Q_c is produced.

How is it possible that the most efficient level of output (Q_b) is not the most profitable level of output? If output expands beyond Q_b, we can see that average costs increase while price remains the same at \$3. Yet, the data from the example of the wheat farmer illustrate that a competitive company will maximize its profits when it produces the level of output where price is equal to marginal cost.

In the example of the wheat farmer, every time an additional bushel of wheat is sold, the farmer earns \$3. Under competitive conditions the farmer can sell as many bushels as he or she wishes at the existing price. As long as the cost of producing one more item (marginal costs) is less than the price, then the sale of that item will add to the total profit of the farmer, causing total profit to rise.

In Figure 7–4 we see that if the farmer produces any level of output from Q_a units to Q_c units of wheat, the marginal costs lie below the price. At any level of output beyond Q_c, marginal costs are greater than the price. Consequently, the farmer will tend to add to his or her profits as output is increased to Q_c, and profits will decline as output is expanded beyond Q_c.

Profit Maximization for a Competitive Company Achieved when a company produces that level of output at which price equals marginal costs

Because of this relationship *profit maximization* results at that level of output where price equals marginal costs ($P = MC$). In Figure 7–4 the farmer will want to sell Q_c, or 3,000 units of wheat.

SELF-TEST

3. Using the figure below identify the profit-maximizing level of output and explain why you made your choice.

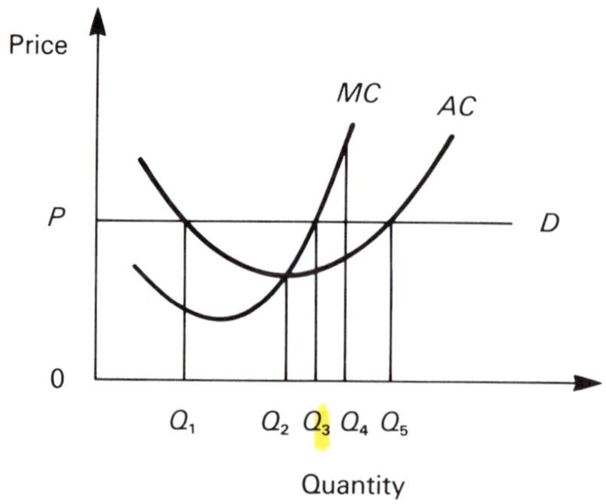

4. If production was to increase to Q_4 (that is, an output level where $P < MC$), would this company be able to earn an economic profit? Why?

FREEDOM OF ENTRY AND LONG-RUN EQUILIBRIUM

So far the example of the wheat farmer has emphasized the importance of the competitive characteristics of many sellers and a similar product. These characteristics cause the company to have a perfectly elastic demand and create the conditions that establish $P = MC$ as the rule for profit maximization. There are, however, two other competitive characteristics that are also very important: freedom of entry and good knowledge of the market. This section will emphasize how these two characteristics interact with the other characteristics and the costs of production to pressure competitive firms to lower their prices and to operate at their lowest cost of production, that is, at their point of maximum technical efficiency.

Let us return to the wheat farmer example and recall that this farmer will earn an economic profit when the farm produces an output level of Q_c. If this farmer and thousands like him or her are profit maximizers, they will choose to produce Q_c amount of output. They will all tend to earn an economic profit (Figure 7–5). Once they have earned that profit, however, a new set of forces begins to operate.

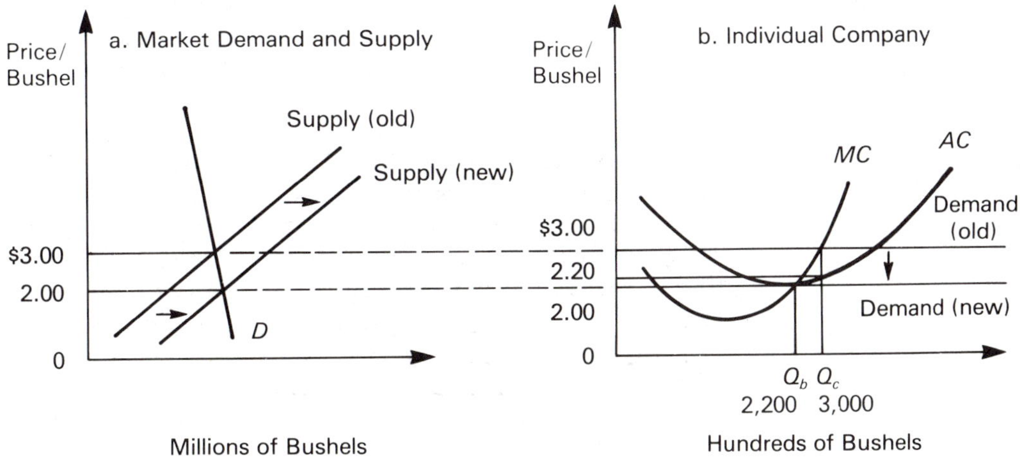

Figure 7–5
Long-Run Adjustments in a Competitive Market

This diagram demonstrates that when a market is in equilibrium ($3 in 7–5a) and when profits are earned by individual companies (7–5b), the market supply will increase (7–5a) until the market price becomes equal to the lowest average cost.

These economic profits become a signal to other farmers to begin producing wheat because they want to share the success of the current wheat farmers. As these new farmers begin to produce wheat, the market supply of wheat increases from the old supply to the new supply (Figure 7–5a). In an economy that adjusts perfectly, the increase in supply will create a new equilibrium price for wheat at $2. (As the supply of wheat increases, a surplus will result at the price of $3, forcing the price down to a new equilibrium of $2.)

The new equilibrium price will become the demand for each farmer. When each farmer was earning an economic profit, the price of wheat was $3 a bushel. Because there is freedom of entry and because most farmers will know that wheat has been profitable, each farmer independently attempts to earn some of that profit by switching his or her production to wheat. It is exactly this knowledge about the profit and the freedom to enter that causes economic profits to drop toward zero.

In Figure 7.5b we can see these changes occur. As the demand curve for the wheat of an individual farmer falls to $2, we find that Q_b is the only level of output that the farmer can produce without sustaining a loss. If the farmer continues to sell Q_c amounts of wheat, the average cost is still $2.20 per bushel, but the price has fallen to $2.00 per bushel. The result will be an economic loss. In the short run the only option available to the farmer is to reduce output from Q_c to Q_b.

Although the individual farmer would prefer the price to remain at $3, society receives some significant benefits from these changes. Look closely at the new equilibrium experienced by the farmer in Figure 7.5b. How does the change in output from Q_c to Q_b alter the economic situation?

First of all, the farmer must produce at Q_b if he or she wishes to avoid an economic loss. Q_b identifies the output where $P = AC$. More important, however, at every other level of output the farmer would experience an economic loss because price would be less than average costs. Thus, the best the farmer can do is cover all economic costs, but he or she cannot earn an economic profit. When price equals the minimum value of average cost, consumers experience the lowest price that a company can afford to charge.

Second, at Q_b we see that average cost equals marginal costs. When the price was $3 per bushel, the individual farmer found it more profitable to produce at a level of output that was not its most efficient level. When price falls to $2, each farmer has no choice. He or she either produces at the most efficient level of production or experiences an economic loss.

The consequences of the pressures that force price to equal average cost and marginal cost are rather dramatic. As consumers we want to pay the lowest price possible for the products we consume. When markets are competitive, consumers can realize that goal because prices will be forced down toward average costs.

When competitive forces push all companies toward a level of output that results in $P = AC = MC$, then all companies in a competitive economy achieve both technical efficiency and economic efficiency. Companies will produce with technical efficiency because $AC = MC$. That is, companies will be using the least amount of resources to produce a particular level of output. Companies will also achieve economic efficiency because $P = MC$. Consumers will pay a price that is just high enough to ensure that the output gets produced. In general, the $P = AC = MC$ relationship identifies how competitive companies achieve technical and economic efficiency.

The preceding paragraph is very important in economic reasoning because it provides us with a specific rule to follow in the search for economic efficiency. As a result of scarce resources, society wants to find that level of production at which consumers are paying a price that is just high enough to make sure that the product gets produced. When price equals marginal cost for all products, we achieve that goal.

SELF-TEST

5. Explain why a competitive company will tend to produce its output efficiently.
6. If the current price falls below the lowest average total costs of production, what changes will occur in the market?

PROFITS AND EFFICIENCY

First of all, we need to recall the definition of economic profit as the difference between total revenue and total costs. From an economic perspective we must consider the use of all resources when we determine the costs of producing a product. For example, the farmer is an economic resource that is essential to produce wheat. If a farmer does not receive sufficient revenue to permit that farmer to receive a sufficient payment for his or her work, he or she may stop producing wheat. If adequate compensation is not received, the farmer may decide that the return from wheat is inadequate and that he or she should plant other crops or get out of farming entirely.

By identifying an adequate payment to the owner as an economic cost we incorporate all payments to the factors of production into the definition of economic costs. Then when a company finds itself in the position of receiving zero economic profit, all resources are receiving the minimum return necessary to continue production. Resources will receive a return that is determined by demand and supply forces in the market. Individual companies have incentive to continue producing the product at zero profit, because they are receiving an adequate payment.

Even though every company desires to earn an economic profit, companies in a competitive economy expect continuing pressure for prices to fall until they equal average costs. If competitive pressures exist in all markets, then there will be a tendency for prices to equal average costs in all companies. As a result, zero economic profit will provide a sufficient payment to resources to maintain production of their respective products.

Nevertheless, maximizing profits still remains the primary motivator in a market economy. When a company encounters zero economic profit, it will search for ways to earn some profits. Because it is a competitive company, the company cannot raise its price for the

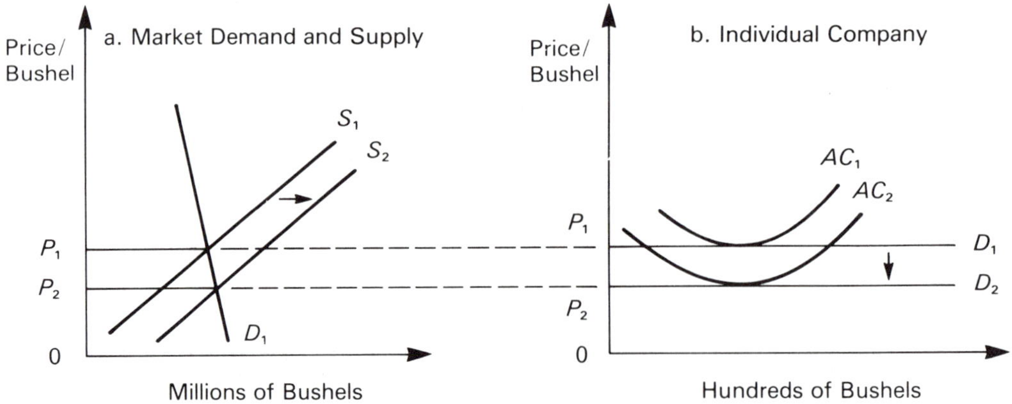

Figure 7–6
Market Adjustment Caused by Increased Efficiency

This diagram demonstrates that increased efficiency will decrease average costs from AC_1 to AC_2. With prices at P_1 the company earns an economic profit. This profit attracts entry and increases supply from S_1 to S_2. The new supply (S_2) causes prices to fall to P_2, which will equal AC_2 at its minimum point.

reason that the company is a price-taker with a perfectly elastic demand curve. Thus, if the company wishes to increase its profits, it must do so by becoming more efficient. The farmer, for example, may discover a new way to use energy that causes average costs to fall (Figure 7–6).

Once the farmer begins using the more efficient method of production, he or she will have the temporary advantage of the price of wheat being greater than its average costs. The farmer can then earn a temporary economic profit.

The beauty of the competitive model, however, is that the process does not stop here. Because this farmer can earn an economic profit, other farmers will be attracted to this market. As these additional farmers begin production with the more efficient means of production, the market supply of wheat will expand from S_1 to S_2 (Figure 7–6a). A new equilibrium price will be established (P_2), and the demand for the wheat of the individual farmer will fall to D_2 (Figure 7–6b). The result will be that the farmer will once again face a situation of zero economic profit and the necessity for producing the wheat in the most efficient manner possible.

SELF-TEST

7. When a competitive company receives zero economic profit, will the owner experience an economic loss? Why?
8. If you are the owner of a competitive business that is earning zero economic profit, explain what action you might take to increase your profits.
9. Explain how your desire to earn economic profit will tend to increase economic efficiency.

RECAP OF EFFICIENCY AND THE COMPETITIVE MARKET

A competitive market is defined as a place where may producers of similar goods and services attempt to sell products for the most profitable prices, and consumers attempt to purchase products at the lowest reasonable prices. These conflicting interests create a dynamic relationship that forces each competitive company to produce its output with maximum technical efficiency.

When companies fail to produce with technical efficiency, they will be forced out of the market. Inefficient companies cannot survive because there is constant pressure in a competitive market for prices to fall toward average total costs. If some companies cannot reduce their average total costs as low as those of other companies, then the market price will tend to drop below the average total costs of these less technically efficient sellers, causing them to experience an economic loss.

When competition exists, businesses understand that there is a tendency for economic profits to fall toward zero because all companies work hard to increase their sales relative to the sales of other companies. Nevertheless, each company has a strong motivation to earn economic profit. Individual companies cannot manipulate the prices of their products (they are price-takers). The only alternatives these companies can pursue to increase their profits are to increase technical efficiency and to improve the quality of the product. Both of these activities are very desirable for the consumers and the economy in general. To the extent that businesses succeed in becoming more technically efficient or in offering improved products to the public, these businesses will earn temporary economic profits.

When all companies within an economy produce with technical efficiency and sell their products at a price equal to their lowest average cost of production, the economy will achieve the goal of economic efficiency. In other words, consumers will be able to purchase the goods and services they wish to consume at a price just high enough to pay the costs that are necessary to ensure that the goods and services get produced.

We have placed great emphasis upon the importance of efficiency as an economic goal. Achieving this goal requires a complex interaction among competitive characteristics. If this interaction does not function properly, the pressures to achieve economic efficiency are no longer automatic. Imperfect competition may permit price-setting power to replace competition. When companies gain price-setting power, certain individuals gain some control over the welfare of others. The next chapter will examine the consequences of imperfect competition on economic efficiency.

ACTIVE REVIEW

1. Assume that you are an Iowa corn farmer who expects the price of corn to equal \$2.50 a bushel. At that price you expect to earn an economic profit, so you plant enough seed to harvest Q_1 bushels of corn. See Figure 7a.

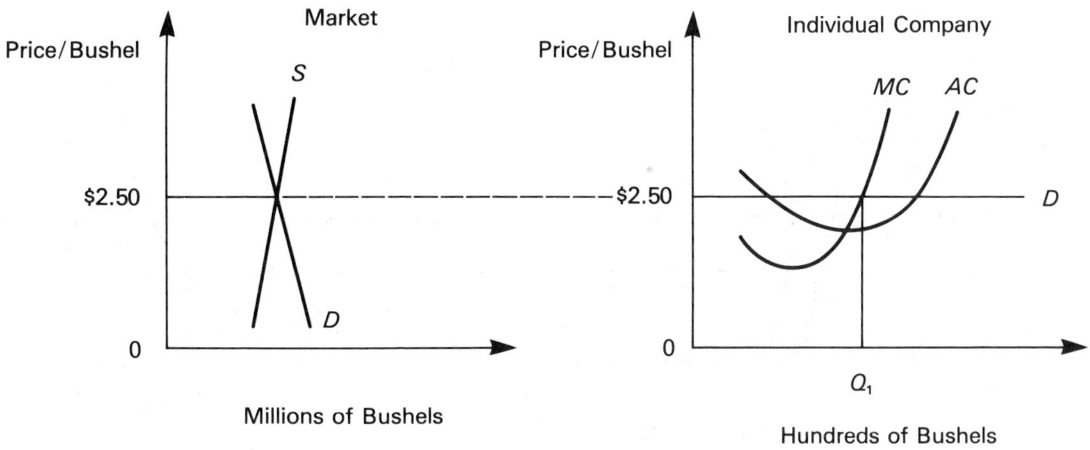

Figure 7a

a. During the planting season you read in the newspaper that the French had a very poor corn harvest last year, and as a result they are now purchasing corn from the United States. With the help of Figure 7a explain what will happen to the market demand and supply and to the demand of the individual seller.

b. Given the consequences you described in question 1a, will you alter your level of production? Explain.

c. Assume that after you have picked and sold your corn, you have earned an economic profit. What can you expect to happen to next year's corn prices? Explain why.

2. Assume that you are a competitive company that is earning zero economic profit. What action can you take to increase your profit? Will this action have any impact upon technical efficiency? Why? Will it improve economic efficiency? Why? If you succeed in improving your economic profit, what will happen to the future price of your product?

ANSWERS TO ACTIVE REVIEW

1a. The increased purchase of corn because of the poor corn harvest in France will cause the market demand for corn to increase. The rightward shift in the demand curve (D_2) will cause a new equilibrium price, for example, \$3 (Figure 7b). As a result, the demand for the corn of the individual seller will increase to \$3 also.

1b. Because the price of corn has increased to \$3 per bushel, individual farmers will discover that they can increase their production. In the short run, companies will increase their output (quantity supplied) only if they will receive an increased price. In this case the higher

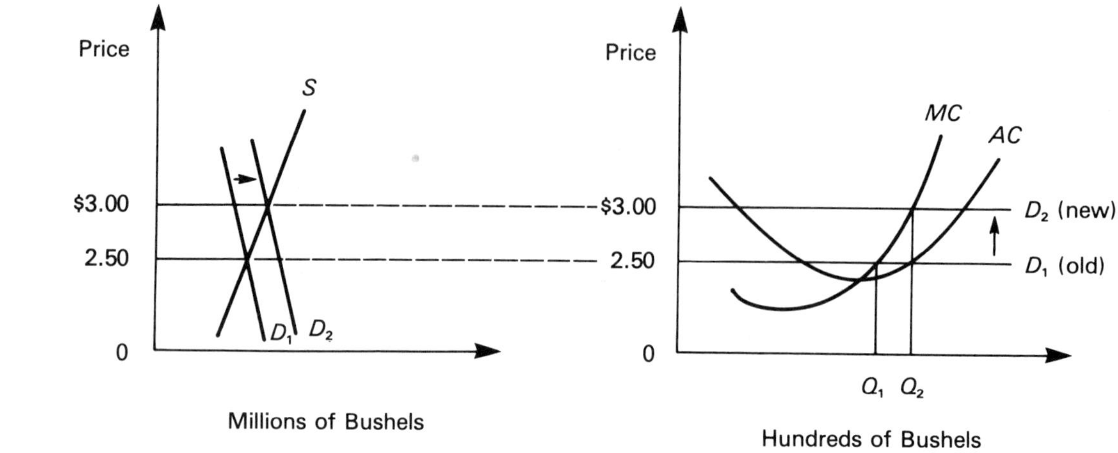

Figure 7b

price of \$3 intersects the marginal cost curve at Q_2 level of output (Figure 7b). Thus, if the company wishes to maximize its profits, it will produce output Q_2.

1c. Since entry into the production of corn is relatively easy, you can expect that these higher profits will attract the entry of more farmers to the production of corn. As these farmers harvest more corn, the market supply of corn will increase. The increase in supply (S_2) will establish a new equilibrium price for corn (Figure 7c). Since this new equilibrium price is lower than the previous equilibrium price, the demand for the corn produced by the individual farmer will fall (D_3). Eventually, the demand for the corn of the individual farmer will reach a level where $P = AC = MC$ at output, Q_3. In this example, the new price is \$2.

Figure 7c

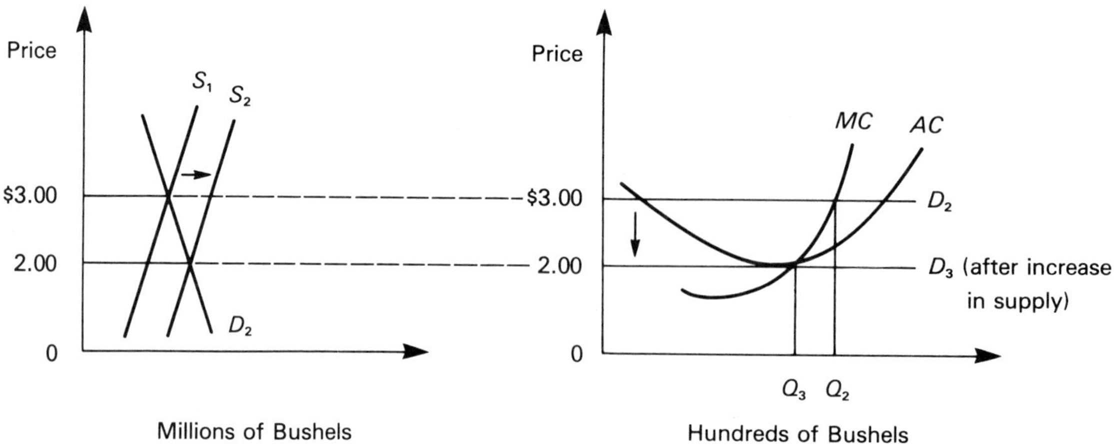

ANSWERS TO SELF-TEST

1. Competitive companies are price-takers because they must accept the price that is set by the interaction of the market demand and supply. More specifically, there is a sufficiently large number of sellers that no one seller can influence or have any impact on the total supply of the product. In addition, since there are so many sellers, consumers will always purchase the product that is sold for the lowest price. Any company that increases its price above the market price will not sell any products, because consumers will purchase the product from one of the many other sellers. Companies cannot gain by decreasing their price, because they can sell the entire output at the existing price (horizontal or perfectly elastic demand). If a company was to decrease its price, it would only decrease its revenues.
2. The demand for your lettuce may fall because the market supply of lettuce may increase or the market demand for lettuce may decrease. If the supply of lettuce increases because farmers use a new fertilizer, there will be a new and lower equilibrium price for lettuce (Figure 7d). If the market demand for lettuce decreases as a result of a claim that fertilizers leave a toxic residue on the lettuce, then there will be a new and lower equilibrium price for lettuce (Figure 7e, p. 104).

Figure 7d

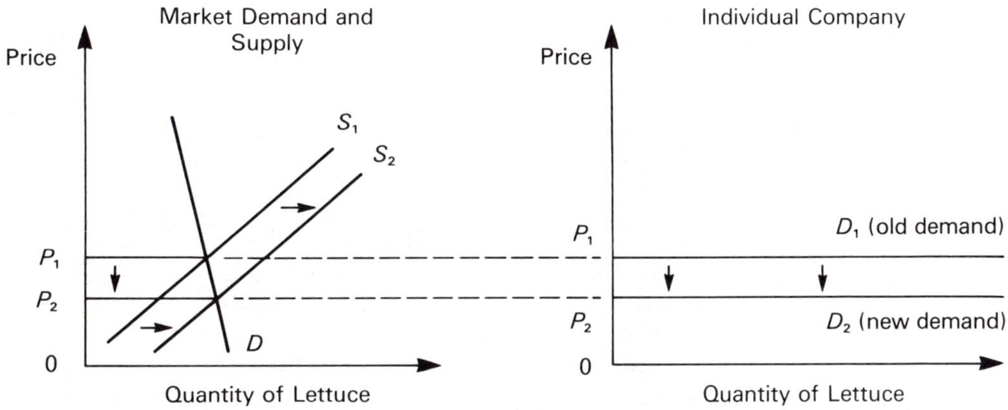

3. The profit-maximizing level of output is Q_3 because Q_3 is the output where $P = MC$. If the company was to choose Q_2, it would discover that $P > MC$ at that level of output. As long as $P > MC$, the sale of that item will generate more revenue for the company than the marginal cost of producing that item. Thus, the company should expand output until $P = MC$.

   Similarly, if the company was to choose Q_4, $MC > P$. That is, the additional cost of producing this level of output is greater than the revenue the company will receive from selling that output. Every time

Figure 7e

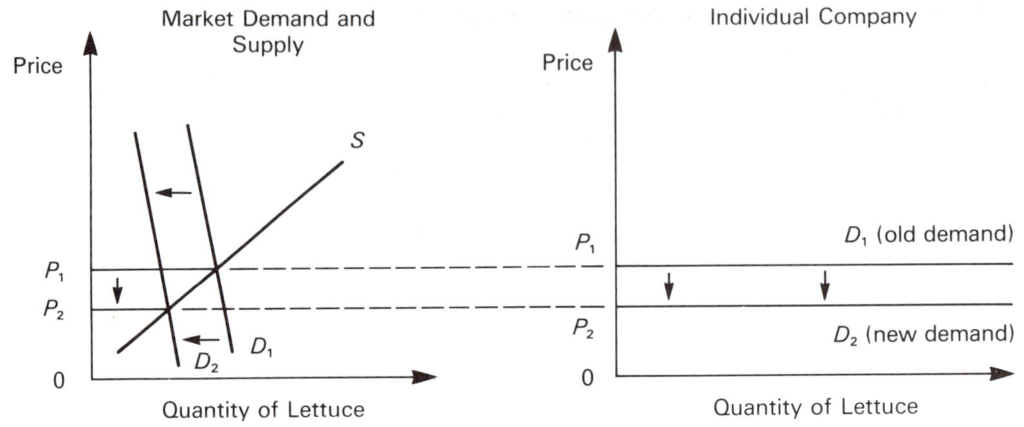

a company sells an output for which $MC > P$, the company will reduce its profits or increase its losses.

4. This particular company will earn an economic profit if it produces output Q_4, but the profits will be less than if the company was to produce the output Q_3. At Q_4 the price is still greater than average cost. Since total revenue equals price times quantity, and total costs equal average cost times quantity, the company will earn economic profit as long as $P > AC$, regardless of the relationship between price and marginal costs. If a company wishes to maximize its profits, the company must sell the output at which $P = MC$.
5. Under competitive conditions a company does not have any choice except to produce efficiently. Because of the competitive characteristics of many sellers, easy entry and good product knowledge, whenever companies earn economic profits, new companies will enter the market, increase the market supply, and decrease the price of the product. Prices will continue to fall until price equals average total cost. Since $P = ATC$ is the zero profit level of output, some companies will discover ways to become more efficient. Since prices will eventually equal the lower costs of these more efficient companies, all companies must become more efficient if they wish to stay in business.
6. Two changes may happen when price falls below average total costs. First, some companies will probably go bankrupt and go out of business. When these companies cease production, market supply will decrease. As a result, the price of the product will rise and improve the profit position for the remaining companies. Second, some companies may improve their efficiency. As these companies improve their efficiency, their costs will fall so that $P = AC$. These efficient companies will remain in business.
7. Economic costs include all payments to the factors of production that are necessary to ensure that output gets produced. Because owners

are factors of production, they require payment. In economics these payments are included in the concept of economic cost. Consequently, when economic profit is zero, the owners are receiving a payment, but they are not receiving anything extra for rewards or risk-taking. When a company earns zero economic profit, the owner receives an income equal to his or her best alternative opportunity.

8. As an owner of a competitive company you can improve your efficiency, improve the quality of your product, and introduce new products. If you improve your efficiency, then your average total costs will fall below the price, at least until other companies do the same thing. If you improve your product or introduce new products, you are likely to earn economic profits as long as the consumers like your products and are willing to pay the price for the improved quality of your products.

9. As you pursue economic profits, your attempts to increase efficiency will tend to improve technical efficiency; that is, you will produce a given output with fewer factors of production. You must become more efficient because you cannot raise your prices. Consequently, you must find ways to lower your costs. In addition, you will search for ways to increase your sales by improving your products. You will search for ways to produce efficiently the output that consumers desire. The tendency toward zero economic profit will force companies to search for higher levels of economic efficiency.

8
Imperfect Competition and Efficiency

The major point in Chapters 4–7 emphasized how competitive characteristics work together to pressure buyers and sellers toward greater economic efficiency. Throughout those chapters we emphasized how the interaction of buyers and sellers causes (1) demand for the products of an individual seller to be perfectly elastic with respect to price and (2) production to be technically efficient. Furthermore, since consumers can choose from among many sellers and products, each company constantly finds the profit motive stimulating it to introduce new products and to identify new ideas for improving technical efficiency. All these pressures tend to cause the production of that combination of goods and services most desired by consumers. In other words, all these pressures are necessary to achieve economic efficiency.

ALTERNATIVE MARKET STRUCTURES

If we examine any economic system, we will find a large number of markets that have few sellers rather than many, differentiated products rather than homogeneous ones, difficult entry rather than easy entry, poor rather than good market knowledge, and varying degrees of price control rather than the powerless price-takers of the competitive model. What impact will these deviations from competition have upon the attainment of economic efficiency? Will any deviation from the characteristics of the strict competitive model significantly alter the pressure on companies to produce efficiently? We will attempt to answer these questions in this chapter.

There are many variations from the competitive model ranging from markets that have only one seller (monopolies) to markets that have many sellers of differentiated products. Each variation poses different complications for attempts to achieve economic efficiency.

Monopoly

Monopoly A market characterized by one seller that controls the market because entry is blocked

Monopoly is at the opposite end of the spectrum of market structures from competition. See Table 8–1. Some monopolies exist because cost conditions dictate that there be only one seller of a product for which there is no reasonable substitute. For example, there is usually only one producer of electricity within a region. If an individual wishes to light a home, watch television, or wash clothes, he or she must purchase the necessary electricity from the one electric company in that area.

In this particular example, entry is blocked because of cost considerations. When we studied economics of scale in Chapter 5, we learned that when economies of scale exist average costs continue to decline as a company expands its plant size. The production of electricity is an illustration of this condition because the high average fixed costs of generating electricity can be reduced substantially as the amount of electricity generated is increased. If more than one electricity company attempted to provide electricity in an area, all companies would experience higher average costs because of the duplication of some production facilities. Under this condition it is likely that a monopolistic electric company has a greater probability of being technically efficient than does a competitive electric company.

Table 8–1 Alternative Market Structures

Competition	Imperfect Competition	Monopoly
1. Many buyers and sellers 2. Easy entry and exit 3. Good product knowledge	1. Few buyers and many sellers 2. Differentiated product 3. Difficult entry or 1. Many buyers and sellers 2. Differentiated product 3. Minor problems with entry	1. One seller and many buyers 2. Entry blocked

Market Power The ability of a company to alter the price of its product in pursuit of economic profit

Because a monopoly is the only seller in a market and because entry into that market is effectively blocked, the monopoly will possess *market power*. Instead of prices falling toward the minimum level of average costs (zero economic profit) as a result of competitive pressures, monopolies have the ability to keep price above average costs and thus to earn economic profit.

If monopolies are able to earn these profits over a considerable period of time, they distort attempts to achieve economic efficiency because consumers have to pay a higher than necessary price for the output of the monopoly. Hence, consumers move up along the demand curve, purchasing a smaller quantity of the product than they would have purchased under competitive conditions.

Oligopoly A market characterized by a few sellers that dominate a market because entry is difficult

Oligopoly An *oligopoly* is similar to a monopoly in that it also possesses some market power. But oligopolies differ from monopolies because the existence of a few sellers creates an interdependence among sellers that does not exist in other markets. Monopolists act independently because there are no other sellers in a monopolistic market. Competitors act independently because the benefits gained from collaboration are very small compared with the difficulty and costs of attempting to organize the collaboration. The output of each competitor is too small to influence the other sellers in the market.

But in an oligopolistic market each seller has a significant influence upon the other sellers in the market. Consequently, when one company alters its price or introduces a new product, the other companies react to those changes, causing some interesting changes in price and cost.

Assume, for example, that four companies equally divide 6,000 units of total sales. Each company sells 1,500 units annually. When one company lowers its price and increases its sales by 15 percent to 1,725 units, the sales of the remaining three companies will, on the average, drop to 1,425 units, or approximately 5 percent of their sales.* Since this 5 percent loss will tend to reduce significantly the profits of these three companies, they will react to the price cut of the first company. In many cases these companies will also lower their prices. If, as a result of this reaction, all four companies decrease their prices, then the original price-cutter will not gain any appreciable advantage by its price cut.

A primary reason the first company would consider a price cut is to gain a significant increase in sales. When a company experiences demand that is price elastic, the company can reduce its price and

*This example does not include the increase in quantity demanded as a result of a price cut. If this increase were included, the numbers would change slightly, but the basic analysis would not.

substantially increase sales as long as the other companies keep their prices constant. If, however, all companies decrease their prices simultaneously, then customers will tend to remain loyal to their brand. No one company will gain a sufficiently large increase in sales to compensate for the price cut.

Companies will tend to act simultaneously when only a few companies dominate a market. Each company understands that its actions will cause reactions from the other sellers. As a result, oligopolistic companies act interdependently rather than independently—as the competitive companies act.

Barriers to Entry Obstacles that make it difficult, if not impossible, for potential producers to enter a market when profits indicate that more production is desired

In addition to interdependence, oligopolies are characterized by *barriers to entry* that are caused by economies of scale, high capital requirements, patents, ownership of raw materials, and product differentiation. If economies of scale dictate that technical efficiency occurs at an output equal to 20 percent of the total market, then only five efficient companies can exist in that market. Even when economic profit exists, new companies will have difficulty entering, because the potential new companies will not be able to attract enough buyers to permit the company to achieve economies of scale. If it costs $20 million to build an efficient production facility, entry is unlikely, because of high capital costs. If a few companies hold the exclusive rights to patents, then no one else can produce the product unless they purchase a license from existing sellers. If existing companies own the existing sources of critical raw materials (for example, iron ore in the case of steel production), then the only way a new company can enter is through purchase of those raw materials from an existing company. Finally, products that are highly differentiated such as laundry detergents, personal-care products, and beer have high promotional expenses that make entry very difficult.

Product Differentiation Ability of a seller to alter its product so that consumers can distinguish one product from another. The distinction may be caused by quality, or it may result from packaging, style, and advertising

When *product differentiation* exists, new sellers must overcome the reputations of established sellers. The reputations of such products as Tide, Budweiser, and Scotch tape require potential new competitors to attempt to reduce consumer loyalty to these brands. Thus, the potential entrant not only has the cost of producing and distributing a new product, but the potential competition must also devote resources to attracting customers away from the existing brands. This endeavor will often cause the costs of the potential entrant to rise above the costs of the established companies and make entry into the market difficult.

As a result of interdependence and difficult entry, oligopolistic companies tend to pursue pricing and output strategies that are significantly different from those used by competitive companies. Because of the high degree of substitutability among products, competitive companies face highly price elastic demand curves. (In perfect competition the demand curve is perfectly elastic.) Individual companies that are highly competitive have little or no control over prices. If a competitive company was to increase the price of its product, the company would lose a substantial proportion of its customers. In perfect competition a price increase would result in a total loss of sales.

Products sold in oligopolistic markets are often differentiated. Advertising is a common practice for companies in oligopolistic markets because companies want to increase their shares of the market without decreasing prices. Because oligopolies have only a few sellers, and they often sell differentiated products, oligopolies face downward sloping demand curves. As a result of the downward sloping demand and some barriers to entry, oligopolies have some market power. They have some discretion in altering their prices in attempts to maximize profits.

Since it is difficult to enter an oligopolistic market, economic profits might not attract new production in the same manner that profits would attract entry into a more competitive market. Higher profits have been achieved because the companies are producing less output than consumers wish to purchase. With this restriction in output the pressure to achieve economic efficiency is reduced.

The dynamic forces of competition that cause markets to work toward the competitive equilibrium of $P = MC = AC$ is reduced. If prices remain above average costs, companies cannot achieve economic efficiency. We will examine how imperfect competition influences efficiency in the following four sections.

SELF-TEST

1. Companies that exist in a competitive market are independent; companies in an oligopolistic market are interdependent. How can this difference exist? Don't farmers talk with one another about the crops they are going to plant?
2. Companies engage in product differentiation because they wish to alter the nature of their demand curves. How can altering a demand curve from a perfectly elastic demand curve to a downward sloping demand curve influence the efficiency of a company?

IMPERFECT COMPETITION AND DEMAND

In a competitive market each company is a price-taker, that is, companies have no influence on the price of the product and must accept the price that is set by the interaction of the market demand and

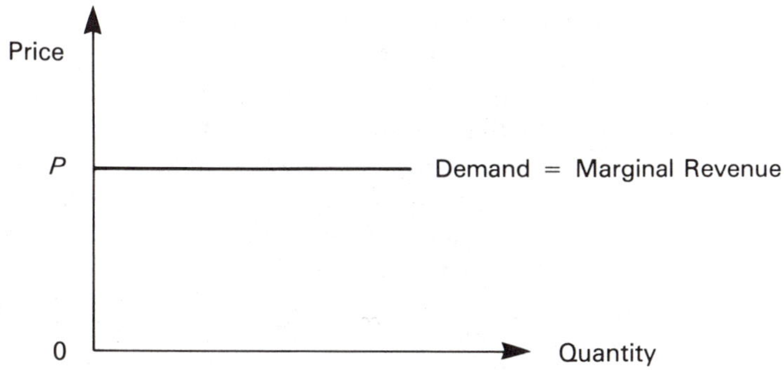

Figure 8–1
Demand Curve for an Individual Competitor
This diagram shows that a company that sells under conditions of perfect competition can sell an indefinite amount of output at the existing price.

supply. In imperfectly competitive markets, individual sellers have some degree of influence over the price. As a result each company faces a demand curve that slopes downward to the right, causing the company to alter the way it determines the level of output that maximizes profit.

In a competitive market each seller has a perfectly elastic demand, indicating that each company can sell as much as it wishes at the market price. Under this condition the price line is the demand curve and the *marginal revenue* curve (Figure 8–1). In imperfect competition the demand curve (the price line) and the marginal revenue curve differ because a company must reduce its price if it wishes to increase sales. More specifically, the marginal revenue curve falls more rapidly than the demand curve as price is decreased (Figure 8–2).

Marginal Revenue
The additional revenue gained from selling one additional unit, *ceteris paribus*

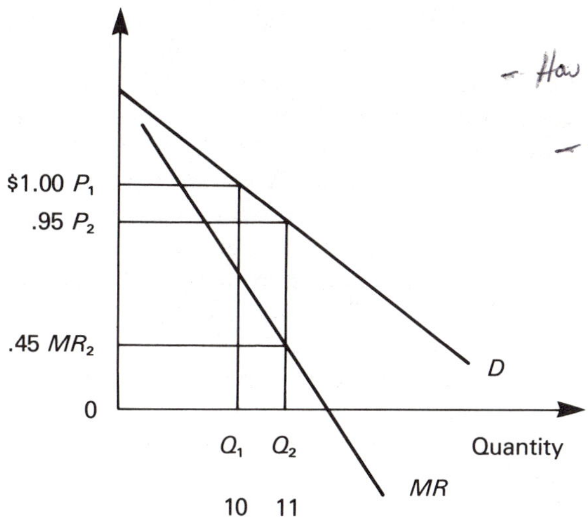

Figure 8–2
Demand Curve for an Individual Imperfect Competitor
This diagram illustrates that a company that sells under conditions of imperfect competition must decrease price to increase the quantity of sales.

Can you explain why marginal revenue is different under conditions of competition than under imperfect competition? You will find the answer in the nature of the two demand curves. With a perfectly competitive demand curve, every sale brings exactly the same revenue: the price. But in imperfect competition, each additional sale is the result of a decrease in the price. Sales increase from Q_1 to Q_2 in Figure 8–2 because the price has fallen from P_1 to P_2 for all units sold. But as Figure 8–2 demonstrates, the price P_2 is paid for all sales, not just for the items between Q_1 and Q_2. As a result, the marginal revenue associated with the change in quantity from Q_1 to Q_2 is MR_2. If, for example, P_1 = \$1.00 and Q_1 = 10 units, then total revenue would equal \$10.00. If price drops to P_2 (\$.95) and quantity increases to Q_2 (11 units), then total revenue would equal \$10.45. By dropping the price from P_1 to P_2, the marginal revenue (MR_2) equals \$.45.

Profit Maximization for an Imperfectly Competitive Company Achieved when a company produces that level of output at which marginal revenue equals marginal costs

As potential profit maximizers, companies will now have to rethink the rule for *profit maximization*. Under competitive conditions, a company would find that level of output at which price was equal to marginal cost ($P = MC$) because at that level of output the company is just able to pay its additional costs (MC) with the revenue received from sale of the last item (P). But in imperfect competition, marginal revenue is less than the price. If an imperfectly competitive company wishes to maximize its profits, it must identify the output that equates its marginal revenue with its marginal costs. If the company equates price to marginal costs, the additional revenue (MR) will be less than the additional costs (MC), profits will be less than the amount that could be earned at the level of output where marginal costs equal marginal revenue. Thus, the profit maximizing rule for companies under conditions of imperfect competition states that companies should operate at that level of output where marginal revenue equals marginal costs ($MR = MC$).

If imperfectly competitive companies do produce at the level of output where $MC = MR$, then it is likely that the company will become technically inefficient. In Figure 8–3, for example, a company producing under competitive conditions will tend to produce output Q_2 at price P_2 and the lowest average cost C_2. At Q_2, price equals marginal cost, which in turn equals average cost. But if imperfect competition exists, a company will tend to produce output Q_1. At this level of output price P_1 is greater than average cost, C_1 and average cost, C_1 is greater than marginal cost, C_3.

Because imperfectly competitive companies tend to choose output Q_1 as their profit-maximizing level of output, we discover that these companies produce with less technical efficiency ($C_1 > C_2$) and less economic efficiency ($P_1 > C_3$). The economy suffers because this

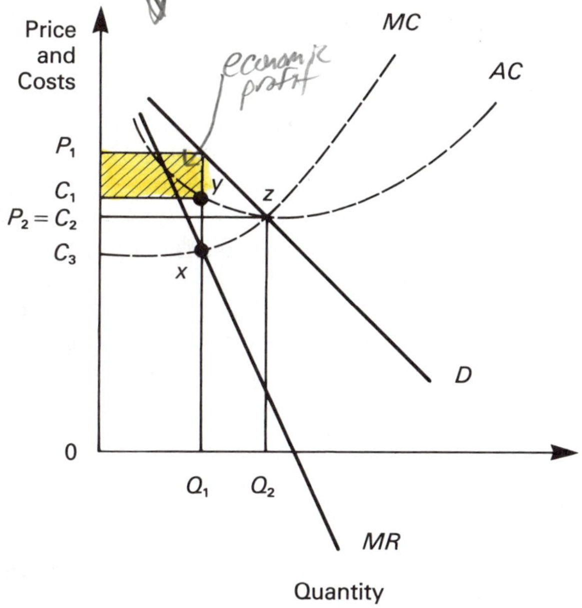

Figure 8–3 Relationship of Price and Costs in an Imperfectly Competitive Company

This diagram illustrates that a company facing a downward-sloping demand curve will tend to experience higher costs, charge higher prices, and reduce output, relative to a company operating under competitive conditions.

level of output is using resources inefficiently and because output is restricted to Q_1. If these companies are typical of a large number of companies in the market, the economy is not receiving the most desirable combination of goods and services.

IMPERFECT COMPETITION AND COSTS

Under competitive conditions, companies are constantly pressured to produce efficiently, because competitive forces push prices down to average costs and toward the position of zero economic profit. But under conditions of imperfect competition the pressures toward zero economic profit are not the same. Companies are not under the same pressure to maintain technical efficiency. If the company has some market power, it may decrease its level of sales to cause its price to increase. (Remember a demand curve for a company in an imperfectly competitive market slopes downward to the right.) At lower levels of output the company is likely to produce less efficiently. The following three sections identify ways in which imperfectly competitive companies may cause costs to be different from those that would exist under competitive conditions.

Barriers and Efficiency

When companies possess significant barriers to entry, the companies have less pressure to produce efficiently. If, for example, a market is dominated by five producers because they possess the patent rights to a manufacturing process, then these companies can attempt to maximize profits without undue concern about attracting entry. The five dominant firms will realize that restricting the amount of sales is in their mutual interests.

In Figure 8–3, we see an example of the demand and cost relationships for a typical company in an oligopolistic market. In this particular example, this company would choose to produce the output Q_1, because marginal revenue equals marginal costs (point X) at that level of output. Since the company chooses to produce Q_1 amount of output, it can charge price P_1 for its product and incur an average cost of C_1. The result of choosing output Q_1 is an economic profit represented by the shaded area.

If this company were operating in a competitive market, the economic profit would attract entry of new companies. This entry would cause the price of the product to fall to P_2 and output to increase to Q_2. In addition, companies would be forced to operate at the minimum point on their average cost curve (Z) because competitive characteristics force companies to produce with technical efficiency.

In an oligopolistic market, however, a company may continue to produce the less efficient output Q_1 rather than output Q_2. At output Q_1 the less efficient average cost is identified by point Y, whereas the average cost of producing output Q_2 is identified by point Z. If the oligopolistic company were more concerned about reaching maximum efficiency, it would also have to increase output to Q_2. Because all companies that sell in a market with imperfect competition face a downward sloping demand curve, the company would have to decrease its price to P_2 in order to increase its sales to Q_2.

Once the company actually reached output Q_2, however, it would not be able to earn economic profit because price P_2 would equal average cost C_2. Since oligopolies have the advantage of restricting entry, they will tend to charge price P_1, sell Q_1 amount of output. The sale of this level of output will earn an economic profit, but result in less efficient production than the production that would occur in a more competitive environment.

SELF-TEST

3. Since a competitive company can sell an indefinite number of units at the existing market price, and since an imperfectly

competitive company must reduce its price to increase sales, will a competitive company be more likely to earn economic profits than an imperfectly competitive company? Why?

4. Companies that operate under oligopolistic conditions might produce inefficiently. Does this mean that oligopolies are not concerned with profit maximization?

Product Differentiation and Efficiency

Under competitive conditions, companies sell products that are sufficiently similar in nature so that consumers can choose their products on the basis of price. When price differences exist, consumers can be confident that higher-priced products are of higher quality. For example, lower-priced corn will contain more water than higher-priced corn. Under conditions of imperfect competition, however, sellers may be able to differentiate their products to gain greater consumer loyalty. Sellers accomplish this differentiation through such activities as changes in product design, style, and advertising. If successful, product differentiation tends to have two effects: (1) The demand for the differentiated product becomes greater and less elastic, and (2) the average costs of producing and selling the product tend to rise.

To demonstrate these two effects, we will use an example of advertising. If you are a company manager, under what conditions would you accept the increased costs associated with a new, more expensive advertising campaign? You would be willing to incur these costs if you expected your sales to increase and customers to become more loyal to your product (that is, your demand becomes less elastic). Successful advertising has this effect because it informs consumers about the availability of your products, and it attempts to convince consumers that your products are the best on the market (see Figure 8–4). If either or both of these results occur, the company might earn enough additional revenue to pay the costs of advertising and still earn more profit than it would have earned in the absence of the advertising campaign.

Long-Run Average Costs Sometimes called planning costs. These costs describe the lowest average costs at which a quantity of output can be produced

It must be noted, however, that advertising does cause the *long-run average costs* to rise from $LRAC_1$ to $LRAC_2$ (Figure 8–4). It is possible that advertising will increase sales for Q_1 to Q_2 because of an increase in demand to D_2 as a result of advertising. Although advertising increases average costs from AC_1 to AC_2, the specific average cost (C_2) of producing output Q_2 may be lower than the average cost (C_1) of producing output Q_1. This result will occur if the adver-

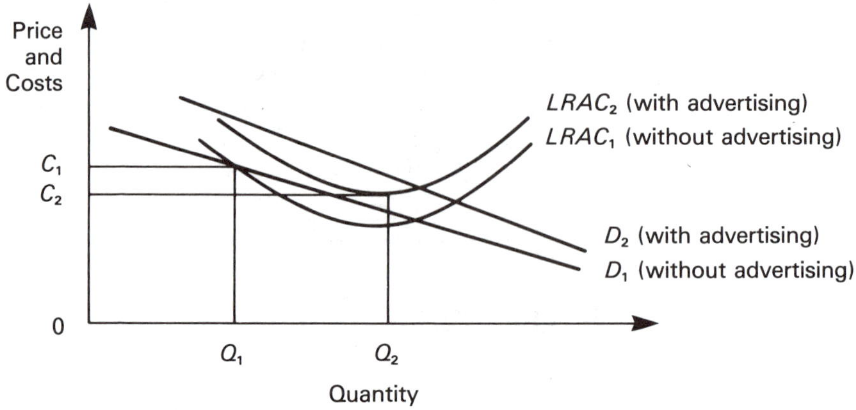

Figure 8–4
Change in Demand and Average Costs as a Result of Increased Advertising
This diagram shows that a company can decrease its average costs through advertising by expanding production to a more efficient level of output.

tising campaign increases demand by a sufficiently large amount to permit a company to achieve greater economies of scale and to produce its output more efficiently.

In an oligopolistic market, however, it is questionable whether advertising can stimulate sales by a sufficient amount to achieve increased efficiency. Because oligopolistic companies are interdependent, individual companies are not likely to achieve significant increases in sales at the expense of their rival companies. Consequently, advertising campaigns are less likely to generate a significant lasting increase in sales. Nevertheless, companies will continue to advertise, often intensively. If they do not follow this behavior, they will lose sales to companies that do advertise more intensively. As a result, companies that advertise intensively are likely to experience an increase (shift upward) in long-run average costs without a significant increase in demand (Figure 8–5).

Since oligopolistic companies are highly interdependent, a successful advertising campaign by one company is likely to be followed by similar advertising campaigns by other companies in the same market. Although this advertising will tend to increase the overall demand for a product, the major impact will more likely be felt by the different brands of a product. For example, advertising may influence whether we drink Coke or Pepsi, wash clothes with Tide or All, or brush our teeth with Crest or Colgate. But a change of brand is not the same as an increase in the total sales of soft drinks, laundry detergents, or toothpastes.

Thus, advertising may help some companies achieve or maintain economies of scale, while other companies may experience no gain in sales or possibly suffer a loss of sales. If there is no gain in sales or a loss of sales, the increased advertising will cause the company to experience increased costs and reduced efficiency. This conse-

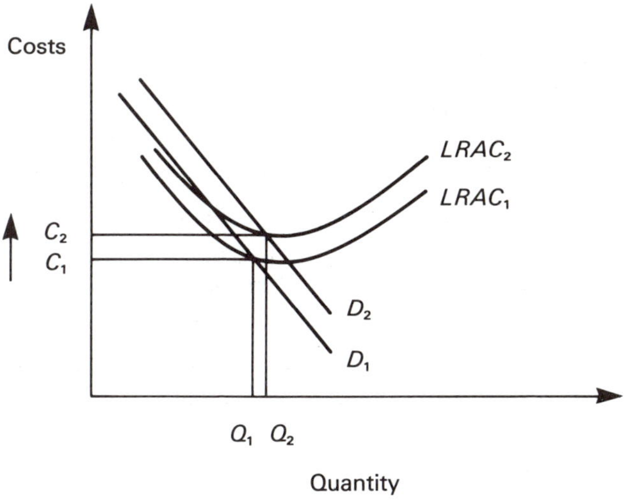

Figure 8–5
Changes in Demand and Average Costs as a Result of Increased Advertising
This diagram demonstrates that a company would not increase its efficiency as it expands output, because it has already achieved an efficient level of output. The diagram also shows an increase in costs as a result of an increase in advertising.

quence is shown by the shift in average costs from $LRAC_1$, to $LRAC_2$ in Figure 8–5.

Economies of Scale and Efficiency

Under competitive conditions, each company produces only a small proportion of the total output for that market, because there are no cost advantages associated with becoming larger. Companies have no significant economies of scale. In some oligopolistic markets, however, companies may possess significant economies of scale, which dictate that as the companies expand the size of their productive facilities, their average costs curves will fall (see Chapter 5, pp. 64–66).

The production of certain types of products is more efficient in large facilities, because companies can gain advantages associated with mass production techniques. A company can use production and distribution methods that lower its average costs as the business grows in size. As a company becomes larger, it is easier for it to use specialized machinery that can increase the overall efficiency of the company. For example, an automobile company can use the assembly line process to increase the efficiency of production. When significant economies of scale exist, companies operating under the competitive conditions of many sellers would experience a cost disadvantage compared with companies that were part of an oligopolistic market.

Figure 8–6 illustrates long-run average cost curve for a product that has significant economies of scale. In this particular example, a company that wishes to make this product efficiently must produce

Figure 8–6
Economies of Scale and Barriers to Entry
This diagram illustrates the cost advantage of producing in plant 3, relative to plants 1 and 2.

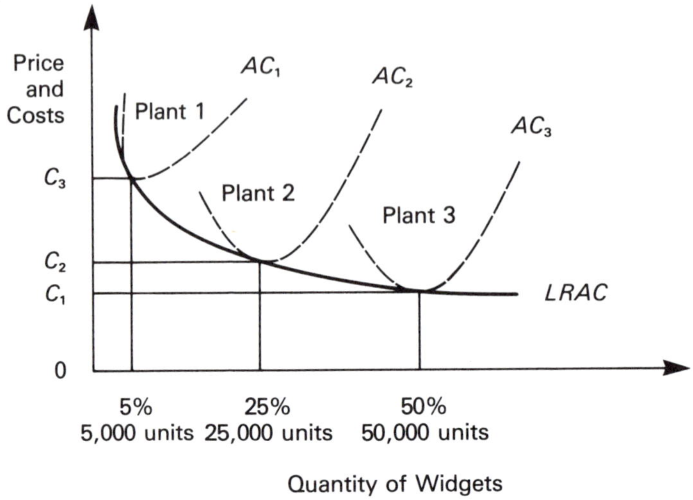

50 percent of all the output. For example, if 100,000 widgets are sold, a company would have to make at least 50,000 widgets if it wanted to produce those items at their lowest average costs. In terms of Figure 8–6, the company would then have to operate in plant 3, because efficient production in that size plant will generate an average cost of C_1. Whereas, if the number of sellers increased so that each seller operated plants the size of 1, their most efficient average cost would be C_3. It is clear from this illustration that the larger companies producing 50,000 units in plants as large as plant 3 are much more efficient than the smaller plants.

Thus, the existence of significant economies of scale creates an interesting dilemma. If companies are motivated to achieving maximum technical efficiency, some companies will grow in size because they possess significant economies of scale. But as these companies become efficient, smaller companies will disappear, and the market will become dominated by a few oligopolistic companies.

In addition, for the same reason that small companies disappear, new companies will discover that entry is very difficult. If the market is left with a few companies and difficult entry conditions, the pressures to operate at the most efficient level of production are reduced. Without this competitive pressure, will companies producing under oligopolistic conditions make their products efficiently? The answer is not clear.

In general, it appears that as market structure moves away from competition and toward oligopoly and monopoly, competitive pressures to produce at maximum efficiency are reduced. When companies function in an oligopolistic structure, there are only a few competing companies and potential new companies to exert downward pressures on prices and costs. Without the competitive characteristics of many sellers and easy entry, some companies will gain sufficient market power to alter prices and earn economic profit. If these companies have significant barriers to entry, they can earn profit without attracting entry by new companies.

This result is very good for the company earning economic profit, but it is not so good for the economy in general. Without the pressure from potential entrants into the market, the profit-earning companies may restrict their sales to charge a higher price, and they may also absorb higher costs associated with product differentiation. Both of these actions may result in the operation of plants at output levels below that of maximum efficiency. In other words, once we lose some of the competitive characteristics of many sellers, standard product, easy entry, and good product knowledge, we also lose the *automatic* pressure for companies to produce at their levels of maximum efficiency.

SELF-TEST

5. Evaluate the following statement: If an advertising campaign increases sales, then the company that did the advertising must earn an increase in economic profit.
6. Explain how economies of scale may give a company market power.

IMPERFECT COMPETITION AND EFFICIENCY SUMMARIZED

As market characteristics diverge from those of a competitive market, we are no longer guaranteed that markets will progress toward the competitive equilibrium of price equal to marginal costs equal to average costs ($P = MC = AC$). These divergences from this equilibrium need not lead to inefficiency if imperfect markets have relatively easy entry and a tendency to develop new products. Under these conditions, consumers can expect that sellers will develop new products, earn some economic profit that will attract entry into the market, and force sellers to lower their prices and produce more efficiently. Although companies that are imperfectly competitive may not achieve the theoretical point of maximum efficiency, they might reach a close approximation of that level of output.

If, however, the imperfectly competitive companies have significant barriers to entry or product differentiation, the pressures to be efficient are lessened. When a market experiences significant barriers to entry, several factors interfere with the mechanisms that can cause companies to produce efficiently. When these interferences become significant, the probability of inefficient production increases significantly.

For example, if existing companies control the known supply of natural resources necessary to manufacture a product, entry will be effectively restricted. Existing companies are free to produce at their profit maximizing level of output. Since entry is difficult, these companies are not compelled to be efficient, and they may become less efficient because they choose to accept more perks than might be permissible in a more competitive environment.

If differentiated products are sold by a few interdependent companies, achieving maximum efficiency is again problematic. Interdependent companies expect other companies in their market to react to changes in their selling strategies. If company A changes the style of its product, company B will probably do likewise. If the changes are simply stylistic, then the cost of providing the product will increase without any increase in the quality of the product. Consequently, the companies will become less efficient.

When companies possess significant economies of scale, they have the ability to be more efficient than many smaller companies operating in the same market. At the same time, however, the economies of scale may cause significant barriers to entry that reduce the necessity to produce efficiently. The potential for inefficiency will depend on the ability of the barriers to restrict actual entry. The weaker the barriers, the more likely the companies will produce efficiently.

There is a sufficiently large number of markets that possess many competitive characteristics. These markets experience prices and costs that resemble prices and costs that we might expect from a competitive market. On the other hand, some economists believe that imperfectly competitive markets have some serious defects and require significant intervention by government to achieve maximum economic efficiency. Chapter 9 will explore these arguments about the need for governmental intervention in various markets.

ACTIVE REVIEW

1. Companies that produce under conditions of imperfect competition create some interesting deviations from the competitive model. They face downward sloping demand curves and may experience economies of scale.

a. Explain why demand tends to slope downward to the right.
b. How do economies of scale influence the number of sellers in a market?
c. Will economies of scale influence the pricing behavior of a company?
d. How will this pricing behavior influence efficiency?

2. Product differentiation influences both demand and costs.
   a. Explain how product differentiation influences demand.
   b. Explain how product differentiation influences cost.
   c. Under what conditions will product differentiation increase efficiency?
   d. Under what conditions will product differentiation decrease efficiency?

ANSWERS TO ACTIVE REVIEW

1a. The demand curve for companies selling under conditions of imperfect competition slopes downward for two possible reasons: (1) When few sellers exist in a market, there are fewer substitutes. In the extreme case of monopoly the only choice available to consumers is whether or not to purchase the product. Thus, the seller can attempt to entice new buyers into the market by lowering prices. This ability is identified by the downward sloping nature of the demand curve. (2) Products are often differentiated. When different brands exist, the products are no longer perfect substitutes. If one company increases the price of its product, the company's sales will decline, but not to zero, as would be the case in competition. Once again, the downward sloping demand curve reflects the decrease in the substitutability of products.

1b. If the most efficient plant size produces 25 percent of the total industry output, then only 4 efficient companies can exist in that market. Whereas, if the most efficient plant size produces only 1 percent of the total industry output, then 100 efficient companies could exist in the market.

1c. If economies of scale create a barrier to entry, then the companies that possess the economies of scale will attempt to set prices above their average costs but below the average cost of the smaller, less efficient companies. This type of pricing behavior will tend to increase profits and keep new companies from entering the market.

1d. If companies with economies of scale are successful in restricting their output to increase their prices and profits, then they are likely to produce a level of output that will be less efficient than if the companies were using their full capacity to produce.

ANSWERS TO SELF-TEST

1. It is true that many companies are likely to talk with one another about what is happening in their businesses, but there is a significant difference in how companies will react to the actions of one another in different industries. In a competitive market, companies are price-takers; that is, individual companies have no influence over prices. Each company must accept the price set in the market. If one company did attempt to change its price or product, the other companies would not experience any significant changes in their prices or sales.

   In an oligopolistic market, however, there are only a few sellers. Each seller has some ability to alter its price and output. Since there are only a few companies in a market, changes in prices and output by one company are likely to have a significant impact on the other sellers. For example, in the extreme case of two sellers, if one company increases its sales from 50 percent to 60 percent of total sales, then the second company will suffer a loss in sales from 50 percent to 40 percent. The second company will most likely react to this loss of sales and take action to recover its losses; the companies are interdependent.

2. If a company is successful in differentiating its product from those of other sellers in a market, then that company is likely to gain some market power. When a company has market power, it will have a downward sloping demand curve. If the product differentiation creates some barriers to entry, then companies will tend to restrict their output in order to increase their prices. When these companies restrict output, they are likely to produce less efficiently, because they will not be using their full production capacity.

3. Competitive companies constantly experience pressures that tend to push their profits toward zero. The horizontal demand curve indicates that sales are indefinite, but not unlimited. In fact, actual sales are definitely limited by the relatively small size of their companies and by their lack of ability to influence prices. Remember that if all or many companies increase their production, the market price will fall.

   In an imperfectly competitive market, however, individual companies do have some control over their prices. They are able to search for the price-output combination that maximizes their profits. Imperfectly competitive companies are more likely to earn economic profits than are competitive companies.

4. Oligopolies are very interested in profit maximization. The point we must remember is that profit maximization is determined by the gap between total revenue and total costs, not by minimization of average cost. Because oliogpolies face a downward sloping demand they will maximize their profits by producing the level of output where marginal revenue is equal to marginal cost. It is very likely that the average cost curve may still be falling at this level of output. That is, the company will not be producing at its minimum costs or most

efficient level of production. See Figure 8a. The oligopoly will tend to produce output Q_2 with an average cost of C_2, which is higher than C_1, the average cost of the most efficient level of production.

Figure 8a

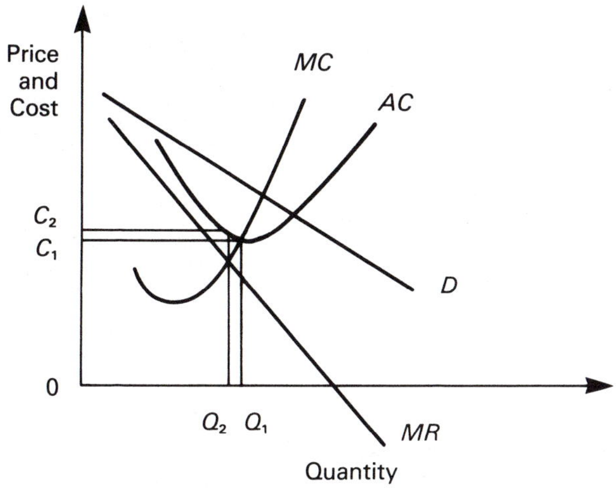

5. It does not necessarily follow that if an advertising campaign increases sales, the company will realize an increase in economic profit. Advertising campaigns increase the costs of production. If the cost of the advertising is greater than the revenue gained from the increased sales, then a company would lose money as a result of the advertising campaign.
6. If a company experiences significant economies of scale, then it produces its output at a lower cost than companies that use a smaller plant to produce smaller amounts of output. The company producing with the larger plant knows that it can set a price up to the level of the smaller companies' costs. Under this condition smaller companies will have difficulty staying in business, because their costs will tend to be higher than their revenues. Consequently, the larger company has considerable market power when economies of scale exist.

9
Role of Government and Efficiency

Throughout Chapters 4–8 we discussed how a market economy works to achieve the goal of economic efficiency. When markets function competitively, there are strong pressures for all resources to produce efficiently. Yet there are circumstances when markets will not generate the pressures to cause companies to produce efficiently.

When markets function under imperfectly competitive conditions, products may be differentiated and entry may be difficult. These conditions may permit costs and prices to rise above their competitive levels. If either costs or prices rise above competitive levels, companies will not achieve economic efficiency.

Even when competitive markets exist, the production process may generate costs that are not included in the usual accounting practices. When these costs appear (for example, run-offs from toxic waste dumps), the economy must find some way to deal with them. If we do not take some specific action, these costs will tend to increase and cause a misallocation of resources.

In other cases a market economy may discover that political forces cause an intervention into the operation of a market. An example of this type of intervention often exists when there is trade between countries. If, for instance, Japan significantly increases the number of automobiles that it sells in the United States, the United States automobile manufacturers, auto workers, and auto dealers may ask government for some form of intervention. Both the trade and the intervention will have influences on economic efficiency.

Since we are committed to achieving efficiency as an economic goal, and since the forces in a market economy may not always achieve the desired level of economic efficiency, we need to examine whether governmental intervention can influence our attainment of this goal. This issue is controversial. There are several aspects we can investigate to appreciate the role of government in achieving economic efficiency. To this end, this chapter examines some of the reasons governmental intervention is advocated and, specifically, the impact of the different types of intervention on efficiency. In the final section of this chapter we will briefly examine a few alternative economic systems to gain an appreciation for their approaches to economic efficiency.

REASONS FOR GOVERNMENTAL INTERVENTION

The United States economy is based upon the principle that individuals should be free to choose the products and services that they wish to produce and consume. The nature of a competitive market indicates that the role of government should be kept small. Yet Chapter 8 explained that there are times when markets may not operate competitively. Under conditions of imperfect competition, companies may exercise market power and cause some resources to produce inefficiently. In other cases companies may possess natural monopolies that make impractical the multiple-sellers characteristic of competition. In both these cases there are significant questions about whether these companies will produce efficiently without some form of governmental intervention.

In addition to governmental intervention designed to influence the degree of competition, governments often intervene in the market process because of social costs and benefits and political forces. For example, when a community decides that the level of pollution has reached an undesirable level, some form of government regulation may be imposed. Government may also be required to provide some goods and services that private companies cannot provide for a profit; for example, city streets. In other circumstances, governments wish to alter the amount and type of trade between countries. Tariffs or quotas are governmental tools that are designed to make adjustments in international trade. These five reasons for interventions will be discussed in the following pages.

Potentially Anticompetitive Practices

When a market is dominated by a few oligopolistic sellers, there is a strong tendency for these companies to act interdependently. Instead of market forces working to decrease costs and prices, oligopolistic, or interdependent, companies may instead develop pressures for increases in costs and prices. For example, let's assume two companies dominate the production of cement blocks. Since cement blocks are physically similar, consumers will buy from the company that sets the lowest price. If these two companies compete with each other, the price for cement blocks will drop to the most efficient cost of producing the blocks. Because these two companies dominate this market, they have high motivation to avoid this competition and to agree on a price that would permit each company to earn economic profit. The companies have the incentive to collude.

If these two companies collude, they will set their prices and outputs in the same manner as a monopolist. The consequence of this collusion will be restriction of output and an increase in price. As these companies restrict their output, they will often experience an increase in their average costs, because they will produce at a less efficient level of output.

In Figure 9–1 we see that under competitive conditions prices and output will be set at P_1 and Q_1. If the two companies collude, they will act as monopolists and maximize profits by reducing production to some output Q_2 and increasing price to P_2. As a result of this action to maximize profits, the companies will be less efficient, because their average costs will rise to C_2.

Another potentially anticompetitive practice is merger of two

Figure 9–1
Price and Costs with Collusion

This diagram shows that collusive companies are likely to experience less-efficient production.

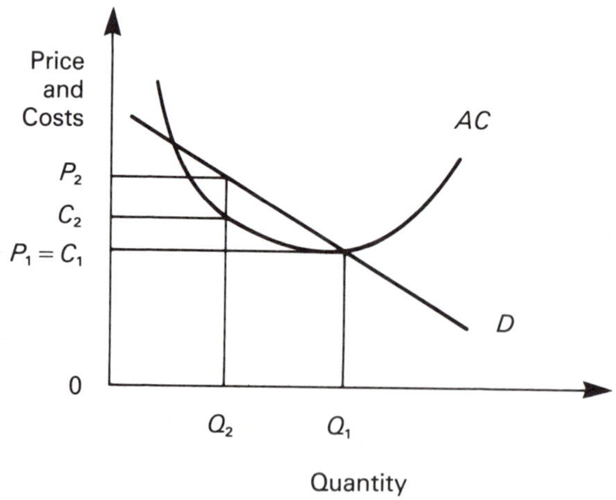

companies to form one larger company. If a merger significantly reduces the number of sellers within a market, then the merger increases the probability that some companies will possess sufficient market power to reduce the quantity of items sold and increase the price of the item. For example, if Coca-Cola and Dr. Pepper were to merge, the resulting company would become the dominant seller in the United States soft drink market. Because Dr. Pepper is now a major rival of Coca-Cola, their merger would significantly reduce the number of companies in the market. The size of the new merged company relative to the other soft drink producers in the market would increase the potential for this new company to exercise its market power and increase prices.

There are several types of mergers with different degrees of potential anticompetitive effects. Although each type of merger deserves additional study, the primary issue here is that mergers may increase the size of companies without increasing their efficiency. If mergers do not increase efficiency, then they do not increase total output in the economy. If the merged companies increase their market power as a result of mergers, the companies gain ability to earn economic profit without fear of entry into the market. In such cases government may need to intervene to maintain competitive pressures.

We should note that not all mergers are anticompetitive. In fact, some mergers may increase efficiency by allowing two smaller companies to achieve economies of scale. In other circumstances mergers may occur between a strong company and a failing one. If this type of merger occurs, efficiency may be increased.

Natural Monopoly

Natural Monopoly Markets in which only one seller can produce efficiently because economies of scale are so significant

In some markets a natural monopoly may be formed because significant economies of scale result as output increases. If more than one seller exists in markets that have characteristics of a *natural monopoly*, there will be inefficient production. If more than one company exists in this type of market, the average costs for each company will rise significantly (see Figure 9–2). If the total market demand (D) for a given product is just large enough to enable one company to produce at its most efficient level of output (Q_2), then the introduction of any additional sellers would cause an increase in the costs of production of all sellers. If a second seller entered the market and sales were divided between the two sellers, their average cost would rise to C_1 because both sellers would use smaller, less efficient plants (AC_1) to produce their output. Because of economies of scale, there is room for only one efficient seller. Thus, from the perspective of efficiency,

Figure 9–2
Natural Monopoly
This diagram illustrates that when economies of scale are very important, only a few efficient companies will exist. In this specific example, only one efficient seller can exist.

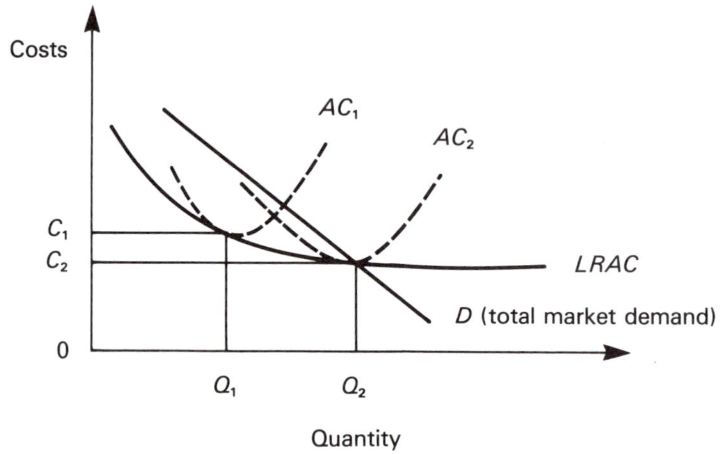

monopoly is capable of providing the most efficient results when significant economies of scale exist in the production of particular products.

If monopoly results from the existence of economies of scale, then the company no longer has the competitive pressure to set its price equal its best cost situation of C_2. Instead the company is likely to reduce its output below Q_2 and to charge some price above average cost C_2 in an attempt to earn an economic profit. Since entry is unlikely because of the inability of entering companies to achieve AC_2, the existing company will not be pressured to produce at maximum technical efficiency. Thus, the company may not achieve some of the efficiency that is possible as a result of the natural monopoly condition. In this instance, as in the other examples of anticompetitive practices, some form of governmental intervention is often advocated.

SELF-TEST

1. Evaluate the following statement: According to the text, two companies that dominate cement block production have the incentive to collude and set monopoly price and output. Since competitive companies sell highly similar products, small groups of sellers in competitive markets will also have the incentive to collude.
2. The profit motive is a primary motivator in a market economy. Two companies will merge because they expect to earn higher profits. Does it follow that the merger will also cause an increase in the efficiency of production?

External Costs

External Costs Costs of production that are paid or absorbed by society rather than by the producer of the product

In a market economy sellers are concerned about minimizing their costs so that they can remain competitive with other companies in the same market. In most circumstances, however, companies will be concerned only about their own direct costs. That is, they will attempt to minimize all their direct costs, such as wages, rent, energy, transportation, materials. Yet, in some cases, companies also create *external costs*. For example, if a company dumps its waste into a river, the people who live along the river experience (and therefore, absorb the costs of) polluted water. The company does not consciously decide to pollute the river. Rather, it decides to build next to a river because a river provides an easy way to remove waste from the plants and keep the private costs from rising.

Consumers do not want pollution either. But since pollution is an external cost that usually is not directly reflected in the price of products, consumers unwittingly accept pollution by purchasing products at their lowest prices. If consumers do not live near the river, they may not be aware (or maybe do not care) that the wastes from production are destroying the river. If a company builds a waste treatment plant to reduce the pollutants that enter the river, the company will experience a higher cost of production, causing an increase in the price of its product.

Consumers, however, do not like higher prices and will search for and purchase products that are lower in price (probably from companies that dump their waste into rivers). Consequently, a company that considers using a waste treatment plant will find itself at a competitive disadvantage unless it pollutes the river just as its competitors are doing. In other words, in market economies, companies have no incentives to reduce external costs. In fact, companies will often increase external costs if that action will reduce private costs.

In terms of economic efficiency, however, the river is an economic resource that is being used to produce an output. If we wish to account for the efficient use of all resources, then we must also consider these external costs. When external costs are few, companies will pay the private costs and ignore external costs because the people affected by the external costs have no way to collect payment from the companies causing the pollution. For instance, people who live downstream from the polluting company have no mechanism to charge the company for killing the fish in the river and making it unsafe for swimming.

If society does not account for the external costs, then we will experience a significant change in economic efficiency. That is, society will produce higher quantities of the polluting products than it would if companies properly included external costs in its calculation of their total costs. In addition, people who did not produce or purchase the polluting product will suffer the costs associated with the pollution. The effect of externalities on our society and on the quality of market decisions is the major emphasis of Chapter 13.

Although we will study externalities in more detail in Chapter 13, it is important to note that an economy that emphasizes individual decision making is unlikely to account properly for the costs and benefits associated with externalities. If we wish to assign the costs and benefits properly, governmental agencies must get involved. For example, government must provide some form of guidance if we wish to reduce pollution.

Public Goods

In a market economy, goods and services are produced because businesses expect to earn economic profit as a result of their production. In some instances, however, a community demands some goods and services, but private businesses will not produce them because the private business cannot earn a profit from the sale of these goods and services. For example, virtually everyone within a community wants a good system of streets and roads. In fact, you have probably complained when the number and size of pot holes have increased. Since there is such an evident demand for good roads, why won't an enterprising person start a business that builds and maintains roads?

At first, this business venture may seem tempting. Currently, there are no private companies in this business. Second, the cost of entry into the maintenance portion of the road business is minimal. The opportunities for success look great until you ask some very important questions, such as What prices will you charge? and How will you get people to pay your prices? As soon as you ask the question, you will realize that no one is likely to pay you to repair the pot holes, and consequently, you will not be able to earn an income.

Nonexclusion Principle The characteristic possessed by some goods and services whereby no buyer can prevent other consumers from enjoying the same good or service.

Can you explain why no one is willing to pay for repairing the pot holes? The answer lies in the concept of the *nonexclusion principle*, which states that for certain goods and services, no one can be excluded from using the good or service once it has been produced. We can see this principle at work in the example of a dam that is built for flood control. All the families who live in a valley that floods every spring know that the flooding can be controlled by a dam. Everyone wants the dam, but no one is willing to build it, because a private owner of the dam would not be able to recover costs and earn a profit. Once the dam is built, everyone is protected. No one in the valley can be excluded from flood control, thus no single consumer has any incentive to pay for the protection provided by the dam. In fact, each person who wishes the dam built has an incentive to claim an unwillingness to pay for the construction of the dam in hope that someone else will pay. Then he or she would be protected by the dam for free. Consequently, if the community wishes to control the floods, some level of government must acquire the money necessary to build the dam by raising taxes.

Many governmental expenditures can be explained by the nonexclusion principle. For example, streets and roads and lighthouses and mosquito control are all services to which the nonexclusion principle applies; hence, they are public goods. The nonexclusion principle applies to a component of each person's education. To the extent that everyone benefits from a more highly educated society, education is a public good. Some benefits of education are clearly personal. The educated person has greater opportunities. Since the consumer of education can exclude others from using these benefits, this component of education is a private good. This distinction may help you understand why elementary and secondary education are paid for by taxes and why higher education is usually paid for by a combination of taxes and private expenditures.

Political Interventions

So far in the examination of economic efficiency, we have discussed the functioning of a market system within the context of a single country—our own. We have not considered what, if any, changes would occur if the United States began trading goods and services with nations such as Canada, Japan, Germany, and Brazil. Theoretically, the competitive process will remain the same. In fact, some people argue that competition from foreign autos, steel, and televisions would increase the competitive pressures and improve the likelihood of achieving a higher level of economic efficiency.

Exports The goods and services that are produced in the United States and sold in other countries

Imports The goods and services that are produced in other countries and sold in the United States

In reality, however, most countries do not see foreign trade as a benefit to their countries unless their *exports* (sales to consumers in other countries) exceed their *imports* (purchases of goods from other countries). Since all countries cannot simultaneously experience greater exports than imports, some countries (maybe all countries) will be threatened by the potential negative consequences of imports. If these countries are sufficiently concerned about the imports, they will erect some type of barriers to reduce imports.

Why do countries behave in this manner? If Austria can make some types of steel more efficiently than the steel mills in the United States, steel-using companies in the United States could reduce their costs by purchasing the foreign steel. With lower costs, these companies could lower prices and probably increase their profits. Since consumers are most interested in lower prices, they will, *ceteris paribus,* purchase the products made with Austrian steel. Most consumers would be unaware that the products contained foreign steel. Thus, foreign trade will tend to improve the overall efficiency of the economy.

In reality foreign trade does not work quite this smoothly. Unless the resources of capital and labor that were used in steel production can be easily transferred to the production of other products, business activity in the United States may in general decline. Workers in the United States may not be able to find alternative employment, and the general level of income in the United States will tend to fall. Thus, the drive to become efficient by purchasing foreign steel may displace some economic resources, at least temporarily.

When displacement occurs as a result of the normal competitive process, resources will move from the production of products that are no longer profitable to ones that are profitable. But when displacement occurs because of international trade, the resources of capital and labor do not easily move from one country to another. That is, steel workers in the United States are not likely to move to Austria to become steelworkers there. As a result, capital and labor in the United States may suffer more serious unemployment problems. If the United States economy cannot find alternative productive uses for these resources, the economy will experience inefficiency and a serious misuse of these resources. When these consequences are encountered, government is often called upon to intervene through some form of protection, such as tariff barriers.

SELF-TEST

3. As the manager of a chemical plant you know that you can increase your efficiency by placing barrels of your chemical waste in a nearby landfill. Yet from the perspective of the society, this form of waste management is inefficient. Explain why this difference exists.

4. The market forces of demand and supply tell us that when a product or service earns a profit, production should increase. When a product or service suffers a loss, production should decrease. Why should the introduction of foreign producers alter our thinking about this process?

GOVERNMENTAL INTERVENTION AND ITS IMPACT ON EFFICIENCY

Throughout the previous section we discussed instances in which a market economy failed to achieve the desired levels of economic efficiency. Because of these apparent market failures, government will often intervene, with the intention of moving the economy closer to the goal of economic efficiency. This section will discuss the impact of these interventions on efficiency.

Attempts to Monopolize

When oligopolies engage in monopolizing practices such as collusion, government can use the antitrust laws to correct this behavior. The primary purpose of the antitrust laws is to restore competitive behavior to markets and to restore economic efficiency. Under provisions of the laws that prohibit conspiracies in the restraint of trade, government can stop collusive practices. With this authority, the appropriate government agencies can stop the anticompetitive practices and fine the companies that engage in illegal practices. But more important, through the use of the antitrust laws, companies are encouraged to behave competitively and efficiently. In essence, the antitrust laws are designed to enforce competitive and, therefore, efficient, behavior.

The antitrust laws also outlaw monopolization and attempts to monopolize. That is, the laws prohibit companies from attempting to acquire such a large share of their markets that they can dominate the other sellers in those markets. For example, if a merger between Coca-Cola and Dr. Pepper were actually to occur, the antitrust agencies would study that merger very closely. If the agencies concluded that the merger would result in too much market power for the new company, they would disallow the merger.

The merging companies may claim that the increased production potential provided by the merger would permit the merged company to produce with greater efficiency. If the antitrust agency agreed that such results were possible, the agency would encourage the companies to expand through internal growth rather than through the acquisition of another leading company in the industry. In all cases, the antitrust laws are designed to protect the many sellers and easy entry characteristics of competition. If the antitrust laws are effective, they encourage the efficient production that results naturally when competition exists.

Natural Monopoly

When one company monopolizes a market because it possesses significant economies of scale or the market is too small to permit more than one company to operate efficiently, governmental intervention to increase the number of companies does not make sense. As demonstrated in Figure 9–2, an increase in the number of sellers in the market will actually decrease the efficiency of production in that market, because each company will be forced to produce in a smaller, less efficient plant. Thus, if government wishes to intervene, it must do so in some other way.

Government usually responds to natural monopoly situations by some form of direct regulation. For example, electricity is provided to a given region by one monopolistic company because the generation and transmission of electricity possess significant economies of scale. The regulatory agency recognizes the technical efficiency that may result from the natural monopoly, but the agency must take specific steps to reduce the possibility that the electric companies will exploit the market power they derive from their monopoly position.

If an electric company wishes to increase its prices, the company must submit a price increase request to the state public utilities commission, which will study the request and determine whether the price increase is justified. (That is, the price increase must correspond to a legitimate increase in costs.) With this procedure government expects to maintain the efficient production gained through the economies of scale and also to achieve prices that approximate minimum average costs. The regulatory activity is successful if electricity is produced and transmitted efficiently and sold at competitive prices.

SELF-TEST

5. When a natural monopoly exists, the company has the power to set a monopoly price by restricting its level of output. In an

attempt to maintain competitive prices and output, government may take action to introduce more competition into these markets, or it can impose some form of direct regulation. If government is going to intervene, which approach is likely to achieve the greatest level of efficiency?

External Costs

Externalities present a dilemma for government. Public surveys clearly indicate that a significant majority of the population wants cleaner air and water and better controls over toxic waste dumps. Yet public opinion surveys also reveal that the general public wants to reduce the level of governmental regulations.

As we discussed earlier in this chapter, individual companies are unlikely to reduce pollution and properly control toxic waste sites, because the profit motive encourages them to reduce only private costs and not external costs. When government takes action that requires companies to include the external costs as part of their total costs of production, companies will generally increase their prices to pay for these costs. If customers do not understand the nature of external costs, they accuse governmental regulations of contributing to inefficiency and higher prices. If we wish to reduce these external costs, what must be done?

Because of the nature of external costs, it is clear that government involvement is essential if we wish to reduce the level of such external costs as pollution and improperly monitored toxic waste dumps. It is also clear that we need to inform the general public that the external costs are actual production costs that must be included in the total costs if we wish to allocate resources efficiently. The challenge to governmental regulators such as the Environmental Protection Agency (EPA) is to determine the optimal level of pollution. Since reducing pollution to zero would cost an exorbitant amount, we need to determine the level of pollution we are willing to tolerate. The EPA can approach this problem by setting pollution standards for all industries, or it can establish a type of pricing system that would permit companies to pay a fee for polluting if they did not wish to eliminate their pollution. These options will be developed in Chapter 13.

It is clear that government must intervene in the private economy if we wish to reduce the problems associated with external costs such as pollution. Without some form of governmental involvement, companies have little incentive to reduce external costs. As a result, consumers will be deceived into thinking that companies are more efficient than they actually are. In fact, failure to account properly for external costs causes economic inefficiency, because society will purchase more of the polluting products than it would if all costs (private and external) were properly measured.

Public Goods

The provision of public goods has an interesting impact on efficiency. In most instances we do not think about how streets, lighthouses, and educational services influence the cost of production. Yet these public goods can have a very important effect. For instance, if a community does not have a good system of streets, businesses will experience higher transportation costs. If lighthouses did not exist, shippers would absorb higher costs because of damage to their ships. If public education did not exist, the quality of the work force would decrease.

Thus, the provision of public goods will often increase efficiency in subtle but important ways. If a community was unwilling to provide these public goods through paying increased taxes, the level of efficiency would decline. Consequently, we need to examine our need for public goods very closely and make sure that we appreciate fully the importance of public goods for the economic welfare of the community.

Barriers to Free Trade

International trade presents another dilemma for governmental agencies. On the surface, trade barriers such as tariffs and quotas restrict the supply and increase the price of the product to the consumers. If free trade can be achieved, it will increase efficiency within the economy, because foreign trade increases competitive pressures that will force companies to produce at their lowest average costs.

When free trade occurs, some domestic workers will either lose their jobs or suffer decreases in wages. Some businesses will become less profitable because they will lose sales to businesses in foreign countries. Labor and management in these areas are likely to lobby Congress for tariffs to protect them from the competitive pressures of international trade. Congress must decide whether it should protect the interests of the workers and managers of the affected industries or whether it should let free trade work and provide lower prices for the economy in general.

As a legislator for the entire economy, can you increase efficiency by restricting free trade? Figure 9–3 suggests that you cannot, but Figure 9–3 assumes that labor and capital are able to move freely from the production of one good to another and, if necessary, from one country to another. In modern society, labor and capital resources do not appear to move that freely. When foreign trade displaces labor and capital in the production of a product (for instance, steel), steelworkers and capital equipment are unlikely to move to Austria, where steel production is apparently more profitable. Instead these resources must find their way into a different market or they will become unemployed. If these resources remained unemployed, the economy will experience significant inefficiency. (See Chapter 4, p. 42, where efficiency is defined.)

When free trade causes unemployment of economic resources, government appears to have two responsibilities: (1) It should encourage, and possibly assist, inefficient domestic producers to become more efficient, and (2) it should assist labor to regain employment. These approaches are more effective than tariff barriers, because the barriers reduce supply to S_2, causing prices to rise to P_2 and quantity to fall to Q_2. These types of interventions also require businesses to cope with competitive pressures that come from foreign competitors.

If, however, free trade does cause a significant increase in unused labor and capital, then government may consider using tariff barriers as a *temporary* measure to permit a reallocation of labor and capital. In addition, government may implement some specific programs to assist the movement of displaced workers and capital from the companies that cannot compete because of foreign trade into the pro-

Figure 9–3
Advantages of Free Trade

This diagram demonstrates that free trade will increase supply and, as a result, increase output and decrease price.

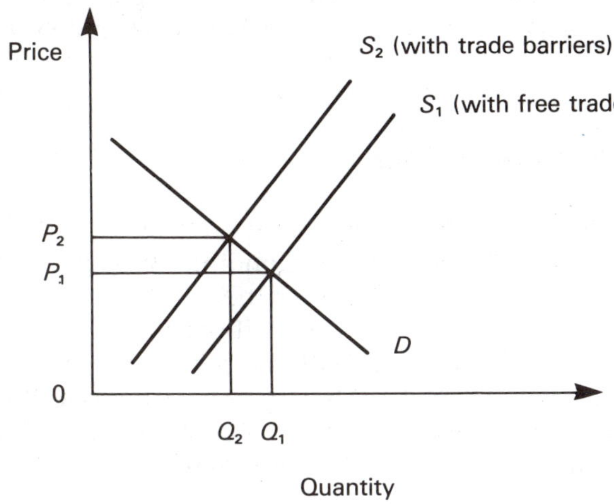

duction of goods and services that are more profitable. For example, movement of labor and capital into businesses that export goods and services would help balance imports and exports. Through this form of intervention, government can enhance the long-run efficient use of resources within the economy.

SELF-TEST

6. When governments create agencies such as the Environmental Protection Agency (EPA), the economy experiences increased costs associated with that agency. How can economists claim that the EPA can increase efficiency?
7. When foreign trade causes business failure and unemployment, can government take any action to improve efficiency?

EFFICIENCY AND OTHER ECONOMIC SYSTEMS

Throughout Chapters 4–9 we have emphasized how a market economy works to achieve economic efficiency. The dynamic process of competition tends to force companies to be efficient, or else they will be pushed into bankruptcy. But in Chapters 8 and 9 we learned that the competitive process does not always work as well as we would like. Imperfect competition may permit companies to produce their output at less than maximum efficiency. A market economy will often experience difficulties caused by foreign trade and external costs. We now need to examine how other economic systems handle these issues.

Market Socialism

Market Socialism
An economic system in which competitive markets function but profits may return to government or to the workers

In the United States we adjust to these problems by asking government to intervene. Other economies respond to the goal of efficiency in a variety of ways. Some of them follow essentially the same process as that in the United States; others respond very differently. The final section of this chapter will take a brief look at *market socialism,* which is the theoretical basis for the economies of Hungary and Yugoslavia, and the business and governmental coordination in Japan.

In most countries that use market socialism, there will be a central planning board that sets rules governing production decisions, chooses the rate at which plants and equipment are increased, fixes the prices for all capital goods (prices of consumer goods and wages are set by the market forces of supply and demand), and influences the price of capital equipment. The planning board does not decide what to produce, how much to produce, or how to produce. These decisions are made primarily by the rules of competition, that is, price should equal marginal costs, and all resources of production should be used efficiently.

Since this economic system incorporates some attributes of a competitive market with those of a planning board, some economists argue that market socialism can be more efficient than a typical capitalist economy like the United States. Advocates of market socialism argue that there are several advantages to this system: A planning board with a broader vision of the economy will enable producers to achieve their equilibrium prices more quickly as a result of fewer trials and errors. A planning board can directly account for external costs. Public ownership of some of the means of production causes income to be distributed more equitably. As a result, there will be a higher degree of consumer sovereignty than exists in a capitalistic market. These advantages should lead to higher levels of efficiency.

Market socialism, however, does have some major problems. The fixing of the prices of capital goods is complex. First, if these prices are not set properly, the use of economic resources will be altered significantly. Second, if the profits go to government, what incentives do managers have to operate efficiently? Also, if workers are paid bonuses according to the success of the entire production unit, what incentive does any one worker have to work efficiently? Under market socialism, cooperation is a more important concept than individual self-satisfaction.

If the economy is democratic and workers believe that the market for consumer goods and the planning board accurately reflect their interests, then workers will generally cooperate, and the economy will function efficiently. If, however, workers do not believe that they have adequate choice among the consumer goods and that they are poorly represented by the planning board, the likelihood of inefficient production rises dramatically. The examples of Hungary and Yugoslavia suggest that in reality both advantages and disadvantages of market socialism exist. The issue of whether market socialism can be more efficient than capitalistic markets depend upon a whole host of additional factors, including cultural characteristics of the individual economies.

Business and Governmental Coordination

The Japanese economy presents another alternative to the capitalistic system of the United States. Where the market system in the United States stresses competition among many sellers, the Japanese system encourages large corporate organizations that are strongly influenced by governmental agencies.

Because a significant proportion of Japan's production occurs in sections dominated by large industrial groups, there is a high degree of coordination among producers at the different stages of production. For example, there is a close relationship between large companies and their suppliers. This relationship helps explain Japan's great efficiency in managing its inventories.

Suppliers know what the large companies are going to order, so the suppliers can adjust their production rates to the needs of the large companies. This level of cooperation reduces the amount of unnecessary production and minimizes the number of times that supplies would be unavailable.

A major form of governmental influence is achieved through the financial system. There is a savings system that encourages companies to deposit savings at the same rate of interest as that in commercial banks. But the governmental savings system provides a tax exemption for the first three million yen earned from the interest on the deposits. This tax exemption provides a strong incentive for businesses to put their savings into the governmental savings system.

The government lends these savings in the form of low interest loans to companies who are willing to expand production in areas targeted by governmental agencies. In this manner government has a direct influence on the types of expansion companies will pursue. Although businesses are free to make their own business decisions, the availability of these low interest loans from the governmental saving system makes it very difficult to ignore the direction set by government. The result of this approach is a form of governmental planning that has been highly efficient.

The Japanese system evolved from an interaction among the cultural, political, and economic forces within that society. These forces are difficult for other societies to copy. In addition the current Japanese system is showing some signs of weakness. Youth are not as dedicated to their employers as are their parents. The financial system does not appear to function as smoothly during periods of economic slowdown. Also, as growth has slowed, there have been signs of decreasing cooperation between workers and management and between suppliers and producers. Thus, we can see that although Japan has had a period of highly efficient production, its system is also strongly influenced by both the economic conditions and cultural and political forces of the time.

ACTIVE REVIEW

1. Chapters 4–8 explained how a market economy works to achieve the goal of economic efficiency. Chapter 9 discussed the importance of government in achieving this goal. To what extent is governmental intervention necessary to achieve economic efficiency? To answer this question, answer the following questions:
   a. Briefly explain how anticompetitive practices, externalities, and foreign trade can affect efficiency.
   b. Governmental intervention is costly. Under what conditions does it make sense to increase costs by involving government with the intention of decreasing costs to society at large (increasing economic efficiency)?
   c. Can government achieve efficiency by altering the economic system?
2. Evaluate the following statement:

   A market economy that operates with the forces of demand and supply is a powerful force toward efficiency. Any attempts to alter the forces of demand and supply by governmental intervention will ultimately result in more inefficiency.

ANSWERS TO ACTIVE REVIEW

1a. If companies can act as monopolists, they will restrict their output to achieve profit maximization. If this restriction in output causes companies to produce at less than full capacity, the companies will experience a higher average cost than if they produced at full capacity.

If companies create external costs, they will impose those costs on society unless some governmental action is taken. If companies do not absorb these external costs, then the economy will experience a misuse or inefficient use of the resources that create the external costs.

When foreign trade causes unemployment, inefficiency results, because an economy is producing less than its potential. It is operating inside its production possibility curve.

1b. To determine the efficiency of governmental intervention, we must determine the cost of the inefficiency caused by monopoly, external costs, foreign trade, etc., and determine whether the governmental intervention reduces that inefficiency by more than the increased costs associated with operating the governmental program. If the gain in efficiency is greater than the cost of the governmental program, then we should advocate intervention.

1c. The text discussed briefly market socialism and business and governmental cooperation. In both cases there is evidence of increased efficiency as a result of governmental intervention. Both cases also describe some potential difficulties in achieving efficiency. There are several ways to pursue economic efficiency, and each one of them is imperfect. It appears, however, that when imperfect markets and externalities exist, governmental action can nudge the economy toward a more efficient allocation of resources. On the other hand, if we are not careful, governmental intervention can cause additional misallocation of resources.

ANSWERS TO SELF-TEST

1. A small group of competitive companies will not collude, because their collusion would be ineffective. When competitive conditions exist, no single seller or small group of sellers dominates the market. There are many sellers, and entry is easy. If a small group of sellers were to collude and raise their prices, customers would purchase the product from other sellers and new sellers would probably enter the market. The colluding companies would lose sales and revenue.

   In an oligopolistic situation described in the text, the two companies dominated the market. In addition, oligopolistic markets have difficult entry. If the two companies were to collude, customers would not have a sufficient number of alternative sellers from whom they could purchase the product.

2. If a merger increases the market power of the merged company, then the new larger company may exercise its market power and restrict output in order to earn higher profits. When output is restricted, the company may move to a less efficient level of production. The merged company may produce on the downward sloping part of its average cost curve. It is possible, however, that a merger may increase efficiency by infusing the better management techniques of the more efficient company into the less efficient one.

   If the merging companies were efficient prior to the merger, the merger is unlikely to increase efficiency, because the combining of the two companies will not cause an increase in the economies of scale. In such a case, market power is likely to increase instead of efficiency.

3. The disposal of chemical wastes presents us with the problem of distinguishing between private and external costs. From the perspective of the individual company, placing the chemical waste in a landfill

is efficient because it minimizes the cost to the individual company. To remain competitive this company will use the landfill, because it wishes to keep its costs as low as possible.

If we examine the costs from the perspective of society, we find that the placing of chemical waste in a landfill may cause some serious health problems for people who live near the landfill. These people experience the external costs associated with the production of chemicals. If the chemical company is not forced to dispose of the chemicals properly, the economy will experience economic inefficiency, because the company has not absorbed all of the costs associated with producing chemicals.

4. Some economists would argue that we should not alter our thinking about demand and supply as a result of international trade. Others argue that it is more difficult for labor and capital to find new employment when they have been displaced by foreign trade. As a consequence, these economists argue that government should assist labor and capital in their search for new and productive employment.
5. If a natural monopoly exists, then by definition only one efficient company can exist in that market. Any attempts to increase the number of sellers in this market would cause all sellers to produce less efficiently. Thus, if government is going to intervene in the market, it must do so with some form of direct regulation.
6. Agencies such as the EPA exist because they are needed to control the external costs associated with production. It is true that there is a cost associated with operating an agency such as the EPA. It is also true that private companies will ignore external costs such as pollution unless laws are passed to control those costs and agencies are formed to monitor compliance with those laws. If the cost of operating agencies such as the EPA is less than the external costs of pollution, then the creation of the EPA can increase efficiency.
7. Economic efficiency is achieved when the factors of production are fully employed and being used to produce with technical efficiency the most desirable combination of goods and services. If foreign trade causes unemployment, and if the unemployment labor and capital have difficulty in finding new employment, then government can increase efficiency by assisting the unemployed labor and capital to find new and productive employment.

10
Economic Freedom

In response to the often quoted statement of President Kennedy, "Ask not what your country can do for you—ask what you can do for your country," Milton Friedman, a well-known economist stated:

> The free man will ask neither what his country can do for him nor what he can do for his country. He will ask rather "What can I and my compatriots do through government" to help us discharge our individual responsibilities, to achieve our several goals and purposes, and above all, to protect our freedom? And he will accompany this question with another: How can we keep the government we create from becoming a Frankenstein that will destroy the very freedom we establish it to protect? Freedom is a rare and delicate plant. Our minds tell us, and history confirms that the great threat to freedom is the concentration of power. Government is necessary to preserve our freedom; yet by concentrating power in political hands, it is also a threat to freedom. Even though the men who wield this power initially be of good will and even though they be not corrupted by power they exercise, the power will both attract and form men of a different stamp.*

The above quote is representative of the importance placed on economic and political freedom by Milton Friedman and many other

*Milton Friedman, *Capitalism and Freedom* (Chicago: University of Chicago Press, 1962), p. 2.

economists. Furthermore, they argue that political freedom can be achieved only if economic freedom is maintained. Thus, we need to explore the meaning of economic freedom and to understand its impact on the economy.

The purpose of this chapter is to define economic freedom and to discuss its importance, as well as to examine several approaches for achieving that goal. The task of defining economic freedom requires us to note the various ways to interpret this goal. The ambiguity of economic freedom is similar to that reflected in our discussion of efficiency and in future discussions of such goals as equity, full employment, and price stability. In each of these cases the goals have more than one potential meaning.

WHAT IS ECONOMIC FREEDOM?

In one sense the question What is economic freedom? seems somewhat silly. We all know that freedom is the ability to do as one chooses within the normal constraints of a social system. For example, we have freedom to speak as long as we do not slander. We have the freedom to go where we please as long as we have the means to get there. And we have the freedom to acquire private property as long as we acquire the property in a fair exchange.

Yet, like most other important concepts, the simple approach is often inaccurate or, at least, incomplete. The comment "to do as one chooses within the normal constraints of a social system" is really a complex comment. How do we determine the extent of the normal constraints in a social system? Should the limits on freedom be determined through the exchange process in a market economy? How do governmental decisions influence the exercise of freedom?

In a market economy like that of the United States, consumers express their freedom by casting dollar votes for goods and services. Their freedom is enhanced when sellers increase the variety of goods and services available for sale and when consumers possess the income necessary to purchase their choice of these goods and services. If the variety of products is reduced, then consumer freedom is reduced.

For example, consumers may possess sufficient income to purchase a reasonable combination of goods and services, but sellers may restrict the quantity of products available. This type of behavior may exist when firms with market power reduce their production for the purpose of increasing the price of their products. This tactic was evident in the 1970s when the Organization of Petroleum Exporting Countries (OPEC) decreased the supply of oil that was available for purchase. When consumers lose control over the market process, they have lost *consumer sovereignty*.

Consumer Sovereignty The power of consumers to decide what goods and services get produced, how many of each are produced, and who produces them

Consumer sovereignty is also constrained by the role of government. When government passes laws that require motorcycle riders to wear helmets, the freedom of individual consumers has been reduced. If government removes a product from the shelves, freedom has been reduced. For example, if government prohibits the sale of saccharin because of its carcinogenic potential, diabetics and weight-conscious consumers lose the freedom to choose this product.

It does not make any difference whether the intention of the governmental action is honorable or not. As Milton Friedman noted in the introductory quote to this chapter, the concentration of power in political hands will lead to an overall reduction of freedom. From his perspective, economic freedom is maximized when a market economy is permitted to function with minimal interference from government.

Those who supply goods and services also prefer a marketplace in which they dominate decisions about what to produce and the price at which output will be sold. When sellers are required by law to install safety equipment and antipollution devices and to implement work rules, sellers lose some *producer sovereignty*. Under these conditions businesses are not free to choose how they wish to use their factors of production. In essence, businesses are forced to absorb higher costs instead of responding to consumer demand by producing goods and services with the lowest possible private costs of production.

Producer Sovereignty The opportunity for businesses to produce goods and services without governmental intervention

Advocates of a free enterprise economy emphasize the importance of providing businesses the freedom to respond to consumer demand by producing a wide range of goods and services. These advocates argue that consumer sovereignty will be enhanced by emphasizing the freedom of sellers, because companies will constantly work to provide consumers with the best possible products at the lowest possible prices. Under these conditions, governmental regulations are unnecessary, because companies respond to competitive pressures by producing the goods and services desired by consumers. Thus, for the purpose of this book, we wish to emphasize that *economic freedom* represents the "absence of coercion."

Economic Freedom The right of individuals to participate in an economy with minimal coercion from public or private sources

Although we have defined economic freedom as the right of individuals to participate in an economy with minimal coercion from public or private sources, we do acknowledge that alternative definitions exist. According to some economists, people must have the knowledge and income necessary to exercise economic freedom. In those cases where product knowledge may be insufficient, such as with pharmaceuticals, it may be difficult to exercise economic freedom if consumers cannot understand the consequences of drugs, especially the potential side effects. Some governmental intervention, through regulation of products and the dissemination of information, may actually enhance economic freedom, used in this sense.

Governmental intervention may also increase economic freedom by improving consumers' power to participate. Although markets generally provide excellent opportunities for the practice of economic freedom, there are circumstances in which the freedom to participate is seriously constrained by consumers' lack of income. Our ability to participate in a market economy is greatly influenced by our level of income—the more income we have, the more freedom of choice we possess.

Some labor markets are not competitive, and some people are unable to compete. Under these circumstances some people will not be able to exercise economic freedom to the same extent as those who gain respectable incomes from competition in the labor markets. (See Chapter 11 for a more thorough discussion of labor markets that are not competitive.)

When some labor markets function noncompetitively, governmental intervention may enhance economic freedom by improving the ability of those affected to participate more effectively in a market economy. Yet we must be careful of this approach because government generally improves the ability of some people to participate by increasing the taxes of others. In other words, the economic freedom of one group may be increased at the expense of the economic freedom of another group.

Although concerns about equity may influence a decision to accept the "power to participate" as the operational definition of economic freedom, we prefer to emphasize the "absence of coercion" definition of economic freedom. The acceptance of this definition provides us with a clear distinction between the goals of economic freedom and equity. Consequently, when we refer to economic freedom throughout the remainder of the text, we mean that individuals have the right to participate in an economy, with minimal coercion from public or private sources.

SELF-TEST

1. A considerable number of tests have demonstrated quite conclusively that the use of seat belts reduces the number of deaths that are related to highway accidents. If government mandates that all people must use seat belts, has economic freedom been reduced?

2. Are there any circumstances under which economic freedom can be enhanced through an increase in governmental intervention?

WHY SHOULD ECONOMIC FREEDOM BE A GOAL?

The study of economics emphasizes the importance of making effective choices. When we studied the goal of efficiency, we learned that the efficient use of labor, capital, and natural resources results in a greater availability of the goods and services that consumers demand. In a similar manner economic freedom enhances the ability of consumers and producers to participate in the process of exchange. Economic freedom allows people to engage in an exchange process in an attempt to earn profit and acquire property. As the level of economic freedom grows, higher levels of participation leads to increased production and higher standards of living.

The goal of economic freedom includes the right to accumulate property. This right provides a primary motivation to engage in economic activity. The acquisition of property makes it easier to earn economic profits, and profit is a primary incentive to engage in productive activities. For example, as the price of farm products increases, we expect farmers to purchase more land, plant more seed, and harvest more crops in an attempt to earn profits and accumulate more property. As people acquire more property, their wealth and their ability to earn even greater levels of income will generally increase.

In Chapter 4 we identified economic efficiency as a goal, because efficiency is essential for the maximum output from a given set of resources. In a similar manner economic freedom is a goal because buyers and sellers need to exercise their choices for goods and services to achieve the proper allocation of resources or, more simply put, to gain the best mix of goods and services.

If economic freedom does not exist, then markets cannot function competitively, and resources will not be allocated properly. If economic freedom does not exist, some individuals will not have legitimate access to private property. Without the right to accumulate property, incentives to take risks will decrease, and the level of economic activity will decline. Thus, economic freedom is desirable because it helps the economy achieve its best allocation of resources.

ROLE OF THE MARKET AND GOVERNMENT IN ACHIEVING ECONOMIC FREEDOM

Economic freedom is a complex concept; there is considerable disagreement about how it is best maximized. It is clear that the right to own property is an important aspect of economic freedom, because the ownership of private property provides the incentives to take risks and increase the productivity of the economy. Advocates of free enterprise claim that if individuals are free to use their income as they please, they will have greater incentives to be more productive and innovative. If individuals must share their income (and, therefore, their right to acquire property) with others, these incentives may decline. In this section of the chapter we want to examine whether the possession of property is the best way to maximize economic freedom.

Potential Special Advantages and Disadvantages of Markets

Throughout this chapter it has been emphasized by advocates of free enterprise that the right to own private property is a critical element in the pursuit of economic freedom. They argue that through the acquisition of property individuals gain the ability to earn more income and economic freedom. We now examine these advantages more closely.

Potential Advantages of a Market Economy In a free enterprise economy, decisions are based upon the income that we earn. Each individual casts dollar votes for the goods and services that he or she wishes to purchase. In a similar manner, individuals are free to sell goods and services that they have produced. The expected result of these freedoms is a great diversity of goods and services. Through the use of the pricing mechanism, consumers can determine which goods and services they can afford. In response to the consumers' decisions, businesses will produce goods and services that provide businesses with a legitimate opportunity to earn economic profits. Advocates of free enterprise argue that when low-income consumers cannot afford certain goods and services, these consumers will have the incentive to earn more income so that they can make these desired purchases.

We can see consumer sovereignty at work in the selling of clothing. General societal norms cause men and women to choose their clothing according to the styles that are generally accepted within their community. Yet we see people who wear radically different clothing, from the very chic to worn jeans and tattered flannel shirts. This wide diversity of clothing exists because sellers can earn acceptable levels of income from selling almost any style of clothing. In some cases the number of buyers is sufficiently large so that prices may be relatively low. Whereas in other cases, the materials may be very expensive or the number of buyers sufficiently small so that prices will be relatively high. Yet if consumers are willing to pay the price, sellers will respond by producing the desired good or service.

With such a wide variety of products available, households should have incentives to earn higher incomes. These incentives should lead to increased productivity and an increase in the standard of living for the entire society.

At the same time that the standard of living increases, the freedom to acquire private property protects individual freedom by keeping economic power dispersed. Since everyone has the right to own property, the power of ownership is spread over millions of people, resulting in no one owner's having any real power over other property owners. In fact, the right to own property provides not only the incentive to increase productivity but also a natural source of restraints so that the marketplace is a form of economic democracy rather than a system dominated by oligopolies. In other words, a free enterprise economy is supposed to provide everyone with the opportunity to be a producer and to earn economic profit. If this system works well, the freedom to earn profits will prevent domination by a relatively small number of large companies.

Potential Disadvantages of a Market Economy In most market economies there are two significant problems that may arise from the emphasis on producer sovereignty. First, the economy may experience some distortions as a result of dominance of some markets by oligopolies. In these cases the distribution of power resulting from the ownership of property becomes uneven. As a consequence there will be an imbalance between consumer sovereignty and producer sovereignty. Because there are only a few sellers, buyers will have a more limited choice and, thus, less consumer sovereignty. With less consumer sovereignty, producers will have greater influence on what goods and services are offered for sale. For example, in the 1950s and 1960s, the major automobile manufacturers were reluctant to produce small cars. Consumers bought either large cars or foreign cars.

An imbalance in the ownership of property will lead to an imbalance of economic freedom. Current property owners will find it easier to accumulate new property than will those with no property. For instance, if you earn $100,000 per year and you own $500,000 in property, you will be able to borrow money more easily than someone who earns $15,000 a year and owns a five-year-old car and some furniture. Even if this second person can get a loan, it will probably be for a much smaller amount and at a considerably higher interest rate than the loans received by those who own a larger amount of property.

Although the ownership of property is no guarantee that you will earn significantly higher levels of income, ownership of property provides you with many more options than those possessed by individuals with virtually no property. Because you have these options, you have greater freedom than others, and there is no automatic mechanism that enables others to gain property equivalent to yours. When there is little or no governmental intervention to alter the market distribution of income, those with low incomes tend to lose some economic freedom.

Second, markets may experience significant external costs. Although the pricing mechanism is an outstanding allocative mechanism for private goods and services, prices do not work well in areas where externalities are involved. For example, the prices we pay for agricultural products typically do not include the costs associated with the run-off of fertilizers into rivers and streams. As the ecology of the river changes because of the fertilizer run-off, those who use the river for revenue, drinking, or recreating will have to pay a higher cost for use of the river. Their economic freedom will be reduced because the property value of the river will have fallen. The price mechanism does not correct the problems of external costs. (See Chapter 13 for a more thorough discussion of external costs.)

A free enterprise economy promotes economic freedom when all the competitive characteristics function effectively. If, however, the distribution of income is not equitable, if some oligopolies dominate markets, or if significant externalities exist, the effectiveness of a free enterprise economy in achieving economic freedom must be questioned.

SELF-TEST

3. Does economic freedom for producers in a competitive market increase the standard of living?
4. How might the ownership of private property reduce economic freedom?

Potential Advantages and Disadvantages of Government

Governments legislate actions in favor of one group and against others. When states passed laws that mandated the use of specific types of child seats for cars, profits increased for those companies that were already making the right type of seat, while the profits of the companies that made other types of seats probably fell. Consumer sovereignty fell because consumers were no longer free to choose whatever type of seat they liked and could afford. Producer sovereignty also decreased, because they had to produce the child seats according to governmental specifications.

If, however, you think of government as an enabling unit, then governmental actions provide additional economic freedom. For example, if your employer decides to move the company to another state or country, you are likely to become unemployed. You will lose your source of income through no direct fault of your own. Government may assist your ability to participate in the economy by giving you access to unemployment compensation and by assisting your move to a different location to get a new job. In this instance, government has helped you maintain some economic freedom.

Potential Advantages of Government An important feature of the United States economy is its emphasis upon the individual and its attempts to maximize individual choices. Yet in many ways it is very difficult to define what is meant by individuality. Everyone is influenced by the culture and social experiences that surround him or her.

People are products of culture, just as they are also producers of culture. For instance, most people in the United States prefer to drive their own cars instead of using public transportation. As a result many areas of the country have very poor public transportation systems. The lack of good public transportation systems makes it very difficult to choose public transportation as an alternative to private transportation. In this sense no one is free to make a totally independent decision.

In democratic societies, governments may be able to improve economic freedom by passing laws that have positive impacts upon the society as a whole, as opposed to having an impact on individuals within the society. For example, we can enhance our freedom by passing laws that require everyone to pay taxes to improve the educational system or laws that require plants to reduce the amount of chemicals they release into the atmosphere. In this manner any restraints that exist are effectively self-imposed and remain under the discretion of those whose lives are governed by them.

It is true that power often corrupts and can destroy economic freedom. Yet, is also true that power is necessary for freedom to be effective. The important point is that power must be effectively distributed. If income and property become inequitably distributed in a market economy, a democratic government can alter the rules that permit the unfair accumulation of property and can encourage a more equitable distribution of income.

A society and the individuals within it have the potential for becoming more free as knowledge and technology expand. Governments can play a key role in achieving this potential by providing a sound educational system. But if government is going to play a key role in the education of the masses, then government must require tax payments. In other words, individuals must sacrifice some freedom to spend their own income for the freedom gained from living and working with people who have received a good education.

Government is also a critical influence on the development of technology through its support of research and development. In this sense government is not the enemy of freedom, but rather it is the instrument through which freedom becomes more meaningful and genuine. Participatory government maximizes the economic freedom of businesses to use the results of governmentally sponsored research and to develop new products for consumers.

The critical role of government in enhancing economic freedom can be clearly demonstrated by the provision of public goods. If a government taxes the public to light the streets at night and repair the highways, it increases the freedom of people to engage in other economic activities. The conditions of modern life are complex and interdependent. Public agencies (government) are necessary to take action that increases the collective good. When government takes action that increases the quantity and quality of public goods, then economic freedom of the community is expanded. Yet, as we have studied previously, individual people and businesses must pay taxes (give up some individual freedom) to allow public goods to be provided.

Potential Disadvantage of Government Economic freedom is enhanced when power is effectively dispersed. When government accurately reflects the will of its constituents, government is an important instrument in ensuring economic freedom. In other words, for government to increase economic freedom it must be a participatory democracy—there must be a high degree of voter participation in the voting process.

If a large percentage of voters become complacent and fail to take an active part in the political process, governmental action may not reflect the desires of the people within the system. If, for example, a small but vocal group of television manufacturers successfully lobbies Congress to pass legislation to prohibit the sale of Japanese televisions in the United States, the economic freedom of that group would soar, while the freedom of consumers would decline dramatically.

Even when there is a high degree of voter participation, governmental action may result in the loss of some freedoms. Collective decision making operates on the principle of majority rule. When 60 percent of the people vote for a particular proposal, 60 percent are satisfied and free to act within the limits of the proposal. Yet there are 40 percent of the voters who must be coerced to follow the rules set by the majority. The effect upon economic freedom depends on the importance of the public goods to the economy as a whole.

Government plays a very important role in providing public goods and services to the general public. When government does an effective job of providing these goods and services, it increases economic freedom. But if the public fails to participate actively in the political process, then either special interest groups will dominate the economy or the political leadership will take control and act in a totalitarian manner. In either case economic freedom decreases.

Added Realism—Interaction Between Government and Market Mechanisms

In today's world there are no economies that are totally free enterprise or totally run by governmental fiat. All economies are a mixture of markets and governmental activities. But it also is true that economies emphasize one type of approach over another. The United States leans toward a market economy, while Russia, China, and Hungary emphasize collective decision making.

Regardless of the emphasis, economic systems must remember that access to property is essential to economic freedom, because property provides a source of power to make choices. But the access to property must be controlled, because too much property gives too much power to its owners relative to others. This concept is true whether the property is controlled by private individuals or by government.

In a mixed economy a type of checks and balances system can exist. The very nature of a market economy emphasizes diversity and individual choices. When an economy that emphasizes free enterprise works effectively, economic freedom for sellers is increased. But history indicates that markets do not necessarily function effectively. Oligopolies and externalities arise. The distribution of income may become inequitable. When these market imperfections occur, governments generally intervene.

In a mixed economy the market mechanism is closely influenced by governmental intervention, but not always for the good of the economy. Special interest groups are generally more likely than the population in general to influence the formulation of laws. If it is not in legislators' interest to reflect the general needs of the society, then laws will be passed to benefit special interest groups, and the members of the society at large may experience a reduction in their economic freedom.

We must remember that in a complex society individual freedoms are restrained for all kinds of reasons. Some of these restraints are actually desirable. As voters, we have instructed our legislators to pass child labor laws and laws that mandate warnings on cigarette packages. We have restricted the use of DDT as a pesticide, but we also provide subsidies to tobacco farmers and pass laws that protect some businesses from legitimate competitive pressures.

In fact, if we took a few minutes, we could generate a long list of governmental actions that we believe unfairly benefit others relative to ourselves. Yet the majority of people do not want a society without extensive governmental intervention. We petition government to pass legislation to keep us responsible. For example, what would our city streets be like without red lights or stop signs? Local residents constantly pressure governments to install flashing lights or gates at railroad crossings. We are often pleased that a Food and Drug Administration oversees the quality of food and drugs we consume. Businesses request governmental intervention to protect contractual rights.

In general, many people want the freedom to make their own choices but realize that they either do not have access to enough knowledge to do so or do not have power to bring a certain good or service (public goods) into existence. Even if they do make good choices, other people may act irresponsibly and cause a significant reduction in the freedom of others. For example, a seller may prepare food in an unsanitary manner or a drug manufacturer may not anticipate or test for all the side effects of a new drug.

In summary, economic freedom emphasizes the power to participate in the economy with a minimum amount of coercion. Some combination of a market economy, governmental intervention, and an informed and involved electorate is necessary to achieve this goal.

The attempt to achieve other economic goals often leads to specific restrictions on economic freedom. For example, if we attempt to redistribute income, there will probably be a change in the tax laws and some people will pay higher taxes. If we want a cleaner environment, some businesses will be restricted in some of their business practices. In essence, when we attempt to maximize economic freedom, we must always ask, Whose freedom are we improving? The basic emphasis of this chapter has been that we wish to improve the economic freedom of sellers so that they can work to provide consumers with a higher quantity and quality of goods and services.

SELF-TEST

5. If people must be coerced to pay taxes, how can governmental intervention in economic activity increase economic freedom?
6. Evaluate the following statement: If any one company or industry increases its economic freedom, then the economic freedom of the entire economy will increase.

INTERNATIONAL COMPARISONS

In Chapter 9 we noted that economies that practice market socialism may use a political process to account for external costs and to cause incomes to be distributed more equitably. If economies such as Sweden, Hungary, and Yugoslavia manage to distribute income more equitably, consumers have greater freedom to influence the goods and services that will be produced.

If, however, the legislators in these economies have a concept of equity that differs significantly from that of the general population, then the system of taxation may reduce economic freedom. Thus, governmental intervention may advance or hinder economic freedom. The critical question about whether a market economy is more effective than market socialism in achieving economic freedom is difficult to answer. To arrive at a conclusion, we must assess the degree of imperfections in a market economy and the effectiveness of legislators in dealing with these imperfections. For example, if as a result of barriers to entry, there is a high degree of concentration in the economy, new companies will not have the freedom to compete. This restriction of freedom must be compared with any losses of freedom that would be caused by political activities.

In an economy such as that of Japan the coordination between business and government has an interesting influence on the producer's freedom to decide what goods and services should be provided. Within the Japanese economy, businesses are free to operate for a profit, but they receive significant influence from government in the form of the financial system described in Chapter 9. Because of significant tax savings, a company will decide to expand production in areas targeted by government rather than by making totally independent decisions.

This coordination with government does not hinder the ability of businesses to earn profits and acquire property. The coordination does influence the degree to which individuals can exercise their property rights without direct influence of others. A system of government and business cooperation does influence how profit is earned. The major question about such a system is whether governmental agencies are more effective in solving particular problems than is a market economy.

ACTIVE REVIEW

1. Economic freedom has been defined as the right of individuals to participate in an economy with minimal coercion from public or private sources. Yet businesses and consumers often appear to have conflicting interests as individuals. Is it possible to achieve consumer sovereignty and producer sovereignty at the same time? If yes, discuss the role of government, if any, in achieving this degree of economic freedom. If no, explain why the two types of freedom cannot be achieved simultaneously.
2. Whenever government gets involved in economic activity, it typically must levy taxes to pay for that activity. Since most people prefer to spend their own money, the taxes become a form of coercion. Is it possible to pay taxes and increase economic freedom at the same time?

ANSWER TO ACTIVE REVIEW

1. Consumer sovereignty is defined as the power of consumers to decide what goods and services get produced. Producer sovereignty is defined as the right of businesses to produce goods and services without government intervention. On the surface it appears that these two forms of sovereignty are directly opposed to one another, but they do not need to be.

   In a market economy we expect a high degree of competition. When competition does exist, there are many sellers who provide consumers with a high level of choice among the goods and services being sold. Easy entry conditions ensure that if consumers choices are reduced because some companies dominate a market, new companies will enter that market and once again provide consumers with a high degree of choice. Thus, competition allows consumer sovereignty to exist.

In a somewhat similar manner competition provides a setting within which companies can practice producer sovereignty. Within a competitive market, companies strive to earn economic profit by increasing their efficiency or by introducing new products. The companies experience no coercion. Thus, companies practice producer sovereignty by introducing new products and more efficient methods of production because of the pressures of competition and not as a result of governmental coercion.

Yet sometimes competitive pressures do not work properly. If consumers cannot gain sufficient information to make rational decisions, then the intervention of governmental agencies such as the Federal Trade Commission and the Food and Drug Administration would be appropriate. These agencies are desired to provide consumers with the information that is necessary to make good consumer choices. Likewise, businesses will typically avoid paying external costs. Government agencies such as the Environmental Protection Agency may enforce laws that require companies to absorb the total costs of production (internal and external costs) and thereby increase the freedom of those who were unfairly affected by the external costs.

ANSWERS TO SELF-TEST

1. Yes, the mandatory installation and use of seat belts does increase economic freedom, especially if we define economic freedom as the right of individuals to participate in an economy with minimal coercion from public or private sources. Mandatory seat belt laws increase the cost of automobiles and thereby make it more difficult for some people to purchase autos. Also, and perhaps more fundamental, seat belt laws reduce the freedom of individuals to choose whether or not to wear the belts. Even though the evidence may be convincing that wearing seat belts increases the probability of surviving an accident, many individuals may prefer to accept that risk. A high level of economic freedom would permit that choice.
2. Although we have decided to emphasize the "absence of coercion" definition of economic freedom, we are aware that occasionally a market economy does not function as smoothly as we may like. When some members of the economy have incomes that are too low to allow them to participate effectively in the economy, some form of income redistribution may assist their economic freedom. When complex goods and services are offered for sale, consumers may need assistance in making appropriate consumer choices. When governmental agencies

such as the Food and Drug Administration provide this function, economic freedom may be increased. Also, economic freedom can be increased when government provides public goods and services such as police and fire protection and mass transportation.

3. In a competitive economy, producers are always searching for ways to encourage consumers to buy their goods and services, because producers are interested in maximizing their profits. If producers succeed in earning profits, they accumulate property and increase their economic freedom. At the same time consumers increase their economic freedom if there is an equitable distribution of income and sufficient competition to keep a handful of companies from dominating the market. If, however, some firms gain market power, the owners of the companies with market power experience an increase in the standard of living, but consumers are more likely to experience a loss of economic freedom.
4. Although access to private property is a critical feature of economic freedom, ownership of private property can also reduce economic freedom. If some people gain more access to property than others, they gain an advantage in the quest for additional property. If a property owner can borrow money at a lower cost than a non–property owner, then the freedom of the nonproperty owner is reduced relative to that of the property owner.
5. It is important to remember that economic freedom is a relative concept. Coercion may result from the activities of businesses in the private sector as well as from governmental activities. If some members of the private sector gain an undue amount of property and power, they can coerce other members of the economy. Governmental agencies can recognize the growth of this power and act to reduce it, for instance by the passage of antitrust laws. Governmental agencies can also recognize the need for public goods and services. Since members of the society desire to have good education, public services, police protection, and so forth, government must tax the public to provide them. The nature of public goods is that they tend to be unprofitable; thus, companies in the private sector will not produce them. If government does not provide the public goods and services, economic freedom will actually decrease.
6. It is tempting to respond to this comment by stating that it is accurate, especially if we equate the "absence of coercion" with freedom from governmental intervention. However, that response would be inaccurate, because coercion can also come from the private sector. If a few companies in an industry gain market power, they achieve greater freedom to set price and quantity, but consumers lose freedom. If companies are permitted to ignore negative externalities such as pollution, their freedom will increase at the expense of the rest of society.

11
Equity: Inequality and the Market Distribution of Income

In the United States, approximately one out of every six persons lives in poverty. Almost half of working-age, adult black males do not have jobs. At the same time, travel agents report that people are increasing their purchases of exotic, expensive vacations. The sale of fur coats and luxury automobiles is booming.

Whether or not these disparities in living conditions are justifiable is the focus of much economic debate. Each country has a consensus answer to that question. That answer provides its definition of *equity*. The acceptability of the answer is always being challenged by those who see the existing distribution of income as inappropriate. Out of habit, rather than logic, we refer to those who wish a greater degree of equality as advocates of equity.

Equity The legitimate distribution of economic resources

Discussions about equity are rarely based on a precise definition of what constitutes a desirable degree of inequality. Almost everyone agrees that some inequality is needed for incentive purposes. It is accepted that certain tasks will be completed only if the person who undertakes them receives a higher than average reward. As a result, the definition of equity is based on a normative assumption about the proper extent of inequality.

Equity could be discussed in several possible formats. For instance, we might analyze the distribution of wealth among various social classes. Wealth is the stock, or accumulation, of assets. It is the value of property accumulated over time. Income, in contrast, is an annual flow of money. For example, your salary is income; any land, real estate, or stock you own is wealth. Wealth is much more unequally distributed than is income. Table 11–1 demonstrates just how unequal it has been distributed during our recent history.

Our distribution of wealth affects income inequality because personal wealth opens opportunities unavailable to those lacking in such assets. The poorest 40 percent of the population has no measurable wealth whatsoever. This statistic means that any property owned by the poorest 40 percent is offset by liabilities, or payments owed to others. Thus, the contacts, credit, training, and power that wealth provides are unavailable to a large portion of the population.

An alternative way to examine inequality would be to analyze racial, gender, or regional income differences. In such an analysis, nonwhites, women, and families in the South would represent the relatively weak and needy. These groups are not full partners in economic activity for various reasons. A complete picture of inequality would explore those reasons.

Instead of these alternatives, we will focus on equity in terms of income distribution. There is some professional debate about whether personal or household income distribution is more relevant. We will not get involved in that debate, for the same generalizations apply to either form of income distribution data.

While the existing distribution of income is not necessarily the proper definition of equity, it is an ideal starting point in the search for a better definition. While the debate about the extent of poverty has been lively, the basic distribution of income in the United States has shown a remarkable persistence since 1960. Table 11–2 reveals the apparent definition of equity used by those who control the distribution of income in the United States. One qualification to this

Table 11–1
Wealth Distribution
This table reveals the sharp inequality of wealth distribution.

Year	Personal Wealth Owned by Richest 1% of Wealth Holders
1945	23.3%
1949	20.8
1953	24.3
1956	26.0
1958	23.8
1962	22.0
1965	23.4
1969	20.1
1972	20.7
1982	21.0

Source: U.S. Bureau of the Census, *Statistical Abstract of the United States, 1979* (Washington, D.C.: GPO, 1978), p. 470; U.S. Bureau of Census, *Statistical Abstract of the United States, 1986* (Washington, D.C.: GPO, 1985), pp. 462, 464.

Table 11–2
Pretax Incomes
This table organizes the pretax family incomes for various years by quintile, or fifths.

Family Income	1960	1965	1970	1975	1981	1984
Lowest fifth	5	5	5	5	5	5
Second fifth	12	12	12	12	12	12
Middle fifth	18	18	18	18	17	16
Fourth fifth	24	24	24	24	24	24
Highest fifth	41	41	41	41	42	43
Top 5%	16	16	16	16	15	16

Source: U.S. Bureau of the Census, *Statistical Abstract of the United States, 1986* (Washington, D.C.: GPO, 1985), pp. 450–55.

statement is that Table 11–2 is in terms of *pretax* income. However, Chapter 12 will make it clear that government makes only minor changes in the pretax distribution.

The poor living conditions and lack of opportunity of those in the lowest fifth of our income distribution pattern are typically the focus of any analysis of equity. While this approach largely ignores the comparative luxury experienced by the richest fifth, it does have the benefit of directing our attention to the relative deprivation experienced by the poor. If there were no one that we believed was poor, the goal of equity would have been reached. The next section explains what poverty is and identifies who the poor are. The remainder of this chapter explains why the market distribution of income creates inequality. Chapter 12 heightens your awareness of the distributional role of government. As you will learn, one of the objectives of governmental taxes and expenditures is to modify the market distribution of income.

SELF-TEST

1. Evaluate the claim that greater equity would never work because some people will always be able to earn more money than will others.
2. Although by themselves the data in Tables 11–1 and 11–2 do not prove that wealth is more unevenly distributed than income, why do they suggest that wealth distribution is more unequal?
3. How would the distribution of wealth affect the distribution of incomes in future time periods?

THE EXTENT AND DISTRIBUTION OF POVERTY

Absolute Poverty Lacking some minimum amount of goods or services that has been specified as necessary for survival

Relative Poverty Falling too far behind the income of others in your economy

The number of poor that we count depends on the definition of poverty we use. The poorest person in the United States may have more material goods than the average citizen in the poorest regions of Asia. Are both poor? Or is one poor only if he or she lacks enough food or shelter for survival? *Absolute poverty* refers to a condition in which a person does not possess some minimum standard of goods and services. For example, a nation might define poverty as being unable to acquire a certain number of calories per day or a shelter with a roof.

Our discussion of poverty focuses on a different kind of poverty, *relative poverty*. Whenever we discuss equity by looking at the distribution of income among different income groups, we are assuming that human well-being is a relative matter. Relative poverty consists of falling too far behind the upper income groups or average income. However poverty is defined, it is based on the belief that we evaluate our own economic condition in terms of how others in our nation are doing.

The reason for emphasizing the relative significance is that our idea of how we are doing in terms of income evolves over time. A high school education and some kind of automobile are now regarded as a necessity by most people. Yet a few decades ago only the affluent could acquire such training and possessions. Our concept of poverty should be modified as our ideas of "making it" are modified by experience and economic growth.

The official poverty line in the United States is a particular amount of income. The line distinguishing a poor family from a nonpoor one varies with the size of the family. The typical number that you hear mentioned is an annual income for families of four. In 1964, when the official poverty line was set at $3,000, 18 percent of the population was poor. The percentage has fallen to as low as 11.6 percent in 1974 and 1977. Since 1979, the number of poor people has risen. The 1984 poverty rate was approximately 15.5 percent. Of course, the poverty line has been adjusted upward to account for inflation. The demarcation for poverty in 1984 was $12,300 for a family of four.

The poor are different from the nonpoor in more respects than just having a low level of income. The probability of being poor is much greater if a person has particular characteristics. As indicated in Table 11–3, the incidence, or distribution, of poverty is not shared by all social groups in similar proportions. One reason for the persistence of poverty is the relative weakness of those groups who make up the bulk of the poor. They tend to lack both market power and political clout.

Table 11–3 Distribution of Poverty, by Age, Gender, and Race, 1983.
This table shows the extent to which various groups are affected by poverty.

Characteristic	Persons Below Poverty Level (%)
All persons	14.4
Race	
White	11.5
Black	33.8
Gender of head of household	
Male	6.6
Female	35.2
Age 65 and over	12.4

Source: U.S. Bureau of the Census, *Statistical Abstract of the United States, 1986* (Washington, D.C.: GPO, 1985), pp. 457–61.

Since we are examining income *distribution*, we must go beyond this description of the poor. Relative poverty cannot be studied without looking at the entire range of incomes in the economy. The goal of equity requires the creation of a balance between the incomes of the poor and the relatively rich. It is the inequality of incomes that shapes our definition of relative poverty as a problem.

INEQUALITY IN THE UNITED STATES

This chapter began by contrasting the life-styles of the poor and the wealthy. Just how large are the income differences that create these contrasts? Before we can make any judgments about how vigorously to pursue greater equality, we need to be aware of the current extent of inequality.

The same incentive system that motivates productive use of resources also makes it possible for some to earn substantially more income than do others. Those who fail for some reason to meet the culture's definition of production may experience extreme amounts of discomfort in the form of homelessness and hunger. In the United States there is a stigma associated with being poor; it is believed that poor people have not contributed their share to production. The stigma is particularly potent in light of the evidence from television that suggests so many are unspeakably comfortable.

Table 11–2 provides a picture of inequality. If income were equally distributed, each 20 percent of income earners would have 20 percent of total income. Instead, the poorest 20 percent persistently have about 5 percent of income, while the richest 20 percent have approximately 42 percent.

As mentioned earlier, this distribution of income has been almost constant since World War II. This persistence in income distribution shares is extremely important for at least two reasons. First, it is inconsistent with the typical impression that inequality is steadily being reduced in the United States. That belief may be what we want to be true, but the facts suggest otherwise. A second important aspect of the stability in our income distribution pattern is that it contrasts with the stated intent of so many governmental expenditures. Many of us incorrectly assume that inequality will surely shrink if programs are adopted to reduce inequality.

To give you a better impression of what the various quintiles actually mean, Table 11–4 provides you with the starting point of each quintile in 1983. Notice that any family earning $63,200 or more is in the upper 5 percent of households. The very rich are those in the upper 0.5 percent of households. To be in this category the household must have an income in excess of $200,000.

TOOLS FOR MEASURING INEQUALITY: GINI COEFFICIENTS AND LORENZ CURVES

As with each of the other economic goals, we would like to be able to compare our performance with respect to equity over several years and with that of other countries. The Gini Coefficient provides the measure we need. However, before we can interpret Gini Coefficients, we need some background information.

Lorenz Curve A graph indicating the proportion of income earned by each percentile of households or individuals

Gini Coefficients are derived from a graph called the Lorenz Curve. The *Lorenz Curve* consists of a series of points, each point indicating the share of income possessed by a particular percentage of households or individuals. The Lorenz Curve gives us a visual representation of inequality at a particular time. Figure 11–1 is a Lorenz Curve constructed with the aid of the data from Table 11–2.

Table 11–4
Income of Family Quintiles, 1983

	1983, Current Dollars (rounded to hundreds)
Mean income, all families	$25,400
Upper limit of each quintile	
Lowest fifth	11,600
Second fifth	20,600
Middle fifth	29,100
Fourth fifth	40,900
Highest 5% (minimum income)	63,200

Source: U.S. Bureau of the Census, *Statistical Abstract of the United States, 1986* (Washington, D.C.: GPO, 1985), pp. 447–51.

Each Lorenz Curve appears on a graph that includes a 45-degree line. That line is the line of perfect equality, indicating what the Lorenz Curve would be if everyone had exactly the same income. Then 20 percent of the population would receive 20 percent of the income; 60 percent of the population would receive 60 percent of the income; and so on.

The 45-degree line thus provides a basis for comparing degrees of inequality. Those Lorenz Curves closer to the 45-degree line indicate a distribution of income closer to perfect equality.

Comparisons of countries or historical periods can be made by drawing Lorenz Curves for each situation. Comparing the Lorenz Curve with the 45-degree line provides a means of measuring the extent of inequality. The *Gini Coefficient* is the area between a particular Lorenz Curve and the 45-degree line. Thus, by comparing Gini Coefficients, we can discuss the relative inequality among historical periods and different economies. A Gini Coefficient of zero would mean that there is perfect equality.

Gini Coefficient The area between the line of perfect equality and a Lorenz Curve

At the conclusion of Chapter 12, when we discuss international performance with respect to equity, we will look at Gini Coefficients for various countries. In terms of the historical record in the United States, our Gini Coefficient since World War II has been remarkably constant, ranging from .379 to .351. This constancy reflects the stability in our distribution of income.

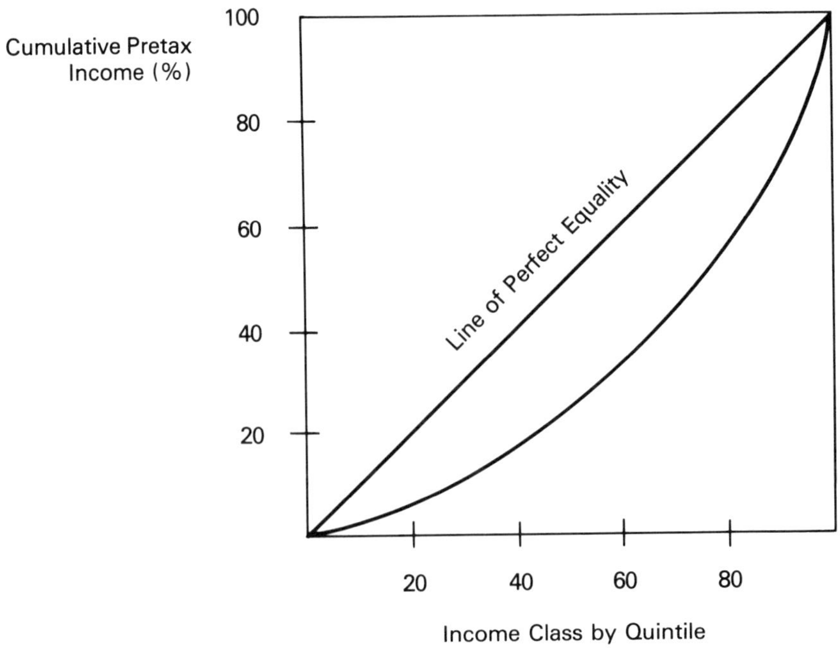

Figure 11–1
Lorenz Curve

This graph measures the deviation of the actual distribution of income from absolute equality of income.

How is this inequality created? Why do some people get rewards from our economic system that are hundreds of times greater than those others receive? The next section begins to answer these questions by examining the economic forces that shape the market distribution of income. The *market distribution of income* is the pattern of income shares that results from the interactions between buyers and sellers in resource markets. The market distribution provides the starting point, or foundation, from which equity is pursued.

Market Distribution of Income Income shares resulting from negotiations in resource markets between those who own resources and those who want to buy them

---

SELF-TEST

4. Explain the reasoning behind the following statement: A Gini Coefficient will not be zero, because we are concerned about motivating resource owners to use their resources for the benefit of others.
5. Why could the poorest 50 percent of households never earn 60 percent of the income?
6. What would happen to a nation's Lorenz Curve if a decision was made to launch a successful fight against poverty?

RESOURCE MARKETS AS SOURCES OF INCOME

Except for that rare individual who gets money from the estate of a relative or from a friend, most of us receive the bulk of our income by selling resources. Those who buy the resources do so because they have some use in mind for them. Those who demand labor, capital goods, or raw materials do so because they believe that the revenue they will make from combining those resources will be greater than the prices that they must pay for those resources. Thus, the demand for resources is a *derived demand.* It is a dependent variable that depends on, among other things, the demand for the goods and services that the resources will eventually be used to create. For example, the demand for auto mechanics depends upon the demand for automobiles. All resources owners are consequently interested in the extent to which total demand in the economy is high and, more specifically, the size of the demand for the outputs for which their resources can be used.

Derived Demand Demand for resources that depends on the demand for those goods and services that the resources will ultimately produce

We have now found two keys to understanding inequality. First, some start the economic game with more resources or more-productive resources than do others. Since resource ownership is the primary source of incomes, we should all be curious about why some start the economic contest with so many more of the income-producing units (resources).

Why does the market distribution of income depend in part on the fact that some start the economic game with more resources than others will have when the game is over? What kind of fairness is provided by such a contest? The explanations for inequality of resource ownership fall into two distinct categories. Some see ownership of resources as the reward for careful planning and hard work in previous years. This view sees individuals as having the power to determine primarily through their choices about education and career the amount of economic resources they will possess.

Others argue that the inequality of resource ownership and the consequent inequality of income are unfair because they are caused by factors over which the individual largely lacks control. To the extent that a person's family, race, gender, ethnic group, national origin, or luck shapes the probability that he or she will acquire economic resources, the resulting distribution is unfair. Income earners then would not be fundamentally responsible for how many resources they possessed at the start of the economic game. This second perspective is the basis for almost all attempts to modify or repair the market distribution of income.

A second key to understanding inequality stems from the concept of derived demand. Income flows more freely from the sale of some resources than from others. The tastes of the society in which resources are sold play a large role in shaping income shares. Everyone owns at least some resources. If nothing else, we each have our own labor to sell. Suppose that the labor you can offer is a talent for designing pet rocks. Unfortunately for you, this is not your year. Your talent would have brought you a sizable income in 1979, but not now.

Alternatively, if you can shoot a basketball through a hoop from 30 feet away with 70 percent accuracy, you have a resource for which contemporary tastes will reward you in grand style. Since demand for resources is derived, the fact that tens of thousands of people will pay $15 to see you use your resource means that resource buyers will want to talk to you. Some basketball players will earn over $1 million per year because many people will buy tickets to watch them play. The point here is that inequality stems in part from having the right resources at the right time.

The demand for resources is easy to understand, but it is even easier to understand the supply of resources. As long as money is the primary motivator, the amount of our resources we will offer for use depends on the size of the income we will receive for that use. If the income (or price) is not right, we will wait for another offer. In the context of a labor market, people will continue to enjoy their leisure until someone pays them a wage that convinces them otherwise. Resources are supplied because offering them for sale is the process by which they are transformed into income.

LABOR MARKETS AS AN ILLUSTRATION

The resource market with which most of us are especially familiar is the market for labor. As in other resource markets some of us have superior resources when we enter the marketplace in search of income. Schooling levels, skills, energy, and personality are all independent variables affecting the wages we will be offered. In addition, the fact that some of our talents are in great demand *given current tastes* may make us particularly attractive candidates for the richest quintile in Table 11–2.

To see how labor markets function, let us start with a simple market, a competitive market, and discover how wages are established. Remember that in a competitive market the seller has no ability to choose the wage at which he or she will sell his or her services. That wage will be shaped by market supply and demand, which are in turn shaped by the factors we looked at in the previous section.

The demand for labor is derived from the expected sale of the worker's output. The quantity of labor demanded falls as the wage rises, because the employer will have greater difficulty in earning enough revenue to pay higher wages. The curve will shift when another relevant independent variable, such as the cost of machinery, or tastes change.

The supply-of-labor curve indicates that higher wages must be paid to convince prospective workers to give up additional units of leisure. The supply of labor curve might shift if unemployment levels changed abruptly. Such a change would alter workers' feelings about the relative value of work and leisure at every possible wage.

In Figure 11–2 the equilibrium quantity is 18 workers; the equilibrium wage is \$4. At any wage other than \$4, there will be an imbalance between demand and supply. If the wage were \$5, the number of workers willing and able to work would exceed the quantity demanded. This excess supply would not last for long, because the employer would sense an opportunity. Why pay \$5 when you can satisfy your labor needs at a lower wage? The wage would be lowered until the equilibrium is reached.

Many factors determine whether the equilibrium wage for you is \$4, as in Figure 11–2, or \$400. We have already mentioned many of these factors—tastes, personality, effort, skill, credentials, gender,

Figure 11–2 Equilibrium in a Competitive Labor Market

This graph demonstrates how wages are established in a labor market in which the resource seller has no market power.

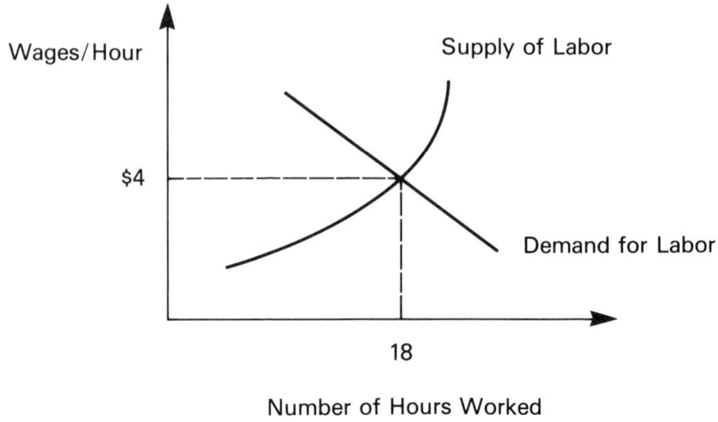

race, and the resources you possessed years before entering the labor market. Other factors that shape inequality are the quality of the other workers with whom you work (the team you are on), the size of the working population who are your age, the level of technology with which you work, and the degree of risk associated with your job. All these factors interact to shape your wage. It is virtually impossible to isolate a single set of causes for inequality. Thus, the fairness of the distributional process is very susceptible to dispute.

SELF-TEST

7. Explain how the equilibrium wage of $4 would be reached if the current wage were $3 in Figure 11–2.
8. Why does it matter whether we believe that wages are shaped primarily by personal choice or by environmental factors over which the worker has little control?
9. How could a person be highly talented and still receive a low wage? Is that possible?

LABOR MARKETS THAT ARE NOT COMPETITIVE

Those who own resources, for example, sellers of goods and services, would like to increase the selling price. One of the techniques by which workers accomplish this objective will remind you of barriers to entry from Chapter 8. You will recall that barriers to entry are designed to preserve the market power of sellers who fear what would happen to their revenue should new competitors thrive.

In labor markets workers similarly try to restrict the supply of those who will be competing with them. If a particular group of workers can figure out some technique for limiting the supply of labor, they will, *ceteris paribus*, raise their income. In effect, they will have caused the supply curve to shift, reflecting the reduced quantity of labor now available at every single wage.

Figure 11–3 illustrates the result. In short, the new equilibrium wage is noticeably higher. *OY* provides more income per hour than workers received at the old equilibrium wage.

How do workers bring about such a result? Many don't. Many workers are not able to gain the market power required to reduce the competitiveness of the resource markets in which they sell their labor. Such employees are at the mercy of demand and supply conditions in their particular markets. No worker likes this lack of control. Some groups of workers have created devices that help them avoid the lower incomes that competitive markets would bring them.

Unions, professional organizations, and licensing requirements are the major techniques by which those who supply labor gain market power. Although only about 20 percent of United States workers belong to unions, these groups have impact on wages and working conditions that extend far beyond their own immediate labor markets. To avoid unionization, employers often improve working conditions for their (currently) nonunion workers. Thus, labor organizations have influence that is much broader than the number of unionized workers would suggest.

Professional associations often act as unions when the income of their membership is threatened. The American Medical Association

Figure 11–3
Restricting Supply in Noncompetitive Labor Markets

This graph shows the shift in supply created by restricting the number of eligible workers.

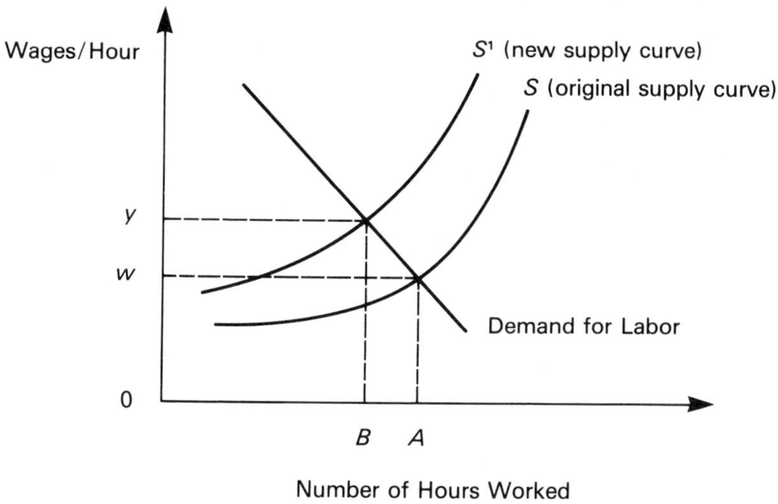

(AMA) does not call strikes, but it vigorously argues that the society would suffer if too many doctors were produced. From the consumer's perspective it is hard to interpret what a glut of doctors would mean. Surely it would mean lower fees and more complete explanations to patients who could easily go elsewhere if their questions are unsatisfactorily answered.

Similarly the AMA has actively resisted the professional associations of nurses who have tried to enlarge the decision-making role of nurses. Such an expansion of the nurse's role would reduce the demand for physicians and expand the demand for nurses.

Both professional associations are trying to adjust the degree of competitiveness of the market to enrich themselves. Doctors may reasonably think that health is not improved by enlarging the role of nurses; nurses may have legitimate professional reasons for wishing to expand their autonomy. However, both sets of arguments receive impetus from the fact that were their advice followed, they would make more money.

Licensing is the third device workers use to "rig" the market. The public justification for licensing is to protect the public. We certainly would not want just anyone, for instance, opening their doors and announcing that they are available to do surgery. The buyer of certain types of services needs protection.

However, licensing also shifts the supply of labor to the left, increasing the incomes of those in that particular resource market. A license prevents those without the license from filling a slot on the supply curve. We should be suspicious of every request for licensing, and support only those where the consumers cannot protect themselves through the market process itself. It is, for instance, more reasonable to license pharmacists than barbers or beauticians.

Every group of workers, with few exceptions, could probably make some kind of argument that their service is potentially dangerous to the public, so licenses should be required. Each such argument should be evaluated on its merits. Can we protect ourselves in this case by simply not buying from the relatively incompetent?

Each group of workers, like each firm, tries to escape the rigors of competition. Competitive labor markets mean that wages are squeezed down to their minimum. Sellers in any market detest competition; workers are no different. Workers, like other sellers, try to restructure their markets so that they can earn larger incomes.

SOURCES OF INEQUALITY

This section provides a summary of the factors that create inequality. Most of the factors will have been discussed in the chapter, but this section brings them together in one location. Notice that some of these factors are under the control of workers; others are not.

1. *Differences in ability and effort.* Some people are more talented than others. Their genes provide them with dexterity, speed, or alertness that translate into higher incomes. Some workers try harder than others. While the reasons for differences in effort are complex, they are usually related to the perceptions of workers about the likelihood that effort will "pay off" for them.

2. *Difficulty of the work.* Jobs that are especially risky, dangerous, or unpleasant often receive income that exceeds that from more normal jobs.

3. *Schooling, training, and credentials.* Employers often do not have the time to examine all the job-related characteristics of applicants for a job. Thus, they may use years of schooling, extent of prior training, or credentials earned as a shorthand technique for deciding whom to hire. Generally, those with more training are presumed to deserve higher incomes.

4. *Luck.* Many people happen to be in the right place at the right time. Others fail through no apparent fault of their own. They train for years to acquire a particular skill, then the demand for that skill disappears, and their dreams are crushed.

5. *Discrimination.* If those who buy resources have a prejudice against women, nonwhites, homosexuals, or youth, the income they will be willing to pay members of those groups will be reduced.

6. *Inherited wealth.* As we said earlier in this chapter, the possession of wealth can be used to generate income-earning opportunities. Most of those in the upper 0.50 percent of income earners reached that status at least partly as a result of large inheritances.

7. *Parents.* The identity of your parents affects many of the activities you will or will not undertake. They are a major factor determining the number of labor market contacts you will have, the schools you will attend, and the experiences you will have prior to working. In addition, they encourage you to have particular work-related attitudes that affect the size of your eventual income.

8. *Demographics.* Those who are born in a year or period during which few others are born will have an advantage two decades later when they enter the labor market. The supply of labor for their group will be farther to the left, *ceteris paribus,* providing them with a larger income.

9. *Extent of control over the labor market.* Those who work with occupational groups that have successfully moderated the effects of a competitive labor market will earn higher incomes. Those required to work where competitive conditions prevail can expect to have their wages squeezed down to the *minimum* amount necessary to get them to come to work.

The next chapter analyzes attempts by government to modify the market distribution that results from these factors. Those who see the labor market as a neutral mechanism simply reflecting the rational choices of resource owners and buyers will see little need for such modifications.

ACTIVE REVIEW

1. Whenever restrictions are placed on entry into a labor market, the public loses. In California, auctioneers, dietitians, those who sell guard dogs, tax preparers, and manicurists are all required to be licensed. In a free society, consumers are well equipped to protect themselves. Those who do not meet the expectations of their customers will not be around to sell their products for long.

   Groups who seek licensing protection from the government are seeking higher incomes. They are creating a shortage that would not be there without the licensing. The freedom of many individuals is limited when such licensing occurs.

   a. Are there justifiable reasons for granting a license to an occupational group?

   b. What assumption does this argument make about the extent to which consumers are informed?

   c. If licenses are just for the purpose of self-enrichment, what alternative strategies could workers use to reach the same goal in their respective labor markets?

   d. Demonstrate graphically how occupational licenses affect the market distribution of income.

2. The number of homeless in our society is a disgrace. For example, in New York City there are approximately 36,000 homeless people. A workable starting point in defining poverty is homelessness.

   The causes of homelessness are numerous. Some of those without homes lost their jobs during the last recession; others simply prefer to roam the nation's streets. The inability to find employment, though, is the major cause of homelessness among young people. In New York City, 40 percent of the men seeking shelter in 1985 were unable to find work.

   a. Does this selection use an absolute or relative definition of poverty?

   b. What is similar about the causes of homelessness and inequality?

   c. What kind of change in the Lorenz Curve for the United States would the author of this passage like to see? Why do you think so?

ANSWERS TO ACTIVE REVIEW

1a. Yes, there are justifiable grounds for granting licenses to certain groups. For some types of activities, the risk of danger from incompetence is so great or the information available to consumers is so incomplete that licensing arrangements are worth their costs. The primary cost is the distributional effect on labor market incomes. Those granted the licenses will have effectively reduced the supply of labor for their services. Their income will consequently rise relative to that for others in more competitive labor markets.

1b. The argument assumes that consumers will possess the information necessary to protect themselves. If consumers are unable to assess correctly the quality of services they receive, for example, psychological therapy, they cannot be expected to protect themselves in the marketplace.

1c. Workers who wish to avoid the relatively low incomes derived from competitive markets can attempt to either restrict the supply of their kind of labor or expand its demand. Forming unions or professional associations is an alternative to licensing as a technique for restricting supply. If the organization can convince or coerce employers to accept only their members as workers, the equilibrium wage will rise. Workers try to increase the demand for their services by claiming that only those trained as they are should be allowed to do many types of work.

1d. Occupational licenses reduce supply compared with what supply would have been in the absence of such provisions. The result, *ceteris paribus*, is a higher wage for those still permitted to participate in that labor market. The incomes of those denied access will fall.

ANSWERS TO SELF-TEST

1. Whoever made this statement is confusing equity with perfect equality. It is almost universally accepted that income differences are necessary for the incentives they provide. Hence, the definition of equity is based on some degree of inequality. While it is true that those who urge us to think about equity usually have greater equality in mind, they do not advocate perfect equality.
2. It would not be possible to infer conclusively from Tables 11–1 and 11–2 that wealth is more unequally distributed than is income. However, the tables would provide support for such a hunch. The richest 20 percent of income earners received from 41 to 46 percent of the income from 1944 to 1981. During the same period of time the richest 1 percent of wealth holders owned between 20 and 26 percent of the wealth. Unless the other 19 percent of wealth holders in the upper quintile held as a unit no more wealth than the richest 1 percent, then

the richest 20 percent of wealth holders surely had a larger share of the wealth than the share of income received by the richest 20 percent of families. Additional information presented in Chapter 11 confirms that wealth distribution is especially unequal.

3. The wealth possessed by one's family affects the amount of economic freedom and opportunity he or she will experience. Wealth permits access to schooling, friends, cultural experiences, training, and role models that may translate into greater success once a person enters the labor market. The distribution of wealth is not the only independent variable affecting the income distribution by any means. It is just one of the more important.
4. The Gini Coefficient is a measure of the area between the Lorenz Curve and the 45-degree line (the line of perfect equality). If that area were equal to zero, the nation would be experiencing complete equality of income. However, as long as we assume that resource owners will not make productive use of their resources unless they are rewarded financially, this condition would create incentive problems. Certain productive endeavors are more risky or more difficult than others. Why would a resource owner do something difficult for the same reward as he or she would earn for an easier task?
5. This question is more an arithmetic than an economic problem. If the poorest 50 percent had 60 percent of the income, the richest 50 percent would have the remaining 40 percent of income. Those numbers do not make sense. Something is wrong! The poorest 50 percent could never have more than 49.9 percent of the income, or they would no longer be the poorest 50 percent.
6. A nation's Lorenz Curve would get closer to the 45 degree line if the fight against poverty was actually successful in creating greater equality. The money to alleviate the conditions of the poor must ultimately come from the nonpoor. The resulting shift of income would reduce inequality and move the Lorenz Curve toward the line of perfect equality.
7. The text provided an illustration of how the equilibrium wage is reached when the existing wage is higher than $4. If the wage is below $4 there is excess demand, more workers are desired at the lower wage than are willing to give up leisure. The firm must raise the wage if it wants more workers. The increase in wages causes a movement along the supply curve. More workers are willing to work at the higher wage. The firm continues to raise the wage until the equilibrium wage is reached.
8. Our feelings about the fairness of the market distribution of income will largely depend on our assessment of the extent to which a person chooses his or her own economic condition. If each worker is in control of what will happen to him or her, the market distribution of income is simply the consequence of those choices. If all workers can select their ultimate wages by their decisions about level of effort, quality

of training, and career, then workers in a sense have selected their incomes.

On the other hand, there is nothing fair about the impact of an environment we did not choose. If parents, for instance, have a significant effect on the size of one's income, we can neither credit nor blame the individual worker for that economic effect. Similarly, if gender is a primary determinant of wages, workers cannot be said to have chosen their economic conditions. Environments that we did not shape would create unfair distributional patterns.

9. It is possible to be talented and make nothing in the form of income. Resources are in demand if their output can be sold. If no one wants the fruits of your particular talent, how talented you are will not affect your income. For example, many currently renowned artists died in poverty. Their fame followed their death.

12 Equity and the Redistributional Role of Government

A brightly colored bumper sticker urges us to "get government off our backs and out of our pockets." What exactly does the owner of the sticker mean? Is the sticker indicating opposition to Pentagon spending, food stamps, *and* the Peace Corps? Do owners of such bumper stickers have only certain government actions in mind as they voice their denunciation of the public sector?

Of course, it is impossible to know exactly what the bumper sticker means. Yet one meaning is likely: Government should not use its expenditures and taxes to reshuffle the income pattern that has resulted from resource market transactions. Those who concur with the sentiments expressed by the bumper sticker have mentally weighed the causes of the inequality resulting from resource market activity and have pronounced it fair. Hence they see equity in terms of defending the existing market distributions of income.

In their view, government is needed for certain allocative and stabilization policies, but government is not needed to reshuffle incomes. Instead, government should attempt to achieve *distributional neutrality*. Governmental actions are distributionally neutral when they do not alter the information in Figure 11–2. If the market distribution of income for the lowest quintile is 4 percent, then that quintile should have 4 percent of the income after government spends and taxes. From this perspective, government has no right to interfere with the resource values that labor, capital, and raw materials mar-

Distributional Neutrality Governmental preservation of the market distribution of income

kets have announced. Thus, the best redistributional policy for government is no policy at all.

The remainder of this chapter is based on the assumption that government does have a positive role to play in shaping the distribution of income. Thus, it is necessary to understand why and how government fulfills this function. Many individual governmental actions have distributional effects. Consequently, it is a good idea, even for advocates of distributional neutrality, to understand the mechanisms whereby the market distribution of income is threatened. The immediate task in this chapter is to survey several of the arguments used to justify a governmental role in the pursuit of equity.

RATIONALE FOR A REDISTRIBUTIONAL ROLE

Many governmental redistribution activities do *not* have as their purpose greater equality. Logrolling behavior, in which one group of legislators supports another group's legislative proposal in return for a guarantee of support when their pet project comes along, is a common occurrence. Governmental subsidies to those who ride trains, college students whose families make more than $40,000 per year, and farmers are vivid examples of redistribution aimed more at satisfying political supporters than at the economic goal of equity.

Despite the many instances when government supports greater inequality, the explicit discussion of government's redistributional role centers on greater equality. Why would anyone desire greater equality in the first place? Several different arguments for greater equality are prominent.

Moral Imperative

This argument starts by claiming that a country's economy should be judged by how it treats those who are weakest. The values of compassion, sharing, and community are highlighted as the most important moral lights available to guide economic policies. The inevitable inequality in the market distribution of income is seen as a reflection of greed and uncontrolled individualism.

Diminishing Marginal Utility of Money

This argument asks you to answer the following question: Does the last $1,000 of income for the person making $100,000 per year provide less, more, or the same pleasure, or utility, as the last $1,000 for the person making $8,000? If we assume that there is a hierarchy of needs that humans have, then the most immediate biological needs (food and shelter) are met first. The next most important needs are satisfied by the next units of income or money.

If this argument is valid, the total pleasure of the society is increased by greater equality. The pain experienced when the richer person loses $1,000 is less than the utility, or satisfaction, gained by the poorer person who receives the $1,000. The marginal gain from additional units of income falls as income rises.

The biggest criticism of this argument for a governmental redistribution role is that it isn't possible to compare the pleasure of different people. Can you be sure that the pain of redistribution from the person with more money is less than the utility gained by the recipient of the governmental transfer? Your answer to this question depends on whether you think there is a hierarchy of needs for all humans. *If* there is a common set of needs for all of us that we fill before thinking about other needs, then this diminishing marginal utility of money argument has merit.

Accidental Factors as the Source of Market Distribution

This argument was discussed in Chapter 11. The more you think that people's incomes result primarily from factors over which they lack control, the less satisfied you will be with the market distribution of income. If you look at rich and poor and say, "There but for fortune go I," then you are likely to support greater equality. There is no good reason for sharp inequality, since the income gaps are not deserved.

Veil of Ignorance

Imagine that you had no idea whether you would be male or female, rich or poor, white or nonwhite, American or non-American, bright or retarded, or who your parents would be. Draw down an imaginary veil of ignorance. Now with this act of imagination it makes sense to start thinking about what our distribution of resources *should* be. Until you draw down a veil of ignorance it is almost impossible for you to be fair while you discuss possible distributions. You already know how you are likely to do under the current distributional rules in the market system. Hence, this argument claims that much opposition to greater equality is based on the weak moral foundation provided by the desire for self-enrichment.

This argument assumes that if you were able to draw down the veil of ignorance, you would be willing to justify inequality very rarely. Perhaps some inequality would be helpful as a stimulus to growth. But each movement away from perfect equality would have to absorb the burden of proof for its existence.

This list of four arguments for a governmental redistributional role is impressive; however, the defenders of the market distribution of income present a forceful case for distributional neutrality by the government.

From the perspective of defenders of market distribution, the costs of greater equality are too high. First, as Chapter 11 pointed out in several places, helping the poor may have negative incentive effects. As more of the poor recognize an expanding safety net, those who are productive will lose their incentive to work at low wages, because they can receive at least some money from social programs. In addition, the children of the poor will lose the ambition to achieve, because they will see that society will provide for them regardless of whether they work.

A second alleged cost of greater equality is reduced savings. Those who will be taxed to help the poor ordinarily save a larger proportion of their income than will be saved by a poor person. Thus a transfer of income to the poor means that there is less total savings to finance investment and growth.

Finally, greater equality violates the consequences of personal choice. People should be individually responsible for their economic condition, since it was their choices that created the condition. People should not be taught that someone will bail them out when they make poor choices. Otherwise, the incentive to make better economic choices has been reduced.

Because we have a relatively high degree of inequality as an economy, the arguments *against* greater equality have apparently prevailed. That is a descriptive observation. Which set of arguments *should* shape government's redistributional role is a question you should struggle with for yourself.

SELF-TEST

1. Evaluate the claim that when government spends money its primary intent is to help the poor.
2. What is the relationship between distributional neutrality and the contention that humans experience a diminishing marginal utility from their money?
3. Why might higher taxes create greater, rather than weaker, incentives to work for some people?

TOOLS FOR REDISTRIBUTION

Those who find the arguments from the previous section convincing look to government for progress toward equity. There are several reasons why government is the chosen instrument for reducing inequality. First, the market has already spoken on the issue of what the correct distribution of income is. Only someone's dissatisfaction with the amount of inequality resulting from market decisions would cause that person to think there is a distributional problem in the first place. In addition, the market has no internal mechanism whereby incomes can be reshuffled once they are received. There is no market where redistribution of a particular amount can be bought and sold. Hence, it is natural to expect government to stimulate greater equity.

A final reason that redistribution is a governmental, rather than a private-sector, function is that government possesses the actual tools for redistribution. The spending and taxing powers of government can be used to redesign the distributional pattern in our economy. When government spends and taxes, the primary intent may be allocation, regulation, stabilization, or redistribution. However, regardless of the primary purpose of these actions, each expenditure or tax has a distributional impact. Only if the impact is distributionally neutral does the government avoid a redistributional result.

Figure 12–1 gives you a picture of the breakdown of governmental expenditures. Approximately one-third of federal expenditures that go for income security and the health and welfare component of state and local expenditures are intentionally redistributional. The fact that they exist in the first place is evidence of the belief that the market distribution of income is not entirely fair. Included in income security are insurance programs such as social security and unemployment compensation, and transfer payments such as food stamps and aid for dependent children.

Transfer Payments Governmental actions that remove income from one group of taxpayers and provide those funds to another group in society

Governmental Expenditures Governmental purchases of goods and services

Transfer payments should be distinguished from governmental expenditures. *Transfer payments* are governmental efforts that take money from one group of taxpayers and channel it directly to another group of taxpayers, for example, subsidies to rice farmers. *Governmental expenditures,* on the other hand, are governmental purchases of specific goods and services. Some of these expenditures, such as salaries for enforcement officers for antidiscrimination laws, are directly redistribution. Others, such as purchases of military aircraft from General Dynamics, fulfill other governmental roles explicitly. Their impact on the market distribution of income is real but rarely discussed.

Expenditures and transfer payments are financed by governmental borrowing and taxes. Not only does the way government spends

Figure 12–1
Allocation of Government Expenditures, 1983

These pie graphs indicate how government spends the borrowed funds and taxes that it receives.

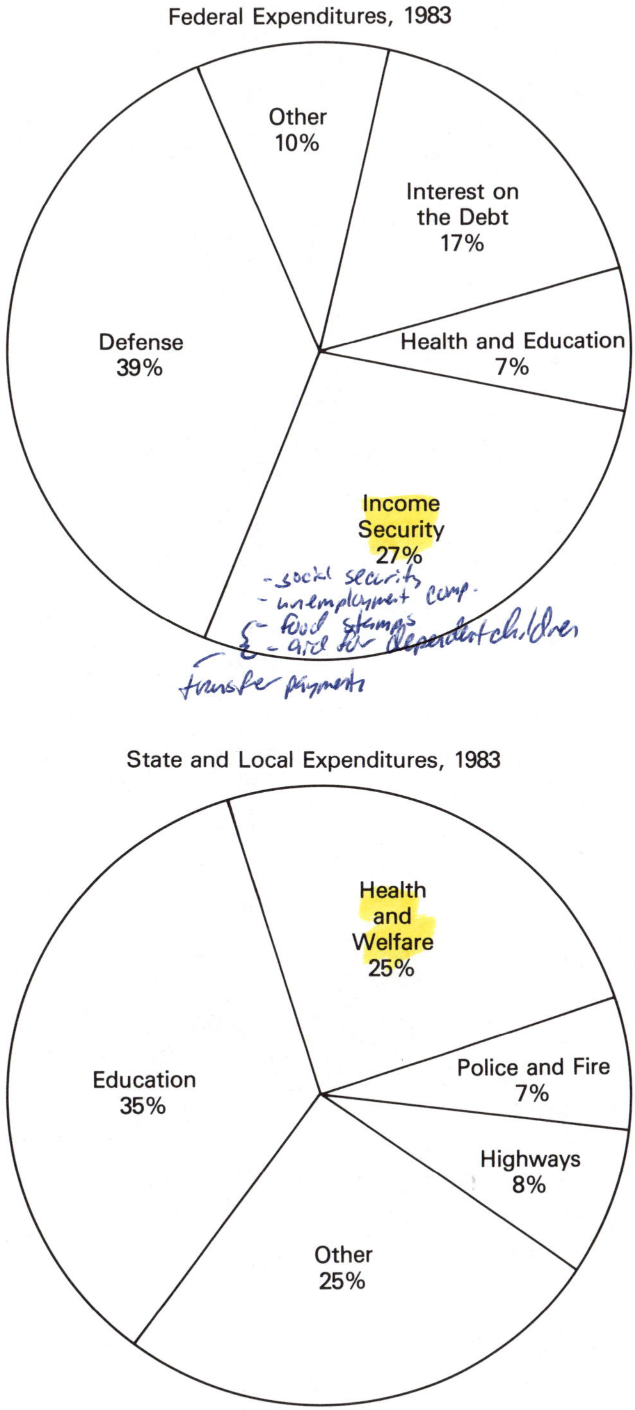

Source: U.S. Bureau of the Census, *Statistical Abstract of the United States, 1986* (Washington, D.C.: GPO, 1985), p. 264.

Figure 12–2
Sources of Government Revenue

These pie graphs demonstrate the proportions of tax revenue from various taxes.

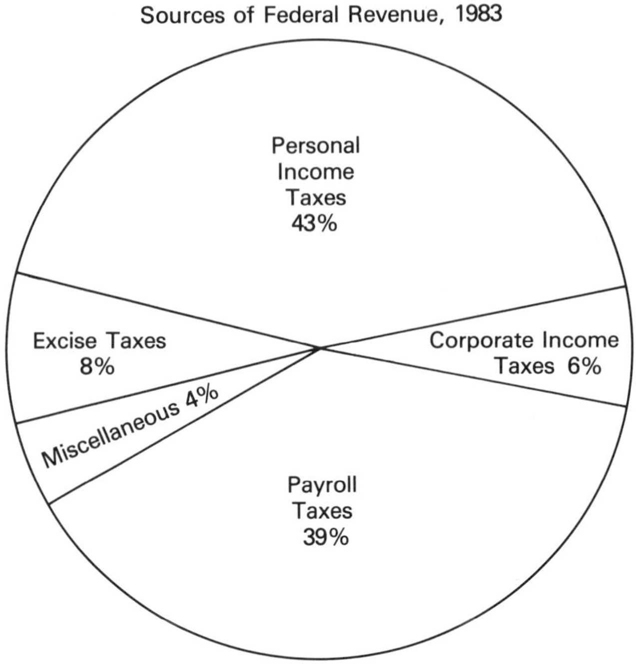

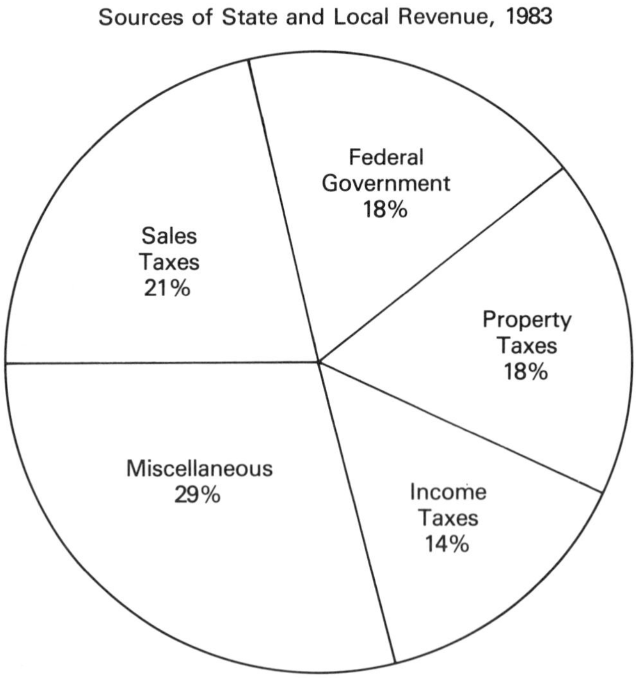

Source: U.S. Bureau of the Census, *Statistical Abstract of the United States, 1986* (Washington, D.C.: GPO, 1985), p. 264.

Table 12–1
Relative Tax Burdens in Selected Countries, 1983
This table indicates the share of national income that is paid in taxes in selected countries.

Country	Taxes as a Percentage of GNP
Sweden	51
Netherlands	47
Italy	41
Great Britain	38
West Germany	37
Switzerland	32
United States	29
Japan	28

Source: U.S. Bureau of the Census, *Statistical Abstract of the United States, 1986* (Washington, D.C.: GPO, 1985), p. 846.

its money have distributional impacts but so does the way government obtains its funds. When government borrows from a particular group in society, the Treasury must pay interest on those loans. The recent growth in the public debt has made interest payments one of the fastest-growing components of the government budget.

Since those who lend money to government are disproportionately the wealthy, the interest payments on the debt tend to create more inequality. However, it would be inappropriate to conclude that the existence of the public debt necessarily creates more inequality. Remember that the debt is used to finance job-creating expenditures that may not have otherwise been made. Those expenditures may stimulate a more equal market distribution of income. The resulting distributional impact of the debt is unclear. We know there is such an effect, but we are not sure whether or how it changes the market distribution of income.

Figure 12–2 describes the proportion of the total tax collected by each form of tax for all levels of government. The many kinds of taxes represent attempts to identify appropriate and varied groups of taxpayers. Another reason for the existence of so many taxes is that division of the tax burden into many parts may reduce our resistance to taxes. Although, as Table 12–1 shows, we are taxed relatively little by international standards, we feel over-taxed.

SELF-TEST

4. Why is the market system not the initiator of income redistribution?
5. Would a governmental expenditure that was designed to redistribute income (for example, medicaid payments for the health needs of the poor) also have an allocational effect?

6. On what basis could a person argue that a simplified tax system would make it *more* difficult for government to fulfill its responsibilities?

TAXES AND REDISTRIBUTION

The distributional effect of taxes depends on who pays what amount of taxes. The first point that must be kept in mind as we look at the burden of taxes on various groups is that the person who is taxed is not necessarily the person who eventually pays the burden of the tax. *Tax incidence* refers to the location of the burden of the tax. Tax incidence will be shifted whenever possible. Those who pay taxes are always hoping to shift the burden of the tax to someone else.

Tax Incidence Location of the ultimate burden of a tax

The lesson from studies of tax incidence is that taxes on homeowners and businesses are not necessarily paid by those institutions. Whenever possible these taxes are shifted to renters, consumers, workers, or stockholders. The type of market structure and the degree of price elasticity of demand have major impacts on the ability of a business to shift its tax burden.

Another concept that is useful when we examine the distributional effect of taxes is the rate structure of a tax. Who is paying the stiffest average rates? What quintile are they in before the tax is paid? To discuss the rate structure of a tax, taxes are classified as being progressive, proportional, or regressive. A *progressive tax* creates more equality, because the average tax rate rises as income rises. *Proportional taxes* attempt to be distributionally neutral. A tax is proportional when the tax rates are the same for all levels of income. Finally, a *regressive tax* creates more inequality than is present in the market distribution of income, since the average tax rate falls as income rises.

Progressive Tax One for which the average tax rate rises as income increases

Proportional Tax One for which tax rates are the same for all income levels

Regressive Tax One for which average tax rates fall as income rises

Two things are important to remember as you try to figure out the degree of progressivity or regressivity of a tax. First, remember that you want to focus on the rate of taxation, not on the total amount of taxes paid. The definitions of various rate structures are in terms of average rates, not the amount of the tax bill. It is possible for a tax to be sharply regressive, yet someone with more income could be paying more actual dollars of taxes. Their proportion of taxes to income will be lower than that for people with less income, but their tax bill could be higher.

Second, you want to examine the taxes actually paid as opposed to the taxes listed in the tax tables. This consideration is especially significant when studying the distributional effects of an income tax. The tax table may say one thing about the degree of progressivity; the actual taxes paid often say something else about the rate struc-

Nominal Tax Rates
The tax rates associated with various incomes in a tax table

Effective Tax Rates
The tax rates that are actually paid

ture. The tax rates in a tax table such as those in Table 12–2 are *nominal tax rates*. These are the rates that would be paid if there were no deductions, exemptions, or exclusions associated with the tax.

The rates that taxpayers actually pay are called *effective tax rates*. Of course, it is the effective tax rate structure that tells you the distributional effect of a tax (assuming that the incidence of the tax is on the person originally taxed). When some income is given preferential treatment in the tax code, the redistributional effect implied by nominal tax rates is misleading.

Both the personal and corporate income taxes are highly progressive from the perspective of the nominal tax rate structure. However, as you might anticipate, most of the special treatment given to particular taxpayers by our tax code benefits upper income groups disproportionately. They have the political power to reduce the progressivity suggested by the nominal rate structure.

The special tax treatment given to certain taxpayers goes by several names. The one you use depends on whether you approve of the beneficiary of the special treatment. Tax breaks that we dislike are usually called *loopholes;* the ones we endorse we call *incentives* or *subsidies.* Each variation from the nominal rates is both a loophole and a subsidy. When taxpayers have their taxes reduced, the tax break encourages them to do more of a particular activity, for example, buy a house or purchase state and local bonds.

Some of the more important tax breaks in the personal income tax law, as of 1986, are tax-exempt securities, capital gains, and deductions for mortgage interest. Many high-income people reduce their income tax liability sharply by shifting their savings to state and local bonds. The interest earned on those securities is tax-free. Capital

Table 12–2
Federal Personal Income Tax Rates, 1982
These are the tax rates for a couple filing a joint return.

Taxable Income	Total Tax	Average Tax Rate
$ 3,400	$ 0	–
5,500	231	4.2%
7,600	504	6.6
11,900	1,149	9.7
16,000	1,846	11.5
20,200	2,644	13.1
24,600	3,656	14.9
29,900	5,034	16.8
35,200	6,624	18.9
45,800	10,334	22.6
60,000	16,014	26.7
85,600	27,278	31.9
109,400	38,702	35.4
162,400	65,202	40.1

gains are increases in the value of property. If the property has been held for at least a year, only 40 percent of the gain in value is counted as taxable income. The consequences of these tax breaks is that the individual income tax is only mildly progressive.

Tax Expenditure A commitment of government funds through changes in the tax law rather than through an appropriation

A revealing way to think about tax breaks is to view them as *tax expenditures*. These expenditures are implicit commitments of governmental funds accomplished not by actual government expenditures, but by changes in the tax law. Just as a governmental expenditure reduces the amount of money the Treasury has for other purposes, so does a tax expenditure. When a tax break is granted, one of two things must happen. Either other people's tax rates rise or governmental expenditures must be decreased.

In one important respect tax expenditures differ from appropriations, spending decisions made by the legislature. Appropriations must be enacted at regular periods. Thus, they must be reexamined periodically. Tax expenditures, however, are not generally reviewed unless a legislator actually initiates an investigation of the desirability of a specific tax break. As a result, tax expenditures do not receive the same kind of public scrutiny as do explicit governmental expenditures and transfer payments.

SELF-TEST

7. Why would we need more information before we reacted to a person's claim that he or she was in the 40 percent tax bracket?
8. Imagine that a tax was imposed on a particular group because the legislature felt that this group had an excessive share of the nation's income. What economic concept would cause you to wonder whether the tax would actually do what its creators intended?
9. The market distribution of income has a particular Gini Coefficient. Some would want government to preserve, not alter, this Gini Coefficient. What type of tax rate structure would such people prefer? Progressive, proportional, or regressive?

INTERNATIONAL PERFORMANCE

The United States has greater inequality than all but a few of the other industrialized countries. This result is not surprising, given our relatively great mistrust of governmental decisions. If we fear governmental reshuffling of income shares, then we are left with the sharp inequality that evolves naturally from resource markets.

If we looked at a spectrum of inequality among developed nations, we would find that the United States and France tend to have the greatest inequality. The Scandinavian countries create the greatest degree of equality. You will remember that the Gini Coefficient in the United States is approximately .36. In Denmark, Norway and Sweden the Gini Coefficient is approximately .25. Although data are unavailable to be sure, it is widely assumed that the income distribution in Israel is even more equal.

A middle category of countries would include the Soviet Union, Japan, West Germany, and the Netherlands. While the data from the Soviet Union are not as systematic as we would like, the information we have does enable us to say that their inequality is less than our own but not as equal as that of some of the other Western democracies.

Another way to look at the same data is by studying the ratio between the highest and lowest deciles (10 percentiles) of the income distribution. In France and the United States, the ratio between the highest and lowest decile is 15:1. This ratio means that for every $1,000 of household income that an average family in the lowest decile has, the average family in the upper decile has $15,000. The equivalent ratios for the Scandinavian countries are approximately 5:1. West Germany and Japan have ratios of 9:1 and 8:1, respectively.

These data are consistent with the Gini Coefficient comparisons. This evidence indicates that the United States does not aggressively pursue the goal of equity.

ACTIVE REVIEW

1. One of the ideas that has generated numerous tax breaks is "trickle-down theory." Those who believe this theory argue that the best way to achieve economic growth is to increase the savings rates of the wealthy. Tax breaks that help the wealthy will cause them to save a greater share of their income.

   How will these piles of savings help anyone else? The answer is that those who invest will now have increased funds to expand plant capacity and modernize their equipment. The projected result is new jobs and improved economic well-being for all.

   a. Would an advocate of trickle-down theory desire distributional neutrality?

   b. Does this suggestion for tax breaks demonstrate that the purpose of government's redistributional role is always to help the poor?

   c. What kind of tax rate structure would result from the proposed tax expenditures?

   d. Will the proposed tax breaks move our Gini Coefficient closer to that of Norway?

2. I believe in rewarding those who take unusual risks with large amounts of income. Even if I had no idea who I was or what condition I would be born into, I would prefer a world of challenge. The only way that I can feel a sense of true accomplishment is when I have risked failure. I have no desire for anyone to fail, but I do believe failure is necessary for success to have any meaning.
   a. If the average citizen in a particular country thought as the author of this statement thinks, what would you expect his or her preferred income distribution to be like?
   b. What argument for greater equality is the statement refuting?
   c. Which argument for a neutral distributional role for government is this paragraph repeating?

ANSWERS TO ACTIVE REVIEW

1a. No, the "trickle-down theory" is a defense of the use of the tax system to create greater inequality *at least initially*. While the objective of trickle-down theory is positive economic growth, the tax breaks that the theory supports have definite distributional impacts.

1b. No, again! Government is a powerful stimulus for economic activity. Because it has such power, government is petitioned by every group with sufficient voice to formulate an appeal. It is incorrect to see government as automatically on the side of the weak and poor. It is not automatically on any group's side.

The suggested tax breaks have upper income groups as their immediate beneficiary. The projected benefits to others are possible; the benefits to the wealthy are a sure thing.

1c. The tax breaks would have the effect of making the tax structure less progressive, that is, more regressive. Their very purpose is to reduce the tax rates on upper income groups.

1d. No, because the tax breaks move us away from the line of perfect equality. They would increase our Gini Coefficient. This increase would increase the gap between our inequality and that of Norway.

ANSWERS TO SELF-TEST

1. Government has many purposes when it spends money. It may be interested primarily in creating new jobs, regulating dangerous market activities, or expanding the number of medical schools. All of these expenditures would have distributional effects. However, those effects may be an unintended consequence.
2. To the extent that I believe that the marginal utility of money diminishes as income rises I will not desire distributional neutrality.

On the contrary, I will urge government to create greater equality as a means for expanding the community's aggregate welfare.

3. We are all familiar with the argument that higher taxes will decrease incentives to work. Why should I work harder if the result is going to be that I will get to keep a smaller proportion of my marginal income?

   We are less familiar, however, with an equally compelling logic for the exact opposite result. If I base my work effort on my desire to keep up a particular standard of living, I may have to work harder to maintain that standard in the face of rising taxes. The fact that I am accustomed to buying certain cuts of meats, going on specific types of vacations, and keeping up with a particular set of Joneses may stimulate me to work harder when taxes rise.

4. The market mechanism has no process that actively encourages reduced inequality. Instead it encourages inequality and then tolerates the even greater inequality that results when income differences create unequal opportunity. Markets have an automatic technique for encouraging efficiency, but the absence of a clear device for reducing inequality is in the eyes of some a distinct weakness of pure market decisions. The result is that the responsibility for achieving equity is given to government. Governments often reject the responsibility, but advocates of greater equality have little choice but to try to enlist government's help next year.

5. Yes, medicaid or other governmental redistributional programs would alter the allocation of goods and services. This answer, like so many others in economics, flows from the concept of scarcity. If more resources flow to hospitals and medical personnel to meet the health needs of the poor, there are opportunity costs. Some other goods or services will necessarily be reduced in magnitude to pay for the redistributional program.

6. One of the alleged purposes of the many types of taxes we have is that their existence reduces resistance to taxes in general. A single, simple tax might accelerate resistance to taxes because the amount of tax being paid would be more obvious. A consequence might be that government would find it more difficult to finance its activities.

7. Typically, when people reveal a tax rate of 40 percent, they expect sympathy. However, whether or not we should be sympathetic depends in part on whether that rate is their nominal or effective rate. The two rates would be identical only if there were no deductions, exemptions, or exclusions. Because tax breaks are numerous, we would want to find out what the effective tax rate is so that we would see the rate that is actually paid.

8. The relevant concept here is tax incidence. When a tax is imposed on someone, all or part of the tax burden may be shifted to someone else. All of us would like to shift our tax burdens, but only some of us are in positions where we have the market power to transfer our tax burden to another taxpayer.

9. If government is to have no effect on the Lorenz Curve, then the tax rate structure should be proportional. By taking the same proportion of everyone's income in the form of taxes, government would be leaving untouched the distributional shares resulting from market transactions. Either progressive or regressive tax rates would alter those shares and, consequently, the Lorenz Curve.

13 Environmental Protection

During a December evening in 1984, toxic gas leaked from a faulty valve at the Union Carbide pesticide plant in Bhopal, India. The gas filled the air in the vicinity of the plant with horrible results. Approximately 2,500 people were killed, and at least 100,000 more allegedly experienced permanent disabilities in the form of blindness, paralysis, sterility, tuberculosis, and brain damage. Suddenly, the air in Bhopal had turned ugly; it was transformed by the leak from a resource into a contaminant.

Closer to home, in 1978, New York state officials ordered the emergency evacuation of 240 families from the Love Canal area of Niagara Falls. The homes of the evacuated families had been constructed over what had previously been a dumping site for industrial wastes. Before covering the dump with soil, Hooker Chemical Company had deposited over 300 million tons of industrial waste in the site. In seeking the evacuation, New York pointed to the unusually high rates of asthma, urinary tract disease, miscarriages, and birth defects among Love Canal residents.

This chapter is designed to give you (1) a better understanding of why such environmental problems exist and (2) an appreciation for the complications inherent in protecting the environment. Environmental protection is the newest member of the list of economic goals. Environmental problems are definitely not new. However, the amount of attention we now pay to these problems is sharply increased. Environmental protection is very much a concern for the *quality* of our life. As economies become richer, citizens pay more attention to how well we are living. These qualitative concerns make their appearance as affluence frees us from the more urgent concerns of food, shelter, and clothing.

WHAT IS ENVIRONMENTAL PROTECTION?

We damage our natural environment just by our daily living. Permitting too many cattle to graze on a piece of land creates soil erosion. Cutting down trees to construct homes reduces our forest resources. Clearing land to grow crops indirectly causes water pollution as chemicals and soil fall into our water supplies. As we think about environmental protection, we begin with the recognition that we cannot protect our environment *absolutely*. Certain resources are going to be damaged by our productive activities. Zero environmental damage is an unrealistic economic goal.

Most of us very much want to enjoy the levels of consumption that affluence has brought our country. Yet we are not willing to pursue that consumption *at any cost*. The prices paid by the residents of Bhopal and Love Canal are too great. Thus, we must seek a balance between the fruits of modern production and the resulting environmental damage they inevitably create.

When we aspire to protect our environment we must have some degree of protection in mind. The degree lies somewhere between zero environmental damage and the amount we have now. It would not be appropriate for us to tell you what the correct degree of environmental protection is. Instead, this chapter will try to inform you of the issues involved in your decision to define the degree of desirable environmental protection.

Environmental Protection Preserving our natural environment so that it can be used and enjoyed by future, as well as current, generations

To help you get an idea of the consensus definition of the proper degree of environmental protection, we are presenting some of the current federal environmental protection standards. These standards do not define how much protection the environment *should be* given. Rather they define what current standards *are*. For instance, the National Environmental Policy Act of 1969 (NEPA) states broadly that Congress desires to "promote the general welfare, to create and maintain conditions under which man and nature can exist in productive harmony." The most concrete step taken in NEPA was the requirement that an *environmental impact statement* outlining the effect on the environment must accompany every proposed federal action that significantly affects the environment.

Under the Clean Air Act amendments of 1977 the administrator of the EPA is required to issue primary standards that spell out the maximum concentration of major pollutants. These standards are based on the administrator's determination of what is sufficient to protect the public against adverse health effects. There are currently six major pollutants for which these standards have been set: sulphur dioxide, particulates, ozone, carbon monoxide, hydrocarbons, nitrogen oxide, and lead. The standards are in terms of micrograms per cubic meter. For instance, the standard for lead is 1.5 micrograms per cubic meter. Violations of these standards result in fines and injunctions.

The main objective of the Clean Water Act as amended in 1977 is to make the waters safe for fishing and swimming by limiting discharges of pollutants. For some pollutants, firms are required to use the "best available pollution-control technology" in restricting emissions. For other pollutants designated in the statute as "toxic pollutants," firms must use the "best available technology, economically achievable." This last standard recognizes the need for flexibility in applying the definition of environmental protection.

Pesticides, toxic substances, and wastes also have specific standards that firms which produce such by-products must obey. All pesticides must be registered to be lawfully sold. For registration, the pesticide must not have "unreasonable adverse effects" on the environment. Any new chemical substance must not present "unreasonable risk of injury" to health or the environment. A waste is considered hazardous if it is toxic, corrosive, flammable, or has the capacity to cause cancer or mutation. A producer of a hazardous waste must keep records of its treatment, storage, transport, and disposal.

These definitions of environmental protection are intentionally imprecise. The goal of environmental protection, like other economic goals, evolves as our knowledge of the goal and our ability to attain it are developed. The remainder of this chapter should make it clear why these standards are so controversial.

SELF-TEST

1. Evaluate the following statement: For environmental protection efforts to be serious we must pledge to halt pollution once and for all.
2. Point out the inadequacy in a very different argument: Love Canal and incidents like it are an inevitable part of our life. Since we pollute when we live, we cannot expect to avoid such

environmental problems, regardless of the misery they may cause.

3. What is similar about the way in which the economic goals of equity and environmental protection are defined? (Refer to Chapter 11, where equity is defined.)

WHY DOES THE ENVIRONMENT REQUIRE PROTECTION?

Typical efforts to provide goods and services should not be viewed as having a starting point—buying resources—and an end point—consumption. Thinking in that fashion ignores the condition of resources when they were purchased *and* what happens to output after it is used. When we use a good or service, it does not simply disappear.

The first basic reason that we have environmental problems is created by a physical law—the law of conservation of matter and energy. This law states that matter and energy may be changed into different forms, but they do not disappear.

The waste disposal problem that we face is a natural result of our affluence. Those resources that we use to satisfy our wants eventually must be recycled or go into the garbage. The "garbage" may take the form of smoke, toxic chemicals, or tin cans. Whatever form our garbage takes, it has been caused by our intentional use of resources to satisfy our material yearnings.

We cannot repeal the law of conservation of matter and energy. Instead, we must live with its effects. This law suggests that environmental problems will not go away when Congress passes a law or when the internal combustion engine becomes more efficient. The goal of environmental protection will be around as long as the physical law that governs our use of resources prevails. Apparently, it will outlast us. There are intelligent responses to our awareness of the law of conservation of matter and energy, such as recycling and greater efficiency in the use of inputs. While neither eliminates the effect of the law, both reduce the *size* of the environmental damage that the law dictates.

A second reason that we need to protect the environment is the definition of progress we have too-frequently used. If we wish to define our progress in terms of greater consumption and control over nature, we will inevitably cause the environmental hazards that flow from the progress we seek. Firms, households, and governments in pursuit of human progress each contribute their share of air, water, and soil problems.

If *more* goods and services are to be our pursuit, it is hard to imagine how we can avoid the environmental problems that their production and consumption cause. Giant dams and reservoirs provide us with needed energy, safety from floods, and weekend recreation opportunities. Unfortunately they also provide a reduced supply of farmland and a changed water table in the area. When we construct our lives around automobiles, we get convenient transportation *and* damaged air. Progress, as we have defined it, does not consider the damage to our environment as a cost. Consequently, unless specific rules are imposed, incentives to preserve the environment are few.

WHAT DO WE OWE FUTURE GENERATIONS?

An additional complication that causes a need for environmental protection is our difficulty in recognizing the needs of future generations. If you glance back at the definition of environmental protection, you will see that its extent depends on how intensely we wish to provide for those who will follow us. Most of the environmental effects of our productive activities will occur later. If environmental decay or catastrophes happened immediately after production or consumption, we would pay more attention to them. Our attention is muted by the fact that we, the beneficiaries of production, may be able to escape the negative by-products of that process. If environmental problems all fell on us, rather than "them," we would assign new importance to environmental protection.

To stimulate your thinking about this point, think about what grabs your attention. When hundreds of people in a foreign country are swallowed up in an earthquake, you are concerned at least a bit. You may even stop eating or reading and glance intently at the tragic picture on the television screen. However, imagine how differently you would react, if you lost a quarter-inch of your finger in an accident in your kitchen. Your attention would be riveted on your condition. In contrast, you pause only briefly to think about the deaths of hundreds when you know none of them.

Similarly, it is difficult to imagine the faces of future generations. You cannot know them, and you might not like them if you did. Consequently, we focus on meeting our material needs. Occasionally we pause to reflect about what life will be like in the future. Basically, however, we are in a rush to consume now. Environmental problems are a natural consequence, but since we don't experience their costs directly, we do not think about these costs or we assume others will pay them.

POLLUTION AND COSTS

Because none of us individually wishes a decaying environment, why does our behavior so naturally produce the tendency for environmental harm? The starting point in answering this question is the recognition that pollution is a cost. We should pay this cost when we live and produce.

The next step in the answer is to think carefully about just who this "we" actually is. Those who pay the costs are hard to identify precisely. "They" are a much broader group than either the producers or consumers of the good or service that results in environmental harm. Although the producers and consumers are the two primary parties concerned about the price and quantity produced of particular goods and services, the effect of the eventual sale extends far beyond the producers and consumers.

Costs from the production and consumption of certain output, such as pesticides, cigarettes, and steel, are experienced by third parties. Third parties are those who are neither buyer nor seller of the output in question but who are nevertheless affected by its existence. For example, the drinking water of a community downstream may be contaminated by agricultural pesticides; patrons in a restaurant may be annoyed by cigarette smokers at the next table; and the smoke from a steel mill will dirty a community. The effects on the third parties that result from a market exchange are called *externalities*. When these effects are harmful, they are referred to as negative externalities.

Externalities
Impacts on third parties from a market transaction

The significant thing about externalities is that those affected by them are not able to influence the market price or the quantity sold directly. Third parties are not involved in the auction or negotiations that create market prices and quantities sold. Hence, the existence of externalities presents a problem for market activity. Governmentally created incentives or programs are the normal way to respond to environmental problems, because the market mechanism has no device for recording the desires of third parties and then modifying output and price figures in response.

You have already encountered a discussion of externalities in Chapter 9. Some costs of production, for example, wages and rent, fall on the firm that is doing the production. Those costs are called private, or internal, costs. Other costs, such as the by-products that create environmental damage, are paid by third parties. Such costs are social, or external, costs. External costs are another name for negative externalities. Whenever external costs exist, some of the costs of production will not be taken into consideration when the firm makes its decisions about how much to produce and what price to charge.

SELF-TEST

4. Are there definitions of progress that would result in less environmental damage than would be created by other versions of progress?
5. Evaluate the following statement: When we take aluminum cans to the recycling center in our neighborhood, we are providing evidence that the law of conservation of energy and matter is not really a law. By recycling, we have avoided an environmental problem that would have otherwise existed.
6. Explain the relationship between private costs and negative externalities.

MARKET BEHAVIOR AND POLLUTION

In the discussion of economic efficiency, you learned that by analyzing its costs at various outputs a firm decides how much it will be willing and able to produce at those prices. Since the firm wants to earn profits, it will produce when the price it can charge for a particular output is at least as large as the average cost of producing that same output. We have just made a related point in the previous section. When firms make their production decisions, they are thinking about only those costs that they themselves will be required to pay. Although the firm is not entirely unconcerned about the external costs from its activities, private costs shape its decision to supply or not supply a given output that consumers want.

We can describe the impact of externalities on market quantities and output with the help of two graphs. Figure 13–1 indicates that for every possible level of output, the firm underestimates the total costs of producing. The firm correctly understands that the average total cost curve (private costs) is the cost concept it needs to study in making its production decisions. The private costs are the only ones it will ordinarily be required to pay. The market mechanism does not force firms to include external costs in its calculations.

So what? How are the firm's activities affected by the discrepancy between private and external costs? Look again at Figure 13–1 for a partial answer. If any firm had to charge a price that covered both private and external costs, the price at all levels of output would

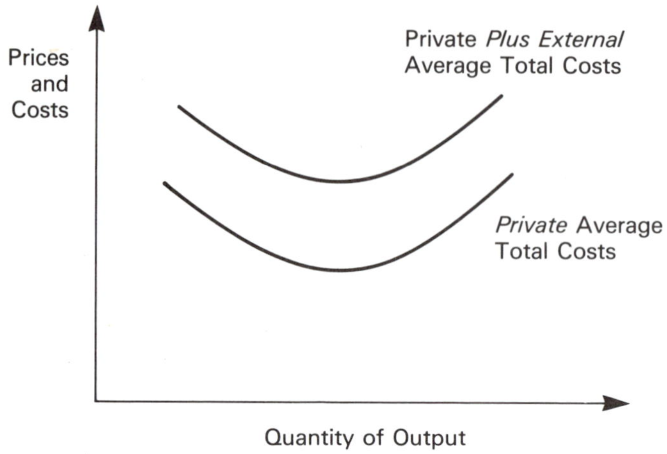

Figure 13–1
Private and External Costs of Production

This graph demonstrates the difference between private and external costs.

probably be higher for the consumer of that output. Otherwise the firm might not be able to cover its now higher level of costs. Thus, one impact of negative externalities is that the firm charges a price that does not reflect the true value of the resources that were used to make the output.

Figure 13–2 illustrates the misallocative effect of externalities. If only private costs are considered, a competitive firm will tend to produce output *OB* at price *OE*. If negative externalities exist, production of output *OB* will be too large and price *OE* will be too low to lead to a proper allocation of resources; the quantity consumed is too large from society's perspective. Study Figure 13–2 to make sure you understand this impact of negative externalities. The cost curves

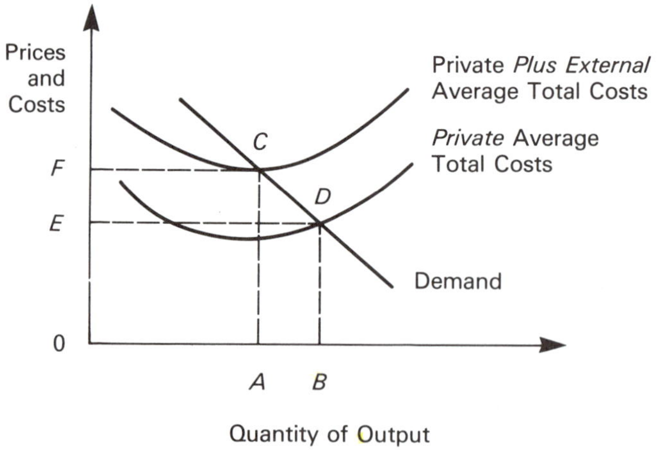

Figure 13–2
Negative Externalities and Misallocation

This graph demonstrates the misallocative effect of negative externalities.

are exactly like those in Figure 13–1. The total costs of production are represented by the higher of the two cost curves. If consumers were asked to pay a price reflecting these private *and* external costs, the demand curve reveals that *OA* units of output would be produced and sold at a price of *OF*. That quantity *OA* would be consistent with a proper allocation of resources, since those who benefited from the output would be absorbing the total cost of transforming those resources into a useful form.

However, the market mechanism would by itself result in a misallocation of resources. The market price would be *OE*, not *OF*. Thus, the firm's consideration of private costs *only* results in a movement along the demand curve from *C* to *D*. The price is lower because the firm does not have to cover external costs. When price falls, quantity demanded increases from *OA* to *OB*. The impact of this movement along the demand curve is a misallocation of resources. Too much of the output is produced and purchased. Notice that *OB* is not "too much" from the perspective of buyers and sellers of that output, but it is "too much" if the interests of all affected parties, including third parties, are included in the cost and price-determination process.

PRIVATE PROPERTY AND CONFLICTING RIGHTS

The last paragraph made an important point. There is sometimes a conflict between the rights and desires of those who produce and consume a product such as cigarettes and the rights of the rest of the community. It is this conflict that creates the heat in environmental protection debates. These conflicts are becoming more acrimonious and numerous as population grows and crowding results. The more of us that are crowded together, the more interdependent we become. This heightened interdependence increases the gap between private costs and external costs shown in Figure 13–1. Individual behavior acquires more of a social flavor when you interact directly with more and more people.

Those who own resources and use them to produce have certain rights that are increasingly questioned as we become more aware of the extent of environmental problems. These rights that resource owners have are private, belonging to them and no one else. The individual rights to use, benefit from, and exclude others from using a resource is what we mean by *property rights*. These rights are always held by individuals. Yet they are constantly being modified by actions of legislatures and courts. Hence, the property rights are private, but at any time the rights may be redistributed so that they are shared with the community.

Property Rights An individual's power to use, benefit from, and exclude others from using particular resources

A given property right is relative. When people own a farm, one of their rights is to use the land as they choose; however, that right is not absolute. For instance, they cannot legally plant marijuana. The right to use the land is restricted by the community; yet, the owner's property rights are still extensive. The number of uses that the owner may pick and choose from are numerous. If the climate and soil permit, a farm owner may choose to plant tomatoes, cotton, soybeans, or any of dozens of other crops.

Why are any limits placed on property rights? The language of private and external costs is useful in forming an answer. When you drive your car, you must pay for the cost of the gas, new tires, and oil changes. However, your driving also imposes costs on third parties. You threaten their safety and health whenever your car and its exhaust fumes approach. These external costs may be entirely ignored when you decide whether to buy an automobile and what price to pay for it. Thus the property rights of others may be abused when individuals fail to consider the full costs of their personal decisions. Limits are placed on property rights to protect against such abuse.

The extent of the limitations and grants of property rights are highly controversial because of the conflicting rights aroused by any modification of existing property rights. A chemical firm cannot be expected to react passively while government tells them that they now must incur millions in new costs because the firm is damaging the environment with its chemical wastes. Similarly, third parties will resist steps that threaten to ignore the longevity and health of their resources. Community groups will protest the creation or expansion of toxic-waste dumps in their communities.

The significance of conflicting property rights is in recognizing that environmental protection consists of negotiating compromises among these rights. Those who pollute are doing more than just polluting. They are also producing output that we demand. As consumers we want to pay as low a price as possible. As individual consumers we will tend to ignore external costs. Because externalities affect third parties, there is a clear dilemma about how much of the externalities we should eliminate. Because of this conflict, externalities will never be reduced to zero.

SELF-TEST

7. Evaluate the assertion that the value of resources used to produce any good or service can be determined by studying a firm's average total cost curve.
8. How is your answer to question 7 related to the concept of conflicting property rights?

9. What happens to the interests of third parties when market demand and supply curves are drawn?

GOVERNMENTAL RESPONSES TO ENVIRONMENTAL DAMAGE

Markets do not by themselves possess a mechanism for forcing the producer or consumer to consider external, as well as internal, costs. Hence, with the exception of the rare voluntary program, environmental protection is an economic goal that requires some governmental regulatory action. These regulations take one of two forms: (1) taxes on pollution and (2) direct restrictions on how a product may be produced or on the amount of pollution the firm is permitted to emit. Notice that after either form of government regulation has been implemented, the market is still functioning. Demand and supply are still in force, shaping the amount produced and the price. However, the regulation has modified the output and price decisions that the firm would have made in the absence of the regulation.

Taxes on pollution are a financial disincentive to the prospective polluter. By imposing the tax that reflects the external costs of pollution, the government is attempting to require the firm to consider the total cost of its production process. The firm retains the decisions about how much and how to produce. Yet its decisions now are based on a more accurate reflection of the worth of the resources it will be using.

In response to this financial disincentive, a firm will presumably reduce its output and, consequently, the amount of pollution it would have emitted. The total costs of production will become known to the firm. In addition, the tax will require them to cover those costs. This form of regulation permits the greatest amount of economic freedom consistent with meeting environmental protection standards. The tax reduces the property rights of the firm but with minimal damage to those rights.

Direct regulations are preferred by those who want immediate regulatory results and who are not especially desirous of protecting the property rights of resource owners. Direct regulations are appealing because they are forceful and appear to be a speedy way to improve environmental conditions. A law specifying (1) pollution limits and (2) penalties for pollution that violates the limits provides a direct assault on the problem in question. Other direct regulation such as a legal limit on the extent of sulfur in coal prevents firms from producing as they would otherwise prefer.

What is not clear about direct regulations is whether they are any more effective than taxes on pollution. The problem with direct regulations is in their enforcement. Taxes on output of polluters can be automatically enforced. There is no need to catch polluters or to win a court case after the polluter has been apprehended. Taxes on output would be paid as a regular part of the taxes paid by firms. In another respect, taxes on pollution are superior to direct controls because they enlist the polluter in the environmental protection effort. The firm can reduce its taxes when it reduces pollution. Thus, the firm has an incentive to help stop at least a portion of the pollution it emits.

There are situations, however, where direct controls are preferable. For instance, any emission that is so dangerous that a zero level of emissions is desirable requires immediate restrictions. If a governor believed that the citizens in his or her state were threatened by a deadly gas emitting from a smokestack, he or she could not wait for a tax to create a disincentive for emissions. The need is substantial and immediate; direct regulations would provide the legal machinery to solve the problem. Especially important for the effectiveness of direct controls is the existence of severe penalties for violators. Otherwise, the merit of direct regulations is limited. If legal enforcement presents costs that are less than those that would have to be paid by the firm to prevent emissions, it cannot be expected that firms will comply. The next section reviews the performance of our combination of pollution taxes and direct regulations.

UNITED STATES AND INTERNATIONAL PERFORMANCE

The relative newness of the goal of environmental protection makes it difficult to assess how the United States or any other country is doing with respect to this economic goal. In addition, there is no single indicator of environmental quality that we can use as a performance measure. Thus, this section provides an impressionistic picture of environmental protection efforts. The data from other countries are particularly sparse.

The first section of this chapter described the legislative standards for environmental protection. The record of meeting these standards is sharply mixed. During the 1970s the Environmental Protection Agency (EPA) reported steady progress in controlling conventional air pollutants. Some locales reported remarkable environmental improvement. In Portland, Oregon, for example, the number of days in which the air quality was "unhealthy" fell from 250 in 1973 to 70 in 1978.

Despite this achievement, two-thirds of people in the United States in 1980 lived in counties that did not meet the legislative requirements for ozone. One-fourth of us resided in areas where the carbon monoxide standard was violated. The air quality standards for those pollutants associated with automotive emissions (carbon monoxide, hydrocarbons, and photochemical oxidents) have been particularly hard to enforce because of the political power of the United States automobile industry. The financial difficulties of that industry and its importance to our economy have combined to pressure Congress into repeatedly postponing the 90 percent reduction deadline that had been imposed on automobile emissions.

Our performance in meeting the standards of the Clean Water Act has been much better. Definite reductions have occurred in the amounts of pollutants that without regulation would have entered the nation's water supply. The total amount of pollutants entering the water from municipal wastewater treatment plants has remained roughly constant since the act was passed, despite a population increase of approximately 20 million. By 1982 a majority of states had met the 1983 goal of fishable and swimmable water in their communities. Industrial discharges dropped dramatically between 1973 and 1977; for example, phosphate emissions fell by 74 percent and oil and grease by 52 percent. Now those emissions appear to have leveled off. The major problems focus on agricultural runoff and permit violations by municipal and industrial polluters. Toxic substances in the water still present enough of a problem to have stimulated partial fishing bans in Lake Ontario, part of the Hudson River, and in Chesapeake Bay.

Toxic wastes remain a serious environmental hazard. In 1982, the EPA placed 114 sites on its priority cleanup list. Unfortunately, the amount of actual cleanup has been small. Budget cuts have hurt the EPA, just as they have other domestic programs. Cleanup costs range from $4 million to $26 million per site. New Jersey and New York alone estimate that they have 30 and 15 hazardous dump sites, respectively. One bright spot has been the 1984 requirement that certain types of wastes be incinerated; this method is the safest means of toxic waste disposal. However, such direct controls are only as strong as the enforcement effort that follows their violation.

One danger you should be aware of is that of believing that pollution occurs only in countries, such as the United States, where private profit is a fundamental motivator of economic behavior. It is true that a firm's profit objectives encourage it to overlook external costs. However, the number of governmental polluters in this country should make us aware that all organizations wish to dispense the costs of their activity to others. *Any* organization that reduces the costs attributed to it has improved its chances of receiving a positive performance rating by shareholders or voters.

The Soviet Union, despite its minimal use of the profit motive as an incentive mechanism, has not escaped pollution. The construction of numerous dams and reservoirs has caused so much evaporation that seashores have been expanding at dangerous rates. In addition, Soviet newspapers on occasion report smoke alerts from air pollution, and fire alerts caused by chemical accumulations in rivers near industrial sites.

In 1979, China indicated for the first time that environmental protection was an important goal of the People's Republic. They passed in that year both a forestry act and a law on environmental protection. No systematic data evaluating the results of these statutes are available. However, the Chinese emphasis on rapid economic growth and their dependence on coal as a source of energy suggest that environmental protection in China will be very gradual.

China has a serious industrial pollution problem. The Chinese rely almost exclusively on direct regulations to control environmental damage. Recognizing that the costs of a national reduction in pollution are prohibitive at the moment, they are emphasizing environmental quality near tourist areas, densely populated places, and water sources.

Since the adoption of their first joint environmental protection policy in 1973, the countries of the European Common Market (EEC) have reaffirmed on two occasions their resolve to resist environmental decay. Competition among member countries has prevented significant environmental improvement. Nevertheless, the EEC has issued directives requiring environmental protection. For example, member states are required to prohibit the marketing of fuels that bring about particular levels of sulphur dioxide pollution. Water pollution has been addressed by prohibiting the marketing of nonbiodegradable detergents. Enforcement efforts have generally been stymied by the claims of member states that their sovereignty is being threatened when EEC rules are stricter than the laws in the offending country.

The goal of environmental protection is being pursued in all economies. However, the vigorousness of the environmental protection efforts seems everywhere to be linked to the performance of that economy with respect to other economic goals. Environmental protection does not currently receive top priority in any economy. Perhaps that assessment is inevitable because the major beneficiaries of environmental protection may be those yet unborn.

ACTIVE REVIEW

1. In 1984 the state of New Jersey attempted to remove asbestos from over 300 schools. The asbestos was in the schools because asbestos fibers are fire-resistant and feature above-average insulating qualities.

Exposure to asbestos is correlated with lung, esophagus, stomach, and colon cancers. The EPA is convinced that any level of asbestos is a health risk. However, they cannot reliably estimate the seriousness of the risk.

The EPA anticipated that once a school was found to have asbestos in the building, the problem would solve itself. Parents, teachers, and concerned citizens would demand removal. A 1984 EPA report found that this expectation was faulty. Only the wealthy school districts acted quickly to remove the asbestos.

a. Why is it unlikely that asbestos will be banned completely as a building material?

b. Once the danger of asbestos became known, why was the problem not immediately resolved?

c. What conflicting property rights are involved in the attempt to remove asbestos from schools?

d. How is the concept of negative externalities related to the problem of asbestos as a health risk?

e. How does the economic goal of equity affect the extent to which particular people embrace the goal of environmental protection?

2. The National Academy of Sciences estimates that over 6 million metric tons of oil is spilled into our marine environment every year. Approximately one-third of that total results from tanker accidents. The United States alone has over 10,000 accidental spills every year.

The oil inflicts damage on many economic interests. Fisherman lose potential catches; marinas lose business; hotels experience reservation cancellations. The public in general faces cleanup costs and damage to marshes and wildlife.

a. What is an example of a direct regulation that would prevent oil spills? How are pollution taxes an alternative solution in this instance?

b. What determines which of the two solutions you described in answering question 2a is better in this instance?

c. Do the cost curves of oil companies reflect the complete cost of their activities?

ANSWERS TO ACTIVE REVIEW

1a. Asbestos is a highly useful building material. As the description of its use indicates, it is fire-resistant and an efficient insulator. Naturally, many builders will wish to make use of it in their construction projects.

A second reason it will probably not be banned is that the precise nature of the health risk associated with asbestos may not be clearly described. Thus, those who produce and use asbestos will always be able to say convincingly, "How can you threaten my bank account on the basis of your hunches?" Buyers and sellers of asbestos or any other good or service will resist attempts to reduce their liberty. For example, you have seen how tobacco firms have argued that the only proof justifying regulations of tobacco consumption is nearly perfect proof.

1b. The problem created by asbestos was not solved, simply because it costs too much money to solve the problem. Awareness of a problem does not create a ground swell of volunteers eager to pay the opportunity cost of a solution. Asbestos firms do not want their demand curve to shift down dramatically. Parents and concerned citizens do not want to pay higher taxes or reduce other public-sector services to pay for the removal of the asbestos.

1c. The conflicting property rights are hinted at in the answer to question 1b. Many people have invested in the future of the asbestos industry. In addition, the industry has many employees whose rights to employment, income, fringe benefits, and retirement are tied to the continued demand for asbestos. These people want the voices of third parties affected by asbestos to be kept to a murmur.

On the other hand, by threatening the health of those exposed to asbestos, the industry is interfering with the property rights of many future workers. The most basic property right is control over the continued existence of one's value as a resource. The damage to children's health certainly restricts this property right.

1d. The cost curves of the asbestos industry do not reflect the complete cost of their activities. The negative externalities associated with the use of asbestos in schools do not appear anywhere in the cost calculations that precede production decisions. Thus, these firms produce more asbestos and charge lower prices than would be justified by a more complete estimate of the value of resources used to produce asbestos.

1e. Even after the problems associated with exposure were announced, some school districts were unable to remove the asbestos. Even the most self-centered parents would probably have had some concern about the danger. Their children are important to them. Yet, only some school districts moved to solve the problem. What stimulated some to act and others to fail to respond to the danger? There were probably many independent variables affecting those decisions; however, the wealth of the districts clearly played some role. The more wealthy the district, the more likely it would be for parents to say, Clean it up!

ANSWERS TO SELF-TEST

1. As attractive as an absolute end to pollution is, such a goal is highly unrealistic. Our daily lives, as well as our productive use of resources, have by-products. Many of these by-products damage nature and its

capacity for beauty and future productivity. Hence, it is inappropriate to expect environmental protection to mean a complete stop to pollution.

2. This statement is as incorrect as the one in question 1, but for a very different reason. To say that pollution is inevitable is certainly *not* to say that Love Canal or any particular environmental catastrophe is inevitable. Building residential units on top of waste dump sites is not a necessary result of our way of life. That particular environmental problem was avoidable. There were alternative methods and locations for storing chemical wastes. The Love Canal incident need not be repeated.

3. Both the economic goals of equity and environmental protection are especially hard to define with precision. Our concept of equity may change as we reevaluate the rights of various groups in the economy or as we gain new evidence about the incentive effects of income differentials. Similarly, the meaning of environmental protection evolves. Our devotion to the rights of future generations changes as we become more affluent as a country and as our knowledge of our interdependence with nature increases.

4. Yes, there are. Certain goods and services produce less environmental damage than others. Thus, if we were more self-conscious about *which* goods or services we should have more of and *which* we should relinquish, we could still define economic progress in terms of more goods and services as we do currently.

   An alternative way to answer this question would be to point out that we do not have to define progress as *more* material goods and services, of any kind. Instead, we could define it in terms of longevity, infant mortality rates, extent of literacy, or elimination of poverty. Allocational decisions could then move us toward "progress" without our necessarily having to expand total output.

5. This statement is based on a misunderstanding of the law of conservation of matter and energy. The law does not state that there must be environmental damage. Instead, it states that resources never disappear. They may change their form from solid into gas, but their presence remains.

   Recycling is not inconsistent with the law. On the contrary, recycling is an attempt to demonstrate an intelligent awareness of the law. By reusing resources, those who recycle are trying to avoid turning productive resources into a garbage heap.

6. Both private costs and negative externalities are costs of production. For production of some goods and services to proceed, these costs must be paid. What distinguishes private costs and external costs is the person or group who does the paying. Private costs are paid initially by the firm that produces the product. On the other hand, negative externalities are paid by third parties. Their desires about the proper level of production and the price are not a component of the normal price-determination process.

7. The average total cost curve does provide a partial measure of the value of resources used by the firm. In some cases where negative externalities are zero or minimal, the cost structure that a firm uses for its production decisions provides a valid measure of resource value.

   The problem with the assertion is that it does not apply to those situations for which external costs are numerous. In these instances the firm's purchase of resources represents only one important element of resource value. Third parties also pay a cost from the contemplated use of resources. Hence, their interests are ignored in the normal market estimates of resource value. Third parties have no mechanism whereby they can adjust the cost curve upward to reflect their attitudes, *unless* government intervenes on their behalf.

8. The struggle between (1) buyers and sellers who want average costs minimized and (2) third parties who want costs to the firm to be adjusted upward to reflect a more complete measure of resource value is a struggle over who will control the use of particular resources. Firms want to be left alone to make production decisions on the basis of prospective costs and benefits *to them*. Third parties demand a voice in those decisions because such an input is necessary to enhance the future use of their resources.

9. When market demand and supply curves are drawn (in the absence of regulation), consumers and producers make their calculations considering private benefits and costs. Third parties are not present literally or symbolically when these decisions are made. Thus, market demand and supply curves typically ignore the effects of output on third parties.

14
The Goal of Economic Growth

Average life expectancy in the United States has increased yearly without exception for decades. In 1920 we were expected to live an average of 54.1 years; that expectation jumped to 70.9 years in 1970, and 74.5 years in 1982. Advances in medical science are enabling us to live longer, healthier lives. The *capacity* to finance these developments is increased by economic growth.

Current medical technology is awe-inspiring. It has resulted in innumerable new procedures that enhance the quality of our existence. A list of such techniques includes: amniocentesis and ultrasound examination, which allow doctors to monitor the development of fetuses with more accuracy than could have been imagined two decades ago; the development of laser surgery, which results in far less damage to healthy human tissue than conventional surgical methods; and more-successful organ transplants and the advent of artificial organ transplants.

As income per capita increases, overall mortality decreases, with especially significant decreases in death from cardiovascular disease, cirrhosis, and suicide. It is the additional resources created by economic growth that provide the basis for investment in new research, hence a healthier population.

The advances that we associate with economic growth have a rich history of causes and effects. The methods by which they are achieved and the economic impacts from these policies comprise the essence of this chapter. As for the other chapters on economic goals, we begin our search for understanding economic growth with an analysis of how the goal is defined and the problems associated with its measurement. Subsequent sections explain how growth is enhanced, outline the limits we face as we attempt to grow, and finally describe how we have done in our efforts to grow more rapidly than other economies.

THE DEFINITION OF ECONOMIC GROWTH

What exactly does it mean for the economy to grow? There are many aspects of an economy that can be enlarged. An economy can grow in terms of the extent of compassion it expresses toward the weaker members of the planet; it can grow in terms of literacy rates; it can enlarge the sense of control or autonomy felt by citizens who participate in that economy.

Economic Growth An increase in the economy's capacity to provide more goods and services for the average person

While economic growth could refer to many different characteristics of the economy, the conventional definition focuses on the capability of the economy to meet the desires of its population for goods and services. Notice that the definition requires some measure of the economy's capacity to provide more goods and services for the average person. If we did not include a measure of the population, we could not understand the significance of growth data. The economy could be expanding, but a typical consumer could be worse off. The population measurement is required so that the capacity can be expressed in terms of an average member of the economy.

Gross National Product The total of all expenditures on final products sold in markets during the current year, or the dollar value of all final goods and services produced in one year

The most commonly used measure of the economy's capacity to fulfill material desires is the nation's gross national product (GNP). Increases in economic growth are expressed in terms of increases in GNP per capita. The GNP is the sum of the money value of all final products produced in a particular year, expressed in current prices. These money values can be calculated by adding purchases of final goods by households, business firms, and governments.

One of the advantages of this definition of economic growth is its availability. GNP figures exist; they can be compared from year to year, and with some adjustments, from country to country. They appear to reveal how we are doing in a cumulative sense.

One initial caution is that GNP statistics do not by themselves permit comparisons over time. If you refer back to the definition of GNP, you will see that the total of all expenditures is expressed in terms of prices for that year. The result is called money GNP.

Accurate comparisons require us to recognize inflation. Price tags change every year. We would not want our measure of production capacity to reflect these changing price tags. A rise or fall in average prices does not necessarily reveal anything about our capacity to produce.

To adjust GNP for price changes, to discover "real GNP," requires us to choose some base period and then to express all GNP figures we are studying in terms of prices for that base year. While the actual calculations are discussed in Chapter 19, it is important for you to recognize the necessity of checking GNP statistics to see whether they are in real or money terms. You can avoid a faulty inference by being careful about the form in which you are being fed GNP numbers.

Figures 14–1 and 14–2 illustrate the importance of distinguishing between money and real GNP data. Both are graphs of GNP data,

Figure 14–1
Money Value of Gross National Product

This figure presents the enormous growth of money GNP during the period from 1946–1983.

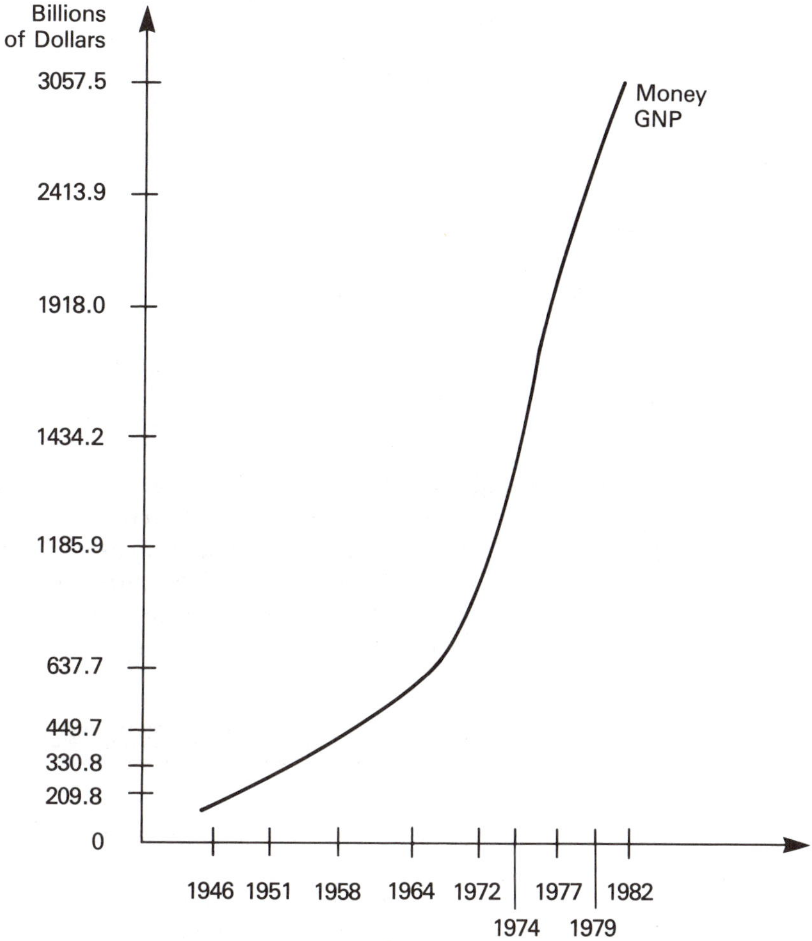

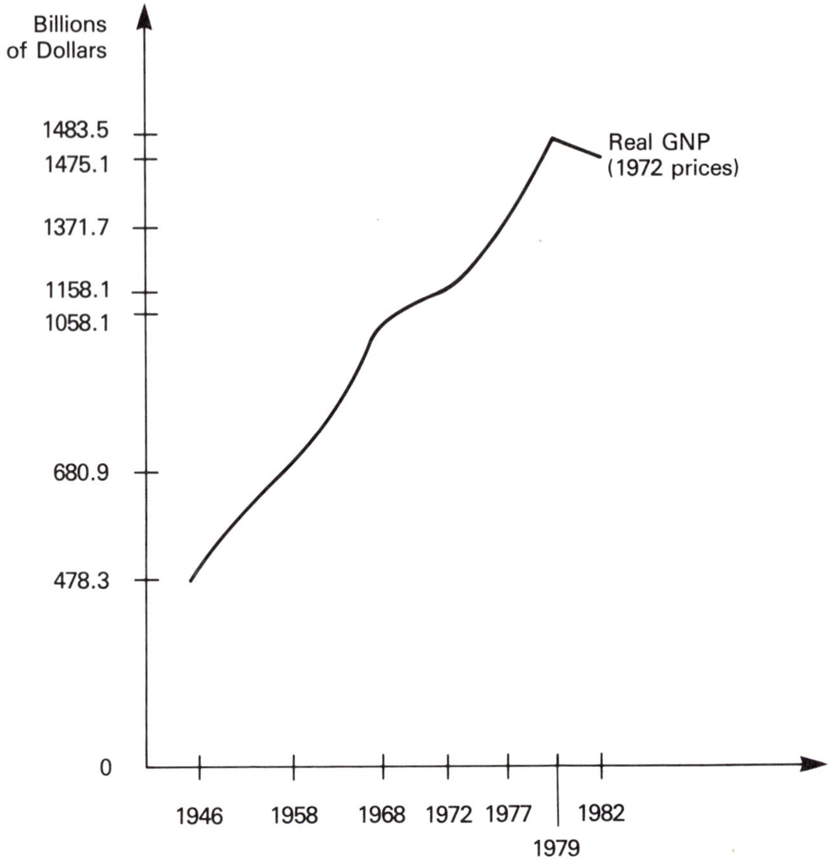

Figure 14–2
Real Value of Gross National Product (1972 prices)

This figure should be compared with Figure 14–1 because the comparison will show the effect of inflation on our measure of economic growth.

and both are for the period from 1946 to 1983. The differences in the numbers are, however, dramatic. Particularly, look at the GNP data for the contemporary period. The real GNP is approximately half of the money GNP. Since GNP is *the* most common indicator of our performance, great caution is required on your part in establishing the type of GNP data you are being asked to interpret.

PROBLEMS ASSOCIATED WITH MEASURING ECONOMIC GROWTH

GNP data promise so much as an indicator of our economic well-being. Presidential elections, such as those in 1960 and 1980, often revolve around claims that we should be doing better. Most of us assume that the implicit standard that we can do better at is growth in GNP per capita. Whenever we have an economic performance measure on which we rely heavily, it is essential that we focus on its weaknesses as a measure of economic health. We have already mentioned one such problem, expressing GNP in money instead of real terms. This section mentions several other potential problems. The purpose of this material is to help you see more clearly exactly what GNP data do and do not mean.

1. *GNP data ignore many aspects of the quality of life*. This particular difficulty was hinted at earlier. The quality of our lives is highly subjective. The weights we individually attach to material goods and services, serenity, beauty, honesty, wisdom, and other noncommercial aspects of life are diverse. Those differential weightings represent just another way of saying that our values differ. Consequently, no measure, whether it be GNP or anything else, will offer a noncontroversial proxy for how our economy is doing.

GNP data assume that what is important is identifiable by measuring what is sold. That is one reasonable perspective. That measurement, however, is an especially important indicator only to those of us who see commercial behavior, the buying and selling of goods and services, as the proper focus for our lives.

2. *Some elements of GNP do not enlarge our capacity to produce*. When GNP statistics are calculated, there is no attempt to make certain that all expenditures expand our ability to produce more goods and services. It something is sold in a market, the sales price is counted for GNP statistics. Brief reflection, though, causes us to recognize that many things we buy merely preserve or rebuild our existing capacity to produce. When you purchase garbage bags to store the remains from your consumption, you have not made a contribution to an enlarged capacity to produce. Nevertheless, our expenditures on such items are all added into GNP right along with expenditures on new plant and equipment.

Many of the expenditures made by governments perform a maintenance, rather than growth-enhancing, function. Grants for cancer research, subsidies to clean up air and water pollution, and expenditures for sewage treatment are all included in GNP. To the extent that these are major components in GNP statistics, we are exaggerating economic growth in terms of an improved ability to produce goods and services.

3. *GNP fails to include some output of new goods and services*. The measurements of GNP are a compilation of market transactions. Thus, any production done at home by a family for its own consumption is not included. Regardless of how productive gardening or housework is, the output never makes its appearance in GNP, because it is not sold in a market. As soon as one hires a gardener or housekeeper to do the same work that was previously done by a member of the

household, GNP rises because the output can now be measured by the amount of the salary.

Underground Economy Economic activities that are not reported to the government

The activities in the *underground economy* also are omitted from GNP calculations. Some of these activities are legal, some illegal. Illegal drug sales, payments in cash to accountants or lawyers, and trading one output directly for a service all fall into this category. Why does the underground economy exist? The reasons for the growth of the underground economy (estimates range from 10–25 percent of GNP) include the understandable desire to avoid prosecution or the payment of taxes on reported income.

The significance of the underground economy for economic growth is that it causes an underestimate in our growth rates. These growth rates are obtained from GNP statistics. When those statistics fail to report activity in the underground economy, they lose some of their accuracy as a measure of our material accomplishments.

4. *GNP reveals nothing about the distribution of goods and services.* To know that average levels of GNP have advanced tells us nothing about who is better off. In terms of both logic and reality, groups with whom you identify can have their income levels harmed by techniques that enlarge GNP per capita. Suppose, for instance, that research in robotics eliminates the need for 80 percent of factory employees and that these developments expand the capacity of the economy to produce goods and services. GNP per capita may lurch upward. Those who sell goods and services to former factory workers can hardly be expected to cheer this particular growth in the economy as their sales revenues plummet because the factory workers have lost their jobs. (We will discuss this problem again in Chapter 15 as structural unemployment.)

Chapter 12 presented some data revealing marked differences in the distribution of resources among various countries. Economic growth in those countries with a Gini Coefficient that is huge will probably mean that the large gap between rich and poor will get larger. Rapid growth in a more egalitarian economy will result in a greater sharing of the benefits from economic growth among all sectors in the economy.

SELF-TEST

1. Why isn't it possible for us to agree about GNP per capita as *the* indicator of how our economy is doing?
2. Explain why someone might reasonably make the following statement: There is no contribution to economic growth from a particular output unless someone *buys* the output.

3. Evaluate the claim that GNP is a measure of the quality and quantity of national output.

HOW GROWTH IS ACHIEVED

There are many worthwhile goals that individuals and cultures can pursue. Wisdom, serenity, sharing, or creating beauty are all meaningful pursuits. Since our energy is limited, growth is a competitor for our attention with all other worthwhile goals. Thus, the most basic of all the prerequisites for economic growth is the will to focus on that goal, to make it a focus of our efforts.

Materialistic Value System

For economic growth to occur, the members of an economy must place a high value on material output. Their time and talents must be dedicated to finding ways to expand the number of things available to be consumed. All of us are trained to do well, to achieve. Yet this motive to achieve has many potential objectives. As mentioned above, one could seek excellence in the arts, physical fitness, or compassion. But these goals are not compatible with materialism. For the achievement motive to propel economic growth, the desired accomplishments must lead to higher levels of consumption of goods and services. People in an economy pursuing economic growth must emphasize the acquisition of wealth and property.

When an economy has a value system that emphasizes material possessions, it possesses one of the factors required for growth. In resource or factor markets, those who sell resources want to assure high levels of potential output from resources they sell so that they can get a high price for those resources. For example, workers want to at least *appear* highly productive so that they can demand a high salary. The high salary would help them purchase greater levels of material satisfaction.

Those who buy resources because they want to produce goods and services will also encourage economic growth if their motive to achieve is directed toward material possessions. They will want to buy the most productive resources at the cheapest cost because they, the producers, want to generate more revenue for themselves. By accelerating the flow of income into their pockets, they will be better able to satisfy their material desires.

Imagine, for instance, that you wish to open a Chinese restaurant. Your basic reason is your desire to have a bigger home and car. When you hire labor, choose a location, or order ingredients, you are very interested in keeping costs low and resource quality high. These motivations will, *ceteris paribus,* stimulate output through a growth in the sales of your Chinese food.

Thus, on both the demand and supply sides of markets, a value system emphasizing material possessions facilitates growth. In the absence of that emphasis, the motivations of resource owners and buyers are altered. Their behavior is consistent with high levels of economic growth only when they are trying to enrich themselves so that they can purchase greater amounts of goods and services.

Long-run Perspective

Motivation to acquire material possessions can be directed toward immediate consumption or eventual consumption. Economic growth is accelerated when those who determine how resources are used focus on long-run consumption activities.

Consumption Good One that is used up after its initial use

Capital Good One that is used to create other goods

Why is growth made easier if an economy postpones consumption? The answer lies in the distinction between *consumption goods* and *capital goods.* For example, a tomato has one primary use—to be eaten alone or combined with other goods to be eaten; it is a consumption good. The tomato is not used to produce other goods and services.

An assembly line, in contrast with a tomato, *is* used to produce other goods. The very reason it is constructed is because it has that capability. Hence, an assembly line is a capital good. Since economic growth is desired precisely because it results in a greater capacity to satisfy our material desires, any economy that focuses on capital goods production will grow more rapidly. Such an economy is using its resources in a manner that expands the output from those resources. An emphasis on capital goods thus encourages economic growth.

To emphasize capital goods, an economy must delay gratification; it must have foresight. Recall an earlier encounter, in Chapter 2, with the idea of opportunity cost and the curve that represents alternative choices and their consequent costs—the opportunity cost curve. The idea behind this concept and curve is that resources cannot be used for multiple purposes. If land, for instance, is used to grow soybeans, it cannot be used at the same time to grow cotton. So choices about what and how much to produce must be made.

It is highly tempting to make those choices with the goal of immediate consumption in mind. Why delay consumption when we can use resources in a manner that will give us some of the things we want right now? Specifically, we can emphasize consumption goods.

A special form of the opportunity cost curve, the production possibilities curve, permits us to visualize clearly the impact of the choice between capital and consumption goods. Notice that in Figure 14–3 consumption goods are on one axis, and capital goods are on the other. Observe further that the curve on the graph is shaped in such a way that there is no way to move from one point to another on the curve and to thereby increase the quantity of both consumption and capital goods. In other words, the graph is consistent with there being a trade-off between the production of consumption goods and capital goods.

On Figure 14–3 *A*, *B*, and *C* represent allocational choices that result in different combinations of capital and consumption goods. Point *A*, for example, yields a higher number of capital goods and fewer consumption goods than would be provided by the allocational choice represented by point *C*. Each point results in the availability of a different mix of goods and services.

But what do these allocational choices between consumption goods and capital goods have to do with economic growth? The answer depends on the distinction between the two types of goods. Capital goods expand the capacity of the economy to make goods and services in the future; they enhance economic growth. In contrast, consumption goods maintain the existing flow of income. They give us satisfaction now while denying us more bountiful consumption at a later time. Whenever we buy albums, the funds we use cannot be spent on machinery and productive capacity. Hence we are reducing the amount

Figure 14–3 Productive Possibilities Curve

This curve demonstrates alternative allocational choices that an economy must make in terms of capital and consumption goods.

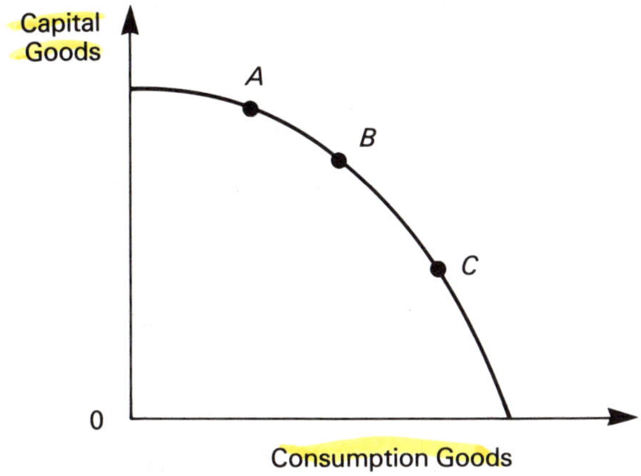

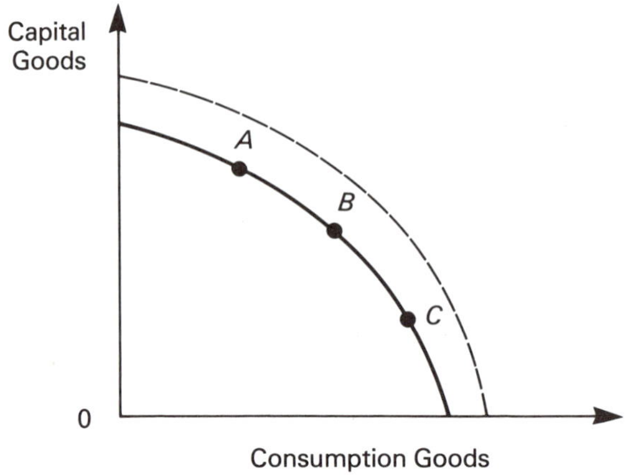

Figure 14–4 Production Possibilities and Growth

This graph provides a visual portrayal of the positive impact of capital goods output on our economic future. Growth is enhanced when capital goods output is substituted for production of consumption goods.

of albums and everything else that could have been available in the future.

In terms of the production possibilities curve, an emphasis on capital goods production provides an avenue whereby we can have more of both consumption and capital goods in the future. Since capital goods expand our capacity to produce, producing capital goods now permits even more goods later. In Figure 14–4 any movement up the curve, from *B* to *A* for instance, results in a greater allocation of resources to capital goods production. This reallocation of resources permits a shift of the entire production possibilities curve farther to the right than would have been possible with the previous allocation of resources.

The shift outward of the production possibilities curve indicates economic growth. Even choice *C* might result in some outward shift, but points above *C* permit more dramatic shifts or economic growth as a result of the greater emphasis on capital production. Choose any point on the new production possibilities curve and compare the potential output of the economy with that represented by a point on the old curve that is either horizontal or vertical to the point you have chosen. What do you notice about the comparison? Right, economic growth means an expanded capacity to produce more goods and services.

Increases in Quantity and Quality of Resources

Since resources are the elements used to create goods and services, increases in their number and improvements in their quality stimulate economic growth. When our population grows or the number of us entering the labor force increases, there are more labor resources available for production purposes. The percentage of us now seeking employment is on the rise. Currently almost 60 out of every potential 100 workers tries to find employment. Should this number rise further, the impact on growth, *ceteris paribus,* would be positive.

When thinking about humans as resources, we should not take the generalization provided above to extremes. Population can and sometimes does grow at such a rapid clip that the economy's resources cannot keep pace with the growth of potential consumers. In this situation an increase in population becomes a drawback, not a stimulus to growth. Economic growth accomplished by population growth also increases the denominator in GNP/capita calculations.

The quality of human resources refers to their productive capabilities measured in terms of market transactions. Techniques that promise to expand the knowledge, energy, achievement motivation, and creativity of potential employees are sources of future economic growth. By improving the quality of a human resource we have expanded productive potential without the draining effect of increasing the *number* of human resources.

Capital goods, like labor, are essential to economic growth. An increasing labor force that was compelled to work with an unchanging amount of capital would soon experience decreasing output per person. Constant stocks of capital therefore result in smaller and smaller amounts of growth as the labor force expands. The quantity of capital is increased, as we saw in the preceding section, by using resources that could have been used for consumption of goods to create more machines, tools, vehicles, and other capital goods.

As with labor resources, capital resources can be improved so that the potential output of resources grows. The quality of capital is enhanced by technological developments that invent new uses for capital. While much about technological achievement remains a mystery, we do know that technology can be expanded through conscious efforts by firms and governments to do research and then discover commercial applications of the research.

High Levels of Total Expenditures in the Economy

Increases in the quantity and quality of resources provide a stimulus to economic growth on the supply side of markets. They make production cheaper and more efficient. However, an increasing productive capacity requires adequate levels of total expenditures before the enlarged productive capacity will be used. Those who produce do so when they have confidence that output will actually be sold. Potential output will become actual output when expenditure levels are high enough to purchase the newly surging output levels.

The Great Depression of the 1930s did not occur because we lacked abundant resources or because the resources we had were of poor quality. The actual decline in real GNP during that period stemmed from, among other things, sharply reduced expenditures. Potential output was not achieved and growth was inhibited. The unemployment of resources caused by low levels of total expenditures not only wastes potential output but also creates confusion and hesitation among those who would ordinarily be willing to purchase the capital goods that could start the movement toward full employment.

SELF-TEST

4. How might a revival of interest in the family serve as a limiting factor on efforts of the economy to grow?
5. Imagine that the economy in which you live is located at point *R* below the following production possibilities curve. Should you be optimistic or pessimistic about the prospects for growth of your economy?

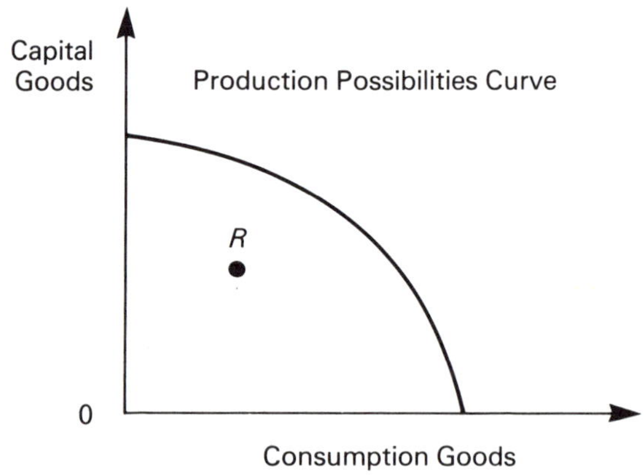

6. Explain why aggregate demand levels affect the extent of economic growth.

LIMITS TO GROWTH: WHY WE CAN'T GROW FASTER

If growth enables us to have a greater supply of goods and services, why can't we grow and grow to solve whatever economic problems we face? We know from looking around us that scarcity cannot be replaced by plenty. Many good and well-intentioned minds have struggled with the economic problem of scarcity, and they have eventually surrendered. Why wouldn't growth cause scarcity to vanish?

The answer can be found be becoming familiar with several characteristics of our world that limit the extent of growth. A given economy might choose to grow at a certain rate, but these limits prevent the goal from being accomplished. These limiting factors prevent us from solving scarcity by ongoing economic growth.

Failure to Employ Our Resources Fully

Resources, or factors of production, are the building blocks with which we create goods and services. When natural resources, labor, or capital exist but go unused, potential output is lost. Hence, any economic events that prevent the use of resources limit the growth of our economy.

On a production possibilities curve, the failure to employ resources fully is represented by any point inside the current production possibilities curve. For example, each of the points labeled in Figure 14–5 is inferior to any point actually on the production possibilities curve in the sense that it represents less output.

An economy that wishes to accelerate its output of consumption and capital goods would be limited in its efforts by decisions that result in unemployment of resources. How could an economy allow this waste to occur? The answer anticipates the final five chapters in this text. Emphasis on certain economic goals can have unemployment as an unintended consequence. When, for instance, those who shape monetary and fiscal policy attempt to achieve price stability by restricting the level of total expenditures in the economy, unemployment is a common result. Accordingly, another way to think

Figure 14–5
Production Possibilities Curve

Each of the allocational choices represented by points inside the production possibilities curve indicates that some available resources are not being employed.

about this limit to growth is to remember that there are conflicting economic goals, the achievement of which may halt efforts to grow.

Recessions, stagnation, and depressions are not ordinarily an objective of those who make economic policy. Yet their regular recurrence in our country and in other economies highlights one important reason the struggle for economic growth is not easy. Severe levels of unemployment not only indicate waste of resources but also create a hesitancy on the part of investors to purchase capital goods. Since these investors are motivated by expectations of profit, they will be less than eager to purchase capital goods for projected use in an uncertain future.

Reduced Supply of Key Resources

The definition of precisely what a resource is and what is a waste product is in constant flux. One of the dreams of modern technology is to be able to turn salt water into plant food, animal excrement into energy to heat homes, and other abundant items in our environment that have no current value as resources into marketable factors of production. Any such transformation makes growth more likely, because it enlarges the number of resources that can be used to generate output.

Unfortunately, however, there is no guarantee that technology's achievements in redefining resources can keep pace with the number of resources we destroy as we produce. Some natural resources are exhaustible; they are available in a fixed supply, and we are using them at a rapid clip. As far as we know, petroleum, natural gas, zinc, copper, iron, and coal supplies are available in limited quantities. Yet these are some of the most basic items we require in a modern economy. Continued growth is threatened by the diminishing supplies of these critical resources.

The problem of limited natural resources hinders growth a long time before supplies of these resources dwindle to nothing. Through discovery efforts we can probably find supplies of these natural resources that have not yet been found. But ask yourself, why have these supplies not been found so far? You are right—the answer lies in the high cost of locating and collecting these additional supplies.

The supplies of exhaustible resources that we have already found are the easiest and cheapest to use for production purposes. Deeper and deeper excursions into the earth's surface in search of more resources require additional outlays by firms attempting to compensate for dwindling supplies. The resulting higher costs of production will, *ceteris paribus,* reduce our capacity to grow. More of our national income will be required to produce the same amount of goods and services that we could produce for less when resources were more abundant.

Short-run Perspective of Economic Decisions

To see the effect of short-run perspectives on economic growth, we can tie together two things you have already learned. First, you encountered earlier in this chapter the idea that capital accumulation is a requirement for economic growth. Furthermore the capital accumulation process is in conflict with our desire to consume now.

Now, put this understanding together with the section in Chapter 13 entitled "What Do We Owe Future Generations?" You recall that it is difficult to visualize future generations and thus very tempting to ignore their projected needs. We are aware of the many goods and services we want. Few of us would not like a nicer car, home, vacation, sweater, or whatever. We feel these desires intensely.

For economic growth to be accelerated, those who make economic decisions must assign great value to future generations. Why else would we deny ourselves what we want and can have at this moment? To choose capital goods production at the expense of current consumption requires an unusual sense of immediate sacrifice. One of the most severe challenges faced by a democracy is how to both permit majority rule and encourage rapid economic growth. Majorities understandably tend to take a short-run perspective. On a primitive level, we know we are alive and eager to consume today. Who knows what tomorrow will bring?

THE RECORD OF ECONOMIC GROWTH

The poor countries on our planet consist of most of Latin America, Africa, and Asia (with the notable exceptions of the Soviet Union and Japan). These countries have the dual problem of growing populations and few resources. Even when there is rapid growth, the relatively small economic base of these countries does not leap forward in absolute terms. A great percentage increase in a tiny capacity to produce goods and services offers long-run hope at best. The 1983 *World Bank Atlas* contains data indicating that over half of the world's population is living in countries where the GNP per person is less than \$360. The same source lists the GNP per person in the United States at \$11,590.

The extent of world poverty can be appreciated by studying the data in Table 14–1. The GNP per capita of countries such as West Germany, Saudi Arabia, the United States, Canada, and Japan provide the resources for the best educational facilities, health services, and communication opportunities available. The GNP per capita of countries such as India and China provide meager consumption and capital accumulation possibilities in comparison. Citizens of these economies must struggle on a daily basis to live. The search for adequate food and shelter occupies the energies and resources of members of these poor economies.

At first when you look at Table 14–1 you may think that the growth rates among industrialized countries are remarkably similar. After all the difference between a 3 percent growth rate and a 1 percent growth rate is a mere 2 percent. But you should think more deeply about economic growth as a process. Growth increases exponentially; the growth rate is multiplied by a steadily rising base. Consequently, over decades there is a huge difference between the effect of a 1 percent growth rate and a 3 percent economic growth rate.

Imagine, for example, that your economy grows at a rate of 1.7 percent. Per capita real income will double in approximately forty years. Suppose, though, that economic policy and events had combined such that your economy grew at a 2.7 percent rate. The result of what appears to be a small difference in growth rates is dramatic. Real per capita GNP would have doubled in only 26 years.

Table 14–1 Comparative Economic Growth Data, 1983

This table demonstrates the sharp contrast in GNP per person in various countries. It also documents great variation in the rates at which GNP per person is changing in selected countries.

Country	GNP per person, 1983	Average annual growth of GNP per person, 1970–80
Switzerland	$15,550	2.7%
United States	13,490	1.7
Sweden	11,850	2.4
Canada	11,535	1.0
West Germany	10,900	2.1
Japan	9,150	3.2
United Kingdom	8,690	1.6
Hungary	6,570	4.1
Venezuela	3,980	1.8
Yugoslavia	2,590	4.4
Mexico	2,000	1.9
Chile	1,890	−0.8
China	380	3.7
India	250	1.2

Source: United States Bureau of the Census, *Statistical Abstract of the United States, 1986* (Washington, D.C.: GPO, 1985), pp. 842–43. All GNP figures are in 1982 United States dollars.

To make these numbers more real to you, make them personal if you can. Each of us has a limited number of 26- to 40-year periods in which to live. We can squeeze three periods of doubled GNP per capita into what would otherwise be just two such periods if we can just figure out how to increase growth from 1.7 to 2.7 percent. The result would be many more of our material dreams fulfilled.

SELF-TEST

7. What are the long-run effects of failure to employ all our resources?
8. Evaluate the following statement: The market system, working through the profit motive, will solve our problem of exhaustible resources. As the supply of needed resources declines, potential profits will drive entrepreneurs to find new resources.
9. Is it fair to claim that those countries in Table 14–1 with low growth rates simply lack achievement motivation?

ACTIVE REVIEW

1. Suppose you were watching the news one evening and you heard the following announcement:

   Well, there's good news tonight. The economy has never looked better. The Commerce Department released information today that heralds a new prosperity for us all. GNP figures shot up in the last year by 3 percent. Apparently, the administration's emphasis on consumption goods has provided just the right stimulus for economic growth.

   As you reflect on the substance of the newscast, answer the following questions:

   a. Is the news actually good?
   b. What aspects of the newscast suggest that whoever wrote it may not understand what he or she is saying?
   c. If the administration is pushing consumption goods production, what are the prospects for future growth?

2. Every poor country has the desire to grow. Its citizens want to have more goods and services to consume. In addition, every economy has some resources. Finally, every beginning text in economics, including this one, spells out the means whereby a country can grow.

   Given the factors mentioned above, economic growth would seem to be abundant in poor countries. Why isn't it?

ANSWERS TO ACTIVE REVIEW

1a. It is impossible to say whether the news is good or bad. We do not know what the rate of inflation is, so we have no way of knowing whether real GNP rose or fell. In addition, we have no population statistics that would permit us to calculate GNP per capita. Hence, it is conceivable that population growth was so extensive that the 3 percent growth in GNP was swallowed by a rapid rise in the number of people requiring productive output.

1b. The newscast places too great an emphasis on a single indicator of our economic performance. Even if economic growth has occurred, there are other economic goals that we would want to analyze before we matched the newsperson's cheer.

The claim that we are all benefited by a 3 percent growth in GNP ignores the fact that GNP figures tell us nothing about how output is distributed. A very small percentage of the population could be the primary beneficiaries of whatever growth in GNP occurs. Alternatively, the fruits of growth might have been broadly distributed.

1c. The prospects for future growth are grim. An emphasis on consumption goods comes at the expense of investment goods. Yet is is investment goods that accelerate prospects for future growth. They provide new capital resources for ongoing output at a later date. Consumption goods do not constitute a resource for later production.

What can cause a 4 percent increase in suicides, a 6 percent increase in homicides, and a 3.5 percent increase in state mental hospital admissions? Unemployment! Studies have shown that all these problems are associated with a 1 percent increase in the unemployment rate in the United States.

When people become unemployed, they often feel worthless—they think that society does not need their talents. The unemployed often blame themselves for their unemployment. They feel that they have let their family and themselves down. This stress associated with job loss and the frustration of job search causes emotional and mental disorders that, in severe cases, have led to suicide. With this type of impact on individuals, why does the United States permit so many people to go unemployed? During the mid-1980s unemployment averaged over 7 percent, causing approximately 8.5 million workers to be unemployed at any one time.*

ANSWERS TO SELF-TEST

1. We cannot be expected to agree about any single judgment concerning our economy. The varied values that we bring to any measurement guarantees that neither applause nor hoots of derision will ever be

*Joint Economic Committee, statement of M. Harvey Brenner, *Achieving the Goals of the Employment Act of 1946* (Washington, D.C.: GPO, 1976), pp. 4–6.

unanimous. This point is the same one we will make when we discuss full employment and equity. Differences of opinion about the optimal level of employment and equality are sharp and predictable. The reason is not that some analysts are fools and others are bright. Instead, the differences reflect the rich variety of our ideals.

Even were it possible to agree on a single indicator as *the* best estimate of how we are collectively doing, it would not necessarily be GNP per capita. First, other economic goals would surely have their advocates who would make persuasive cases for the overwhelming significance of some other economic goal. Second, GNP per capita has a materialistic orientation to it that for some would disqualify it as the most fundamental goal of all.

2. An output shows up in GNP when it results in a purchase. Otherwise the market value of a final output could not be determined. GNP is calculated by summing actual expenditures. Thus, to be an element of GNP an output must be sold to someone.

   This characteristic of GNP explains why the work of housewives or househusbands and the output in the underground economy are not included in GNP figures. No one purchased them, at least not in legal markets.

3. The quality of our national output is reflected in GNP only to the degree that the market correctly measures that quality. The market makes mistakes, as we have learned in other chapters, when one party to a market transaction has market power, when there is lack of product information, when externalities exist, when the income distribution is unfair, or when decisions fail to reflect the long-run interests of the community. When these conditions are not present, the market provides a reasonably good estimate of the quality of our output.

   The quantity of our output is not adequately captured when either the underground economy or production for use rather than sale is widespread. Such outputs never reach the marketplace, where they can be measured and counted as GNP.

4. To grow at a rapid rate, a country must focus on the acquisition of goods and services. If any alternative objective deflects energy from the materialistic drive, growth is retarded, *ceteris paribus*. Strengthening the family requires time and attention. These efforts are not devoted to marketable output. Thus, a revival of interest in the family could make it more difficult for an economy to grow.

5. Two characteristics of point R have an impact on your prospects for growth. Initially notice that point R is not even on the production possibilities curve; it lies below the curve. Resources available for productive activity are not being employed. The failure to employ these resources reduces the prospects for future economic growth.

   An offsetting characteristic of point R is its location, indicating an emphasis on capital goods rather than on consumption goods. This emphasis is healthy in terms of the likelihood that economic growth will occur later.

6. When aggregate demand levels are adequate to purchase the output made possible by the quantity and quality of employed resources, the potential output will be produced and sold. In the case when aggregate demand is low, purchases will lag behind productive potential. The result will be a slumbering growth rate.
7. The most immediate effect of unemployment is the waste involved. Actual output is below potential output. There are other effects, however, that limit growth for years thereafter. Unemployed human resources, for instance, often lose their desire to improve themselves as workers. They lose hope and surrender to their plight. Their future productivity can be permanently limited by a long bout with unemployment.

   Capital accumulation is also slowed by unemployment. Investors will hesitate to purchase capital goods when existing resources are not being used. Unemployment is generally associated with low levels of aggregate demand. Investors recognize this relationship and may lose interest in the capital goods purchases they were contemplating. Low levels of aggregate demand make it difficult for investors to earn the profits that would motivate their capital goods purchases.
8. The market system *will* create profit opportunities when there is a shortage of resources. This process is not necessarily enough, however, to solve the limitation on growth provided by exhaustible resources. First, there is no guarantee that natural resources are available to be discovered. Profits will stimulate the search; they do not assure actual discovery. Second, the higher costs associated with new supplies of natural resources have a negative impact on future growth because, *ceteris paribus*, these higher costs reduce the economy's capacity to produce goods and services.
9. There are many factors required for growth. Achievement motivation directed toward acquiring goods and services is a necessary but not sufficient precondition for growth. Countries with low growth rates may well have the necessary motivation but lack the resources or long-run perspective required for successful growth records.

15
The Goal of Full Employment

Clearly anyone who wants to work should be permitted to do so, especially since production is the source of all economic income. Employment improves not only the well-being of individuals but also the quantity of goods and services available to the entire society. Yet, from 1970 to 1983 the unemployment rate averaged 6.9 percent. In 1982 and 1983 the unemployment rate rose to about 10 percent. If full employment is such an obvious goal, why did we permit approximately 11 million workers to sit idle during these two years? By failing to use these laborers, the economy sacrificed a great amount of output.

From research done by Arthur Okun we know that a 1 percent drop in the rate of unemployment will increase the annual output of the economy (GNP) by 2 to 3 percent, or what would have been approximately $60 to $90 billion in 1983.

In 1946 with the Full Employment Act and again in 1978 with the Humphrey-Hawkins Bill, Congress identified 4 percent unemployment as the full employment target. If we accept 4 percent as the full employment target, then the GNP in 1982 could have been approximately $360 billion to 540 billion larger. The result of this increased GNP would have been our enjoyment of $350 billion to $540 billion worth of additional goods and services. If we extend this reasoning over the 1970–1982 period, the economy could have produced over $2 trillion of additional output (in 1983 dollars) had we kept unemployment at the 4 percent level. Certainly, the laborers who would have earned this $2 trillion would have loved the opportunity to spend the income generated from this potential production. However, these workers were not employed, and the income and output they would have generated is no longer available. We have permanently lost the opportunity to enjoy that potential production.

The focus of this chapter is on full employment—what it is, why it is desirable, and why it may be undesirable. The objective of this chapter is to provide you with an appreciation of why full employment is an important goal. The following two chapters will emphasize how economic policy can be used to achieve the goal of full employment. Although many strategies may be used to achieve full employment, Chapters 16 and 17 emphasize the use of taxes and governmental spending to achieve this goal. The role of money and its impact on price stability and employment are emphasized in Chapters 19–21. The first part of Chapter 15 emphasizes what full employment is, and the second part is a discussion of how full employment is attained.

We have divided the material in this manner to simplify our discussion of goals and economic principles. There is no question that changes in tax rates, governmental spending, and the supply of money can be and have been used to alter employment levels and rates of price change. It is also true that there are trade-offs in the use of the different economic tools just as there are trade-offs in pursuing full employment instead of price stability. Nevertheless, the chapters on full employment emphasize the role of government in the search for full employment and price stability, and the chapters on price stability emphasize the role of the monetary system.

SELF-TEST

1. If I have a job, why should I be concerned about others who are unemployed?

WHAT IS FULL EMPLOYMENT?

One common definition of full employment states that it is the condition in which everyone who wishes a job has one; however, the technical definition of full employment is actually more complex. Economic resources of labor, capital, and raw materials must fit together perfectly if production is to occur in a fully employed economy. But as hard as a society may try, reaching zero unemployment is difficult. In fact, attempting to attain zero unemployment may impose undesirable costs on society. If some workers decide to change jobs, they may find it necessary to get additional training before they are qualified for new jobs. Or if they do not need training, they may have to relocate from one part of the country to another. Another roadblock to zero unemployment occurs when individual businesses decide to reduce output or shut down, causing many workers to search for alternative employment.

There are many reasons individuals may want jobs but not have them. In a world in which economic resources are complex and varied, the probability of failing to match jobs with those people who wish them is relatively high. Consequently, it is unrealistic to define full employment as the condition where 100 percent of the labor force is employed. One purpose of this chapter is to determine what level of unemployment is acceptable as our full-employment goal.

The United States attempted to define its concept of an attainable full-employment goal through congressional action with the 1946 Employment Act. This law stated that the federal government has the responsibility "to use all practicable means consistent with its needs and obligations and other essential considerations of national policy, . . . to promote maximum employment, production, and purchasing power."* In compliance with the spirit of this act the United States government, throughout the 1950s and 1960s, generally pursued 4 percent unemployment as its full-employment goal. However, our actual unemployment rate has increased such that today some economists suggest that a 6 or 7 percent unemployment rate may be the acceptable full-employment goal.

A major reason for identifying 4 percent unemployment as a full-employment goal is the historical relationship between the level of unemployment and the rate of increase in prices. As we will see in Chapter 20, there is a definite trade-off between the goal of full employment and that of price stability.

A typical relationship between the levels of unemployment and prices is described in Figure 15–1. From approximately 1946 to 1969, prices generally rose as employment rose and output increased. Typically, as the unemployment rate fell to 4 percent or below, the inflationary rate rose to 3 percent or more.

During this period an unemployment rate of 4 percent tended to coexist with an inflationary rate of approximately 2 to 3 percent. If unemployment rose to 6 or 7 percent, the inflationary rate fell to approximately 1 percent. A reduction in unemployment to 3 percent

*_United States Statutes at Large,_ 1946, vol. 6, pt. 1, _Public Law and Reorganization Plans_ (Washington, D.C.: GPO, 1947), p. 23.

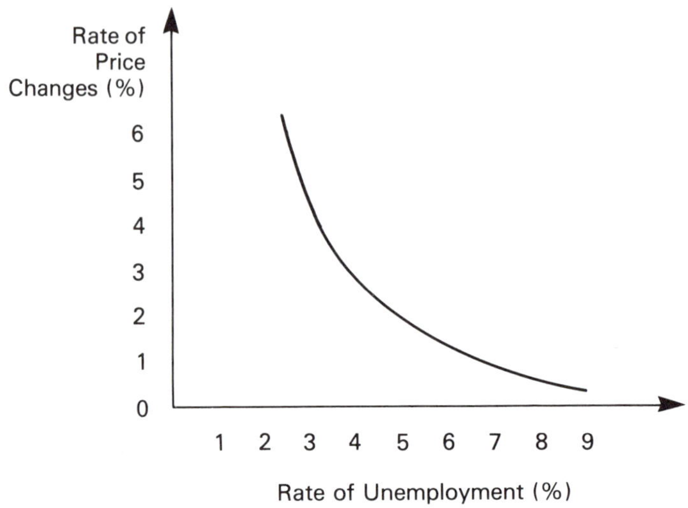

Figure 15–1 Historical Relationship of Prices and Employment

This diagram demonstrates the typical relationship between the level of employment and the rate of price changes from World War II until 1969.

generally caused prices to increase at the rate of 5 percent. Congress apparently believed that the trade-off of 4 percent unemployment and a 2 percent increase in prices was more acceptable than the alternatives. Thus, 4 percent unemployment became the full-employment goal.

Since 1969, unemployment and inflation have not demonstrated these typical trade-offs. In some years since 1969 the rates of unemployment and inflation have both been higher than desirable, increasing the complexity of the meaning of full employment and what the economy should do to achieve it. It seems important, therefore, to know exactly what we mean by employment.

SELF-TEST

2. Since there appears to be a trade-off between unemployment and inflation, can you identify some reasons why emphasis upon employment may be more desirable than emphasis on price stability? Can you think of any problems associated with this emphasis?

FULL EMPLOYMENT: WHO GETS COUNTED?

To understand the meaning of full employment, we need to have some appreciation for how employment is measured. The population is divided into two parts: the labor force and those who are not in the labor force. The following groups are not considered part of the labor force and, thus, are not officially unemployed: homemakers, students, those unable to work because of long-term disabilities, the retired (over the age of 64), the voluntarily idle (failed to search actively for work during the four weeks prior to collection of the data), and the unpaid workers in a family enterprise working less than 15 hours per week. These people are not counted because they are considered to be out of the labor force.

Rate of Employment Percentage of the work force between the ages of 16 and 64 who are engaged in the production of goods and services for a wage or salary

The labor force is divided into two parts: the employed and the unemployed. More specifically, to an economist, being employed means the service rendered by individuals between the ages of 16 and 64 in the production of goods and services for a wage or salary.

This definition immediately excludes any workers who produce goods and services for personal consumption. For example, homemakers, who care for children, clean clothes, and prepare meals are not considered part of the labor force because wages are not exchanged. Individuals who remodel their own homes or build a personal computer are not included as part of the labor force because they have not received payment for their services. (Of course, if these individuals work at other jobs for a wage or salary, they are included as part of the labor force because of those jobs.) Mentally and physically handicapped workers, and retired workers who wish to earn additional income to supplement their retirement benefits are also not included in the labor force. Consequently, when we examine the significance of the unemployment rate, we must remember that the labor statistics exclude certain individuals.

Now that we have some idea about who is included in the labor force, we still have the problem of attempting to measure the actual levels of employment and unemployment. An individual is considered employed if he or she has worked at least one hour during the week in which the data are collected. If the individual has not worked during that week because of illness, bad weather, or strike, he or she is still considered employed. The unemployed are those who did not work at all during the week the data are gathered and who are currently available for work. In addition, to be classified as unemployed a person must have actively looked for work during the previous four weeks.

Because there are some significant measurement problems, even with these distinctions, we still are not clear about what we mean by full employment or who is actually included in each classification. To be considered employed, a person need work only one hour a week. Is that classification proper if the individual wishes to work more hours? In 1975 approximately 3.5 million (4 percent of the work force) of 10.6 million part-time workers wanted full-time work but were unable to get it because their job search had been unsuccessful or because their work week had been reduced as a result of a weak economy.*

Similarly, many seasonal workers, young people seeking summer employment, and women are apt to withdraw from the labor force after a brief search for a job, even though they would work if they thought jobs were available. Women often withdraw from the labor force because low-paying jobs do not compensate enough to cover the cost of child care and other expenses associated with working. At those times when these individuals are not working, they are not considered unemployed. According to the definition of unemployment these individuals are not part of the labor force. These measurement problems are portrayed in Table 15–1, which shows how the level of unemployment changes as its measurement changes.

*_Employment and Training Report of the President_ (Washington, D.C.: GPO, 1976), pp. 181–183.

Table 15–1
Range of Unemployment Indicators Reflecting Value Judgments about Significance of Unemployment, 1974–82

	U-1 through U-7	Annual Averages 1974	1975	1980	1981	1982
U-1	Persons unemployed 15 weeks or longer as a percentage of total civilian labor force	1.0	2.7	1.8	2.0	3.2
U-2	Job losers as a percentage of civilian labor force	2.4	4.7	3.7	3.9	5.7
U-3	Unemployed household heads as a percentage of the household head labor force	3.3	5.8	4.4	4.5	7.0
U-4	Unemployed full-time job seekers as a percentage of the full-time labor force (including those employed part time for economic reasons)	5.1	8.1	6.9	7.3	9.6
U-5	Total unemployed as a percentage of civilian labor force (official measure)	5.6	8.5	7.1	7.6	9.7
U-6	Total full-time job seekers plus half part-time job seekers plus half total on part time for economic reasons as a percentage of civilian labor force less half part-time labor force	6.9	10.3	15.7	16.2	18.8
U-7	Total full-time job seekers plus half part-time job seekers plus half total on part time for economic reasons plus discouraged workers as a percentage of civilian labor force plus discouraged workers less half of part-time labor force	7.7	11.5	18.1	18.8	20.7

Source: Julius Shiskin, "Employment and Unemployment: The Doughnut or the Hole?" _Monthly Labor Review_, 99 (February 1976), 4; Bureau of Labor Statistics, _Handbook of Labor Statistics_ (Washington, D.C.: GPO, 1983), pp. 12, 23, 34, 73, 79; and _Economic Report of the President_ (Washington, D.C.: GPO, 1983), p. 200.

By redefining who should be included among the unemployed, the unemployment rate varies greatly, The definition that is the most appropriate depends heavily upon the goals and values of the society. The reasoning behind each classification is as follows:

- **U-1** If a person has been unemployed for 15 weeks or more, the unemployment is considered a serious problem that is causing financial hardship.
- **U-2** This classification measures the percentage of workers who have lost their jobs in the last year. The implication is that someone who has lost his or her job will experience more-serious problems than someone entering or reentering the labor market.
- **U-3** This classification measures the heads of households who are unemployed, assuming that loss of the income of the major income-earner is the more serious problem.
- **U-4** This measure represents the percentage of persons seeking full-time jobs. This statistic assumes that persons looking for full-time work are more attached to the labor force and that their unemployment is more meaningful than that of marginally attached workers.
- **U-5** This is the official, regularly published series that includes the rate of unemployment for all workers between 16 and 64 who are actively seeking work but cannot find jobs.
- **U-6** This measure includes unemployed persons seeking full-time and part-time work; in addition, it includes one-half of the persons who are involuntarily working at part-time jobs. The significance of this classification is that it assumes that an involuntarily part-time worker should be counted as partially unemployed.
- **U-7** This classification adds the number of discouraged workers to both the unemployed and labor force components. The assumption is that discouraged workers are not looking for jobs because they believe no work is available for them.*

Critics of the current unemployment rate come from both ends of the philosophical spectrum. Market-oriented critics prefer a measure of unemployment that would include only what they consider serious cases of joblessness, ones that we know cause extreme hardship for the household. For example, these critics might like to see the following changes:

*Julius Shiskin, "Employment and Unemployment: The Doughnut or the Hole?" *Monthly Labor Review,* 99 (February 1976), 4.

1. Do not count as unemployed anyone who has a working spouse.
2. Do not count as unemployed any teenager who is living at home with a parent who has a job.
3. Do not count as unemployed anyone who has been unemployed for less than five weeks. If the individuals are looking for their first jobs, the period of exclusion should be even longer.
4. Tighten the definition of "looking for work" to guarantee that those who say they are looking for work are actually doing so.
5. Exclude from the unemployment figures persons whose lack of education or previous job experience make them unqualified for most jobs.

Other economists would like to see different changes in the definition of unemployment. They advocate the following:

1. Everyone who wants full-time work but who can find only part-time work should be counted as at least part of an unemployed person.
2. Discouraged workers, those who would work if they thought jobs were available, should be counted as part of the labor force and unemployed.
3. Persons who are working in public employment programs, that is, jobs specifically created to relieve unemployment, should be counted as unemployed, because they have been unable to find any job in the private sector.

Conservative economists prefer unemployment rates U-1 through U-4 over the official rate U-5; more liberal economists prefer U-6 or U-7. Philosophical leanings strongly influence one's choice of a definition of unemployment.

The conservative reasoning places heavy responsibility upon the individual to search for and obtain employment. If an individual is without a job, he or she must search for one. If no job seems available, the individual should offer to work for a lower wage or salary, improve his or her job skills, move to a new location, or get a better education. In every case, the individual is the one who experiences the rewards that accompany employment as well as the costs associated with unemployment. The conservative assumption is that an unemployed person will actively pursue new sources of work because without work there is no new income and no real chance for economic advancement.

Liberal economists have a very different philosophy: Instead of emphasizing individual responsibilities, liberals argue that often people lose their jobs through little fault of their own and that the ability to find new jobs is influenced by societal forces beyond the control of the individual. For example, when someone loses his or her job because the employer goes out of business, a liberal may argue that society (government) should assist (with our tax money) that worker's search for a new job by providing some form of income support and by assisting in job training and relocation.

There is little agreement about whether those who are working should pay taxes to provide some form of public assistance to those who are not working. Would the unemployed get back into the stream of production more rapidly if they received more (or less) support from government? Would the general economic health of the society be better if the government took steps to keep the unemployment rate as low as possible, say 4 percent? What are some of the benefits and costs of pursuing such a policy?

The answers to these questions are very complex. The choice of which employment policy we wish to pursue depends very heavily upon our priorities among the economic goals. In a similar manner the choice of economic tools to change the rate of unemployment depends upon those same priorities. With these differences in mind we need to examine some of the issues that surround unemployment.

SELF-TEST

3. Explain what the Bureau of Labor Statistics (BLS) means when it reports an unemployment rate of 7.2 percent.
4. Evaluate the following statement: Discouraged workers are relatively unimportant economic resources to business firms because they have poor attachment to the labor force.

WHAT ARE THE TYPES OF UNEMPLOYMENT?

In a society that prides itself on the value of the work ethic and where an individual's personal worth is typically measured by what he or she earns, the vast majority of individuals do want jobs. In fact, they *must* work, because except for government assistance programs, family support, and crime, the only way an individual can receive an income is by contributing to production. Access to a decent standard of living depends upon working. More important, people need to work continuously and in upwardly mobile jobs to increase their incomes and stature in the community. Yet during the past decade, we have seen the unemployment rate rise to 10 percent, a rate that indicates unemployment of over 11 million workers. The length of unemployment lines increased, general productivity of the economy fell, the average number of hours worked declined, and the call for government assistance rose. Why?

As we have already indicated, the answer is not simple. It is highly improbable that we could point to just one or a few causes and claim a thorough understanding of the unemployment problem. However, we can simplify the complexity by categorizing unemployment into different types, and we can identify some different influences affecting the employment potential of people who fall into those types. Policy recommendations will also be affected by the extent to which more than one cause influences the level of unemployment. Initially, we need to define three causes of unemployment and how they differ from one another.

Frictional Unemployment

In a perfect economy, all the units of labor, capital, and natural resources would blend together smoothly so that each factor of production would be contributing as efficiently as possible to the productive capacity of the economy. (This outcome is the consequence of the competitive equilibrium of $P = MC$ discussed in Chapter 5.) In this type of economy, unemployment cannot exist because there is no friction in the society; that is, all attempts to use the factors of production fully will result in a perfect matching of the available labor with capital and natural resources. Workers will be able to find jobs at wages that equate the demand for labor with the supply of labor. If workers wish to change jobs, they will quit their current jobs and accept employment with other employers. Because all resources are highly compatible, there is no reason for any delay in reemployment, therefore, no *frictional unemployment*.

Frictional Unemployment Short periods of unemployment that are experienced by people who are moving between jobs or entering the labor market.

However, we all recognize that this perfect economy is not very descriptive of the world in which we live. People who want to work may have difficulty locating jobs that match their skills and interests. The time between the start of a job search and the acquisition of a job often presents the economy with costs that are unavoidable. Attempts to reduce the costs of linking those workers with jobs often cause those costs to increase and lead to an increase in the general level of prices.

Potentially, the harder we try to reduce the time that people take to move from job to job or search for their first job, the greater the upward pressure on prices is likely to be. Thus, we get the term *frictional unemployment* from attempts to reduce this type of unemployment. As unemployment moves toward zero, friction will heat up the economy in the form of higher prices.

For example, as the economy expands toward its full-employment level of output, consumers will earn more income and increase their spending. As consumers' spending increases, firms will attempt to expand production and, consequently, hire more workers. However, because the economy is approaching its full-employment potential, the available workers may not have the proper skills or be in the right geographic location for the job.

Even when the employer is ready to hire, both the employer and the potential employee may experience delays in making contact and actually completing the hiring. These delays cause friction in the economy that results in increases in prices. If, for example, company A needs more workers to expand production, company A may entice workers to quit their jobs with other companies and take jobs at company A for higher wages. These higher wages will increase costs without increasing productivity. These higher costs will force prices to rise and cause inflation.

As a result of this friction, society has generally accepted the view that 100 percent employment of all those people who wish to work is an unrealistic goal. Some potential workers will get caught in this frictional struggle and experience some unemployment. Fortunately, the percentage of workers who fall into this category is generally small (this point is debatable, and we will examine it more closely later in this chapter) and the length of unemployment is generally short.

Workers who become frictionally unemployed fall into the following categories:

1. A worker who has resigned to look for another job
2. An individual who is a new entrant into the labor market and who has some difficulty in making a first job connection
3. A worker who has been laid off but experiences only a short period of unemployment
4. A worker who is temporarily out of work because of the seasonal nature of the job, for example, construction.

These characteristics of frictionally unemployed workers suggest that the hardship caused by this type of unemployment will be temporary and not unduly severe. For example, a person who quits one job to find another generally will not take that action unless he or she expects to find a new job quickly. A seasonal worker may or may not like the idea that a particular type of work such as construction slows down during the cold months, but typically jobs will become available again as soon as the weather changes.

Most economists agree that there is very little that can or should be done about frictional unemployment. In fact, most economists argue that we should not try to reduce frictional unemployment, because the relatively small gain in reduced unemployment would not be worth the significant increase in inflation that might result from attempts to reach the theoretical full-employment output.

The major debate about frictional unemployment concerns the number of people who actually fall into this category. For example, some economists argue that changes in the age and sex composition of the labor force have caused an increase in the frictional unemployment rate. A possible cause of such an increase would be the expanded number of women and youth who have recently entered the labor force, resulting in a general increase in the degree of competition for jobs. Thus the average unemployment rate tends to be higher today than it would have been if the rates of women's and youth's participation in the labor force had not changed.

If part of the increase in the rate of unemployment in the 1970s was caused by the increased number of women and youth in the labor force, then, some economists argue, we simply must accept a higher rate of frictional unemployment or risk greater inflationary pressures. Other economists argue, however, that the new workers are an important source of production, so we need to find ways to integrate them into the production cycle of the economy. In either case, your task as a student of economics is to appreciate some of the consequences of using different definitions of frictional unemployment and to evaluate economic policy recommendations in light of these consequences. You will be given this opportunity in Chapter 18.

SELF-TEST

5. Explain why it is important to understand that some unemployment is considered frictional.
6. Can you explain what benefits the economy may experience if we accept a low rate (2%–4%) of frictional unemployment?
7. What might be some benefits of a high rate (5%–6%)?
8. Assume a presidential advisor has argued that since many households have more than one income-earner, temporary unemployment is not a serious problem. In fact, she argued that these workers will typically take a longer time to select a new

job. Consequently, she believes a 6 percent frictional unemployment rate is acceptable. Evaluate this statement.

Cyclical Unemployment

Recession An economic period when the level of real output and employment has declined for two successive quarters

Cyclical Unemployment Unemployment resulting from an inadequate level of total demand for all goods and services

Probably the most commonly reported cause of unemployment is the change in the level of business activity. When the economy is experiencing a high level of economic activity, unemployment tends to be lower than when the economy is experiencing a *recession.* Typically, *cyclical unemployment* will increase as a result of a reduction in the level of total production in the economy. For some reason consumers purchase less and business decreases the level of its spending on new plants and equipment. Consequently, sales of all types of products will decline, business inventories will rise, and firms will not need as many workers. The result will be increased layoffs.

Cyclical unemployment results when the demand for workers falls below the available supply of labor at the existing wage rates. For example, during a recession fewer people buy automobiles, and auto production is reduced. Auto workers who lose their jobs because of this reduced production will most likely look for work at other auto plants and auto-related manufacturers. But if employment is down at one auto company, it may be down at all auto plants and auto-related companies. As a result, we find unemployed workers who want jobs but who usually resign themselves to the idea that acceptable job opportunities will not occur until the recession is over. The demand for work is greater than the supply of jobs.

Cyclical unemployment is considered a more serious problem than frictional unemployment because it is involuntary and it lasts longer. Consequently, cyclical unemployment results in considerable disruption to the families of the unemployed and has a significant negative effect on the level of production in the entire economy. The cost of cyclical unemployment includes this loss of output as well as the personal hardship that is experienced by those who have lost their jobs and their primary source of income.

The labor force numbers over 110 million workers. When the economy experiences an economic slowdown, over 1 million additional workers lose their jobs every time the unemployment rate increases by one percentage point. Since many of these unemployed workers are heads of households, not only do those workers lose their source of income but so also do the family dependents. When unemployment lasts for more than a few months, entire household units suffer a significant reduction in their standard of living.

Virtually all economists agree that we should keep the rate of cyclical unemployment at a minimum. But as we identified previously, there is disagreement over where frictional unemployment ends and cyclical unemployment begins. If we accept 4 percent unemployment as frictional unemployment, then we will be more assertive about reducing a 6 percent unemployment rate than if we believe that frictional unemployment is best represented by a 5.5 percent unemployment rate. Thus, thinking about alternative definitions is critical to evaluating employment policies. The acceptance of a particular definition is dependent upon how you prioritize the economic goals.

SELF-TEST

9. How does cyclical unemployment differ from frictional unemployment?
10. If you were unemployed, would you prefer the cause to be labeled as cyclical or frictional? Why?
11. From the perspective of the entire economy, what are the consequences of reduced cyclical unemployment? frictional unemployment? Why are these consequences different?

Structural Unemployment

Frictional unemployment may be associated with job-hopping or temporary periods of unemployment that are endured while individuals search for the right job. In many cases the demand for and supply of jobs are equal, but there is often a temporary adjustment period that occurs as workers and employers arrive at the best mutual arrangement. This type of unemployment is usually considered unavoidable and not very threatening to the economy.

Cyclical unemployment results from a decline in economic activity, a recession, that leaves the demand for jobs higher than the supply of jobs. Workers want jobs, but a sufficient number of vacancies do not exist. The level of cyclical unemployment is directly linked to the level of economic activity. Most economists agree that cyclical unemployment is a more serious concern than frictional unemployment.

A third potential source of unemployment is structural changes in the economy that may cause differences between the skills possessed by the unemployed and the skills demanded by employers. For example, in the early 1970s the United States government dramatically reduced its space efforts, causing a significant reduction in the need for physicists and aerospace engineers. Also, throughout the 1970s and 1980s, United States industry reduced its use of domestically produced steel and increased its use of substitute metals and plastics and foreign steel. This change in the demand for steel caused a significant reduction in the demand for American steel workers.

Both examples demonstrate how a change in demand is likely to have long-term effects on the availability of certain types of jobs. Although the physicists and aerospace engineers were highly trained, well paid, and willing to move to new locations, they had serious difficulty in finding comparable jobs after the reduction in space exploration. In fact, many of them experienced significant periods of unemployment. The steelworkers also experienced unemployment problems because jobs requiring their skills and interests were and are often not available.

Workers may also lose their jobs because of technological changes. For instance, as some manufacturers increase their use of robots, the number of workers necessary in those firms may decrease. It is true that there will be an increased demand for workers to help build and maintain the robots, but the required skills for these new jobs are often dramatically different from the skills necessary to perform the jobs that are now handled by robots. Consequently, while demand for one type of worker (usually workers with very specific skills) increases, the demand for other workers (often semi-skilled or skilled in very different areas) declines.

Regardless of whether the society has experienced significant changes in demand (for example, space and steel) or changes in technology (for example, robots), we may find a mismatch of the demand for and supply of labor. Employers often have job openings, and workers are looking for work; yet the skills demanded by the employer are not possessed by the unemployed. When this mismatch occurs, the economy suffers from *structural unemployment*.

Structural Unemployment
Unemployment caused by a mismatch of the characteristics of the unemployed and the characteristics desired by the potential employer

Another potential cause of structural unemployment is the changing composition of the labor force. Since the mid-1960s, the age and sex composition of the labor force has changed significantly. During the past two decades the number of youth entering the labor force has increased dramatically because of the post-World War II baby boom. As these youths began looking for work, there were more relatively unskilled workers attempting to get jobs than the economy was accustomed to hiring. The baby boom caused a change in the expected availability of labor, especially that of relatively unskilled and inexperienced workers.

Coincidentally, the women's movement gained strength in the United States. Women entered the labor force at an increased rate. In 1960 only 37.6 percent of women over 20 years old participated in the labor force, but by 1983, 53.1% of women were participating. According to labor statistics over the past ten years, the unemployment rate has grown because the increased labor participation by youth and women has made it more difficult for all workers to get jobs. To the extent that these changes do not seem to be flashy trends that will disappear in a year or two, we appear to be experiencing a significant change in the structure of the labor force. In addition, to the extent that these new workers are relatively unskilled, particularly youths, these new workers add to the increasing mismatch of the skills needed by employees and the skills possessed by the workers. The result has been substantial structural unemployment.

There is some controversy about this view of structural unemployment. Some economists claim that structural unemployment is no more than frictional unemployment. They argue that the rapid rise in the number of youth and women in the labor force simply increased the difficulty of the job search because of greater competition among workers. Since many of the new entrants were not the primary income earners in a household, they could take a longer time to find a job, and they might quit a job more readily. Consequently, these economists argue that both the changing composition of the labor force and the changing skill levels required by technological advances increase the rate of frictional unemployment. These economists view this tendency to experience a higher unemployment rate as normal and an acceptable cost of a technological society.

Advocates of this position argue that we should accept a higher unemploymemt rate as a full-employment goal. By doing so we will create fewer inflationary pressures on the economy. Also, by claiming that it is more difficult to absorb all the workers into the labor force, those who accept a higher level of unemployment as normal or natural permit policymakers to ignore the unemployment problem rather than adopt some form of direct governmental intervention to decrease unemployment and increase the level of national output.

To the extent that structural factors are considered significant causes of unemployment, we need to consider specific policies to attempt to reduce them. Since the causes of structural unemployment differ from the causes of cyclical unemployment, stimulating the economy to expand output is not likely to reduce the unemployment caused by structural forces. Even though an expansion in output is likely to increase job opportunities, the structurally unemployed worker is unlikely to possess the proper skills to perform the tasks required by the job.

For example, if the economy experiences a significant expansion in total demand, it is still unlikely that the demand for aerospace engineers will increase. Other areas of production, such as housing, autos, and clothing, are likely to expand because of the demand stimulus. Since the employers of these products do not need aerospace engineers, the worker with these skills will not be able to find a new job. However, as the demand for construction and auto workers expands, there will be a relative shortage of workers with these skills, and the wages in these markets will tend to rise. As a consequence a general stimulus to the economy as a solution to structural unemployment is more likely to cause inflation than it is to reduce structural unemployment.

Previously we stated that attempts to reduce frictional unemployment would result in inflation, and we concluded that society should not attempt to reduce the percentage of workers who are frictionally unemployed. If we reached this conclusion about frictional unemployment, should we reach the same conclusion about structural unemployment? And if we do reach the same conclusion, why should we distinguish between frictional and structural unemployment?

Structural unemployment differs from frictional unemployment with respect to causes and duration. In addition, many economists believe that structural unemployment can be reduced without undue pressure on inflation. Frictionally unemployed workers are usually in transition, between jobs. Any given worker does not experience long periods of unemployment. On the other hand, structurally unemployed workers will have significantly greater difficulty in locating new jobs, especially at comparable wages.

Thus, the cost to the employed are substantially higher for structurally unemployed workers than for frictionally unemployed workers. If structurally unemployed workers acquire appropriate skills, their unemployment will be reduced; total output will increase; and the economy will not experience undue inflationary pressures.

A major policy question we must resolve is whether the economy should direct resources toward reducing structural unemployment or whether the economy should concentrate on increasing total output and assume that the resulting unemployment rate is the most desirable rate for the economy. Before we can make this decision we need to examine how an economic system functions and why it experiences periods of unemployment. Then we can study how we can use economic tools to reduce unemployment. These issues will be the focus of the next chapter.

SELF-TEST

12. How does structural unemployment differ from cyclical unemployment?
13. If you were experiencing unemployment, would you prefer the cause to be labeled cyclical or structural? Why?
14. Evaluate the following statement: After reading this material on the types of unemployment, I have discovered that frictional unemployment and structural unemployment are the same, in that job vacancies exist, but available workers do not match up with the jobs. Also, for both types of unemployment, if we stimulate demand, unemployment is unlikely to fall, but inflation will probably rise. Since these two types of unemployment are so similar, we should not treat them differently.

ACTIVE REVIEW

1. Virtually everyone agrees that full employment is desirable, yet around the world different countries appear to have different levels of success in achieving that goal. It would seem likely that if some countries can achieve relatively low unemployment rates, the United States could do so also. Yet, our unemployment rate is typically higher than that of many European countries. In the halls of the University of Excellence two professors raised the following points about this problem:

   PROFESSOR SWARTZ. I was examining the rate of unemployment in the United States and discovered that although the average rate for the past 5 years is higher today than the average unemployment rate during the 1950s, we should not be unduly concerned, because the primary wage earners are being employed at approximately the same rate over the two periods.

   PROFESSOR ANDERSEN. It is true that the composition of the labor force has changed over time, but how can you ignore the potential output that is lost as a result of keeping labor resources idle? Regardless of whether individuals are the primary wage earners or not, if they are unemployed, they are not contributing to the GNP.

   PROFESSOR SWARTZ. In the abstract you are correct, Andersen, but you must consider the reality of modern-day societies. Not all people are ready to work when you and I think they should be working. Instead they take some time to assess job alternatives before they rush into a new employment commitment.

   PROFESSOR ANDERSEN. It is true that some workers will experience temporary bouts of unemployment because of what we call frictional unemployment. However, we cannot explain the increased level of unemployment by claiming that it is just more difficult today to match workers with jobs. The very nature of the demand for labor is changing.

PROFESSOR SWARTZ. Oh, you are claiming that there has been an increase in structural unemployment. Maybe you are right, but I do not understand why you are so concerned. As the demand for increasing numbers of skilled workers expand, the wages of workers with those skills will also rise. These higher wages will encourage more workers to gain the appropriate skills necessary for these jobs. As more and more workers gain these skills, the so-called structural problem will disappear.

a. How does Professor Swartz's idea of unemployment compare with the official rate of unemployment that is used by the Bureau of Labor Statistics? Why might Professor Swartz think that this distinction is useful?

b. Does Professor Andersen also disagree with the official definition? If he does disagree, are his unemployment rates likely to be higher or lower than the official rates? If his definition is similar to the official, explain why.

c. Professor Swartz basically believes that much of our current unemployment is unavoidable because the workers have chosen to remain unemployed. Under what conditions does this position make sense?

d. Do the labels of *frictional unemployment* and *structural unemployment* really identify different types of unemployment? Explain.

e. Evaluate Professor Swartz's final statement, which argues that the normal competitive forces of demand and supply will correct any problems associated with structural unemployment.

2. Evaluate the following statement: During times of economic growth and prosperity, the rate of cyclical unemployment will be very low, but at the same time the economy could experience frictional and structural unemployment. If high levels of economic activity will not reduce frictional and structural unemployment, then these two types of unemployment must be impossible to reduce.

ANSWERS TO ACTIVE REVIEW

1a. If we were to use Professor Swartz' definition of unemployment, the rate of unemployment would be lower than the official rate. Swartz argues that we need to be concerned about unemployment only when it causes hardship. In his mind a family can still maintain an adequate standard of living if the head of the household is still employed.

Swartz finds this distinction important because he does not want to interfere with market activity unless he believes that the costs associated with unemployment are sufficiently high. He apparently equates costs with personal and household loss of income rather than with output lost to the entire economy. By making this distinction Professor Swartz can reduce his concern about unemployment and increase his concern about other economic goals.

1b. Given what Professor Andersen has said, she probably agrees with the official definition that anyone between the ages of 16 and 64 who is looking for work should be considered unemployed. She sees these unemployed workers as individuals who wish to contribute to production but cannot because they are unable to find employment.

1c. Professor Swartz believes that many unemployed workers are willing to exchange work for leisure at the existing wage rate. Also, assuming that another member of the household is working, the unemployed are willing to take a longer period of time to search for the "right" job. If workers are able to do without their incomes while they are experiencing unemployment, then, according to Swartz, they must not be in great need. If workers still cannot find employment, even at lower wages, then Swartz would agree that unemployment is a significant problem.

1d. Both frictional and structural unemployment identify a condition where jobs exist, but unemployed workers have not linked up with those jobs. However, there is a major difference in the time it takes to accomplish the linking of the unemployed workers with the jobs that are vacant. Professor Swartz apparently believes that most unemployment is frictional and that this matching of workers to jobs is a relatively simple process. Consequently, he argues that governmental officials should not take any special action to speed up the process of reducing unemployment.

Professor Andersen argues that a significant percentage of the unemployed workers do not have jobs because of structural reasons. Employers want to hire workers with specific skills, but the unemployed do not possess those skills. In many cases workers may need a year or two of training to acquire the necessary skills. If unemployment is caused by such a mismatch in the demand for and supply of these skills, then the problems associated with reaching full employment are more complex.

1e. Professor Swartz has described the basic functioning of demand and supply curves, *ceteris paribus*. As the demand for specifically skilled workers increases from D_1 to D_2, wages for those workers will rise from W_1 to W_2. Workers who do not have these skills will be motivated by the higher wage rate (W_2) to learn the appropriate skills. As they learn these skills, the quantity of skilled labor will increase Q_2, and the unemployment problem will diminish (see Figure 15a).

However, Professor Swartz has made a critical *ceteris paribus* assumption. In this case he is assuming that the anticipation of a

Figure 15a

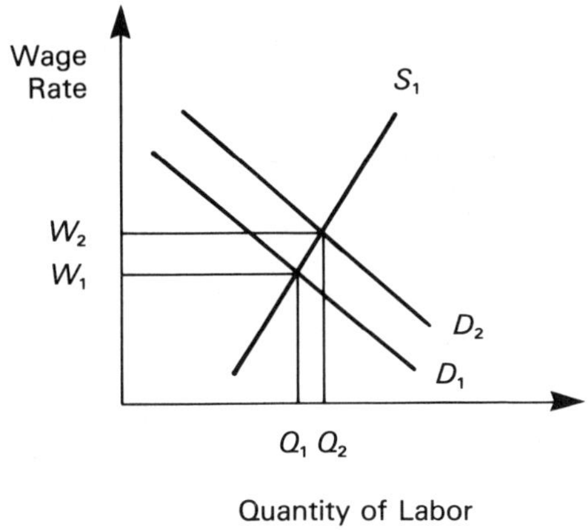

higher wage will attract more workers to these jobs that require specific skills. If these skills require two years of training, how are unemployed workers going to pay for the training and still care for their families at the same time? Professor Swartz is assuming that the costs associated with getting the new jobs are insignificant. If he is incorrect in this assumption, then the use of simple demand and supply analysis is inappropriate, because a training barrier hinders the entry of new workers.

If unemployment is structural as Andersen suggests, the supply of these specifically skilled workers will not increase as Swartz argued. Rather, the properly skilled workers will receive higher wages, and the improperly skilled workers will not have jobs. The anticipated higher wages will not pay for the training or put food on the table. The long training period will dramatically reduce the ability of workers to gain the appropriate skills.

ANSWERS TO SELF-TEST

1. If someone is unemployed, we should be concerned for reasons of compassion, but we also have some good, economic reason to be concerned. First of all, if people are unemployed, they obviously are not producing goods and services that could increase the GNP and the general standard of living in the economy. As the proportion of the labor force that is working increases, the probability of my standard of living increasing also rises. Second, as unemployment falls, the level of government support payments will also fall. Consequently, there will be a reduced need for higher taxes as well as an increased capacity to meet other social needs.
2. Whenever a trade-off exists there must be both positive and negative consequences to the pursuit of one goal over another. Some major

reasons for giving full employment priority over price stability are (1) the impact on GNP (a 1 percent increase in the rate of unemployment will decrease GNP by 2 to 3%), (2) higher standard of living for the entire economy, and (3) decreased governmental spending on support programs as the number of unemployed drops. However, if the attempt to reach full employment is not watched carefully, the economy may experience significant inflationary pressures, which may cause some negative consequences, especially with respect to production decisions by business.

3. The BLS defines an unemployed worker as anyone between the ages of 16 and 64 who is actively looking for work but cannot find a job. This person can be any member of a household who has contacted potential employers some time during the previous four weeks. A person who has worked at all, even one hour for pay during the previous four weeks, is considered to be employed.

4. According to this statement discouraged workers are not very important because they have poor work commitments. If they really wanted jobs, they would look harder for work, and they would be willing to accept lower pay. However, this position ignores the argument that if the discouraged workers had jobs, they could add to the production of the economy. The major issue is whether the discouraged workers could be productive. If so, then the statement is inaccurate.

5. If we do not recognize that movement between jobs does not always occur simultaneously or that job interests and skills do not always match the job vacancies, then we place undue emphasis on the desirability of reducing unemployment to zero. More specifically, since frictional unemployment is caused by workers moving from job to job, attempts to reduce this unemployment may force workers who wish to move to different locations to stay where they are. Employers may be forced to hire workers who are not properly trained, because as employment drops toward zero the available supply of trained workers will also decrease. In both cases there will be an upward pressure on wages, which will probably cause inflation.

6. The preceding answer suggests that attempts to reduce the number of workers who are frictionally unemployed will lead to inflation. Yet that answer does not indicate whether frictional unemployment should be set at 2 percent, 4 percent, 5 percent, or whatever. If we as a society are capable of minimizing the problems of matching the unemployed to jobs, then we have, in effect, released more resources for productive use. As more workers can be employed productively, the general level of production in the economy will expand. Consequently, if an economy is capable of removing some of the causes of frictional unemployment, then the probability of reducing unemployment and increasing production without stimulating inflation is very high.

7. If frictional unemployment is caused by societal conditions that are not likely to be corrected (for example, more women entering the labor market, increased social payments such as unemployment compensation, and increased demand for highly trained labor), then attempts to reduce that rate will typically result in inflation rather than reduced unemployment. If we accept the argument that frictional unemployment cannot be reduced below 6 percent, we can devote our energy to attempting to keep inflation under control. In essence, we would be admitting that this higher percentage of workers will not have jobs, but justify the high level of unemployment on the grounds that its existence permits the economy to function more smoothly.
8. This presidential advisor prefers the U-3 definition of unemployment, which emphasizes household income rather than the income of an individual. She emphasizes that other income-earners in the household will keep the families from suffering unduly. But even though a household does have more than one income-earner, unemployment of one of the members may result in loss of half of their income. Just as important, the economy has lost the productive service of the unemployed. Especially in relation to this last point, the presidential advisor is correct only if the unemployed were unproductive workers.
9. Cyclical unemployment results from a reduction in economic activity. When businesses experience reduced sales, they tend to decrease the number of workers they are willing to employ. The workers tend to remain unemployed until economic activity improves. Frictional unemployment, on the other hand, typically occurs as a result of *temporary* adjustments in the labor market. For example, (1) if workers change jobs, there may be a period of time before a new job is found, (2) new workers entering the job market may have some difficulty in securing their first jobs, and (3) some workers will be temporarily unemployed because of seasonal changes. However, in most cases workers who are considered frictionally unemployed will be able to gain employment more easily than workers who are unemployed because of cyclical reasons.
10. A frictionally unemployed worker is likely to experience unemployment that is voluntary and of relatively short duration because jobs are available and he or she has access to those jobs. The primary reasons workers experience cyclical unemployment are because unemployment is typically involuntary and jobs are less available during a recession. Thus, if you must experience unemployment, you would prefer to be identified as frictionally unemployed because you would expect that the probability of getting a job would be better.
11. As we reduce the number of workers who are cyclically unemployed, there should be a direct increase in output (GNP). Because cyclical unemployment causes a reduction in the use of all factors of production, there are idle productive resources waiting to be used when

employment increases. As a result, an increase in cyclical employment causes an increase in real output (GNP) without causing an increase in inflation. Whereas, these idle resources are not as available when only frictional unemployment exists. Frictionally unemployed workers may not be unemployed for long periods, but there are large numbers of workers affected. Frictional unemployment is associated with labor movement or transition rather than with a lack of jobs. Even if the economy wanted to hire more workers, frictional unemployment would still exist. Consequently, if action is taken to stimulate the economy when only frictional unemployment exists, we are likely to experience inflationary pressure.

12. Structurally unemployed workers may lose their jobs even when general economic activity is strong, because of either a change in demand for products or a technological change. When the United States decreased its space efforts, the need for aerospace engineers dropped dramatically. These workers had trouble finding engineering jobs because relatively few were available even though the general level of economic activity had not changed.

    In a similar vein the introduction of more computers into the workplace reduces the need for people to do repetitive work, but computers require an increase in the number of workers with particular skills. If the less skilled workers do not learn these new skills, they will probably become structurally unemployed.

    Stimulating economic activity is not likely to produce the same results for the structurally unemployed as it is for cyclically unemployed workers, because the structurally unemployed workers are not likely to have the appropriate skills for the available jobs. If a significant training period exists, then the economy will experience inflationary pressure at least until the structurally unemployed workers gain the appropriate skills. In contrast, cyclical unemployment is caused by a recession. Under this condition cyclically unemployed workers should be able to regain the jobs they vacated and begin producing efficiently as soon as they are rehired, without any need for additional training.

13. Structural unemployment requires workers to gain additional training that may require several months or years and may be very expensive. If you are a 40-year-old worker with a family and you become structurally unemployed, where will you find the money to finance your job training? As a cyclically unemployed worker, you find it difficult to live on the reduced income of unemployment benefits. How will you manage to support yourself on unemployment benefits and pay for training at the same time? If you have to be unemployed and have your choice, it is preferable to be unemployed for cyclical reasons.

14. On the surface this statement is accurate. Nevertheless, there is a significant difference between the two types of unemployment. In the case of frictional unemployment, the time necessary to locate a

new job or acquire appropriate skills is relatively short. For example, a worker may gain his or her new skill by receiving training while on the job.

In the case of structural unemployment, the time necessary to locate a new job or acquire appropriate skills is significantly longer and requires considerable expense. However, structural unemployment can be reduced and real GNP can be increased if specific action is taken to assist structurally unemployed workers to gain appropriate skills. Similar attempts to reduce frictional unemployment are unlikely to produce corresponding results, because workers who are frictionally unemployed are likely to move from job to job regardless of the economic conditions.

16

Fundamental Economic Relationships and Full Employment

In the previous chapter we discussed the importance of full employment as a goal, but we did not discuss any methods for achieving that goal. A primary reason for delaying that discussion is the need to use this chapter to study certain relationships that exist within an economic system. Once we understand these relationships, we will gain a greater appreciation for the beauty and complexity of our economic system, and we will be prepared to grapple with many of the questions that surround the goal of full employment.

HOW CAN WE ACHIEVE FULL EMPLOYMENT?

The answer to this question requires us to understand some basic relationships that exist within any type of economic society. Although these relationships can become very complex in our modern world, there are fundamental principles that explain employment. Understanding them should help us gain a better grasp of why we experience periodic bouts of unemployment and why certain types of action may be needed to achieve more desirable levels of employment.

The most basic economic rule is that virtually all economic activity begins with production. If you remember the concept of scarcity in Chapter 1, you know that we desire to have more goods and services than are available. We used a production-possibility curve to help us understand that even when we are producing to our maximum ability, we experience opportunity costs as we alter the composition of the goods and services that we wish to consume.

Furthermore, in Chapter 15 we learned that if our economy is producing a level of output that is inside the production-possibility curve, we are experiencing unemployment and significant losses to the standard of living. (Remember, Okun's Law states that every increase in unemployment by 1 percent causes the GNP to fall by 2 to 3 percent.) Thus, there seems to be a clear need to keep production levels as high as possible. Yet the United States has not been particularly adept at maintaining a high employment and production level (see Table 16–1).

If we assume that an economy that functions close to its potential full employment will approach full utilization of its manufacturing capacity, then utilization rates below 90 percent would indicate that the economy is sacrificing a considerable level of production. Only

Table 16–1 Relationship of Capacity Utilization and Unemployment, 1960–83
This table shows the rate at which we have used our productive resources.

	Capacity Utilization Rate in Manufacturing	Unemployment Rate
1960	80.2%	5.5%
1961	77.4	6.7
1962	81.6	5.5
1963	83.5	5.7
1964	85.6	5.2
1965	89.6	4.5
1966	91.1	3.8
1967	86.9	3.8
1968	87.1	3.6
1969	86.2	3.5
1970	79.3	4.9
1971	78.4	5.9
1972	83.5	5.6
1973	87.6	4.9
1974	83.6	5.6
1975	72.9	8.5
1976	79.5	7.7
1977	81.9	7.1
1978	84.4	6.1
1979	85.7	5.8
1980	79.1	7.1
1981	78.5	7.6
1982	71.1	9.7
1983	75.3	9.6
1984	81.8	7.5
1985	80.7	7.2

Source: *Economic Report of the President* (Washington, D.C.: GPO, 1986), pp. 271, 283.

during the Vietnam buildup (1966) did utilization of manufacturing capacity rise above 90 percent, and during seven years (33 percent of the time between 1960 and 1981) capacity utilization fell below 80 percent. These output data match the resulting unemployment rates. As the rate of capacity utilization rises, the rate of unemployment tends to fall, and when capacity utilization falls, the rate of unemployment tends to rise. This relationship demonstrates Okun's law that a change in the rate of unemployment has a significant effect on the level of GNP, because the level of GNP falls when the rate of capacity utilization falls and vice versa.

It seems intuitively sound that businesses do not want 10 percent of their productive capacity lying idle. It also seems obvious that workers prefer to work and earn income rather than to be unemployed and not earn income. Thus, there must be some explanation of why economies suffer periodic bouts of unemployment.

Theoretically, we can make the argument that production will generate the income necessary to purchase all production. In a perfectly functioning economy, production is the source of all income, and income is the source of all spending. Because people tend to spend their income on production, we find a natural circular relationship among these three concepts.

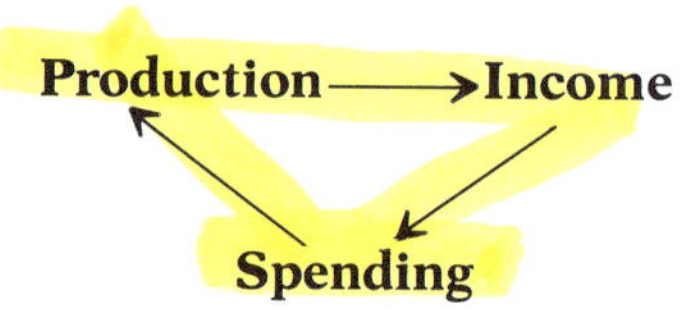

If this relationship functions smoothly, then an economy could not experience unemployment, because producers would always want to keep production levels high, since they know that their production will generate the income necessary to permit the purchase of their products. If all production is not purchased, it is apparent that some of the income is not being transformed into spending, reducing the need for production. If production is decreased, income will fall. This decline in income will most likely cause a further reduction in spending.

HOUSEHOLD AND BUSINESS SECTORS

We can build on this basic relationship between production, income, and spending by adding some sectors to this simple economic model. In any economic community individuals are both producers and consumers.

On the one hand, individuals are producers, because they provide labor and other factors of production to businesses. On the other hand, those same individuals are also consumers, because they spend their income on goods and services. For example, the president and employees of IBM are responsible for getting the proper number and quality of computers to those who wish to purchase them. But at the same time the president and employees are also purchasing clothing, cars, stereos, medical care, etc. By recognizing that each individual plays a dual role in an economy, we can appreciate the circular relationship between the three activities of production, income and spending.

This basic relationship is demonstrated in Figure 16–1. Because of the interactive nature of this model, it is not clear who actually starts the process. In reality, simultaneous decisions are made. But for purposes of simplification, we will begin the process with households that (1) demand goods and services from businesses. The households register this demand by offering to spend their income (2) on goods and services (3) that businesses are willing to sell. In response to this demand (1) the businesses (3) supply the goods and services to the households. This interaction between households and businesses occurs in the product market that was described in Chapter 4, where we discussed the efficient operation of a business.

This relationship is not complete, however, until we explain how

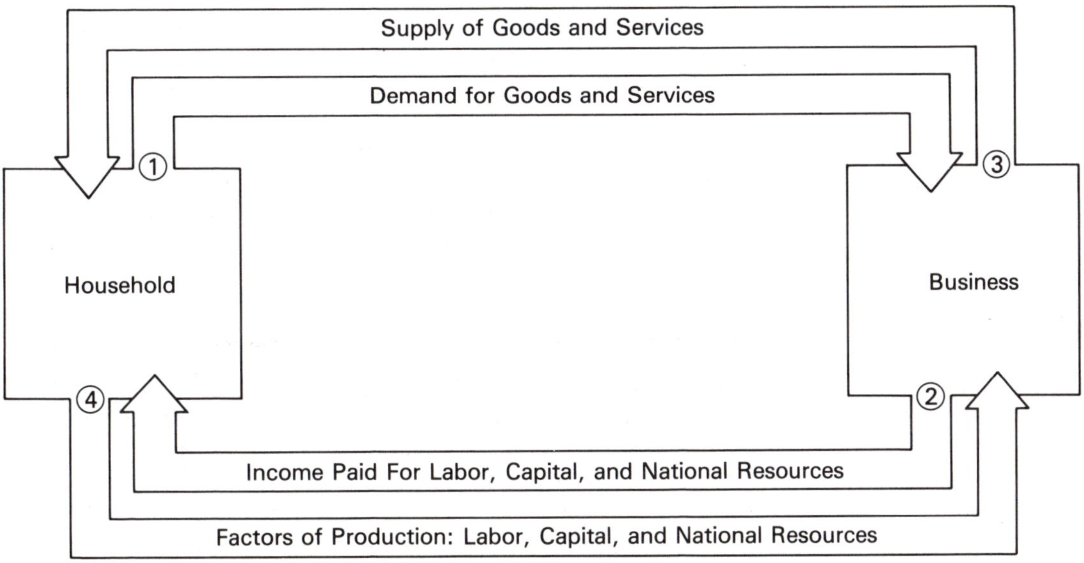

Figure 16–1
Circular Flow of Income

This diagram shows the relationship between the buying and selling of products and the buying and selling of the factors of production.

Factors of Production
The resources of labor, capital, and raw materials that are necessary to produce goods and services

businesses produce the goods and services that are sold to the households. A business responds to this demand by purchasing *factors of production* (2) from the households. In essence, businesses offer households income (2) in the form of wages, salaries, interest, rent, and profit. Businesses are able to pay this income because households have spent their income on goods and services identified in step (1).

Because households wish to spend, they are willing to contribute to the production process by providing businesses with the factors of production (4) (labor, capital, and natural resources) that are necessary for producing the goods and services (3) demanded by households. Hence, we have a circular relationship indicating that households cannot consume (1) unless they earn income (2) by contributing to the production process (4), and businesses will not produce (4) unless households are willing to spend their income (2) on the goods and services (3) produced by those businesses. By using this simple model we restate the importance of the production-income-spending relationship and how changes in any one of the variables will have an effect upon the other two variables.

SELF-TEST

1. Explain why the value of production must equal the value of income.
2. Evaluate the following statement: John and Maria are discussing the economy and its unacceptably high unemployment rates. John states that all we need to do is increase the level of spending, and employment levels will expand. But Maria argues that we need to stimulate production first. What do you think?

SAVING AND INVESTMENT

If we constantly remind ourselves that production, income, and spending are related in a dynamic way, we will be able to gain a greater appreciation of how the economy functions. As long as the spending level in the economy continues to equal the value of production, income will flow smoothly through the economy from consumer to producer and back to the consumer in the form of income.

In addition, if the economy is operating on its production possibilities curve (described in Chapter 2), there will be full employment. However, as you may have guessed, the economy doesn't operate quite that smoothly. There is no guarantee that the economy will be operating on its production possibilities curve. Although production, income, and spending will always be equal, the economy may be functioning at a level below its potential. Consequently, we need to expand our model to understand how unemployment may occur.

If we reflect for a moment we will quickly realize that consumption is not the only way the members of an economy spend their income. Businesses spend through investment activities, and government spends on social goods and services. When businesses expand the size of their production facilities, they generally need financial resources beyond what they earn from selling goods and services. Yet, the model presented in Figure 16–1 does not include any additional sources of revenue for investment purposes. Obviously, that model is incomplete, and we must add a source of investment funds.

Investment A form of spending that causes a change in the ability to produce goods and services and to earn future income

Before we identify that source of funds, we need to define investment. This term causes confusion because economists use it differently from virtually everyone else. In economic terms *investment* is activity that creates additional capacity to produce goods and services. If IBM builds a new production facility, investment has increased. If General Motors adds robots to its production process, investment has increased. If a contractor builds a new home, investment has increased. If K mart increases its toy inventory in May and June in preparation for the Christmas season, investment has increased.

In each of these examples of investment, something physical has happened because a firm has altered its capacity to produce and its ability to earn future income. However, if you purchase ten shares of IBM stock, you have *not* invested. Your purchase has changed the ownership of the stock, but it has not altered the productive capacity of IBM. You have completed a financial transaction, not a physical one.

Saving That portion of income that is voluntarily withheld from current consumption of goods and services

This distinction between financial and physical exchanges is where the confusion lies. Almost everyone will call financial transactions investments, but because financial transactions do not create additional capacity to produce, we must avoid labeling them as investments. In fact, instead of these financial activities being investments, we will shortly see that they are a form of *savings*. The term *investment must* be reserved for physical activities that change productive capacity, for instance, the expansion of a plant.

When a business decides to invest, the income and factors of production necessary to expand its plant and equipment (capital) must come from the production, income, and spending relationship that we have been discussing. In essence, households must decide to withhold some of their income and to purchase fewer goods and services, and companies must retain some of their earnings. In other words, households and companies must save.

Households can accomplish the act of saving by spending less than their current income on goods and services. For example, we all know that if a household deposits $100 each month into a savings account, some form of saving is occurring. But if a household purchases some shares of stocks or bonds or buys some insurance or real estate, the household is also saving, because it has foregone some current consumption. The purchase of stock is not investment, because there has been no resulting change in the capacity of a company to produce its products; only the ownership of the product has changed.

These examples should lead us to the conclusion that saving occurs whenever a component of current income is not spent on goods and services. In essence, saving is an act of postponing consumption. We may put money into a savings account because we know that we will have future educational expenses. We may purchase some stocks and bonds because we hope to build a nice retirement income. In each example, some income has been diverted from the flow of spending and reduces the level of spending in the economy. Unless some additional action is taken to counteract the saving, the economy will experience a decline in much the same way that a tire will go flat if a leak is not plugged.

In Fig. 16–2 we have added household saving (5) and business saving (6) to our earlier model. In both cases the saving has reduced the amount of income available for spending. For a household, any act of saving will reduce the amount of goods and services that the household can currently purchase. For a business an act of saving will reduce the amount of labor, capital, and natural resources it can purchase to produce its goods and services.

If nothing else happens to these savings, income will leak from the economy, and the level of production and spending will fall. But as Figure 16–2 indicates, most saving occurs through the use of financial institutions such as banks, insurance companies, and stock brokerages. These institutions *attempt to* convert the saving into spending, specifically investment, by lending this saving to businesses.

If the amount of income saved by households and businesses is exactly equal to the amount of investment spending, the circular relationship is complete once again. The only change that has occurred is that spending occurs in two sections of the economy: The household consumes (C) goods and services, and businesses expand their plants and equipment, that is, capital investment (I). Given the economy as we have described it, this relationship may be expressed as $C + I =$ GNP.

You may be thinking that this relationship is very nice, but why should we expect the value of saving to exactly equal the value of

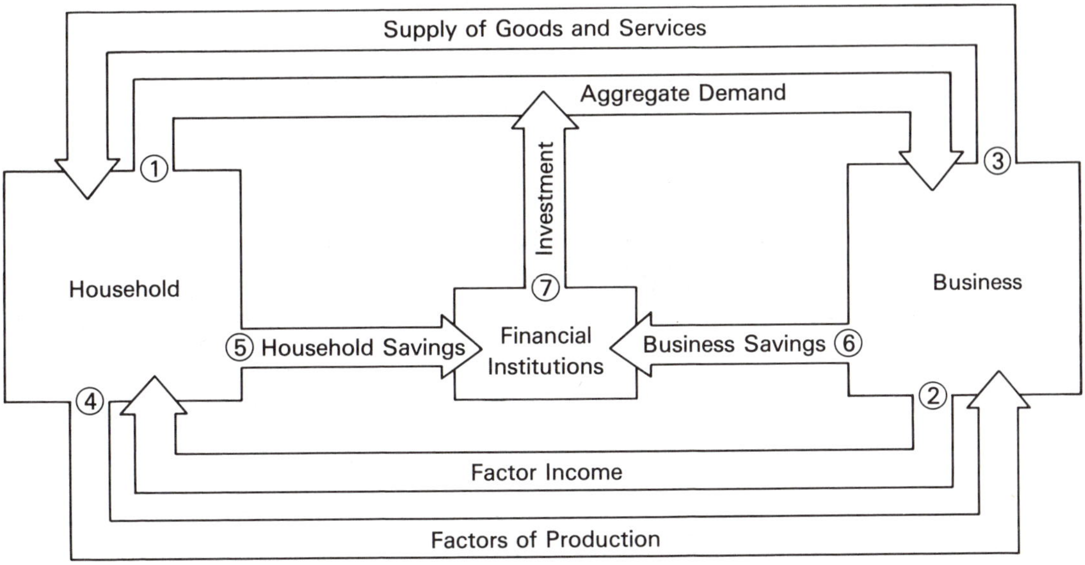

Figure 16–2
Circular Flow of Income, Including Investment and Saving
The diagram shows that even if some income does not get spent as consumption, it may still become a form of spending called investment.

investment? The reasons households and businesses save are very different from the reasons businesses invest. When income is saved, spending power is withdrawn from the economy. When businesses invest, they are expanding their ability to produce and sell merchandise. Businesses expect income to be spent on their products. In this sense, saving and investment seem to be working against each other in the same manner that demand and supply conflict with each other as described in Chapter 4. But just as demand and supply are equated at a specific price, investment and saving will also tend to equal one another at a specific price or interest rate.

This relationship between investment and saving exists because the demand for investment slopes downward to the right and the supply of loanable funds (savings) slopes upward to the right. The downward sloping investment curve demonstrates that businesses will be more willing to expand their plant size when the cost of borrowing (interest rate) falls. The motivation to save money is just the opposite, however. Consumers and businesses may be willing to postpone current spending if they can receive a higher rate of interest for saving their money.

We can see how this relationship works in Figure 16–3. For example, if households and businesses expand their rate of savings, the

Figure 16–3

This diagram demonstrates the tendency for saving to equal investment when interest rates are flexible.

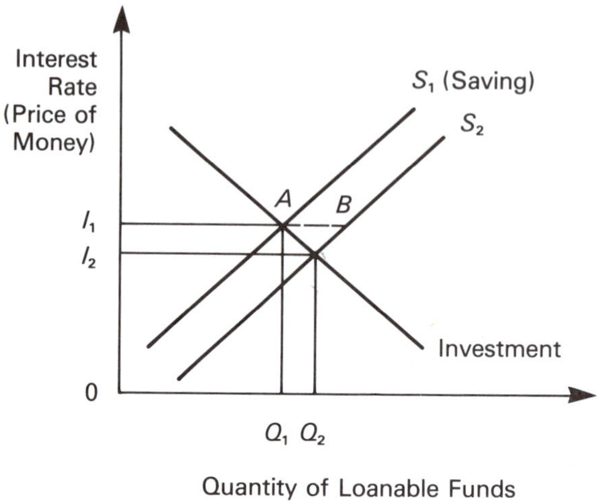

supply of money available for loans will increase; that is, the savings curve will shift from S_1 to S_2. Since investment decisions are influenced by stimuli different from those influencing saving decisions, investment decisions should remain the same; that is, the demand for funds to engage in investment (I) will not shift. When demand for investment funds is I and the supply of funds or savings is S_1, investment will equal saving at the interest rate (or price) of i_1. Investment and saving are equal in that Q_1 amounts of loanable funds will be saved and invested at interest rate i_1.

When savings increases to S_2, there will be more savings available at the interest of i_1 than businesses want to use for investment. This increase in savings will cause the surplus AB. As a result of normal competitive pressures, the interest rate will fall to i_2, where investment (I) and the new level of saving (S_2) will be equal at Q_2.

This relationship between saving and investment is very important as we try to understand how we can work toward achieving the goal of full employment. For now, however, all we need to know is that the circular-flow model assumes that the fundamental forces of competition will tend to equate saving with investment through the process of fluctuating interest rates.

SELF-TEST

3. Explain why your purchase of some IBM stock is not considered economic investment.
4. Indicate what is faulty about the reasoning in the following statement: We have all been told that it is important to save.

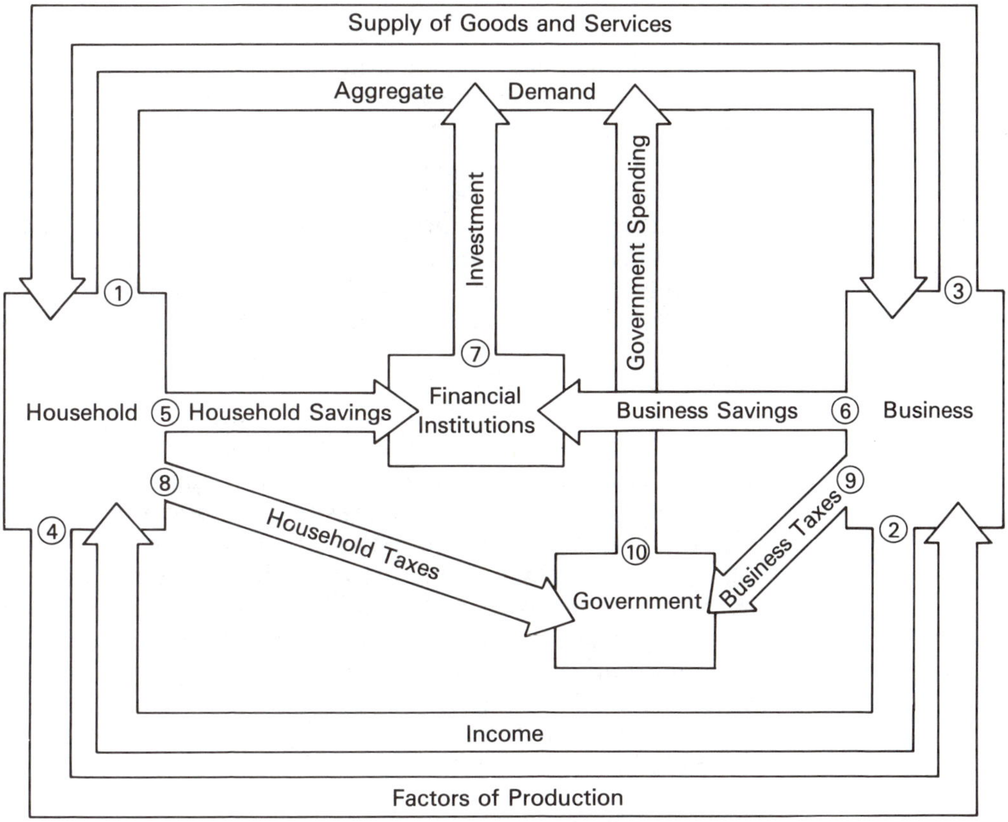

Figure 16–4
Circular Flow of Income, Including Investment and Government

This diagram demonstrates that spending and income will continue to equal each other even though household and business spending will be reduced by savings and taxes.

Yet if we save, there is a withdrawal of spending from the economy, and there will be a tendency for the economy to experience a recession. Thus, instead of saving, we should spend every dollar we earn as quickly as we can if we wish to have a prosperous economy.

TAXES AND GOVERNMENTAL SPENDING

In the preceding section we recognized that in addition to the buying and selling activities of households and businesses, the economy also engages in investment activities. If we reflect for a moment or two, we will identify governmental spending as another important aspect of economic activity. Government gets most of its revenue from households and businesses through taxation. If government collects taxes and does not spend the revenue, the economy will experience an economic decline similar to what would happen if there was too much saving relative to investment. In contrast, if government attempts to spend more than what it receives in taxes, there will be an economic stimulus. In terms of Figure 16–4, the taxes collected from households (8) and businesses (9) should be equal to the amount of governmental spending (10) on social goods and services. Now the basic relationship of the circular analysis shows that total spending ($C + I + G$) is equal to total income, which is equal to the total value of current production (GNP), or $C + I + G = GNP$.

Two additional points need to be made about this simple model: (1) This particular economy is self-contained; that is, it does not engage in international trade. As Chapter 8 indicated, international trade does introduce some interesting complications, but it does not alter the basic relationships that the circular-flow model presents. (2) In Chapter 17 we will study the influence of governmental deficit spending (governmental expenditures that exceed the revenue from taxation). The circular-flow relationship that we see in Figure 16–4 assumes that government spending will equal the revenue from taxes. When we study the tools that are used to influence the economy, in Chapter 17, we will learn that some of the tools require government to spend beyond its means.

SELF-TEST

5. According to the $C + I + G = GNP$ model just presented, there is a natural tendency for total spending to equal total output. Can you explain why?

It is important to remember that an economy must save if it wishes to expand its productive capacity through investment. It is also important to note that some forms of governmental spending are forms of investments; for example, expansion of the highway system and improvements in education. Thus, although savings and taxes are withdrawals from the economy, they both are important sources of funds for private and public sector investment. Without a proper level of investment and governmental spending, the economy would tend to falter. Private businesses would reduce investment in new technology, and governmental agencies would not be able to maintain necessary social expenditures. As a result, GNP and employment would stop growing and eventually decline.

Chapter 17 will emphasize how economic tools can be used to alter the level of economic activity. In every case we must remember the circular-flow-of-income analysis and be careful to examine how changes in any of the variables such as consumption, investment, saving, government spending, and taxes will influence one another.

ACTIVE REVIEW

1. Evaluate the following comment: Our economy is hopelessly confused. We are told to save for the future. But if we increase our savings, we reduce the level of total spending, GNP, and employment. How can we prudently plan for the future without seriously harming the economy?
2. In the circular-flow-of-income model, the three major forms of spending are consumption, investment, and governmental spending. In Figure 16–4, it is clear that households are able to purchase goods and services because they earn income through their use of the factors of production. But where do businesses and government get their income to spend? According to the circular-flow model, only households earn income.

ANSWER TO ACTIVE REVIEW

1. The person expressing this confusion has forgotten the relationship between saving and investment. If savings were dropped into a black hole, that person would have legitimate reasons for concern. However, savings provide the source of funds that are used for investment. *If* the level of saving is equal to the level of investment, the level of total spending will not fall. The level of total spending and GNP will change when the levels of saving and investment are not equal.

ANSWERS TO SELF-TEST

1. In a barter economy products exchange for products, for example, shoes exchange for wheat and eggs. Because the process of bartering is cumbersome, money has been introduced into most economic systems to facilitate the exchange process. However, no matter how much money exists within an economy we cannot buy more products than are produced. Consequently, the value of the wages and salaries (income) that we receive from working (producing goods and services) must equal the value of what we produce. If we receive an income that is greater than the value of the goods and services produced, the prices of those goods and services will rise until the dollar value of those products equals the income we have to spend.

2. In a very simple world both John and Maria are correct. An increase in the level of spending will stimulate businesses to use their idle resources to increase production and thereby increase employment. On the other hand, an increase in production will cause an increase in income. Households will spend that income, which will result in more production and employment. Unfortunately, the economy does not work quite as smoothly or simply as we may like. We already know that the ability of the economy to produce is affected by the significance of frictional and structural unemployment. Even if significant unemployment does exist, a demand stimulus is unlikely to reduce certain kinds of unemployment significantly. Especially in the short run, structurally unemployed workers are not prepared to take the available jobs, which require different skills than those possessed by the unemployed workers.

   The basic relationship between production and income tells us that if production increases, so will income and vice versa. However, the relationship does not tell us anything about the possibility of how much or how easily production can increase. If the economy has problems such as structural unemployment, resources cannot adjust smoothly. Increased income (spending power) will increase the tendency of consumers to purchase more goods and services, but real output may not be able to expand. Consequently, the economy may experience only a rise in prices and not an increase in real output. In a similar way increased production may not cause the desired effect on employment if production occurs through capital-intensive rather than labor-intensive means of production.

3. For an activity to be considered an economic investment there must be a change in the capacity of companies to produce goods and services. When you purchase shares of IBM stock, you are simply transferring ownership from the previous owner of the stock to yourself. You are not directly adding to IBM's ability to produce computers. In fact, your purchase is not really a purchase in an economic sense. You have engaged in a saving activity, because the purpose of your acquiring the IBM stock is to accumulate income for use at some future time. Investment activities expand the capacity of companies to produce.

4. It is true that savings are a leak in the spending stream of the economy, but we must be careful not to assume that the savings always lie dormant. Saving typically occurs through financial institutions, such as banks and insurance companies, which are willing to take your savings because they plan to lend it to others. If other people, particularly businesses, are not willing to borrow the money that the economy saves, then the total level of spending in the economy will fall, and the general level of economic activity will decline. On the other hand, if we spend every dollar we earn on consumption, then businesses will not have an adequate supply of funds to expand their productive capacity. Consequently, instead of stimulating a prosperous economy by consuming 100 percent of our income, we would

eventually cause an economic decline, because businesses would not be able to expand to meet the demands of consumers. The likely result would be inflation; production would not increase as fast as spending. To have a smoothly functioning economy, there must be a significant level of saving and investment.

5. The circular-flow-of-income model ($C + I + G = GNP$) states that total spending ($C + I + G$) must equal total output (GNP). Yet we know that there are leaks in the model. Savings and taxes are forms of nonspending. If income is saved or used to pay taxes and not spent in some other manner, total spending must fall; and if total spending falls, total output will also fall because households will not spend enough to cover the costs of production. However, there is a tendency for businesses to borrow the money that is saved so that they can engage in investment activities, which will return income to the spending stream. In a similar manner, if government uses taxes to supply public goods and services, governmental spending is likely to equal the level of taxation. In any case, if the level of total spending ($C + I + G$) declines, the level of output (GNP) will decline, because businesses will not receive enough revenue to pay the factors of production. Also, if total spending increases, total output will also increase, because businesses will want to increase sales to match the increased demand. (This point assumes that the economy has the ability to expand.)

17
Fiscal Policy and Full Employment

When an economy experiences an undesirable rate of unemployment, governmental agencies can attempt to remedy the problem by altering the rate of taxation and the level of governmental spending. The rate of unemployment can also be influenced by changes in the supply of money. Because both approaches are complex, we have decided to emphasize the role of taxation and governmental spending as we study approaches to achieve full employment. We will study the monetary system when we examine price stability in Chapters 19 through 22. It is important, however, to understand, that both approaches can and are used to influence the level of employment in the economy.

Before we begin an analysis of policies designed to achieve full employment, we must emphasize that there are several methods that can be used. Two major methods stem from different philosophical assumptions about how the economy works. One approach assumes that the competitive process discussed in Chapters 4–7 works very well, and if it is permitted to function freely (without unnecessary governmental intervention), unemployment and problems associated with it will be minimized.

Another approach assumes that there are some flaws in the competitive system (as indicated in Chapters 8 and 9) and that government needs to be directly involved in influencing the economic system to achieve the desired level of employment. This chapter discusses the evolution of the second approach from the first one.

CLASSICAL VIEW

Classical Economists Economists who assert that the basic forces of supply and demand will cause the economy to self-adjust, assuring the maintenance of full employment

Economists do not always agree about whether $C + I + G = \text{GNP}$ always results in full employment. *Classical,* or market-oriented, *economists* emphasize the economic system described in 1776 by Adam Smith in *Wealth of Nations,* which explains that the basic forces of competition with flexible prices and wages will adjust to changes in demand and supply and that the economy will always tend toward full employment. For example, if the economy experiences a decline in total demand, businesses experience declines in sales. Because these businesses do not want to see their sales decline, they have a tendency to decrease their prices to encourage consumers to increase their consumption. (Remember that in Chapter 4 we learned that if a firm lowered its price, the quantity of sales would increase.)

If, however, the firms wish to avoid losing money as they drop prices, they must either reduce wages or increase unemployment. Initially, workers will be reluctant to accept wage cuts, and as a result, some workers will lose their jobs. As the number of unemployed people increases, the competition for jobs will increase. Workers who have become unemployed will offer to work at lower wages. As new workers get hired at lower wages, there will be a tendency for all wages to fall.

During periods of full employment, households earn income that permits a sufficiently strong level of consumption to purchase the goods and services produced by business. In addition, the household savings provide businesses with funds for investment that permits these companies to expand their capabilities to produce. (Remember the circular-flow analysis in Figure 16–3.) But what happens when aggregate demand falls? If consumers or businesses decide to decrease their expenditures, what will be the effect on the level of employment?

When economic activity is high and the economy is functioning well, the aggregate demand for labor (D_{L_1}) is also high, because households, businesses, and government are spending at a relatively high level (Figure 17-1). But when total spending decreases, the demand for labor will fall (D_{L_2}) because employers no longer need as many workers to produce a lower quantity of goods and services. As a result, Q_1 workers want jobs at the wage of W_1, but employers want to hire only Q_2 workers. The difference between Q_1 and Q_2 will be unemployed workers.

Figure 17–1
The Impact of a Decrease in the Aggregate Demand for Labor on the Level of Employment and Wages

This diagram shows that a decrease in the demand for labor will result in a new equilibrium between the demand for and supply of labor *if wages are flexible.* Full employment will be achieved at Q_3, and wages will fall to W_2.

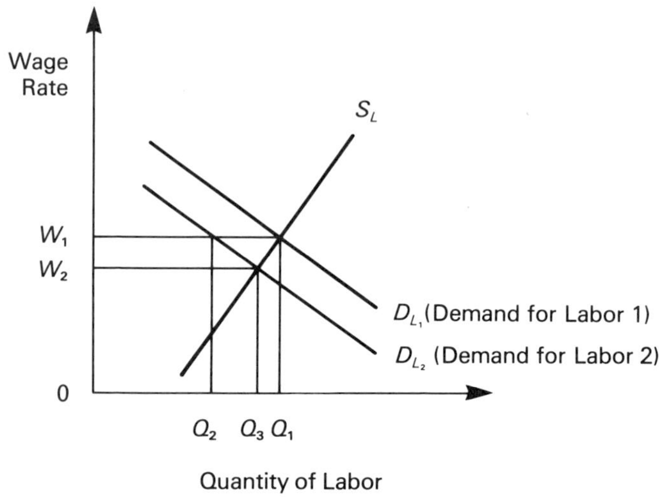

As Figure 17–1 indicates, however, a decrease in demand from D_{L_1} to D_{L_2} will cause the market for labor to experience a disequilibrium at W_1. Just as a seller of any product will have to lower prices to prevent a buildup of inventories (a surplus), labor will have to lower its wages if it wishes to reduce the unemployment (a surplus) indicated by the gap between the labor demanded (Q_1) and the labor supplied (Q_2) at the wage of W_1. Under competitive conditions, wages will fall to W_2. The level of employment will stabilize at Q_3, meaning that everyone who wishes to work at wage W_2 will have a job (in other words, there will be full employment).

Obviously, Q_3 is lower than Q_1, but according to the concept of supply, laborers who are not willing to work at the lower wage are not really committed to the labor force. If such workers become unemployed, the economy will not experience any negative consequences. (This type of reasoning is consistent with the reasoning of those who prefer unemployment definitions U = 1 through U = 4 discussed in Chapter 15.) The equilibrium of the demand for and supply of labor at Q_3 indicates that all workers who really want jobs at W_2 will have them.

In essence, this reasoning supports earlier suggestions that potential full employment output be pegged at a higher unemployment rate in recognition of the claim that some workers prefer not to work at a wage rate of W_2 and will not seek jobs. This argument also emphasizes that if we leave the competitive market mechanism alone, there will be automatic adjustments that will tend to correct the unemployment. As soon as competitive adjustments occur, new wages will be set, and all who want jobs at the new wage will be able to get them.

SELF-TEST

1. Explain how flexible prices and wages will work to keep the economy fully employed.
2. According to classical economists, as the wage rate falls, the number of people who wish to work declines. With fewer people in the labor market, full employment can be reached by actually employing fewer workers. Can you explain why this reasoning makes sense?

KEYNESIAN VIEW

Keynesian Economists Economists who assert that the basic forces of supply and demand do not always self-adjust and that governmental intervention is necessary to maintain a fully employed economy

As neat and simple as this argument sounds, many economists strongly disagree with it. They point to the Great Depression or, more recently, to the very high unemployment rates of the 1980s and argue that the actual market mechanism does not work as smoothly as classical economists would like it to work. These economists base their reasoning upon the work of John Maynard Keynes (sounds like "canes") who, in 1938, presented an economic theory in his book, *The General Theory of Employment, Interest, and Money*. The *Keynesian economists* argue that many prices and wages are not very flexible in the downward direction. Companies resist pressures to reduce the prices of their products, and workers resist attempts to decrease their wages. These economists believe that imperfections such as monopoly and time lags exist in a market economy. Because of these imperfections governmental adjustments in total spending are necessary to maintain a desirable level of employment.

History has taught us that many prices and wages will not fall unless the economy experiences dramatically high levels of unemployment, as we did during the Great Depression and in the early 1980s. In addition, even when prices and wages do fall, we may not recover automatically from the unemployment. The price cuts may not adjust quickly enough to prevent real income from falling. If real income does decline, total spending will fall, and companies will experience additional pressure to reduce employment.

This point can be clarified by returning to circular-flow-of-income analysis. The fundamental relationship is that production, income, and spending must always be equal. If something disturbs the economy so that spending declines (if, for example, we spend more money on foreign autos so that less money is available for spending on domestically produced products), businesses will receive less revenue and will be less able to pay their wages and salaries.* As a result, businesses will either reduce the number of workers they employ or reduce the wages they will pay or both. Although these actions may temporarily solve the problems for the employers, they do not solve the unemployment problems for the entire economy.

As workers experience reduced income from either their lower wages or their unemployment, they will have less income to spend, causing a further reduction in spending. With less spending the circular process starts all over again, resulting in higher levels of unemployment. Not until unemployment reaches relatively high levels will workers experience sufficient competitive pressure to accept a decrease in wages.

In the early 1980s, wages were sufficiently inflexible in a downward direction that unemployment rose to over 10 percent before wages started to fall. Although these wage decreases may start the economy back toward full employment, we have already seen that any level of unemployment greater than our defined goal imposes tremendous costs on the economy in terms of lost output. In addition there is no guarantee that the economy will automatically begin a return to full employment when wages begin to fall.

KEYNESIAN ANALYSIS AND CIRCULAR FLOW

When we examined the reasoning of the classical economists, we saw that market forces and flexible prices and wages allowed the economy to adjust automatically to full employment. In the eyes of Keynesian economists, however, imperfections in a market economy prevent an automatic adjustment. By using the circular-flow analysis, we should be able to understand this relationship more clearly.

Figure 17–2 demonstrates how unemployment may occur. In stage 1 the economy is operating smoothly, with domestic spending of $100 billion equal to $100 billion of income (and therefore, output). In stage 2 the economy experiences a reduction in the demand for the goods and services produced by businesses in the United States, because of increasing spending on foreign autos. Because the $10 billion

*In a dynamic economic system, there are always short-run and long-run consequences to any actions. The example of increased purchases of foreign autos emphasizes the short-run consequences of decreased demand for domestic production. The example is designed to emphasize the consequences of decreased domestic demand for goods and services. It is not designed to deal with the complexities of foreign trade.

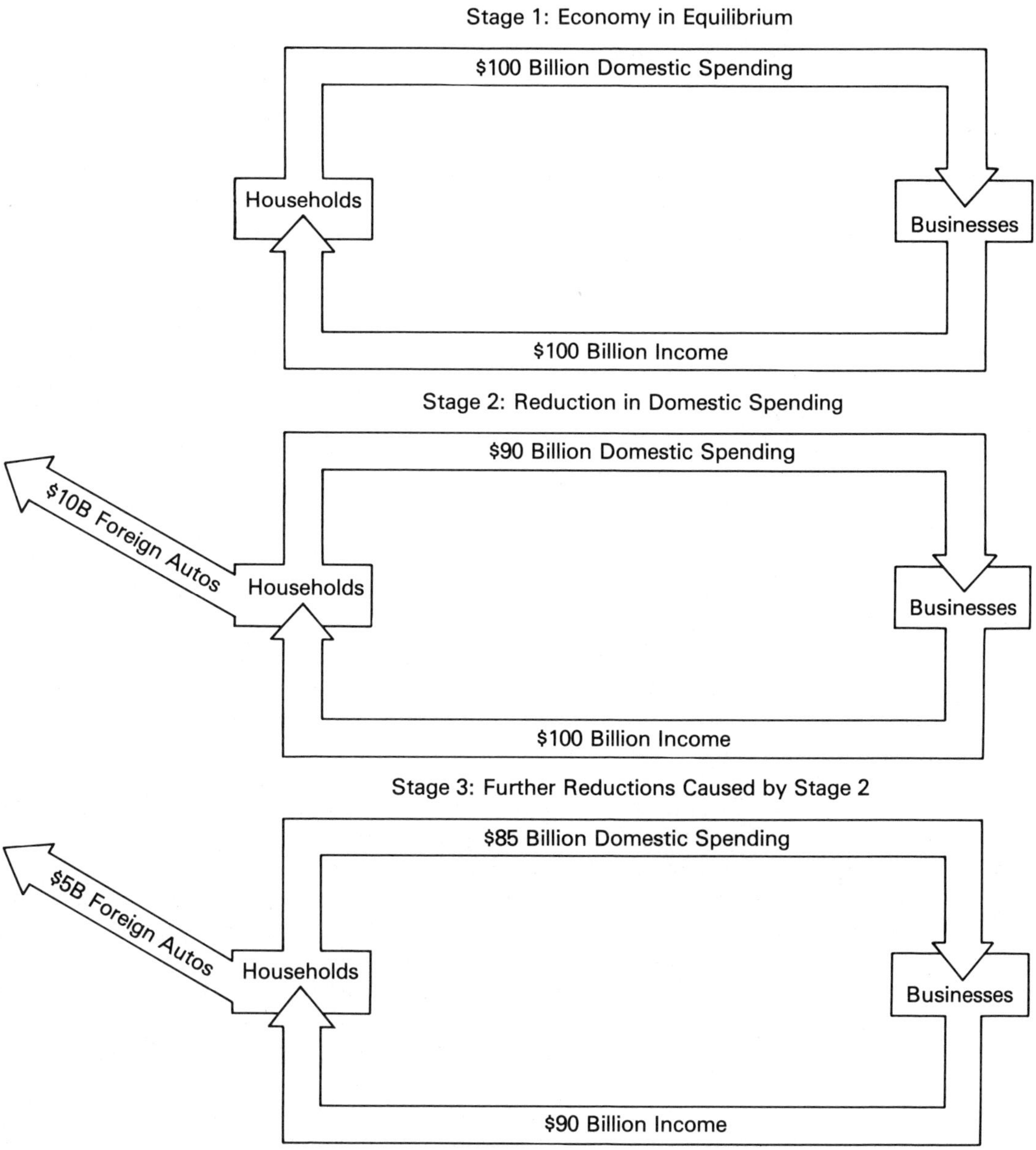

Figure 17–2
Consequences of a Reduction in Domestic Spending

This three-stage diagram illustrates that a reduction in domestic spending will result in less economic activity and unemployment.

spent on these foreign autos will not become part of the revenues received by businesses in the United States, total domestic spending falls to $90 billion.

As a result of the decrease in domestic spending, businesses have only $90 billion to pay labor and other factors of production. Businesses typically will reduce production because they are now selling only $90 billion of goods and services rather than the previous $100 billion. Because businesses are producing less, they do not need as many laborers. As a result the unnecessary workers will be laid off, and the unemployment rate will increase, especially if the wage rate does not fall.

The increase in unemployment is unlikely to stop at this point. In stage 3, households will be earning only $90 billion of income instead of $100 billion. If they continue to prefer some foreign autos over domestic autos, their spending on domestic goods and services will have to decline again. For example, if households spend $5 billion on foreign autos in stage 3, they can spend only $85 billion on domestic products. Since households have spent less, businesses will earn less revenue and will have to reduce the amount they can pay to labor and the other factors of production. Businesses will then reduce production again and lay off additional workers.

The tendency for unemployment to increase will continue as long as some activity drains spending from the domestic economy. Even if the workers are willing to accept lower wages to prevent unemployment from growing, the income level of households will continue to fall until all household income equals some form of spending. Then unemployment will stop growing. But the economy still faces the problem of how to increase employment, because there is no reason to believe that a return to higher levels of employment will occur solely as a result of market forces.

Instead of the economy's correcting itself, it will tend to fall into deeper recession with higher levels of unemployment. A major reason Keynesians believe that unemployment will increase as income decreases is that wages and prices are not likely to fall. Businesses find themselves with a surplus of labor and products at the prevailing wages and prices. Because businesses must find ways to reduce costs, they will usually reduce the number of workers they employ, resulting in an increase in unemployment. Eventually wages and prices will decline, but Keynesians argue that the resulting equilibrium will exclude workers who are willing and able to work at higher wages. They also argue that the loss of output because of exclusion of these workers will cause a significant reduction in the standard of living in the economy.

SELF-TEST

3. If wages do not decline when total demand decreases, what is likely to happen? Explain why.
4. Assume that you live in an economy where total production (GNP) equals $200 billion, total income equals $200 billion, and total spending ($C + I + G$) equals $200 billion. For some reason businesses become uneasy about the future and decrease their investment spending by $20 billion. Explain what is likely to happen to the economy if we accept the reasoning of Keynesian economists.

CLASSICAL ECONOMICS REVISITED

The classical economists claim that governmental intervention in the economy has contributed to the downward inflexibility of wages and prices. If government were to decrease its intervention, the economy would function more smoothly. The classical reasoning can be demonstrated by Figures 17–3 and 17–4.

Aggregate Demand The total spending in the economy from the major components of consumption, investment, and government

We can begin this analysis in the same manner that we began the Keynesian example. Assume that there has been a decline in total spending, or *aggregate demand,* within the economy. In Figure 17–3 this decrease is represented by a shift in aggregate demand from AD_1 to AD_2. This decrease in aggregate demand will cause a decrease in the price level from P_1 to P_2 because businesses will want to reduce their inventories that have been caused by the decreased aggregate demand.

The decline in the general price level will correspond with a lower level of output, Q_2. Individual companies will experience less demand for their individual products, resulting in lower prices and lower units of sales. Because of this decrease in aggregate demand, companies will not be able to pay the same wage rate to their employees. This change in their ability to pay wages will cause the demand for labor to fall from D_{L_1} to D_{L_2} (Figure 17–4). As a result of the decreased demand for labor, the wage level will fall to W_2, and the number of workers employed will fall to Q_{L_2}.

Aggregate Supply The total output of the economy, or GNP, that will be produced at different price levels

The process of change does not stop here, however. The lower wage rate will decrease the costs of production and will cause *aggregate supply* to increase from AS_1 to AS_2 (Figure 17–3). In this particular example the general price level falls to P_3, and the quantity of goods and services increases to Q_1. Although the price has fallen, the in-

Figure 17–3
Aggregate Demand for and Supply of Products

This diagram demonstrates how aggregate demand and aggregate supply will change as a consequence of the dynamic interaction in a market economy.

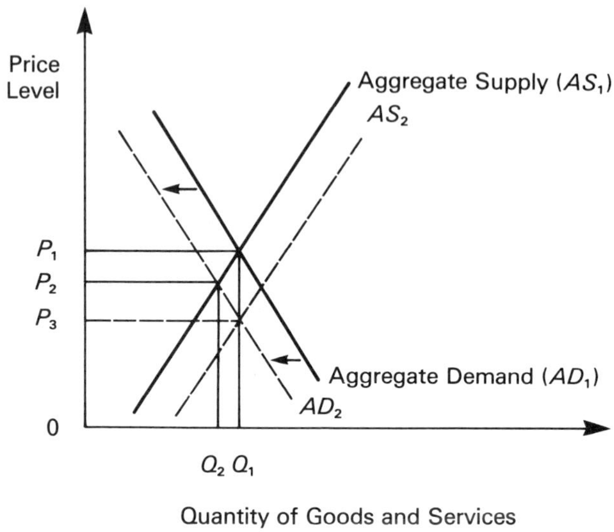

creased quantity demanded for goods and services will cause the demand for labor to increase to D_{L_3} (Figure 17–4). The result will be an economy that has lower prices but full employment. That is, all the workers who want jobs at W_3 instead of W_1 (Figure 17–4) will be able to find work. Consequently, classical economists argue, government should not interfere with the economy.

This chapter has presented two views about how the economy works. One view (classical economics) relies upon a market economy

Figure 17–4
Aggregate Demand for and Supply of Labor

This diagram demonstrates how changes in the labor market are influenced by changes in the product market and vice versa.

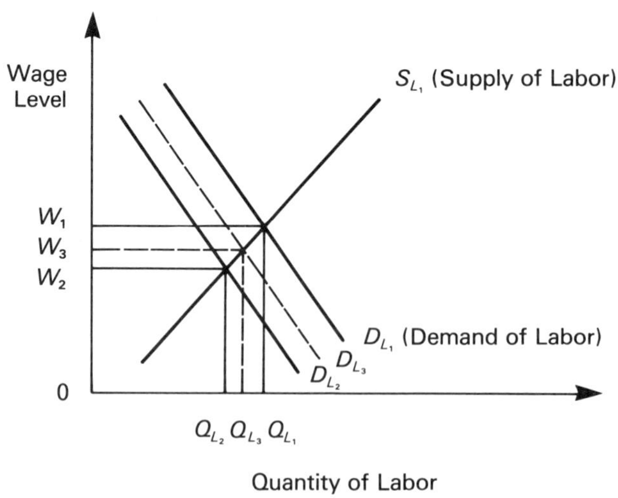

to make appropriate adjustments when there are changes in the relationship between total spending and total output. The second view (Keynesian economics) claims that the market economy has some flaws, especially prices and wages that resist market forces and tend to remain constant or even rise when we would expect them to fall. As a result, the economy does not make automatic adjustments to achieve full employment.

These two different views make it apparent that there will be different approaches to achieving full employment. Chapter 18 will examine some of these approaches and explain how they relate to the different views.

ACTIVE REVIEW

1. Explain why you agree or disagree with this statement: The circular-flow model tells us that the levels of production, income, and spending will always be equal. An economy that relies upon market-determined prices and wages will always tend to operate at a full employment equilibrium. Consequently, society should not be concerned about its level of employment, because the two characteristics above indicate that the economy will automatically adjust to full employment.
2. If aggregate demand falls, companies will decrease their production of goods and services. If production falls, it seems probable that the demand for labor will fall and unemployment will increase. Do you agree? Explain why.

ANSWER TO ACTIVE REVIEW

1. We can agree or disagree with this statement. If we accept the principles of the classical approach, this statement is accurate. If aggregate demand decreases, wages will fall because the demand for workers has fallen relative to the supply of workers. But when wages fall, the costs of production fall. These reduced costs tend to increase aggregate supply, resulting in a lower price level and a higher level of output being produced. The increased production increases wages and employment. Thus, flexible prices and wages tend toward an equilibrium that will be identified as a full employment equilibrium.

   Keynesian economists, however, disagree with the assumption that prices and wages are flexible. Typically, a reduction in spending will result in a level of unemployment higher than that described by classical economists. As unemployment increases, incomes fall, purchasing power falls, and total spending falls. Each time total spending declines, unemployment is likely to increase.

ANSWERS TO SELF-TEST

1. In a competitive economy all prices and wages are flexible. If the economy experiences an increase in the level of unemployment, a surplus of labor will exist at the current wage rate. In a competitive market, when a price (wage) does not cause the demand for and supply of labor to be equal, the price must change. In this case, the price (wage) will fall until the demand for and supply of labor are equal again. When this happens in all labor markets, the economy will be fully employed. Everyone who wants to work at the lower wage will have a job.
2. The question seems to indicate that an economy can experience two different levels of employment and claim they both represent full employment. That claim appears contradictory, but it is not. Reconsider the meaning of the supply of labor. This concept tells us that different numbers of workers will look for jobs as the wage rate changes. If wages decline, fewer people want to work. If wages increase, more people want to work. Thus, the number of employed workers that is necessary to achieve full employment will vary as the wage rate changes.
3. When total demand decreases, firms will experience a reduction in revenues, which they use to pay the factors of production, including labor. With less revenue, firms must reduce costs. If wages do not decline, employers will reduce costs by dismissing more workers, thereby increasing the level of unemployment.
4. In this example, the decline in investment will cause a decline in aggregate demand. The decrease in total spending will reduce the ability of businesses to pay the same level of income to the factors of production. Since Keynesians believe that wages and prices are inflexible in a downward direction, businesses cannot cut their payments to the factors of production by decreasing wages. Consequently, business will decrease these payments by increasing unemployment. As people lose their jobs, their income will fall, resulting in a decrease in aggregate demand because of a decrease in consumer spending. This decline in consumption will cause another increase in unemployment. The economy will tend to repeat this cycle several times.

18
Controlling Economic Fluctuations

The preceding discussion presented two scenarios for an economy that experienced a significant reduction in total spending. To accept a classical view of the economy, we need to be sure that wages and prices are sufficiently flexible. If they are flexible, then no special action is required to achieve full employment. If we accept a Keynesian view of the economy, however, there are actions that we can take to prevent the increase in unemployment and to stimulate progress toward the goal of full employment. Essentially there are two major policy tools that are used to achieve this goal: *fiscal policy* and monetary policy.

Fiscal Policy Changes in governmental spending or rates of taxation or both for the purpose of creating full employment and price stability

Fiscal policy is designed to influence the levels of output, employment, and income by changing the level of governmental spending and rate of taxation. In both instances the decisions must be formulated and implemented through both the legislative and executive branches of government.

If the president or Congress believes that the economy needs to be stimulated to increase the level of output and employment, then Congress must act. It will either increase its expenditures on social goods and services such as defense, highway, education, space, and job training programs or decrease the rate of taxes paid by households and businesses. In both cases the action is designed to increase total spending in the economy by increasing the spending of households, businesses, or government or any combination of the three.

Monetary Policy Activities by the Federal Reserve System to alter the supply of money for the purpose of changing aggregate demand

Monetary policy is designed to influence the level of total spending in the economy through changes in the supply of money. These changes occur through the Federal Reserve System and the banking community, not directly through governmental action. If the Federal Reserve System believes that the economy needs to be stimulated to increase the level of output and employment, the banking system must take action to increase the supply of money. As the amount of money in the economy increases, the level of spending should also increase. As indicated in Chapter 15, monetary policy is an important toll for altering the level of employment. Nevertheless, by postponing a more detailed discussion of monetary policy until Chapters 19 through 21 potential confusion will be minimized.

THE MECHANICS OF FISCAL POLICY

In Chapter 17 we emphasized the importance of the relationship between production, income, and spending. In Figure 17–2 we saw that if spending is less than the income earned in the economy, the level of economic activity would begin to decline. In fact, Keynesian economists argue that if the society does not take some deliberate action, the level of economic activity will continue to decline until severe levels of unemployment are reached. To avoid these unacceptably high rates of unemployment, government can use fiscal tools to inject additional spending into the economy.

Basically, the process works very simply. If we assume that an economy in a state of full employment is capable of producing a GNP of $100 billion, and if we assume further that the economy is producing only $85 billion of GNP, then we know that the actual spending in the economy is less than the potential level of output. Under these circumstances the government can engage in some *expansionary fiscal policies* designed to increase spending. Because the economy is operating below its potential full-employment output, the spending increase should not cause significant inflationary pressures. The increased spending simply stimulates increased production with the use of idle or unemployed resources. The important questions revolve around what types of fiscal stimulus should be used and how much total spending can be increased before we experience unsatisfactory levels of inflation.

Expansionary Fiscal Policies Decreases in taxes and increases in governmental spending that are designed to stimulate total spending in the economy

The Multiplier

The task of choosing the proper level of stimulus is tricky because an increase in spending will have a multiple effect upon the economy. An increase in spending will cause production to expand by an amount greater than the initial increase in spending. The reason this multiple expansion occurs can be found in the relationship of production, income, and spending. Because all three must eventually be equal, a change in one of the components must cause a change in the other two.

The Multiplier The factor by which an initial change in spending will alter total spending through a series of spending cycles

A hypothetical example will illustrate the *multiplier* concept. Suppose the federal government decides to increase its spending on interstate highways by $1 billion. When the highway construction is completed, the contractors will have been paid $1 billion in income for the work they have just completed. Total spending, total production, and total income have increased by $1 billion because the federal government injected into the economy $1 billion that was not previously being spent.

As a result of this new building activity, construction companies have $1 billion that they did not have prior to the increase in government spending. When the companies receive this income, they are likely to spend a large portion of it on, for example, new earth-moving equipment. If these companies spend $800 million on this new equipment, they have injected an additional $800 million into total spending that could not have occurred if the federal government had not spent the initial $1 billion on the highway project.* Thus, the original $1 billion has become $1.8 billion ($1 billion highway project plus $800 million earth-moving equipment).

The process seems almost magical. If we can inject new spending into the economy, the spending will multiply and expand economic activity. But does the expansion stop? What happens to the $800 million that was spent on earth-moving equipment? Just as construction companies received new income and spent a substantial portion of it, the earth-moving equipment companies will also receive income and spend most of it. If the equipment companies pay $640 million in wages to their workers, the income of those workers will rise by $640 million. Total spending has now increased by $2.44 billion ($1 billion highway project plus $8 million earth-moving equipment plus $640 million in wages).

The initial injection of $1 billion will continue to expand as long as each new income recipient spends a portion of that income. In this particular example, each income recipient spent 80 percent of that income. If we were to continue the example with all income recipients spending 80 percent of their increased income, the initial injection of $1 billion would grow to $5 billion. In other words, the multiplier would be 5. The multiplier process is summarized in Table 18–1.

When economists consider different types of fiscal policy rec-

*The actual increase in spending depends upon how society divides its additional income between spending and saving. This example assumes that businesses will spend 80 percent of their new income.

Table 18–1

Step	Source of Spending	Amount (millions)
1	Increased spending on highways	$1,000
2	Purchase of land moving equipment	800
3	Payment of wages	640
4		512
5		410
		328
		.
		.
		.
	Total new spending	$5,000

ommendations, they must be able to predict the size of this multiplying impact, or multiplier. If, for example, policymakers estimate the multiplier to be 2 (that is, the initial spending will expand two times), a $5 billion increase in spending on research for alternative energy sources would generate an increase of $10 billion of new production and income. The actual size of the multiplier depends upon the relationship between consumption and savings and the type of fiscal stimulus the policymakers wish to implement.

Reduction in the Rate of Taxation

As indicated earlier in this chapter, legislators can consider two general ways to stimulate output and employment levels of the economy: decrease taxes on households or businesses (or both) or increase spending on governmental activities. For example, if Congress votes to decrease taxes on personal income, the amount of money households have to spend (disposable income) will increase. When the *disposable income* of households increases, it is highly probable that the level of household spending will also increase.

Disposable Income The amount of income that households have to spend or save after taxes have been deducted.

As the level of spending increases, the level of output must expand to meet the level of total demand caused by this increase in spending. In terms of the spending ($C + I + G$) and output (GNP) relationship, a reduction in the rate of personal income tax will cause disposable income to rise. When disposable income increases, households have the ability to increase consumption ($\uparrow C$). As a result of the increase in consumption, GNP must rise ($\uparrow C + I + G = \uparrow$ GNP). This conclusion follows because of the *ceteris paribus* assumption that the level of investment and governmental spending do not change.

If, as we assumed previously, the economy is functioning below its potential full-employment output, the increased demand will stimulate businesses to use their idle machines and employees to increase production and expand real GNP rather than cause unwanted pressure for prices to increase.

This increase in production will generate additional income that will have a renewed effect upon spending and production. This multiplying effect will continue as long as the increases in spending cause businesses to expand output with the use of idle resources. As the economy approaches its full-employment output potential, any further expansion in spending will cause inflation, because production will not be able to expand as rapidly as the expansion in spending.

The above analysis is summarized in the following example:

1. Assume that total spending causes output to be below potential full employment output;
2. government decreases taxes on household income;
3. disposable income increases, which causes consumption to increase;
4. $\uparrow C$ causes $C' + I + G = GNP'$,* which approaches potential full employment output;
5. GNP′ causes consumption to increase again (remember the multiplier);
6. $\uparrow C$ causes $C'' + I + G = GNP''$, which is moving even closer to the potential full-employment output;
7. the cycle of an increase in consumption causing an increase in GNP will continue as long as income generated by the new GNP gets spent (multiplier);
8. when total spending $(C + I + G)$ expands beyond the potential full employment output, the economy will experience inflation.

If the legislature decides to use an increase in governmental spending on social goods and services as an expansionary policy, a similar cycle will occur. For instance, if governmental spending on education increases, total spending in the economy will initially expand by the amount of the increase in governmental spending.

As resources such as teachers and books are used to meet the increased demand for education, incomes of the teachers and sellers of the books will also increase. With this higher level of income,

*The use of superscripts in C', GNP′, C'', and GNP″ indicate that the values of these items are changing.

households will increase their spending. This new spending will cause an additional increase in production and income. Hence, the initial increase in governmental spending will be multiplied. The result of this multiplied spending will be an increase in the total income and output of the economy that will be larger than the initial increase in spending.

SELF-TEST

1. Explain how a cut in the rate of taxes paid by households will reduce the rate of unemployment if the economy is experiencing an undesirable rate of unemployment.
2. Will an increase in spending by either households or government always result in a reduction of unemployment?
3. Explain why the following statement is inaccurate: Fiscal policy is not very complex. If the actual GNP of the economy is $50 billion below its potential full-employment output, policymakers must increase spending by $50 billion to stimulate production up to the level of potential full employment output.

POTENTIAL COMPLICATIONS WITH FISCAL POLICY

The preceding discussion made the operation of fiscal policy seem so sufficiently clear and straightforward that you may be wondering why we ever experience unemployment. The answer to that concern exists in the realization that the actual economy rarely operates as smoothly as such simple models suggest. At least three significant factors may influence the success of fiscal policy: time lags, deficit spending, and identification of the source of unemployment.

Time Lags

Being able to predict when the economy is going to experience a recession is very critical to effective use of fiscal policy. If fiscal policy is to work most effectively, then fiscal stimulus should begin before the economy actually finds itself in a recession. Yet, even if all our indicators were perfect and we knew that in three months the economy would be in a recession, governmental officials would still have problems putting the proper fiscal policy to work on time. There will be a time lag caused by the need to formulate a policy and get that policy passed by Congress.

There is no standard formula that can be used for every economic downturn. The number of independent variables that affect GNP is incredibly great. Each decline may be caused by a different combination of forces. Consequently, the president and Congress must come to some agreement on what type of fiscal policy is most appropriate for dealing with the current economic situation. Unfortunately, this decision is a difficult one. Under ordinary conditions there will be months of hearings, committee meetings, and debates before a policy is formulated. When a decision about the appropriate fiscal policy is reached, the economy may already be in the middle of a recession rather than anticipating one. Thus, fiscal policy will generally need to be designed to correct existing unemployment rather to prevent its existence.

A second time lag often occurs when government attempts to implement the policy. If part of the fiscal strategy is a reduction in the tax rate, the impact of that action will be delayed by the length of time it takes households and businesses to increase their purchases. For example, a typical tax cut would increase disposable income by a relatively small amount each payday. The increased spending that we expect from the tax cut may take from 6 to 12 months to work itself through the economy; that is, the multiplier effect requires time to reach its full impact. Thus, the effectiveness of fiscal policy is complicated by the existence of these two time lags. In fact, some economists argue that the time lags may cause the stimulus to spending to take effect when the economy is already recovering. These economists argue that instead of causing full employment, fiscal policy contributes to inflation.

Deficit Spending

Deficit Spending An imbalance created by government's spending of an amount greater than it receives in revenues from taxation in a given year

Deficit spending presents the second major problem encountered when fiscal policy is used. If, for example, government decides to stimulate the economy by decreasing the rate of taxation, that stimulation tends to occur only if consumption is increased *ceteris paribus*. The level of governmental spending must remain constant as the level of consumption is increased. (Remember, the earlier example emphasized the importance of consumption's increasing to C' while governmental spending remained constant.) If governmental spending decreases by an amount similar to the increase in consumption, the decline in governmental spending tends to negate the stimulus caused by the increased consumption. Yet, if tax rates are decreased, the level of governmental revenues must also decrease, at least temporarily.*

For government to maintain its spending at the level prior to the tax cut, government will have to borrow money. Government's budget will be out of balance because the level of spending will be greater than the level of revenue. A major concern that we must face is whether this borrowing by government will have a negative impact upon the spending levels of consumers and businesses. (A sophisticated appreciation of this process necessitates an understanding of the monetary system and the importance of interest rates, which will be explained in Chapter 21.)

During a recession one major problem is the insufficient level of total spending by consumers, businesses, and government. Businesses are unlikely to expand the size of their plant and equipment if consumers are not purchasing all the goods and services that are currently being produced. In fact, businesses may actually reduce their levels of production, causing the level of unemployment to rise. If unemployment increases, businesses generally are not interested in borrowing. Thus, money available for business to borrow for the purpose of expanding the size of business plant and equipment will become available for government to borrow.

Stated differently, deficit spending may not be a problem if the economy is operating below its potential full-employment output. When unemployment exists, businesses do not wish to borrow as much as when the economy is operating closer to full employment. If government decides to borrow when business borrowing is reduced, one type of borrowing simply replaces another. Under this condition there will not be any undue competition between the business firm's demand for borrowing and a similar demand by government. The increase in borrowing by government when the level of unemployment is high will not cause an increase in the interest rate as long as private businesses have decreased their borrowing activity. In fact, Keynesians argue that deficit spending by government might actually be desirable when private spending by households and businesses has declined.

However, we need to be careful not to fall into the trap of believing that deficit spending is always desirable. Two major problems may be caused by deficits. First of all, as the economy expands toward

*When we examine supply-side economics in Chapter 19, we will learn that some economists argue that a cut in taxes will cause such a positive incentive effect that productivity will increase significantly. If productivity does increase significantly, then the economy may still experience an economic stimulus even if governmental spending is reduced.

its potential full-employment output, inflationary pressures will grow. If deficit spending is not watched carefully, it may lead us into an inflationary period. (This issue will be discussed more thoroughly in Chapter 21.) Second, we need to be aware of how the deficit is being spent. As governmental spending increases we need to consider the importance of that spending relative to spending by consumers and businesses. More specifically, we need to ask whether the goods and services that government would buy with deficit spending are more desirable than what would be bought by consumers and businesses with the same money. If the governmental spending is not more desirable, then steps should be taken to stimulate consumption and investment rather than governmental spending.

The issue of whether private spending is more desirable or more efficient than governmental spending is a complex one that requires an understanding of the importance of social goods. If a society identifies social needs, then government must be involved in providing those needs. The question is no longer whether the spending should be done by the private or public sector, because, by definition, the public sector provides social goods. The real issue is how can governmental agencies furnish social goods in the most efficient manner.

The National Debt
The total accumulation of deficit spending by the federal government

National Debt Finally, we have a potential problem with the accumulation of deficits, or the *national debt.* As the size of the national debt grows, so do the interest payments that must be paid to finance the debt. For example, according to Table 18–2 the 1985 national debt was $1,945.9 billion, and the federal government paid $129.4 billion in interest payments to people and institutions who had lent money to the federal government. These interest payments accounted for approximately 14 percent of federal governmental spending in 1985.

A major criticism of a debt of this size is that the $129.4 billion of tax revenues could have been spent on projects such as schools, hospitals, and veteran benefits instead of making payments on borrowed money. When government must use tax revenues to pay interest on the debt, it cannot spend as much on other projects without increasing taxes. If taxes are increased, the level of consumption and investment is likely to decline. These decreases in aggregate demand will lead to a decrease in GNP.

The size of the public debt is provided in Table 18–2. By 1985 the public debt had risen to over $1,945 billion, and the GNP had reached almost $4,000 billion. While these numbers appear to be enormous, we need to put them into context. A strong economy, one that has a large and growing GNP, has a greater ability to incur and carry a larger public debt than does an economy that has a smaller

Table 18–2
The Public Debt and Interest Payments in Relation to GNP, 1929–85

(1) Year	(2) Public Debt (billions)	(3) Gross National Product (billions)	(4) Interest Payments (billions)	(5) Public Debt as Percentage of GNP[a]	(6) Interest Payments as Percentage of GNP[b]
1929	$ 16.3	$ 103.4	$ 0.7	16%	0.7%
1940	50.9	100.0	1.1	51	1.1
1946	259.5	209.8	4.2	124	2.0
1950	256.7	286.5	4.5	90	1.6
1954	278.8	366.8	5.0	76	1.4
1958	283.0	449.7	5.4	63	1.2
1962	304.0	565.0	7.6	54	1.3
1967	322.3	799.6	9.6	40	1.2
1972	425.4	1,185.9	14.0	36	1.2
1976	619.3	1,718.0	25.2	36	1.7
1979	819.0	2,417.8	40.6	34	1.7
1982	1,140.9	3,057.5	82.5	37	2.7
1983	1,410.7	3,304.8	89.8	43	2.7
1984	1,633.0	3,774.7	111.1	44	2.9
1985	1,945.9	3,988.5	129.4	49	3.2

Source: *Economic Report of the President* (Washington, D.C.: GPO, 1983) and *Federal Reserve Bulletin*, Washington, D.C.: Publication Services, Board of Governors, Federal Reserve System, 1985).
[a]Interest payments divided by gross national product.
[b]Public debt divided by gross national product.

GNP. If we examine both the size of the debt and its interest payments relative to the size of GNP, the vastness of the debt looks different.

Since 1946 there has been a general downward trend in the relative size of the debt and the interest payments in comparison with GNP. In 1946, during World War II, our debt was actually larger than the GNP. After 1946, however, the ratio of debt to GNP continually declined until the 1980s. During the early part of the 1980s there was an increase in the size of the debt relative to GNP. This change in direction deserves some close observation.

In a similar manner we should investigate the size of interest payments on the debt relative to GNP. Here we find a high degree of stability. From 1929 to 1979 the ratio of interest payments to GNP varied between 1 and 2 percent. The disturbing point is that this ratio has been increasing over the past decade. In 1985 the ratio reached 3.2 percent.

If the size of the debt relative to GNP or the interest payments relative to GNP continues to increase, there can be significant impact upon the level of unemployment. If the public interprets this high debt and its accompanying high interest payments as a sign of economic mismanagement, businesses may reduce their incentives to take risks, to innovate, and to invest. Laborers may have less incentive to work hard and be productive. If these reductions in incentives occur, production will decline and unemployment will increase.

Another problem with the debt is the increasing amount of foreign ownership. In 1960 only about 5 percent of the public debt was foreign-owned. That percentage grew to the point that by the early 1980s about 15 percent of the debt was foreign-owned. This increase is significant because the current interest payments on the foreign-owned debt (approximately $12 billion annually) are sources of income that leave the United States.

If the public debt were totally owned by people and institutions within the United States, income earned from the interest payments would stay within the United States economy and be a source of spending on domestic production. Because approximately 12 percent of the debt is now foreign-owned, a significant portion of the interest income from the debt flows out of the country and causes reduced spending in this country. As spending decreases, unemployment will tend to increase.

The preceding discussion of the deficit and debt tells us that although deficit spending can be an important tool in attempting to reduce unemployment, this type of spending must be used cautiously. There are definite constraints upon its effectiveness as a means of reducing unemployment. If deficit spending is misused, it can contribute to inflation. If the absolute size of the debt is permitted to grow relative to the size of the GNP, the size of that debt may also contribute to increased unemployment.

Sources of Unemployment

As we have studied fiscal policy the emphasis has been placed upon the ability of government to alter the level of total demand in the economy. Yet some economists argue that unemployment may be caused by changes in the structure of the economy. For example, the rapidly increasing use of computers is causing a reduction in the need for workers to perform repetitive tasks but increasing the demand for workers who have skills necessary to run and maintain the computers. If this phenomenon is happening throughout the economy, there may be an increase in unemployment. Workers with low-level skills will lose their jobs faster than employers can find and hire workers with higher-level skills.

If fiscal policy is used to stimulate demand when this type of structural unemployment exists, the economy may experience rising inflation rather than falling unemployment. This type of unemployment is not caused by insufficient demand, but by a difference in the skills possessed by the unemployed and the skills desired by employers. If demand is stimulated, the demand for skilled workers will expand beyond its current level. Because training takes time (maybe a year or more), production will not increase to meet the increased demand. The result will be inflation. A more detailed examination of this problem will occur in Chapter 24.

SELF-TEST

4. Assume you are responsible for implementing fiscal policy. Can you identify the best time to stimulate total spending?
5. Define *deficit spending*. Explain why government is likely to deficit spend when fiscal policy is used to reduce the level of unemployment.
6. If unemployment is caused by some phenomenon other than insufficient demand, will stimulating total demand be effective in reducing unemployment? Why?
7. Evaluate this statement: Whenever the level of unemployment is higher than acceptable, the fiscal authorities can increase governmental spending, and unemployment will tend to fall.

RECAP OF FISCAL POLICY

The purpose of Chapters 15–18 is to explain the significance of full employment as a goal and how governmental intervention in the economy may assist in achieving that goal. In the process of understanding some basic economic relationships we learned that production, income, and spending are tightly linked. If the level of total spending in the economy declines, production and employment will typically decline.

We also learned that government has the power to use fiscal policy to reduce the level of unemployment. Essentially, fiscal policy consists of governmental actions that change either the rate of taxation or the level of governmental spending. In either case, when an undesirable level of unemployment exists, fiscal policy is designed primarily to stimulate the level of spending in the economy. The expectation is that as total spending increases, production will also increase to meet the new demand. This increase in production will cause an increase in the level of employment. The expansion of production and employment will continue until the economy reaches its potential full-employment output.

If the economy was experiencing inflation rather than unacceptably high unemployment, fiscal policy could be used to contract the level of total spending in the economy. Instead of cutting taxes or increasing governmental spending, the policymakers would increase taxes or decrease governmental spending. These actions tend to reverse the stimulating actions described in this chapter.

INTERNATIONAL COMPARISONS

Certainly every economy wishes to keep its unemployment rate as low as possible, yet the effectiveness of different industrial nations in achieving low unemployment have been varied. Table 18–3 indicates that these differences are persistent and significant. Typically, the United States and Canada have had much higher unemployment rates than Italy, Japan, Sweden, or West Germany. All countries seem to experience negative employment effects when business activity declines (recession), but some countries appear to do a better job of moderating the ups and downs of this activity and its resultant impact on employment.

It is curious that in any given year some countries are able to employ a greater percentage of their work force than does the United States. We should discover why these different performances exist. If countries such as West Germany and Sweden use different economic policies than those used in the United States, we will want to determine whether their policies are responsible for their ability to keep unemployment relatively low.

Several factors create differences in the unemployment rates of

Table 18–3 Civilian Unemployment, Percentages, Approximating United States Concepts in Ten Countries from 1974–81

This chart compares the unemployment rates of selected industrialized countries.

Year	U.S.	Can.	Austrl.	Japan	France	W. Ger.	Gr. Brit.	Italy	Neth.	Sweden
1974	5.6	5.3	2.7	1.4	2.9	1.6	3.1	2.8	3.8	2.0
1975	8.5	6.9	4.9	1.9	4.2	3.5	4.6	3.2	5.2	1.6
1976	7.7	7.1	4.8	2.0	4.6	3.5	6.0	3.6	5.4	1.6
1977	7.1	8.1	5.6	2.0	5.0	3.5	6.4	3.6	5.1	1.8
1978	6.1	8.4	6.3	2.3	5.4	3.4	6.3	3.7	5.2	2.2
1979	5.8	7.5	6.2	2.1	6.1	3.0	5.7	3.9	5.3	2.1
1980	7.1	7.5	6.1	2.0	6.5	3.0	7.3	3.9	6.1	2.0
1981	7.6	7.6	5.8	2.2	7.7	4.2	11.3	4.2	8.9	2.5

Source: Joyanna May, "Unemployment and Labor Force Trends in 10 Industrial Nations: An Update," *Monthly Labor Review*, U.S. Department of Labor, Bureau of Labor Statistics, November 1982, p. 20.

countries. One major factor is that many European countries appear to emphasize compassion relative to personal responsibility. The consequence of emphasizing this value is the development of income maintenance programs and educational programs that are specifically designed to keep unemployment low. Other important factors are differences in the rate of increase in the size of the labor force, cyclical flows of foreign workers, degrees of governmental intervention, and cultural influences.

Most European countries provide higher levels of unemployment benefits than the United States. However, the United States pays benefits for a comparatively long time. In some foreign countries there are bonuses paid to the workers for quick reemployment, and in other countries there is a reduction of benefits after a certain length of time. These last two features may help keep unemployment rates lower than the rate in the United States.

The educational system in the United States is different from that in Europe. European educational and labor market institutions tend to encourage students into training for narrow specialities, while American youth tend to get a more general education. This more specialized training usually results in lower unemployment but less mobility, *ceteris paribus.* This reduced mobility may discourage worker movement from job to job.

Between 1960 and 1980 the United States experienced a more rapid increase in the size of its labor force than did most other industrial economies. A significant proportion of this increase was the result of the post–World War II baby boom. This fact may help explain why the rate of teenage unemployment is higher in the United States than it is in other countries. Yet in the early 1960s, when other countries had a higher proportion of teenagers in the labor force than did the United States, their unemployment rates were still lower than those of the United States.*

The European countries and Japan discourage layoffs by requiring employers to notify workers several months prior to actual layoff. During this period of notification employers are required to assist employees in their search for alternative employment. In these countries, workers are usually much more attached to their jobs than are workers in the United States. Workers are more reluctant to change jobs in search of higher wages or better working conditions. Because of the intervention of government the general labor force in Europe and Japan has greater job security and less fear of unemployment than their counterparts in the United States. Yet, temporary or sea-

*U.S. Bureau of Labor Statistics, *International Comparisons of Unemployment,* August 1978, pp. 67–68.

sonal workers and new entrants in Europe and Japan tend to experience great employment difficulties.

The cultural and social patterns in Japan and Europe indicate that these countries have a stronger traditional preference for job security as opposed to the job mobility that tends to be emphasized in the United States. Because of these cultural and social patterns we can appreciate why these governments are more willing than United States politicians to take action to reduce the threat of unemployment.

This brief look at other countries tells us that unemployment can be kept at lower levels than those achieved by the United States. In most cases the countries with better employment records have instituted policies that have broad social and economic implications that are currently not part of the way people in the United States think about these issues. When we examine trade-offs, in the second part of this book, we will examine these implications more closely.

ACTIVE REVIEW

1. Assume that the United States economy is experiencing a 10 percent unemployment rate and that everyone, regardless of his or her economic philosophy, agrees that the level of unemployment should be reduced. After significant deliberation, Congress votes to reduce personal income taxes to cause an economic stimulus. However, even though Congress agrees that a tax cut is desirable, there are several other issues that must be resolved.
   a. According to economic estimates the economy is losing over $250 billion of output (GNP) annually as a result of the unemployment. Consultants from Economics, Inc., argue that Congress should, therefore, reduce personal income taxes by $250 billion so that consumers will increase their spending and thereby reduce unemployment. Do you agree with this plan? Explain. (Hint: How will the multiplier concept influence your decision?)
   b. Consultants from the American Institute of Economics argue that the tax cut needs to be smaller, say $125 billion, but that government must also reduce its spending by $125 billion to make sure that the governmental deficit does not increase. Evaluate this strategy.
   c. If structural forces are significant reasons for the high unemployment rate, will a decrease in the rate of personal income tax solve the problem?
2. Deficit spending presents some interesting and potentially conflicting problems for economists. Keynesians argue that deficits can stimulate

aggregate demand and move the economy closer to full employment. On the other hand, deficit spending could cause inflation, and it could also cause some increase in unemployment. Thus, can we tell whether deficits can have a positive influence on the economy? Answers to the following questions may help reduce the confusion.

a. Why might deficit spending increase GNP without increasing inflation?

b. If the economy is currently operating close to its full-employment potential, will deficit spending increase GNP even more, or will it increase the pressure on inflation?

c. What do economists mean when they say that the debt is too large? Explain why this view makes sense.

ANSWERS TO ACTIVE REVIEW

1a. If the economy is currently producing an output that is $250 billion less than the potential full-employment output, there are some strong reasons for cutting income taxes to increase aggregate demand. It is not necessary, however, to decrease taxes by the entire $250 billion. For example, if households increase their spending by $50 billion as the result of a tax cut, and the multiplier is 5, then that $50 billion will be multiplied to $250 billion ($50 billion of new spending times 5, the multiplier, equals $250 billion). Taxes would have to be cut enough to create the $50 billion increase in spending. This tax cut would be much closer to $50 billion than $250 billion.

1b. If the multiplier were 2, then a tax cut of $125 billion would generate approximately $250 billion of increased production as long as government spending remained constant. (Remember that $C + I + G = GNP$. If C increases but G decreases, the two changes will tend to offset one another.) Under certain circumstances when governmental spending is sufficiently large so that it causes negative incentives, some reductions in governmental spending tend to increase GNP. But it is unlikely that tax cuts and cuts in governmental spending of the same size would enable the economy to achieve its goal of a fully employed economy.

1c. Structural unemployment is defined as unemployment that is caused by a mismatch of the skills of the workers and the skills needed by employers. If workers are unemployed for structural reasons, then the economy needs to improve the training of workers more than it needs to stimulate aggregate demand. If taxes are cut, households will spend more money. Businesses will try to increase production as a result of this increased aggregate demand. They will have difficulty expanding production, because unemployed workers will not have the skills necessary to fill these jobs. Consequently, instead of reducing unemployment, a cut in taxes in this situation is more likely to cause inflation.

ANSWERS TO SELF-TEST

1. A cut in taxes paid by households will increase the disposable income that households have to spend on goods and services. As households increase their spending, firms will increase production. As production increases, firms will need to hire more workers; this hiring activity will reduce the level of unemployment.
2. The effectiveness of a stimulus in spending is dependent upon how close to its potential full-employment output the economy is operating. If spending is stimulated when the economy is close to full employment, we are likely to experience inflation rather than more employment. If the economy is operating below its potential full employment, then an increase in spending is likely to increase employment as employers expand production.
3. The major problem with increasing total spending by $50 billion to close a $50 billion gap in GNP is that this approach ignores the multiplier effect. An increase in total spending will tend to increase GNP. However, this increase in GNP will, in turn, cause spending to increase. As spending increases, so will GNP. Consequently, a $50 billion increase in total spending will cause GNP to increase by much more than $50 billion. In this particular example, if GNP increases by more than $50 billion, the economy will experience inflation.
4. Timing the implementation of fiscal policy is a complex problem. First of all, policymakers must agree when unemployment is most likely to begin increasing. Although economists have indicators that predict when a recession is likely to occur, in a democratic country such as the United States there will usually be a significant period of time before the appropriate agencies will be able to agree that a recession is near. Second, once the proper authorities do agree that we are in a recession and do implement fiscal policy (for example, a tax cut), the full impact of the policy will not be felt for 6 to 12 months. Consequently, if we had perfect information, we should implement fiscal policy approximately 12 months prior to the expected unemployment. In reality this precise timing will never happen.
5. Deficit spending is spending by government that exceeds the level of tax revenues being received by government. Deficit spending is likely to occur when government engages in a fiscal stimulus, because the intent of the stimulus is to expand total spending. Taxes are cut to increase the spending of households. If government cut its spending to match the reduction in tax revenues, the decrease in governmental spending would tend to offset the increase in household spending. If

the economy experienced a spending stimulus, it would be a weaker stimulus than if the economy engaged in deficit spending.

6. If unemployment is caused by a change in the structure of the economy, then stimulating demand may cause inflation rather than reduce unemployment. When employers cannot find enough workers with the proper skills, production cannot expand as smoothly as an employer would like. In fact, increases in production probably would not keep pace with increases in spending. Even though producers want to increase production, they are not likely to hire workers who do not have the proper skills. They may hire the most trainable workers, but because of the long training period required, production is not likely to increase for a year or more, or until the workers are properly trained. In the meantime, a demand stimulus is likely to cause inflation rather than reduce unemployment. The employer wants to respond to the increased demand and chooses price increases as the response, since expansion of employment is not practical.
7. Whenever an undesirable level of unemployment exists, policymakers must decide the causes of unemployment, and they must also consider the side effects of their policy suggestions. If unemployment is caused by a recession, then increasing governmental spending may be an appropriate policy.

   However, unemployment may be caused by structural forces. Under this condition an increase in governmental spending is not likely to reduce unemployment unless the spending is directed toward job training. If governmental spending is increased for highways or defense, there will be inflationary pressure rather than a reduction in unemployment. Because of structural unemployment, highway construction and defense production will not expand smoothly, since workers will not be properly skilled. Thus, anyone who argues that an increase in spending will always correct unemployment is likely to be in error.

19
The Goal of Price Stability

Most of us want to own a home. To us, owning a home symbolizes security, privacy, and success. Our ability to achieve this dream is being hampered by the astronomical prices of the new homes we desire. These prices are high and rising. The median sales price of a newly constructed home was $20,000 in 1965. Five years later this figure was $23,400, a paltry figure compared with the $69,300 price tag on the average home in 1982. Certainly these ballooning prices inhibit many prospective home buyers. While prices are just one of several independent variables that affect housing sales, one-family home sales fell from 819,000 in 1977 to 412,000 in 1982.

Steadily rising prices present obstacles in many other sectors of the economy. Almost all consumers lament the expanding of their grocery bills. Food costs for a family of four (two children between the ages of 6 and 11) increased between 1975 and 1981 from an average of $63.00 per week to $90.70 per week. The implication of these numbers is that one dollar does not buy as much now as it did in previous years. Consumers feel the resulting loss of purchasing power if their incomes do not rise as fast as prices.

In modern economies virtually every economy activity is based on relative prices. If you plan to purchase a house, you consider whether you can afford to purchase a $60,000, $80,000 or $100,000 home. When shopping for cars, you may consider autos priced from

$6,000 to $12,000. If you wish to purchase a gallon of milk, you might face a charge of from $1.69 to $2.19. If you wish to get your hair cut, you could pay anywhere between $5.00 and $25.00. Whatever the goods or services you wish to purchase, you will investigate the prices before you buy, because *money* provides us with a standard of value. The prices provide us with some indication of the quality of goods and services.

Money Anything that is accepted in payment for goods and services, because it is a medium of exchange and a standard of value

In Chapter 7 we learned that prices were an essential part of the competitive market model. Rising prices in pure competition indicate that consumer demand has increased relative to supply. Higher prices mean, *ceteris paribus,* that producers earn greater profits. As profits rise, production tends to increase. This increase in supply will usually cause prices to fall and in competitive markets will result in reducing profits (see Figure 7–5). When prices of particular goods and services fluctuate in this manner, we know that markets are adjusting to competitive pressures. Under these conditions consumers can be confident that higher-priced goods and services are higher-quality goods and services.

What happens when the general level of prices rises? Do price increases in the economy cause behavior similar to that predicted by the competitive model? What will happen to money as a standard of value? Will consumers continue to use money as a medium of exchange? How will changes in the value of money influence the functioning of the general economy? What steps can be taken to reduce these general price increases and the problems associated with them? The next three chapters will attempt to provide answers to these questions. We should anticipate that the answers are not simple and that economists disagree about many of them. Nevertheless, by studying prices and money we can gain a greater appreciation of the relationship between price stability and the level of economic activity.

WHAT IS PRICE STABILITY?

Definition of Inflation

In Chapter 15 we asked a similar question about full employment, and we discovered that considerable controversy existed about the acceptable level of unemployment. There was even disagreement about how we should measure who is employed, who is not, and who is looking for work but has not found a job. Similar questions exist

Price Stability Maintaining the general price level at a low and stable rate of inflation

Inflation The rate of increase in the general level of prices

about the definition of *price stability*. Most people believe that *inflation* (price instability) is a rise in the general level (or average) of prices in the economy. Price stability is thus disrupted by inflation.

Inflation is a recurring problem. In the 40 years after 1945 prices quadrupled: A typical item that cost $10 in 1945 had a price tag of about $40 in 1985. These price increases make people feel poorer, because each dollar that they earn buys fewer and fewer goods and services. Consumers would obviously prefer lower rates of inflation because they believe that as prices rise their standard of living falls.

Inflation introduces an increased degree of uncertainty into a market. Although participants in a market economy accept the possibility that they may fail, inflation adds to the uncertainty by increasing the risk. If you expect inflation but do not know whether the rate will be 5 percent or 15 percent, how should you behave? A typical response is to purchase more products today to take advantage of the lower prices. Although this strategy seems to make sense, there are two serious problems with it:

1. If everyone behaves in the same manner, there will be an increase in aggregate demand without a comparable expansion in an aggregate supply. As a consequence inflation will increase even more than was expected.
2. If you borrow money to make your purchases, you expect to repay the loan with dollars cheaper (dollars with less purchasing power) than the ones you borrowed. This strategy may backfire, however. Because inflation increases uncertainty, the economy may experience a recession, and you could lose your source of income through unemployment. Then you are in danger of losing the property that you purchased with borrowed money. Farmers, for example, faced these problems in the 1980s. They borrowed to purchase more land and equipment. When the price of food and farm land fell significantly, many farmers were forced to sell their farms.

Inflation is sometimes feared more than unemployment because people inaccurately assume that inflation has a negative impact upon everyone while unemployment affects only that small percentage of workers who are unemployed. But we learned in Chapter 15 that unemployment has a very pronounced effect upon the entire economy. In this chapter we will learn that inflation also has an economy-wide impact, but its impact, like that of unemployment, is uneven. Under some conditions certain groups may actually gain from inflation, and others may lose purchasing power.

SELF-TEST

1. Why is inflation a problem?
2. A market economy by its very nature is uncertain. Why should inflation make the functioning of the economy any different?

Measures of Inflation

Because inflation is a rise in the general price level, we cannot look at the price increases of one product, even a major product such as energy, and claim that the increase in the price of that product is equivalent to the rate of inflation. We need to establish price indices to help us determine how fast prices are changing. The three most commonly used price indices are the Consumer Price Index, the Producer Price Index, and the GNP Deflator.

Price Index A measurement of price changes relative to a specific period or base year

Base Year The year against which other prices are compared

A *price index* is developed by measuring the prices of a specific group of goods and services in one year and comparing those prices with the prices of the same group of products in another year. Table 19–1 shows how a price index is calculated. Assume that year 3 is the *base year*. Thus, the price index for year 3 is 100, because purchase price of goods and services in year 3 ($875) is divided by the base year price of $875 (that is, $875/875 = 100).

If we want to know the rate of inflation from year 3 to year 4, we should note that the price index in year 4 is 104 as compared with 100 in year 3. We know that prices increased by 4 percent during year 4 (104/100). The rate of inflation between year 4 and year 5 is determined either by dividing the prices in year 5 by the prices in year 4 ($940/$910) or by dividing the indices in the two years (107.4/104). In either case your answer will be 1.033, which indicates that

Table 19–1
Price Index

Year	Purchase Price of a Group of Goods and Services	Price Index	Annual Rate of Inflation
1	$800	91.4	
2	850	97.1	6.3%
3	875	100.0	3.0
4	910	104.0	4.0
5	940	107.4	3.3

the inflation in year 5 measures 3.3 percent; that is, the prices in year 5 are 3.3 percent higher than in the previous year. The index of 107.4 tells us that prices have risen by 7.4 percent since year 3.

Consumer Price Index A measure of price changes for purchases of products such as food, shelter, clothing, and medical care by a typical urban family

The *Consumer Price Index* (CPI) is the most commonly used price index because it attempts to measure price changes in goods and services that are commonly purchased by all consumers. On the average, typical urban wage earners spend their incomes on shelter, transportation, food and beverages, medical care, clothing, other goods and services, and entertainment. To define the weights to be attached to each price in the price index, statisticians examine each item according to its importance as a typical consumer expenditure. The prices of these key items are examined monthly, and their average change is reported as the CPI. By following this procedure the CPI provides consumers with a rough guide to how fast prices in general are changing.

Producer Price Index A measure of price changes of the goods and services a typical business must purchase to produce its products

The *Producer Price Index* (PPI) provides an indication of changes in prices of the goods and services that producers use to manufacture products. The PPI is an important index because it helps us predict what will happen to prices of consumer goods and services. Since the prices producers pay are very likely to influence the prices of products they sell, increases in the Producer Price Index are likely to appear later on as increases in the Consumer Price Index. By studying the Producer Price Index economists may be able to take some action to reduce potential inflationary pressure.

GNP Deflator A measure of price changes for the entire economy regardless of whether the price changes affect consumers, producers, or government

Money GNP Annual output of the economy measured in terms of current prices

Real GNP Annual output of the economy measured in constant dollars, that is, with inflationary changes removed

The third major price index is called the *GNP Deflator*. The primary purpose of GNP Deflator is to remove the inflationary influence from the annually reported GNP figures. That is, it distinguishes the *money GNP* from the *real GNP*. The real GNP permits us to measure the year-to-year changes in production independent of changes in prices. This measurement helps us avoid the problem of incorrectly measuring the level of economic activity. For example, if the money GNP is $1 trillion in year 1 and $1.06 trillion in year 2, it appears as if the economy is performing very well because it has expanded by 6 percent. Most observers would state that this high rate of increase in production should make the economy very healthy.

If, however, the economy also experienced a 6 percent rate of inflation, then the increase in production is really an illusion. Instead of finding a 6 percent increase in production, we find that production did not rise at all. The 6 percent increase occurred only in prices and not in production. Thus, the economy has not grown. By using the GNP deflator we get a much clearer picture of the actual changes in output.

All three of these price indices are important and are used all the time when we wish to analyze the economy seriously. But we must use these indices carefully because they, too, have shortcomings. All the indices use a base year for comparison. In doing so we report that if the price of lettuce is $.75 in year 1 and $.90 in year 2, there has been a 20 percent increase in the price of lettuce. This report makes sense for lettuce because it is highly unlikely that the quality of a head of lettuce has changed from one year to the next. Thus, we can be confident that we are paying 20 percent more for the same quality of lettuce.

But this generalization may not hold true for other products, such as refrigerators. They may also experience a 20 percent price increase, but that increase may be the result of an improvement in quality of the product by an increase in its energy efficiency. In this case the product has improved its quality, and the price increase may simply reflect that change in quality. Price indices cannot detect quality changes. Thus, if we are not careful, we may interpret all price increases as inflationary, when in some cases the price changes are reflecting an improvement in the economy through increases in quality.

A second major problem with price indices is that they assume that the combination of goods and services that is consumed today is essentially the same as the combination that was consumed in the base year. This assumption can create some serious problems if we attempt to measure inflation over a long period of time. If we are not careful, we will be comparing rubber-biased tires with steel-belted radial tires, convection ovens with microwave ovens, jet airplanes with propeller airplanes, and computers with adding machines. To minimize this problem, economic analysts change the base year on a regular basis.

SELF-TEST

3. When should you study the Producer Price Index more than the Consumer Price Index?
4. Evaluate the following statement: The distinction between real GNP and money GNP is a phony one. If I and other consumers pay the higher price associated with inflation, it must be because we are more pleased with the output than we were at the preinflation price.

Types of Inflation

Now that we understand how inflation is measured, we need to study the causes of inflation. Then we can examine different policies to correct the inflation. In a very general sense inflation can be defined as too many dollars chasing too few goods. If the money supply in the economy always increased or decreased by the same amount that production increased or decreased, inflation would not be a problem. In a modern economy, however, it is virtually impossible to keep the money supply and level of production changing at the same rate, because the two variables are interactive. That is, an increase in the money supply *may* cause an increase in production, and an increase in production *may* influence an increase in the money supply.

In addition, there are other variables that influence the level of production and the size of the money supply. Because it is difficult to regulate the supply of money relative to the level of production, the economy will often experience an imbalance between the money supply and the level of production. When we experience too many dollars chasing too few goods, inflation is the consequence.

Demand-Pull Inflation A type of inflation caused by an increase in aggregate demand relative to aggregate supply

Demand-Pull Inflation When we describe inflation as too many dollars chasing too few goods, we are discussing *demand-pull inflation.* If members of an economy attempt to purchase more goods and services than are available for consumption, we have a classic case of an imbalance between aggregate demand and aggregate supply. Just as the price of houses will rise when demand for those houses rises faster than their supply, the general level of prices will rise as aggregate demand increases faster than aggregate supply.

Demand-pull inflation is closely related to the amount of money in the economy. If the supply of money increases at a pace faster than the increase in production, then prices tend to rise. This condition is likely to occur as the economy approaches full employment.

When consumers attempt to spend increasing amounts of money, businesses experience increasing difficulty in expanding their production. As the unemployment rate falls, businesses encounter greater difficulty in acquiring labor and other resources necessary to increase production. To hire more labor and other resources, businesses generally must pay higher wages and prices for resources. As a result these businesses must raise their prices to pay these higher costs. Since consumers have more money than production, they can afford to pay the higher prices—thus, inflation. This relationship was discussed in Figure 15–1.

When unemployment is relatively high, an expansion in the money supply relative to production generally is not inflationary. The increase in the money supply will strengthen consumer demand. Businesses will want to enlarge production to satisfy this demand. Since there is relatively high unemployment, businesses can hire more workers without increasing wages. Consequently, production should expand without increases in inflation.

When trying to solve unemployment by increasing aggregate de-

Inflationary Expectations A change in buyer and seller behavior caused by the expectation that prices will continue to rise

mand, we generally consider inflation between 1 and 3 percent to be acceptable. But if we are not careful, *inflationary expectations* may cause inflation to gain a life of its own. Consumers will begin to reexamine their purchasing habits. If they expect inflation to continue, it makes sense to purchase today, when prices are relatively low, rather than in the future, when prices will be relatively high. This change in purchasing behavior will increase aggregate demand and will probably aggravate the inflationary pressures.

Cost-Push Inflation A type of inflation caused by an increase in the cost of production rather than by an increase in demand

Cost-Push Inflation Although many people think of inflation in terms of excess demand, we also need to be aware of *cost-push inflation.* It is possible for inflationary pressures to exist even though aggregate demand has not expanded faster than aggregate supply. Cost-push inflation typically occurs when either the supply of some critical products unexpectedly decline or the cost of the factors of production rise without a corresponding increase in the value of the products. An upward pressure on prices could come from increased costs of profit, labor, fuel, raw materials, borrowing, or any other costs of business. In the case where market power exists, businesses may raise prices to increase profits even though excess demand does not exist.

In the last 20 years several factors have stimulated periods of cost-push inflation. For instance, wage-price spirals occur when labor organizations attempt to maintain their purchasing power in face of inflation. That is, if inflation for the year was 7 percent, labor organizations would attempt to gain at least a 7 percent in their wage contracts to maintain their purchasing power. If a 7 percent wage increase is granted, the businesses will experience an increase in the cost of production because it is unlikely that the productivity of labor will have increased by 7 percent. Businesses will then attempt to increase their prices to compensate for the increased costs. If businesses succeed in raising their prices, there will be an increase in inflationary pressure.

The problem can become more complex if labor organizations are able to negotiate cost of living allowances (COLAs). This type of contract automatically adjusts the wage rates according to the rate of inflation. For example, if inflation is 8 percent, then wages may be automatically adjusted upward by as much as 8 percent. The actual adjustments depends upon the nature of the labor contract. Costs, and therefore prices, are forced upward. If COLAs are prohibited, workers absorb the costs of inflation. If COLAs are permitted, we must find ways to increase productivity to alleviate the resulting inflationary pressures.

Another cause of cost-push inflation has been commodity shortages. When the economy experiences shortage in some critical areas

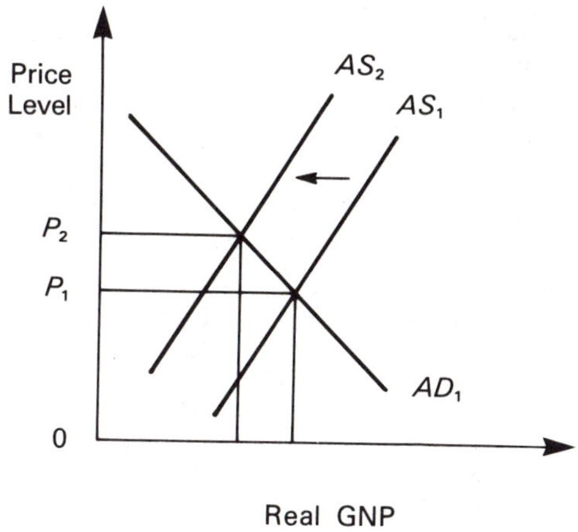

Figure 19–1
Cost-Push Inflation
This diagram demonstrates that a reduction in the output of the economy relative to demand will cause an increase in the general level or prices.

such as energy and agricultural goods, we may experience another form of cost-push inflation. During the 1970s a group of oil producing nations joined together to form the Organization of Petroleum Exporting Countries (OPEC). By forming this group OPEC gained market power over the price of oil. OPEC increased the price of oil by restricting its supply.

Because oil is an essential source of energy, businesses immediately experienced an increase in their costs of production. Oil is also an important factor in a substantial number of our products, such as foods, records and fertilizers. The reduced supply of oil increased the production costs of these products. Thus we experienced a classical example of a shift in supply (Figure 19–1). As the aggregate supply shifted from AS_1 to AS_2, the general price level rose from P_1 to P_2, depicting an increase in inflation, *ceteris paribus*.

In today's economy it is likely that inflation will result from a combination of demand and supply conditions. We will want to determine the major sources of the inflation, because the methods to control inflation may change as the sources change.

SELF-TEST

5. Explain the difference between demand-pull and cost-push inflation.
6. If the money supply were held constant, would it still be possible to experience inflation?

WHY SHOULD PRICE STABILITY BE A GOAL?

The previous section has begun our answer to this question. Because inflation causes instability, consumer and producer behavior become more difficult to predict. Consumers may increase their purchases, because they wish to beat the inflationary price increases. If consumers do increase their level of consumption, profit opportunities for businesses may expand. If businesses are able to expand their production of goods and services, the economy would grow stronger.

Consumers and businesses are just as likely to curtail purchases because they fear an economic recession. They do not want to get stuck with goods and property that they cannot afford or cannot sell. If consumers and businesses do, in fact, reduce their purchases, the economy will experience a recession.

With these conflicting tendencies the business community is likely to be cautious. If the rate of inflation is relatively low, say 1 or 2 percent, and stable, businesses may be more willing to risk expansion. But they will do so cautiously, because they believe that further increases in the rate of inflation are sure signals of economic problems. Thus, even though businesses may be experiencing profits, they do not want to risk expansion if there is a good probability that the profits will turn to losses because of an economic downturn. Thus, inflation, like unemployment, can cause significant economic loss to the society.

Economic uncertainty is not the only problem caused by inflation. In the beginning of this chapter we talked about how inflation reduces the purchasing power of money and how most people believe that they are worse off because of this inflation. The reasons for this belief are quite simple. Assume you earn $100 and you make the following purchases:

Preinflationary Prices				Postinflationary Prices			
2–$20	shirts	=	$ 40	2–$22	shirts	=	$ 44
1–$10	tie	=	10	1–$11	tie	=	11
1–$40	jacket	=	40	1–$44	jacket	=	44
2–$5	pr socks	=	10	2–$5.50	pr socks	=	11
			$100				$110

If prices rise by 10 percent, then your projected expenditures will rise from $100 to $110. Since you have only $100 to spend, you can no longer afford the combination of clothing you had desired to purchase. You may alter your purchase to the following combination:

Postinflationary Prices

2–$22	shirts	=	$ 44
1–$11	tie	=	11
1–$44	jacket	=	44
0–$5.50	pr socks	=	0
			$ 99

This example demonstrates that although your income remains at $100, your purchasing power has fallen by 10 percent, or, in this case, by two pairs of socks.

The key to this loss of purchasing power is that prices went up while income remained constant. Yet, is income likely to remain constant? Who gets the income from the higher prices? In the above example, the clothing producers receive $110 for the same goods that had previously sold for $100. In other words, their income has risen by the 10 percent that prices rose. If all incomes rose by 10 percent, then each consumer would have $110 to purchase the $110 combination of clothing. In this particular case, the *real income,* or purchasing power, of the consumers has remained constant even though prices rose by 10 percent. Inflation has had no impact upon purchasing power.

Real Income Actual purchasing power of one's monetary income

In most cases, however, changes in prices and incomes do not occur so evenly. Some people receive fixed incomes (for example, the elderly on pensions), others receive income that generally rises more slowly than the rate of inflation (for example, educators), and others may receive income that rises faster than the rate of inflation. (This group is hard to identify, but it often includes those income earners who can set their own fees.) When incomes change unevenly, inflation has an uneven impact. Individuals or families who receive fixed or slowly changing incomes will experience a reduction in real income (purchasing power) as a result of inflation. Whereas individuals and families who receive increases in their income that exceed the rate of inflation will actually experience an increase in real income.

We can see that inflation also causes a redistribution of income. Through no fault or activity of their own, some families become poorer while others become wealthier. As the distribution of income changes, businesses become more uncertain about future business opportunities. If businesses believe that the risk of increasing production is too great, they may reduce their business spending and cause a recession. Thus, inflation may hurt some people, because their purchasing power may decrease. Inflation may also lead to recession and reduce production within the economy.

From the preceding discussion it should be clear that inflation can cause serious problems for the economy. If we could maintain price stability, the economy would function much more smoothly. If we were to examine the historical record, we would discover that the United States was very successful in achieving price stability in the 1950s and 1960s. But our success changed dramatically in the 1970s. We need to examine why this change occurred.

Chapter 20 will start us on that path by explaining the role of money within an economic system. More specifically, we will study how the money supply can be used to influence the rate of inflation.

ACTIVE REVIEW

1. During the past year the GNP of country X expanded by $10 billion, which was a 10 percent increase in GNP over the previous year. The citizens were elated because a 10 percent increase in GNP indicates that their economy is prospering. However, upon further investigation economists revealed that the Consumer Price Index rose from 100 to 105 over the same period. With this information do you believe that the citizens should be elated about the vitality of their economy?
2. If every time I purchase a product someone else receives additional income, incomes must rise as prices (inflation) rise. If incomes increase at the same rate as inflation, the inflation will not reduce purchasing power. If purchasing power does not fall, inflation is not a problem. Evaluate this statement.

ANSWER TO ACTIVE REVIEW

1. Although money GNP rose by $10 billion, real GNP rose by only 4.8 percent (see calculations below). The 5 percent inflation cut the 10 percent money GNP virtually in half. Although a 4.8 percent increase is generally considered to be very good, it certainly is not as good as 10 percent.

   A potential major problem facing this economy is inflationary expectations. Consumers initially thought they had earned a 10 percent gain, but inflation reduced that gain to approximately 5 percent. If consumers begin to worry that this rate of inflation will continue to increase, they are likely to make purchases today that they had previously decided to postpone. If enough consumers alter their purchasing decisions, they will cause an increase in aggregate demand and actually cause an expansion of demand-pull inflation. If demand-pull inflation occurs, future economic expansion will be negatively influenced.

If the 5 percent inflation is under control, inflationary expectations are less likely to be a problem. The economy should then concentrate on expanding production beyond the real rate of 4.8 percent.

	Money GNP (billions)	Rate of Inflation*	Real GNP**
Year 1	$100	100%	$100
Year 2	110	105	104.8

*The rate of inflation is equivalent to the GNP deflator.
**The real GNP is determined by dividing the money GNP by the GNP deflator ($110 billion/105 = $104.8 billion).

ANSWERS TO SELF-TEST

1. Inflation causes two significant economic problems: It reduces the purchasing power of some members of the society, and it increases business uncertainty that may lead to a recession. As prices rise faster than the income of some members of the economy, the purchasing power of those members falls. As a consequence the standard of living of those people falls. If a substantially large proportion of the economy experiences reduced purchasing power, aggregate demand will fall, and unemployment will rise (assuming that wages are unlikely to fall).

   If business uncertainty rises, businesses will be less willing to accept the risks associated with new business ventures. If businesses become unwilling to accept these risks, business spending will decline, and the economy is likely to experience a recession.
2. It is true that a market economy operates on the principle of trial and error and that businesses accept the reality that some of their business ventures will fail. Inflation, however, increases the uncertainty. When price stability exists, businesses attempt to minimize their errors by producing their goods and services efficiently and by performing market surveys to determine what goods and services consumers are willing to purchase. When the economy experiences inflation, businesses become less able to predict the purchasing behavior of consumers. If businesses anticipate that the consumers of their products will experience a reduction in purchasing power, the businesses are unlikely to accept the risks associated with increased production.
3. If you are attempting to understand what will happen to *future* prices of consumer goods, then it is more appropriate to study the Producer Price Index. Price changes in PPI precede changes in the Consumer Price Index. If PPI is not rising, economic planners can predict that inflation in consumer goods and services should decline.

   If you studied only the CPI, you would learn how consumer prices had changed the previous month, but you would not know whether these prices are likely to continue to rise during the current month. The PPI is a better predictor.

4. The statement is erroneous. Consumers' ability and desire to purchase goods and services depends upon the income they have available. If prices and income increase by the same percentage, consumers can purchase exactly the same quantity of goods and services as they did prior to the price increase. The quality of the products has not increased nor has consumer satisfaction. The only way our standard of living will increase is if there is an actual increase in goods and services. Increases in prices generally do not indicate an improvement in production.
5. Demand-pull inflation occurs when the ability of consumers to spend rises more rapidly than actual production of goods and services. Cost-push inflation occurs when production is reduced relative to its former level. The spending power of consumers has not increased, but the supply of goods and services has decreased. Although the causes are different, both types of inflation result in the condition of too many dollars chasing too few goods. In Chapter 21, we will see that different policies should be used to combat the two types of inflation.
6. Cost-push inflation could occur when the money supply is held constant. If an important commodity becomes less available (such as oil in the 1970s), real output decreases. If the supply of money remains at its previous level, the money supply will become greater than the level of production. We again face too many dollars chasing too few goods. Under this condition, however, the problem exists because production declined, not because the money supply expanded too rapidly.

20
Price Stability and the Monetary System

In Chapter 19 we learned that price stability is an important goal because when it is achieved, purchasing power is preserved and business decisions can be made with more certainty. We also learned that price stability can be maintained if an economy can manage to keep its supply of money and the level of output changing at the same rate.

Since price stability is an important economic goal and since we simply need to equate the rate of change of the money supply with that of output, why then do we allow our economy to experience high levels of inflation? If inflation is often considered the major economic problem of the society, why don't we keep inflation under control?

Recurring inflation is caused by many diverse forces, including the supply of money. An economy may experience a spurt in aggregate demand without a corresponding increase in aggregate supply. Businesses with market power may push prices up to increase profits. The costs of production may suddenly increase because of an unexpected decline in production. We may experience inflation because as a society we decide to pursue some other economic goal.

During the 1970s and early 1980s the rate of inflation fluctuated between 3.3 and 13.57 percent. These rates of inflation are significantly higher than the average inflationary rate of 2.3 percent that we experienced between 1950 and 1970. How did we manage to let the level of production and the supply of money get so far out of alignment?

The purpose of this chapter is to examine the relationship between the money supply and price stability. We will study different functions of money as they relate to price stability; we will examine the different ways to measure money; we will illustrate how the banking system creates money; and finally, we will identify the tools that monetary authorities can use to control the supply of money.

PRODUCTION, SPENDING, AND MONEY SUPPLY

In Chapter 16 we established that economic systems can be described as a circular flow and that all economic activity begins with production. In primitive economies this circular flow occurs when people engage in barter. Members of the economy exchange their production with one another. Even in segments of industrial economies such as the United States individuals barter. For example, one farmer may harvest wheat for a second farmer, and in return the second farmer may give the first farmer a side of beef. But in most segments of our economy, barter is not a very effective method for exchanging production. Generally, producers earn income from the sale of their goods and services, and they use that income to purchase other goods and services.

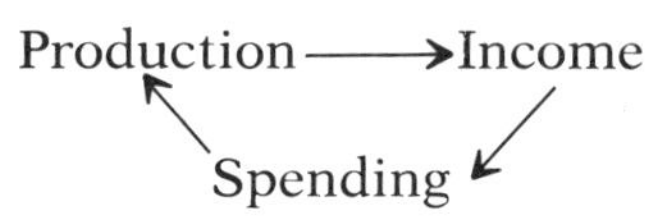

To operate an economy in this manner there must be a monetary system. Money must exist to facilitate the exchange of goods and services. In other words, money is a medium of exchange. Individuals will accept money (dollars, francs, rubles, and so forth) in payment for goods and services because they are confident that other sellers will accept that same money from them as payment for goods and services.

Why does this system work? Why are you confident that someone will sell you a sweater for $40 or a stereo unit for $500? Why do the sellers prefer the money over commodities such as gold or silver? One answer is that the system works because everyone believes it will work. Silly as it sounds, this answer is accurate. Yet we still need to investigate *why* people have confidence in paper money.

The answer to this question is found by examining the relationship between level of output in the economy and the supply of money. If the supply of money increases and the level of production does not, the price of the product will increase, but the quality of the product will not increase. To demonstrate, let's develop a very simple example. Assume you live in a very small community that produces only one crop, wheat. In year 1 your economy produces 10,000 bushels and it has $10,000 with which to purchase the wheat. Under these conditions the wheat will sell for $1 per bushel.

In year 2 the economy produces 10,000 bushels again, but the money supply increases to $20,000. What happens? The price of wheat doubles to $2 per bushel, but the quantity and quality of the wheat remain the same. As a result of the doubling of the money supply, the purchasing power of the dollar dropped by one-half. If the money supply dropped to $5,000, then the price of wheat would fall to $.50 per bushel. Does this drop in price mean that the quality of the wheat has fallen?

In each example the quantity and quality of wheat have remained constant while the supply of money has changed. The price of wheat varied directly with the change in the money supply. That is, when the money supply increased, the price of wheat increased. When the money supply decreased, the price of wheat fell. Furthermore, under these conditions, as the price of wheat rises, the value of money falls because each dollar will buy fewer products.

If we broaden the example to include many goods and services, the same relationship would exist. When the money supply rises faster than the general level of production, inflation occurs. Prices remain relatively stable as long as the supply of money changes at approximately the same rate as the level of production.

Consumers and producers maintain their confidence in money as long as it maintains a relatively consistent relationship with the level of production. It does not make a great deal of difference if price of wheat is $.50, $1.00, $2.00, or $5.00 a bushel as long as the prices do not fluctuate widely. If the price of wheat stays around $2.00, the monetary system will function effectively. If, however, the price of wheat changes from $1.00 to $1.50 to $4.00 to $6.50 over a three-year period, producers and consumers will lose confidence in the dollar. They cannot use the dollar to approximate the value of wheat. Money will lose its acceptability because people will not know how to use it effectively to exchange goods and services.

SELF-TEST

1. The monetary system in the United States appears to have no relationship to the amount of gold in the economy. If money is not backed by gold or some other precious metal, then what gives money its value?

FUNCTIONS OF MONEY

It has been implied throughout the preceding section that money functions in three ways: as a medium of exchange, a measure of value, and a store of value. Money is valued for what it does rather than for what it is. Curious as it may seem money has very little intrinsic value. Money permits an economy to operate more smoothly, much like lubricating oil facilitates the working of an automobile engine. If the engine has too little oil, the engine will work sluggishly and may even stop. If there is too much oil, the engine will again act improperly. When the money supply is kept at its proper level, the economy tends to operate very smoothly. We can understand this relationship by studying the three functions of money more carefully.

Medium of Exchange

Because bartering is cumbersome, modern economies have searched for ways to make the exchange process easier. Although it may make sense for one farmer to exchange a side of beef for the harvesting of his or her wheat, it does not make sense to pay an auto worker with auto parts that he or she must then exchange for goods and services. A complex economy such as that of the United States needs money facilitate exchanges. In other words, an economy need a *medium of exchange.*

Medium of Exchange Anything that is generally acceptable as a means of payment for goods and services

Money may be any commodity. If we do a historical search we will find that such diverse items as cowrie shells, boar tusks, bars of salt, tobacco, and gold have all been used as money. But what made these items acceptable? Initially, their intrinsic worth and relative scarcity were important, but once the items were used in trading, the very fact that others would accept boar tusks for food or shells for clothing made these items an important part of the exchange process.

The same reasoning holds true for money in today's economies. Buyers and sellers have confidence that the supply of money will be relatively scarce because it will change at approximately the same rate as the level of national output. Money will continue to function as a medium of exchange as long as the relationship between the supply of money and the level of production remains relatively stable. If the money supply expands too rapidly, people will return to forms of barter to make their exchanges.

Measure of Value

In a barter economy, goods and services are exchanged for one another. There is no standard unit of comparison. For example, if you are a wheat farmer, what can you expect in trade for a bushel of wheat? If you want eggs, you will need to negotiate with an egg producer, and if you need butter, you will need to negotiate with a dairy farmer. In both instances your negotiations depend more upon your skills as a negotiator than on the intrinsic value of wheat. Whereas in a modern market economy we can expect the price or exchange value of wheat to remain relatively similar whether it is sold in Nebraska or in Pennsylvania.

If a monetary system exists, the dollar, franc, pound, or ruble acts as a measuring rod that identifies the values of different goods and services. Typically, we talk about the value of a product in terms of its monetary unit. That is, haircuts are worth $10, refrigerators are worth $500, and automobiles are worth $10,000. Because money is accepted as a means of payment, money also becomes a way to identify value.

This point is especially true when an economy is functioning in a relatively competitive manner. For example, if you go shopping for meat and you find that one cut of meat is more expensive than another, you can be confident that the higher priced cut of meat is a better (more tender and tasty) cut of meat than the lower priced cut. Similarly, if a pound of hamburger is $1.09 and a pound of ground chuck is $1.39, you can assume that the hamburger has more fat content. Consequently, when you cook the hamburger, your dinner will contain more fat and there will be less to eat because of the shrinkage of the meat after the fat is cooked out. Money as a *measure of value* helps us make better decisions.

Measure of Value Function of money that provides a standard for measuring the value of goods and services

Store of Value

Store of Value The function of money that permits an accumulation of wealth to be used for future purchases

Because money is a medium of exchange that can be used to purchase goods and services at virtually any time, money is a convenient form in which to store wealth (assets) for later purchases. Money is attractive as a *store of value* because it is easily converted into other assets; that is, money is highly liquid. For example, if you save $10,000 and wish to purchase a car, you simply take your money to an auto dealer and exchange money for the auto. People save money for future purchases because money is a store of value.

All assets are stores of value, but none of them is as convenient as money. Other assets, such as stocks, bonds, and homes, must be converted to money before they can be spent. On the other hand, other assets tend to earn income. For example, stocks earn dividends, bonds earn interest, and homes tend to appreciate in value. Thus money is a store of value because it is easy to use, but it is a potentially costly store of value because it does not earn income. Consequently, people tend to store their wealth in some combination of money and other assets.

Money and Price Stability

The three functions of money perform very effectively when the economy is experiencing price stability. When prices become unstable however, there is a pronounced effect on the ability of money to function as we just described. To demonstrate this point, let us examine the functions of money in reverse order.

If inflation becomes a chronic problem within an economy, money may cease to function as a store of value. When inflation occurs, the purchasing power of money (dollars) falls. Households and businesses realize that holding money as a store of value for future purchases does not make sense, because each dollar saved will purchase fewer goods and services in the future than it will today. As a result, people are likely to increase their rate of spending. This increased spending will add pressure that could cause demand-pull inflation.

In addition, as the level of savings decreases, the amount of money available for borrowing and investing decreases. Less savings result in higher costs of investing. If these higher costs cause businesses to reduce their level of spending on plant and equipment, a recession becomes probable. Thus, when money loses its ability to function as a store of value, the economy is likely to experience the additional instability of a recession.

Price instability will also influence money as a measure of value. If all prices increased at the same rate, money would continue to function as a measure of value, because prices would maintain their relative positions to one another. For example, in period 1 the price of bread is $1 a loaf and the price of sirloin steak is $3 per pound. In period 2 the price of bread rises to $2 a loaf and the sirloin increases to $6 per pound. Under these circumstances the price of both products has doubled, but the price of steak is still three times more than the price of bread. Money still measures the relative worth of these products.

Unfortunately, inflation generally does not affect all prices in the same way. Although inflation is defined as an increase in the general level of prices, some prices will increase more rapidly than others. When prices rise unevenly, money loses its effectiveness as a measure of value. For example, if as a result of inflation the price of bread rises from $1 to $2 and the price of sirloin rises from $3 to $5, the price relationship between the two products has changed. Prior to inflation the prices told us that sirloin was three times more valuable than bread. After inflation, prices indicate that sirloin is only two and one-half times more valuable than bread.

This latter relationship may be misleading, however, because only prices, not quality, have changed. The longer inflation continues, the more likely that money will cease to function as a measure of value, because the price relationships among products will change as a consequence of prices rising at different rates.

Finally, inflation distorts the ability of money to function as a medium of exchange. When prices are stable, money is by far the most convenient way to exchange goods and services. When inflation occurs, this relationship changes. As consumers, we need to question whether money will enable us to purchase the appropriate value. As sellers, we are uncertain about whether we should accept money in payment for goods and services, because the future purchase power of money is declining.

If inflation rises rapidly or continues over a period of years, people will lose confidence in money as a medium of exchange. Forms of barter will reappear. Farmers may start accepting seed and fertilizers for their grain. Doctors may begin accepting goods and services for their medical diagnoses or surgery. In general, inflation makes a monetary system less effective and causes the economy to function less smoothly.

SELF-TEST

2. Explain the difference between money as a store of value and money as a measure of value.
3. Evaluate the following comment: It does not make any difference if the price of bread is $1, $2, $5, or $20 as long as the prices of all other products rise at the same rate.

TYPES OF MONEY

Up to this point in the chapter we have referred to money as if it were a well-defined unit. Yet in most countries money is defined in several ways, and different definitions are used to study different aspects of the economy. If you were asked to identify money, what would you answer? It is a safe bet that you would start with coins and dollars, but this answer would be only partially correct. In fact, currency (coins and paper money) is only a small portion of the total supply of money. A much more important source of money is money on deposit in banks, called *checkable deposits.**

Checkable Deposits Accounts in banks on which checks can be written

Checkable deposits are popularly identified as checking accounts. When you deposit currency into a checking account, you still possess the right to use those deposits as money. When you write a check, the majority of businesses will accept the check as a means of payment. That is, the check is a medium of exchange. Because you can use your checks in the same way as currency, checkable deposits are also measures of value and stores of value.

Checks are so easy to use and important as records of business transactions. As a result checkable deposits have become the most significant part of the money supply. Consequently, our money supply is influenced more by changes in the size of checkable deposits that it is by the printing of dollars. (This point will be explained a little later in the chapter.)

Federal Reserve System A system of central banks that regulates the money supply and other banking activities

Because of the changing role of financial institutions, the *Federal Reserve System* has four designations for money, M-1, M-2, M-3, and L. The designations and their relationships are shown in Table 20–1.

There is some controversy over the definition of money and how to measure the nation's money supply. The most common designation is M-1, which includes currency, demand deposits, other checkable deposits, and travelers checks. Some economists believe, however, that M-1 is too narrow a definition. They argue that many people use savings accounts like checkable deposits.

The following example demonstrates their reasoning. Suppose you have $500 in your savings account to help pay your living expenses while at school. Is this $500 money? According to the M-1 definition, savings are not a medium of exchange, because you must convert them to cash or demand deposits before you can spend the savings. Other disagree, claiming that savings are easily converted to cash or checkable deposits. As a result, the student and others use the savings deposits as if they were cash. Under this condition the savings should be considered to be money. If this premise is accepted, money is designated M-2.

As Table 20–1 indicates, money is also defined as M-3 and L. In

*In today's economy the definition of banks has become blurred. Prior to 1980 we could easily distinguish between commercial banks and savings and loan institutions. Today, however, savings and loan institutions perform many of the same functions as banks. For this reason we will refer to banks, but we wish to include under this heading all financial institutions that lend money and accept checkable deposits.

Table 20–1
Measure of Money Supply (Dec. 1984)

Designation	Components	Seasonally Adjusted Dollars (billions)
M-1	Currency Demand deposits Other checkable deposits Travelers checks	558.5
M-2	M-1 plus Savings deposits Other small time-deposits	2,371.7
M-3	M-2 plus Large denomination time-deposits	2,995.0
L	M-3 plus Liquid Treasury obligations	3,543.8

Source: *Federal Reserve Bulletin* (Washington, D.C.: Publication services, Board of Governors, Federal Reserve System, 1985).

each case the definition includes more items. When additional items are added to the definition of money, the supply of money becomes less flexible, or less liquid. For this reason most economists prefer the M-1 definition of money. You should be aware, however, that the different definitions could cause significant differences in analyzing the supply of money. For example, in 1984, M-1 was $558.5 billion, M-2 was $2,371.7 billion, M-3 was $2,995.0 billion, and L was $3,543.8 billion. For the purpose of our analysis we will assume M-1 as the appropriate designation.

SELF-TEST

4. Traditionally money has been defined as currency and demand deposits, but today economists typically define money as currency, demand deposits, other checkable deposits, and travelers checks. Why does this change in composition make sense?

BANKING SYSTEM AND CREATION OF MONEY

The banking system in the United States is a complex structure of many types of financial institutions, ranging from relatively small credit unions to the Federal Reserve System. In one way or another all these institutions affect the supply of money in the economy. It is important to understand how the banking system functions, because price stability depends upon the ability to control the supply of money within the banking system.

This point needs to be emphasized. There is a common myth that the federal government controls the supply of money through the process of printing and destroying money. The myth continues by claiming that inflation can be controlled by reducing the number of dollars the United States Treasury prints.

It is true that when the Treasury prints new dollars, more money is added to the total supply of money. It is also true that printing dollars could be a major cause of inflation. In the United States, however, the supply of dollars has not been the major culprit in inflation. We need to remember that the supply of currency is only 28 percent of the total supply of money and that checkable deposits make up the majority of the difference. Thus, attempts to control the supply of money require changes within the banking system rather than changes within the United States Treasury.

In the United States the banking system consists of many financial institutions, such as commerical banks, savings and loan institutions, and credit unions, that are linked together by a system of central banks called the Federal Reserve System. The institutions within the banking systems accept checkable deposits (checking accounts) and time deposits (savings accounts). They also grant loans and purchase securities such as treasury notes and corporate bonds. Through the use of these loans and securities the banking system is able to create money.

Federal Reserve System

The Federal Reserve System (FRS) consists of 12 regional Federal Reserve Banks and a board of governors who oversee the money supply. The board of governors has the responsibility of coordinating the operations of financial institutions and regulating the relationship between deposits and loans. Through these activities the FRS attempts to control the supply of money.

The Federal Reserve Banks are not like the other members of the banking system. A typical depositor cannot do his or her banking at one of the Federal Reserve Banks. Instead of working with deposits from individuals, the Federal Reserve Banks serve as the bank for commercial banks, savings and loans, and the United States government. The Federal Reserve Banks perform these services by holding reserves, or deposits, clearing checks, and granting loans to financial institutions.

All financial institutions belonging to the FRS are required to

Reserve Account Percentage of a bank's deposits that are placed in a Federal Reserve Bank

hold a specified fraction of their deposits as reserves. Part of these reserves is held in a Federal Reserve Bank in a *reserve account.* The amount that a financial institution must deposit with a Federal Reserve Bank will vary according to the type of deposit. Financial institutions that hold checkable deposits must hold a greater percentage of their deposits on reserve than must institutions that hold savings and time deposits. These reserve requirements are influenced by the functions of the financial institutions and play an important role in controlling the supply of money. (We will examine this feature more thoroughly in the next section.)

The Federal Reserve Banks clear checks. When you write a check to pay your tuition, your university has to get its money from your deposits in your local bank. The FRS provides a check-clearing service to facilitate these transactions. Just imagine the confusion if every single business had to worry about collecting the money for each check. Under that condition your university would probably have to contact banks all over the country. Because the FRS provides this service, your university will simply deposit your check in its bank, which will then send the check to its regional Federal Reserve Bank. The regional Federal Reserve Bank then transfers the checks to the proper accounts. Today this process is done electronically.

Fractional Reserves

Before economies began to use paper money, people would often ask goldsmiths to hold or store gold. After performing this service for a while, goldsmiths realized that when they stored relatively large amounts of gold, they gained the flexibility to lend some of that gold. As long as they always kept enough gold available to meet the day-to-day requests of the depositors, the goldsmiths could lend the remaining gold to others and thereby earn some income from interest payments.

The people who borrowed the gold used it to expand their business activities. Thus, the goldsmiths performed an important service for their communities. They kept gold in safekeeping for those who had surpluses, and they lent gold to those who wished to expand their business activities. In essence, goldsmiths were the early bankers.

In a similar manner today's bankers know that generally all depositers will not demand their money on the same day. With proper management banks can hold a fraction of their reserves, lend the remainder of the deposits to people who are willing to borrow, and still return money to depositors upon their request.

This system works because new deposits are constantly being

made at the same time old deposits are being withdrawn. Although these amounts are unlikely to be equal, bankers learn through experience that the two amounts are similar enough so that banks need to keep only a relatively small proportion of actual deposits to cover day-to-day transactions.

Fractional Reserves Banking practice in which only a portion of deposits are kept in banks. The remainder of the deposits is used to make loans and to purchase securities.

Keeping only a portion of actual deposits is known as *fractional reserve* banking. This practice is a critical feature in the monetary system because banks can earn profit from these loans. The more money banks lend, the greater the profit they can earn from the interest payments. Thus, banks have an incentive to increase their lending activities as much as possible.

On the other hand, banks must be careful to keep from lending too much money. If they let the reserves fall too low and cannot respond to depositors' requests for their own money, the banks will fail. When banks fail, there is danger that the monetary system may collapse. As a result, the Federal Reserve System sets specific rules on the percentage of deposits that a bank must hold.

Fractional reserves are an essential feature of the banking system. If properly managed, the fractional reserves are safe and effective. They provide bankers the flexibility to respond to the monetary needs of the economy.

SELF-TEST

5. If ordinary people like you and me cannot deposit money in the Federal Reserve Banks, why are they necessary?
6. Evaluate the following comment: I put my money in banks because I know that I can withdraw my deposits whenever I please. If I ever thought that a bank did not have my money on hand, I would stop using that bank as soon as possible.

Creation of Money

Excess Reserves Funds that are available for loans as determined by the difference between actual reserves (money from deposits) and required reserves

We mentioned earlier in this chapter that the banking system has more influence over the supply of money than does the United States Treasury. The reason for this influence is the relative importance of checkable deposits as money.

Because banks use the practice of fractional reserves, they can alter the supply of money by using the *excess reserves* to increase their loans. By using fractional reserves, banks can use one deposit as the basis for several deposits. For example, Joe deposits $1,000 in his local bank. As a result of the fractional reserve concept, his local bank decides to keep $250 in reserve and to identify $750 as excess reserves. Mary may approach the same bank and request a $750 loan. If the bank grants the loan to Mary, the money supply will increase by $750. Joe still has the right to use his $1,000 whenever he wishes. In addition, Mary has the same right with her borrowed $750.

In a rudimentary way we have just described the basics of the creation of money. There are more steps to the process, however. We need to know that the Federal Reserve System requires banks to maintain a specific percentage of their deposits as assets. That is, banks are required to hold a percentage of the deposits cash or as a deposit in a Federal Reserve Bank. These reserves are called *required reserves*.

Required Reserves Specified percentage of checkable deposits that must be kept as an asset, either as cash or as a deposit in a Federal Reserve Bank

Fractional Reserves and a Single Bank Are you confused? If so, let us approach the same information from a different perspective. We will take a glance at what may happen in a fictitious bank, Security National. Assume that you have just made a $2,000 deposit to your checking account at Security National. Can you explain what Security National will do with your deposit?

Your deposit causes the bank to make two entries in its books. First, your $2,000 deposit is a liability to the bank in that the bank must return that money to you whenever your request it. Second, your deposit has also created an asset, because Security National can use your $2,000 to earn income. At the time of your deposit, Security National has an additional $2,000 of deposits and additional reserves of $2,000 (step 1 in Table 20–2).

The officials of Security National know that the Federal Reserve System requires them to hold a percentage of their deposits on reserve. In this example we will assume that the percentage is 25 per-

Table 20–2 Potential Money Expansion at a Single Bank (Security National)

Step	Assets		Liabilities	
1	Reserves	$2,000	Checkable deposits	$2,000
2	Required reserves	500	Checkable deposits	2,000
	Excess reserves	1,500		
3	Required reserves	875	Checkable deposits	2,000
	Excess reserves	1,125	Checkable deposits for Alex	1,500
	Loan to Alex	1,500		
4	Required reserves	2,000	Checkable deposits	8,000
	Loans to Alex	6,000		

Assumes a required reserve ratio of 25 percent.

cent. In other words, Security National must hold $500 of your $2,000 deposit in cash or on deposit at a Federal Reserve Bank. This requirement means that Security National must identify its assets as $500 worth of required reserves and $1,500 as excess reserves (see step 2 in Table 20–2).

Security National may lend the $1,500 of excess reserves to other customers. Let us assume that Alex, another customer of Security National, requests a $1,500 loan. If the loan is granted, Security National will increase Alex's checking account by $1,500, thus increasing deposits in Security National to $3,500. At the same time, however, the bank's assets will increase by $1,500 because Alex promises to repay the loan (step 3).

But what has happened to the relationship between excess reserves and required reserves? Security National has $3,500 in demand deposits. Therefore, they are required to keep $875 in required reserves ($3,500 × .25 = $875). The difference between the original $2,000 deposit and $875 required reserve becomes $1,125 of excess reserves (see step 3 in Table 20–2).

Since Security National still has $1,125 in excess reserves it can continue to make new loans. In fact, Security National can continue to lend money until its required reserves equal its total reserves. In this example, when deposits equal $8,000, required reserves will equal $2,000 ($8,000 × .25 = $2,000). Thus, the initial $2,000 deposit has grown to $8,000 because the fractional reserve system permitted Security National to expand its lending activity by $6,000 (step 4).

Although this example is basically accurate, it is a little deceptive because it refers to only one bank, Security National. When we study one bank, we should expect people who borrow money to withdraw their deposits. For example, if Alex borrowed the $1,500 for some home repairs, then he probably would write a $1,500 check to his contractor very shortly after he received the loan. When Security National honors the check, both its deposits and excess reserves will drop by $1,500. Hence, Security National has not expanded its deposits and can lend only the amount of its excess reserves.

Fractional Reserves and the Entire Banking System Single banks cannot increase checkable deposits, because borrowers will withdraw their money from the bank soon after they receive loans. But this consequence does not hold true for the entire banking system. When Alex pays his contractor $1,500, what is the contractor likely to do? In most instances the contractor will place the $1,500 in a checking account at another bank, say First Fidelity. That is, the reduction in deposits at Security National is matched by an increase in deposits at First Fidelity. This point is important because it illustrates that although Security National cannot lend any more money First Fidelity can increase its loans because it now has excess reserves of $1,125. (Can you explain how we arrived at this figure? Hint: What are the required reserves for the $1,500 deposit?)

The entire banking system tends to recapture deposits that are withdrawn from any one bank. In the banking system checkable deposits that are withdrawn from one bank tend to be deposited in another bank. As long as consumers and businesses pay most of their bills by checks, money will move from account to account, but it will tend to stay within the banking system. If the money stays within the banking system, then the general level of checkable deposits and their reserves will not decline every time someone writes a check. If the reserves do not decline, then the banking system can expand checkable deposits by a multiple of new deposits (net additions).

SELF-TEST

7. Explain why a single bank in a multi-bank system cannot create money, but all banks working together within the banking system can create money.
8. Throughout this chapter the text explained that banks can increase the money supply by increasing their loans. Won't this practice cause inflation by letting too much money into the economy?

Money Multiplier

By this stage you should be aware that an initial checkable deposit in a bank can expand to several times its original size. In like manner a reduction in checkable deposits will cause the money supply to contract by a multiple of the original reduction. These changes are influenced by the size of the initial deposits and by the *required reserve ratio.*

Required Reserve Ratio Amount of money that must be held in a reserve account divided by the total checkable deposits

The Federal Reserve System controls the size of the required reserve ratio because it has the responsibility to control the expansion and contraction of the money supply. The required reserve ratio determines the extent to which a change in the size of deposits will be multiplied. If the Federal Reserve System increases the size of the required reserve ratio, the supply of money will experience smaller expansions and contractions. The opposite occurs if the size of the required reserve ratio is decreased.

This relationship can be illustrated more clearly by identifying

Money Multiplier Maximum possible change in the money supply caused by a change in the level of the deposits within the system

the *money multiplier* as the reciprocal of the required reserve ratio. That is: money multiplier = 1/required ratio. For example, if the Federal Reserve System sets the required reserve ratio at 25 percent, the money multiplier will be 4 (money multiplier = 1/.25 = 4). If the required reserve ratio is set at 20 percent, the money multiplier will be 5 (money multiplier = 1/.20 = 5).

Assume that the Federal Reserve System sets the required reserve ratio at 20 percent. The multiplier tells us that if $1 million of new checkable deposits are injected into the banking system, those deposits will expand to a maximum of $5 million. In a similar manner, if checkable deposits are decreased by $1 million, the deposits will decrease by a maximum of $5 million. Thus, the multiplier helps us understand what happens to the money supply when the economy experiences changes in the level of its checkable deposits.

The expansion of the money supply is illustrated in Table 20–3. Step 1: Someone, say Hank Jones, deposits $5,000 in Security National. Because the required reserve ratio is 20 percent, Security National must keep at least $1,000 of the $5,000 on reserve. Amelia Johnson requests a $4,000 loan to purchase a computer. Security National grants the loan because it has $4,000 in excess reserves.

Step 2: Amelia purchases the computer from Computer Specialists, who deposit Amelia's check in its bank, First Fidelity. The required reserves for First Fidelity increase by $800, and its excess reserves expand by $3,200. First Fidelity is now able to lend Barney Jacobs $3,200 for some home repairs.

Step 3: Barney's contractor, Homes Renewed, deposits its $3,200 in Central Trust, whose required reserves increase by $640, and its excess reserves, by $2,560. Central Trust lends the $2,560 to Dr. Wendy Welsh who needs to purchase some new equipment for her dental practice.

Step 4: Dental Equipment, Inc., takes Wendy's check and deposits it in Bank of the Nation, whose required reserves increase by $512,

Table 20–3
Illustration of the Money Creation Process

Step	Financial Institution	Checkable Deposits	Required Reserves (20%)	Loans
1	Security National	$ 5,000	$1,000	$ 4,000
2	First Fidelity	4,000	800	3,200
3	Central Trust	3,200	640	2,560
4	Bank of the Nation	2,560	512	2,048
5	All other financial institutions	10,240	2,048	8,192
	TOTALS	$25,000	$5,000	$20,000

and its excess reserves, by $2,408. Bank of the Nation can now lend $2,048 to Harold Peterson to repair his car.

Step 5: The depositing and lending process will continue throughout the banking system. Each time a deposit is made, the amount that can be lent will equal 80 percent of the deposit (20 percent must be kept as required reserves). Eventually the new deposits and loans will approach zero. When they do, the money supply will have expanded to its maximum amount. In this example the initial deposit of $5,000 was multiplied by 5 to a total of $25,000 of deposits or money.

Some Qualifications

The previous section suggests that altering the money supply is a relatively easy process. We need to know how much money we wish to inject into the system during times of unemployment or how much money to withdraw during times of inflation. We also need to know the required reserve ratio so that we can calculate the multiplier. Unfortunately, there are complications. Banks do not always lend all their excess reserves, people do not always want to borrow all the money banks want to lend, and some people do not always deposit their money; they may keep some in cash.

Some banks do not lend all their excess reserves because they wish to be a little cautious. They may want to protect themselves against unexpectedly large withdrawals. Although this policy may be a sound management practice for individual banks, it complicates the multiplier process. Holding excess reserves makes it difficult to calculate the multiplier, because we do not know the actual percentage of deposits that the financial institutions are holding. If we have difficulty in calculating the multiplier, then we will not be able to make accurate predictions about changes in the money supply.

Expansion of the money supply cannot occur unless qualified borrowers apply for the loans. Especially during recessions businesses are often reluctant to take risks on new ventures and consumers often postpone their purchases of cars, televisions, and other durable goods. Thus there are times when financial institutions want to lend money, but borrowers do not respond in sufficiently large numbers to borrow all the excess reserves. When this circumstance arises, the money multiplier will not reach its maximum effect.

Finally, the multiplier process that we discussed assumes that all financial transactions occur with checks. We know that this assumption is inaccurate because 28 percent of the money supply is currency. When people buy and sell in cash or if people hold cash, then the size of checking deposits will decrease. If the size of deposits decreases, then the actual money multiplier will be smaller than the theoretical limit that we defined as the reciprocal of the required reserve ratio.

It is important to remember these qualifications because changing the amount of reserves is the principal method of operating monetary policy. If we have some difficulty in controlling these reserves, we will have some difficulty implementing *monetary policy*. We will study the effectiveness of this policy in the next chapter.

Monetary Policy Activities by the Federal Reserve System to alter the supply of money for the purpose of changing aggregate demand

SELF-TEST

9. A money multiplier of 5 says that a checkable deposit of $1,000 will be expanded five times, to a total of $5,000 of checkable deposits. How can that expansion occur? How can we create $5,000 of checkable deposits when the banks have only $1,000 in reserves to support those deposits?
10. Assume that you are the head of the board of governors for the Federal Reserve Banks. Assume further that there is $5 billion more money in the economy than there is national output. With a 20 percent required reserve ratio should you direct the banking system to reduce reserves by $1 billion?

TOOLS OF THE FEDERAL RESERVE SYSTEM

We mentioned earlier that the Federal Reserve System, not the United States Treasury, is the primary agency for controlling the supply of money. The FRS influences the supply of money through its monetary policy, which is designed to influence the ability of banks to lend money. That is, monetary policy is directed toward altering the size of bank reserves. As the size of reserves increases, banks can increase their loans and create money.

Because the supply of money in the economy affects the degree of inflation, the FRS has the responsibility to adjust the supply of money to keep the rate of change of the money supply approximately equal to the rate of change of GNP. For instance, if real GNP increases by 3 percent and the supply of money increases by 3 percent, the economy will not experience any significant inflationary pressures. Similarly, if GNP fails to grow and the money supply is held steady, prices should remain stable.

The FRS has three primary tools to alter the money supply: open market operations, the discount rate, and the reserve requirements.

The FRS will use any one or a combination of these tools to keep inflation under control.

Open Market Operations The buying and selling of government securities for the purpose of altering the money supply

Open-Market Operations

In addition to lending money, banks also use excess reserves to purchase securities. That is, banks buy stocks and bonds of corporations and United States government securities such as three- and six-month treasury bills. (The United States government sells these securities to finance the national debt.) These securities earn income through the receipt of interest payments in a manner similar to the receipt of income from the interest on loans.

The FRS has the responsibility of buying and selling these government securities to banks, investment companies, business firms, pension funds, and individuals. When the FRS buys or sells these securities, there is a change in the excess reserves that banks are holding. As the reserves change, there tends to be a change in the supply of money.

Let's be more specific. Assume that the economy is experiencing an undesirable rate of inflation and that the FRS wishes to reduce the supply of money to decrease the inflationary pressure. The most common action that the FRS uses to combat the inflationary pressures is to sell some government securities. When banks purchase these securities, excess reserves will fall because banks use their excess reserves to purchase the securities. As a result banks will have to reduce their lending activities, causing fewer deposits to be created. If banks hold fewer checkable deposits, the money supply will decrease by a multiple of the initial decrease in checkable deposits.

The following example will illustrate how open-market operations are used to reduce the supply of money. Suppose the Federal Reserve Bank of New York sells $2 million of government securities to banks in its region. To pay for these securities, the banks transfer $2 million from their excess reserves to the Federal Reserve Bank of New York. Prior to the purchase of these securities the banks could have lent the $2 million and created $10 million of new deposits (money), assuming a required reserve ratio of 20 percent. But because the banks did purchase the securities, they no longer have that $2 million of excess reserves. As a result, the money supply tends to decline by $10 million.

If the FRS wished to stimulate the economy, it would reverse the process. Instead of selling securities, the FRS would buy them from banks and companies. These purchases would increase the reserves of the banks. When the FRS buys from a bank, reserves increase directly. When the FRS buys securities from companies, the companies are likely to deposit their revenue in their local banks. When a bank's checkable deposits increase, there will also be an increase in reserves. Because banks operate with fractional reserves, they can use the excess reserves to increase loans and expand the money supply even further.

The open-market operations are the most frequently used tool of the FRS. Government securities can be bought or sold on a daily basis, permitting the FRS to make frequent adjustments to the money supply.

Discount Rate

When a bank is short of reserves, it must sell securities, reduce the amount of loans, or borrow money from the FRS. If banks believe that their shortage of reserves is a temporary problem, they will often borrow from the FRS. When the banks borrow from the FRS, they must pay an interest rate that is called the *discount rate.*

Discount rate The rate of interest that the Federal Reserve System charges banks when these banks borrow from the FRS

The FRS can use the discount rate to help regulate the supply of money. For example, if the economy is experiencing inflation, the FRS might increase the discount rate. The higher rate will discourage banks from borrowing. If banks decrease their borrowing from the FRS, their excess reserves will tend to decline, causing the money supply to decline.

The FRS tends to use the discount rate as its second tool for controlling the money supply. When the FRS does use the discount rate, for example, by increasing that rate, the banking community takes this action as a clear message that the FRS is attempting to tighten the money supply and reduce inflationary pressures. The reverse signal would be given if the FRS reduced the discount rate. A reduction would, *ceteris paribus,* expand aggregate demand.

Reserve Requirement

Reserve Requirement Policy tool that permits the Federal Reserve System to alter the required reserves to influence the money supply

In 1980 Congress passed the Monetary Control Act, giving the FRS authority over all depository institutions. Prior to that date the FRS had only limited authority over the reserves of lending institutions. This act gives the FRS increased capability to control bank credit and the supply of money. Specifically, the FRS sets the *reserve requirement,* which has direct influence on the lending ability of financial institutions.

The reserve requirement is the most powerful tool of the FRS and, consequently, is used infrequently and cautiously. The power of this tool lies in its impact on the money multiplier. In our previous examples, we have assumed that the required reserve ratio was 20 percent, giving us a money multiplier of 5 (1/.20 = 5). If the FRS decides to increase the reserve requirement to 21 percent because inflation has become a very serious problem, the money multiplier falls to 4.76 (1/.21 = 4.76). In the case where banks have $100 million of checkable deposits, their required reserves increase from $20 million to $21 million. More important, however, the ability of banks to expand checkable deposits will drop because banks will have fewer excess reserves. With a 20 percent reserve requirement, banks could expand deposits by $400 million to a total of $500 million of checkable deposits. When the reserve requirement increases to 21 percent, bank deposits will expand by only $376 million to a total of $476 million of checkable deposits. By this simple act the FRS has reduced the money supply by $24 million.

When the FRS raises the reserve requirement in conjunction with the open-market operations and the discount rate, there is a major reduction in the ability of banks to lend money. For those banks that have excess reserves prior to the increased requirements, it is highly likely that these excess reserves will disappear. Banks that do not have excess reserves must reduce their lending activities. The consequence of both of these changes is a significant reduction in the supply of money.

The three tools of monetary policy can be used in conjunction with fiscal policy to help control fluctuations in the economy. We must now examine the effectiveness of monetary policy in promoting price stability. Chapter 21 will explore this issue.

SELF-TEST

11. If you were a governor of the Federal Reserve Banks and the economy was experiencing mild inflation, what monetary tool or tools would you use to correct the inflation? Why?

ACTIVE REVIEW

1. Imagine yourself as the leader of a small economy that is just beginning to develop. At the moment, you do not have an established monetary system, and banks do not exist. Explain how you would set up a monetary system and how you would use that system to control the supply of money.

2. When you borrow money, the financial institution literally writes the amount of money you are borrowing on a deposit slip or on a check and says that the money is yours. If you wish, you could convert that money to cash immediately. How can banks appear to create deposits (money) from nothing? Won't that activity cause too much money to enter the economy and cause inflation?

ANSWERS TO ACTIVE REVIEW

1. In establishing a monetary system, it is essential to remember that no matter what you identify as money, you must make sure that the supply of money changes at the same rate as production within your economy. If your monetary unit is permitted to expand at a more rapid pace than the rate of increase in production, your economy will experience inflation. Thus, your money unit must be some commodity that is relatively scarce and whose supply is controllable.

   If you observe these conditions, your economy could print some money (you need to make counterfeiting very difficult) and pass a law stating that the money must be accepted as a means of payment. In other words, laborers must accept this new money as payment for their work, and businesses must accept the money as payment for their products. In this way, money facilitates exchange so long as banks do not expand or change the money supply more rapidly than the supply of goods and services in the economy.

   Once the monetary unit is established, people will look for institutions to hold, or save, their money. You can then establish a bank. You can encourage people to leave, or deposit, their money with you (you might even pay them some interest). After you have collected a relatively large number of deposits, you can begin lending some of that money to others. As you lend the money you must be careful to keep enough money on reserve to meet the needs of day-to-day transactions. You will learn that new deposits and withdrawals will be made daily, and sometimes withdrawals will outnumber deposits. At these times your bank must have reserves to honor the requests of depositors to withdraw their money.

   Because your bank has the ability to expand or contract the size of deposits through the lending process, the bank can have a very significant impact on the supply of money. If the bank is not careful, it can expand the money supply too rapidly and cause inflation. For this reason you need to control the expansion and contraction of the money supply by establishing a specific percentage of deposits that your bank must keep on reserve. By taking this action you actually accomplish two objectives: (1) You help keep your bank safe, and (2) you can control the expansion of money by controlling the size of the reserves.

ANSWERS TO SELF-TEST

1. Money has value because it facilitates the exchange of goods and services, not because it can be exchanged for gold or some other precious metal. We accept money as payment for our work because we know that other people will accept money as payment for our purchases. The general acceptance of money is directly linked to the relationship between the amount of money and the level of production in the economy. If this relationship changes over time, members of the economy may begin to question the value of money. For example, if the supply of money increases more rapidly than the level of production, inflation will result. If inflation gets out of control, people will be less willing to accept money in exchange for production.
2. When prices remain stable over time, buyers know that money they save today can be used to make purchases in the future. That is, $500 in money can be easily converted into a stereo. Buyers can be confident that the money they hold contains the value of a stereo or other products they wish to purchase whether they purchase the product today or some time in the future.

   When buyers are confronted with a choice of which items they should purchase, money becomes a measure of value. For example, if in addition to the $500 stereo unit, you would like to purchase a $300 airline ticket and a $400 repair on your car, money will assist your decision in choosing which item you wish to purchase. The different prices give you an estimate of the different values of the products. You make your purchase on the basis of the value of the product (or how much money you wish to spend.)
3. This comment makes some sense if we are concerned about money only as a measure of value. In this case prices of goods and services are increasing, but they maintain their positions relative to one another. For example, if the price of eggs rises from $1 to $2 a dozen and the price of sweaters rises from $20 to $40, the sweaters still are twenty times more expensive or valuable. Money still functions as a measure of value.

   If, however, prices rise as the comment indicates, money will have difficulty functioning as a store of value and a medium of exchange. As prices rise, people become reluctant to hold money, because money loses its purchasing power during inflation. In addition, rising prices make buyers and sellers suspicious about money as a medium of exchange. Buyers may refuse to accept money because inflation is causing money to lose its purchasing power. Finally, if members of the economy decrease their savings because of increasing inflation, the cost of investing in new plants and equipment will increase. If businesses reduce their investment activities, the economy is likely to experience a recession.
4. Prior to the Monetary Control act of 1980 the only checkable deposits were demand deposits. In other words, if you wanted to establish a

bank account upon which you could write checks whenever you wished, you had no choice but to open a checking account by depositing your money in a demand deposit at a commercial bank. After the passage of the 1980 Monetary Control Act, savings and loan institutions and credit unions were given the authority to open accounts, such as NOW (negotiable order of withdrawal) accounts, that were almost the same as checking accounts. Depositors could use the demand deposits and NOW accounts just as if they were currency. In essence, the other checkable deposits became a medium of exchange, a measure of value, and a store of value. In other words, other checkable deposits are money.

5. The Federal Reserve Banks are a group of 12 banks that act as a central bank to oversee and control the financial institutions within the banking system. If the Federal Reserve System did not exist, it is highly likely that the monetary system would not function properly. Without the FRS there would be no way to control increases or decreases in the supply of money. Without control over the supply of money it would be very difficult to keep inflation and unemployment under control.
6. The comment is accurate to the extent that individuals should be confident that they can withdraw their deposits whenever they wish. But banks do not need to maintain 100 percent of their reserves to guarantee depositors that they can make withdrawals at any time. The experience of goldsmiths has taught us that depositors will not request to withdraw all their money at the same time (unless some banking crisis occurs). Because of this experience, banks practice fractional reserves, whereby they keep only a portion of your deposits on hand and lend the remainder to people who wish to borrow.
7. When a single bank lends money, it is highly probable that the borrower will withdraw that money immediately to complete some economic transaction such as the purchase of a house, car, appliance, or college education. As soon as borrowers withdraw their money, the bank's excess reserves decrease. As a result the bank's ability to lend also falls.

   If we consider the entire banking system, the excess reserves will not fall immediately after the loan is made. For example, if the first bank lends money to Alissa to purchase a car, she will most likely write a check to the auto dealer. At this moment the reserves at the first bank drop by the amount of the check. The auto dealer, however, will probably deposit the check in its bank, bank 2. As soon as the deposit is made in bank 2, the reserves and, therefore the lending capability of bank 2 increases. If bank 2 increases its loans, money will be created. The reason money is created is because the entire banking system does not lose reserves as a single bank loses reserves.
8. When we explained that currency amounts to only about 28 percent of the money supply, we implied that the remaining 72 percent of the money supply is checkable deposits that can be increased or

decreased by banks changing their levels of lending activities. If banks indiscriminately increased their lending activities, inflation could become a serious problem. Banks are unlikely to behave indiscriminately because of state and federal regulations, and because banks would find that excess lending activity is a bad business practice.

We must remember that money has value because it has a consistent relationship with the level of national output. As long as the Federal Reserve System controls the supply of money and keeps its rate of change approximately equal to the rate of change of national output, inflation will not be a problem.

9. The creation of money does bring about a situation where an initial deposit ($1,000 in this case) increases reserves that support a total of $5,000 of deposits. In other words, many people have legitimate claims to the initial $1,000. This multiple expansion does not create any problems because banks operate on the principle of fractional reserves. Experience has taught bankers that deposits are made and withdrawn continuously. When one person withdraws some money, it is highly probably that other people are depositing money.

   Bankers have learned through experience that they must keep a small percentage (20 percent in our example) of deposits on reserve to handle day-to-day transaction. Once they can guarantee the handling of day-to-day transactions, banks can lend the excess reserves without any real fear that they are endangering the monetary system.

10. Given the standard formula for the money multiplier, the act of reducing reserves by $1 billion should reduce the overall supply of money by $5 billion. Unfortunately, in reality the money is likely to decrease by less than $5 billion because there are several leaks in the process of creating and destroying money.

    Financial institutions may hold more than the required reserves. If they hold more reserves than the minimum required, then a reduction in their reserves accounts will not necessarily force these institutions to reduce their lending activities. The reduction in reserves is likely to increase the cost of borrowing, because less money will be available to lend.

    A second reason the money supply may not decline by as much as the money multiplier predicts is that approximately 28 percent of the money supply is held in currency. The money held in cash is not affected by the amount of money in reserve accounts. Consequently, if we wish to reduce the supply of money by $5 billion, we will need to reduce the reserve account by more than $1 billion.

11. It is possible to use any or all of the three monetary tools. It is most probable that you would choose to use the open-market operations because they are more flexible. The Federal Reserve System can sell relatively small amounts of securities to cause minor adjustments in

the rate of inflation. If you chose either the discount rate or the reserve requirement to attack inflation, you would have increasing difficulty in making small adjustments. Both of these tools tend to have stronger impacts on the supply of money. This caution is especially true for the reserve requirement because of the direct link between the reserve account and the creation of money.

21
Monetary Policy and Control of Inflation

Throughout the last two chapters we have discussed the general relationship between money and inflation, the nature of money, and the creation of money. In this chapter we examine how manipulation of the money supply can influence the level of inflation within an economy.

We know that inflation occurs when the money supply grows more rapidly than national output. We also know that the supply of money can be controlled (at least strongly influenced) by the actions of the Federal Reserve System. What we do not know is how changes in the supply of money actually influence the levels of demand and output within the economy.

RELATIONSHIP BETWEEN MONEY SUPPLY, INVESTMENT, AND INFLATION

Most economists agree that price stability and full employment are very desirable economic goals. We learned in Chapter 17 that in spite of this agreement it is difficult to achieve these goals simultaneously. When we approach the goal of full employment, we tend to experience inflation. When we have managed to keep prices stable, we typically have experienced an unacceptably high level of unemployment. There also have been times like those of the 1970s and early 1980's when we experienced unacceptably high rates of unemployment *and* inflation. Within the context of these trade-offs we need to examine monetary policy more closely to determine the influence of money in achieving these goals, especially the goal of price stability.

In Chapter 20 we learned that the Federal Reserve System has the ability to reduce the supply of money in the economy by reducing the amount of excess reserves that are held by banks. By reducing these excess reserves the FRS limits the ability of banks to make loans and thereby create money. When there is less money in the economy, inflation is less likely to occur.

The act of reducing the money supply has an impact on aggregate demand through investment spending. More specifically, changes in the supply of money will influence the price of money (interest rate), which will in turn affect the level of investment in the economy.

Demand for Money

Demand for Money Desire to hold money as an asset to facilitate future transactions, provide flexibility for unexpected transactions, and provide the opportunity to speculate.

To understand the importance of fluctuating interest rates we need to understand the concept of demand for money. Can you explain what is meant by the term *demand for money?* Our guess is that you would equate the demand for money with the desire to earn more income. If you believe the demand for money and the desire to earn more income are the same, you are making a common and understandable error.

We desire income so that we can consume more goods and services such as clothing, autos, food, and shelter. We demand money because it is an asset we want to hold. The *demand for money* refers to the currency we have in our pockets, cookie jars, and checkable deposits. Our demand for money is represented by the income that we are not spending on some other form of assets.

You may wonder if we are talking in riddles. Why would people want money that they just hold? We can answer this question by thinking of money as an asset with great flexibility. By holding money we gain the flexibility to make purchases whenever we wish. For example, if it is announced that Bruce Springsteen concert tickets will go on sale tomorrow, you will be able to purchase some of those tickets if you have held some money. If your car brakes need to be repaired, you can get the brakes fixed immediately if you have held some money. If, however, you put your money in a 90-day money market account, you do not have that same flexibility. You will have to make a withdrawal that will include a penalty fee.

The major point is that money is an asset just like a piece of art, a painting, or shares of IBM stock, but money has much greater flexibility. We can spend money immediately, whereas we would have to convert paintings and stock to cash. When people hold money, they have the flexibility to take advantage of unexpected opportunities or to pay for unexpected expenses.

This flexibility has a price associated with it. If we hold money, we experience the opportunity cost of foregoing the purchase of alternative assets. If instead of holding money we purchase some IBM stock, we would earn income from that stock in the form of interest or dividends. By holding money we give up the opportunity to earn that interest. It follows, therefore, that as interest rates increase, people tend to convert their money into other, interest-bearing assets such as stocks, bonds, and government securities. For similar reasons people tend to hold more money when interest rates fall. Thus, the demand to hold money looks similar to the demand for other products in that it slopes downward to the right (see Figure 21–1).

Changes in the Supply of Money and Interest Rates

In the previous chapter we studied how the FRS could alter the supply of money. Now we need to investigate how those changes in supply may affect the level of output in the economy.

Assume that the FRS instructs the open-market committee to sell securities. What happens? We know that the selling of securities by the FRS will reduce the amount of excess reserves held by banks. As illustrated by the shift from S_{M_1} to S_{M_2} in Figure 21–2, when excess

Figure 21–1
Demand for Money

This diagram shows that people are willing to hold greater quantities of money when the interest rate is low than when it is high.

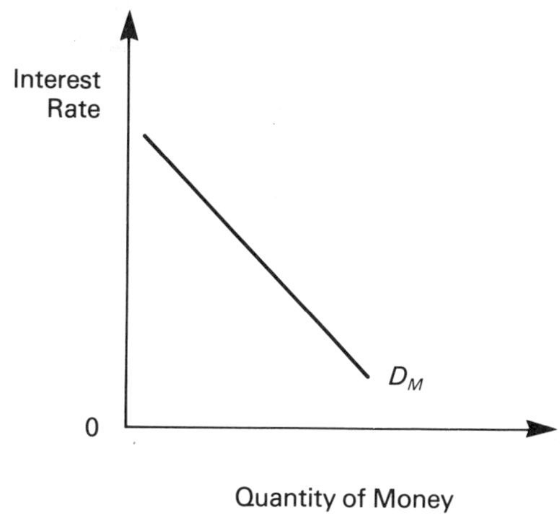

Figure 21–2
Demand and Supply of Money

This diagram illustrates that the rate of interest will increase when the supply of money is decreased.

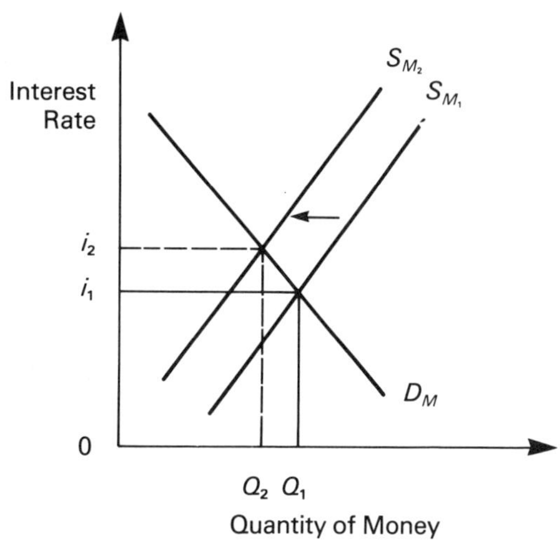

reserves fall the supply of money will generally fall. This decrease in the supply of money will cause the interest rate to rise from i_1 to i_2.

This increase in interest rates will have an important impact on the level of aggregate spending (consumption + investment + government) in the economy. The essence of this impact can be seen in Figure 16–3. The circular flow of income illustrates that savings flow from households and businesses to financial institutions and back into the spending stream through investment. This analysis stated that investment is an important component of aggregate demand and that the rate of interest influences the level of investment.

The higher interest rate illustrated by i_2 increases the cost of borrowing money. As the cost rises, businesses will reassess their plans for investment. In those cases where they decide that the higher rate of interest will eliminate the expected profits from a business activity, businesses will reduce their investment spending. When investment spending falls, aggregate demand will also fall. In the times when the economy is experiencing demand-pull inflation, the reduction in investment spending will reduce the inflationary pressure.

According to Figure 21–3 the equilibrium of aggregate supply (AS_1) and aggregate demand (AD_1) indicates that the economy is experiencing inflation. Can you explain how we know that equilibrium *A* is inflationary? Take a close look at the aggregate supply curve. Over the flat range of the *AS* curve there is unemployment in the economy. When production increases in this range of the curve, there

Figure 21–3
Monetary Policy and Inflation

This diagram demonstrates that a reduction in aggregate demand, caused by a decrease in investment, will reduce demand-pull inflation.

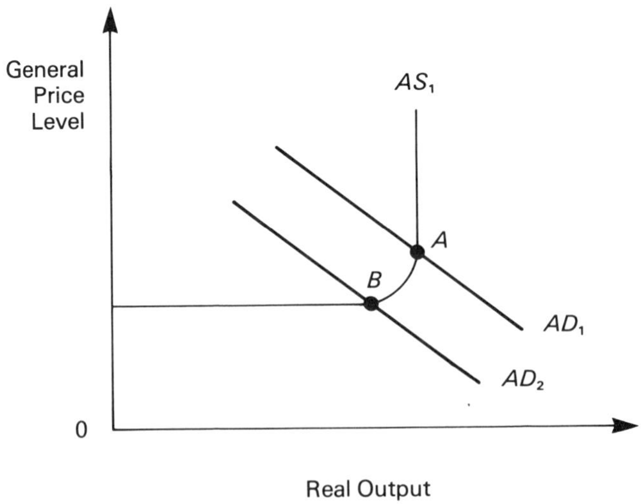

is very little inflationary pressure, because unemployed workers can be given jobs without raising prices. Additional employment in this range increases production.

When production approaches its potential level, the *AS* curve will begin to swing upward to the right. When the economy cannot expand production because it is using all its productive resources fully, the *AS* curve will be vertical. Any attempts to increase aggregate demand when aggregate supply is rising will cause inflation. Thus, equilibrium *A* reflects an inflationary position because we are attempting to demand more than the society is capable of producing.

When the economy is operating at point *A*, action should be taken to decrease aggregate demand. The FRS can cause aggregate demand to fall by instructing the open-market committee to sell securities. As a result the money supply falls, interest rates rise, and investment tends to decrease. A drop in the level of investment reduces aggregate demand and creates a new equilibrium at some point *B*. The actual magnitude of the decrease in aggregate demand will depend upon the amount that FRS reduces the money supply and the extent to which businesses actually reduce their investment spending.

Figure 21–4 demonstrates the importance of the FRS actions. If the economy is currently operating at point *A* and the FRS causes aggregate demand to drop to AD_2 (point *B*), monetary policy has worked very well. Prices have dropped without causing any significant reduction in output; that is, an increase in unemployment is unlikely. If, however, the FRS action causes aggregate demand to fall

Figure 21–4
Potential Impact of Monetary Policy

This diagram illustrates that reductions in aggregate demand *can* cause price stability without significant unemployment, or it *can* cause significant unemployment.

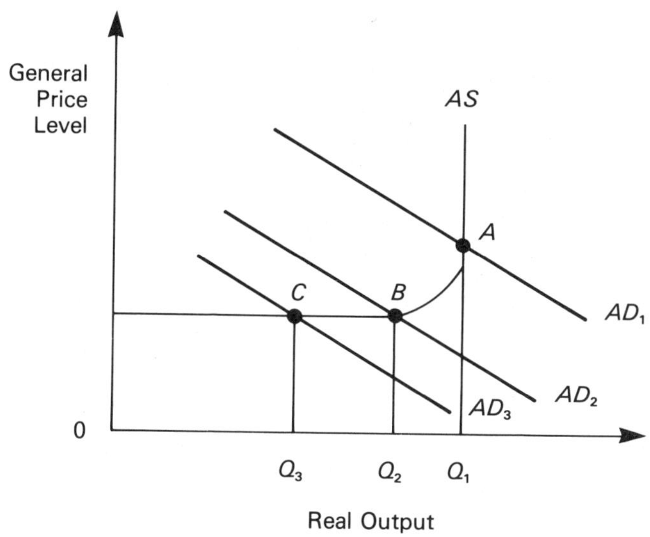

to AD_3 (point *C*), prices stop falling, and the economy experiences a significant decrease in real output. In this case the money supply has decreased too far. It is clear that the monetary authorities want to achieve point *B*, but incorrect judgments and imprecise tools can lead an economy to point *C*.

SELF-TEST

1. Is there a difference between the demand for money and the demand for goods and services? Explain.
2. Why would an increase in the rate of interest cause individuals to reduce the amount of money they are willing to hold?
3. Evaluate the following statement: Monetary policy is an excellent way to reduce inflationary pressures, because reducing the supply of money will not cause a significant increase in unemployment.

An Alternate, or Monetarist, View

Monetarists Economists who argue that changes in the money supply will directly affect the level of national output

A group of economists called *monetarists* believe that changes in the supply of money have a direct impact on aggregate demand. They state that economic activity can be explained by the equation of exchange: $MV = PQ$. In this equation P equals the general level of prices in the economy, and Q equals the real national output of the economy. Together they equal the money GNP. On the left side of the equation is a measure of the economy's ability to spend. M equals the money supply, and V equals velocity, or the number of times each dollar is spent in a year. Thus, if $P \times Q$ equals \$400 billion and M equals \$100 billion, then each dollar must have been spent four times, meaning that $V = 4$ during a given year.

Monetarists argue that velocity is relatively stable and highly predictable. They argue further that since we can predict velocity, changes in the money supply are the major reason for economic instability. Inflation, according to the monetarists, is always preceded by a significant increase in the money supply, whereas recession is always preceded by a significant decrease in the money supply.

In Figure 21–5a we see an increase in the money supply from S_{M_1} to S_{M_2}. As a result people will tend to hold M_3 amounts of money at i_1 instead of the desired amount, M_1, causing a surplus of money balances. Given the demand for money, DM_1, people do not want to

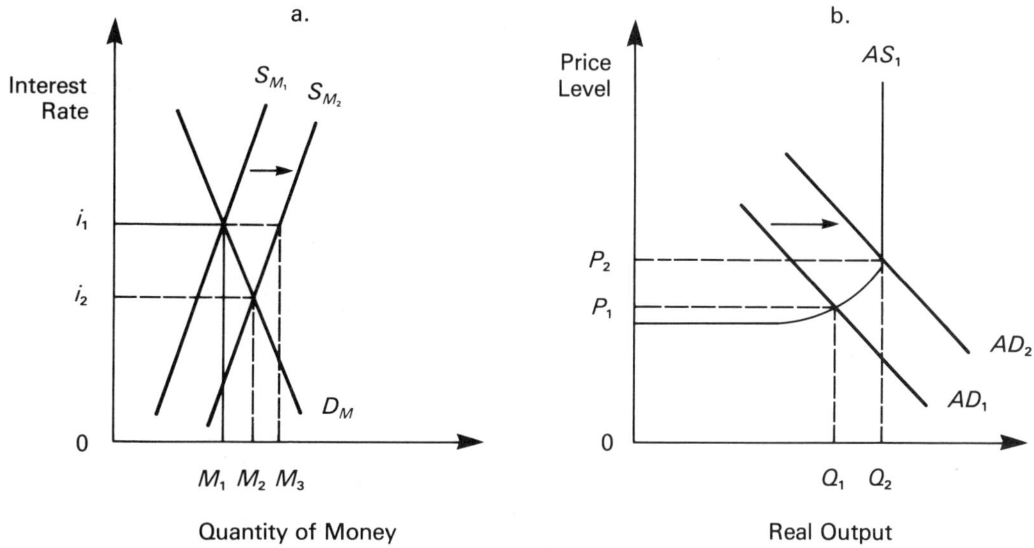

Figure 21–5
Consequence of Change in Money Supply (Monetarist View)

This figure demonstrates the direct impact of the money supply on the level of economic activity.

hold this surplus, so they increase their spending. That is, the increase in the supply of money causes an increase in aggregate demand from AD_1 to AD_2 in Figure 21.5b. The increase in aggregate demand causes the general level of prices to rise from P_1 to P_2.

To prevent this type of inflationary pressure, monetarists argue, we must control the money supply so that it increases as real national output increases. We cannot let the money supply increase before production increases, because the increased money will simply lead to inflation.

The basic stabilization strategy of a monetarist is to determine the average rate of increase in the level of national output. They would then instruct the FRS to increase the supply of money every year by that percentage. Monetarists claim that although there will be times when the economy has too much money (for example, when the money supply expands by 4 percent and the economy by 2 percent) and vice versa, the degree of inflation (or unemployment) will be kept under control.

If the money supply is allowed to expand and contract according to the discretion of the FRS, there is a high probability that the money supply will miss its target and that the monetary authorities will have incorrectly predicted economic conditions. Consequently, monetarists argue that we can maintain much better control of the economy if the money supply is increased at a consistent rate instead of manipulated as economic conditions change.

Problems with Monetary Policy

Easy-Money Policy
A monetary policy that increases the supply of money and decreases the interest rate

Monetary policy affects the general level of economic activity by influencing the rate of interest. But some economists argue that an *easy-money* policy is not as effective in stimulating aggregate demand as monetary policy is in reducing demand-pull inflation. These economists argue that lower interest rates caused by an increase in the supply of money will not cause an increase in aggregate demand. Businesses are more likely to borrow money to increase investment when the economy is growing and profit opportunities are good. When the economy is stagnant, the lower interest rates do not create sufficient incentives to compensate for the poor profit opportunities. Thus, aggregate demand will not expand if businesses are unwilling to borrow.

Tight-Money Policy
A monetary policy that decreases the supply of money and increases the interest rate

During inflationary periods, the use of a *tight-money* policy does effectively decrease spending by reducing the money supply. If the FRS takes action that reduces excess reserves, banks must decrease their lending activities. With fewer excess reserves banks will increase their interest rates. Some businesses will decide that the interest rates are too high and decrease their borrowing. As these businesses decrease their borrowing, investment and, thus, aggregate demand will fall. A decline in aggregate demand should lead to a decrease in inflation.

Economists who wish to use monetary policy to control inflation still must be cautious because there are several potential problems associated with a tight-money policy. First, tight money affects some sections of the economy more strongly than others. Businesses that rely on borrowed money are expecially hurt. For example, farmers, auto buyers, and home buyers use substantial amounts of credit in their purchases and, therefore, are very sensitive to changes in interest rates. As interest rates increase producers of farm equipment, auto companies, and home sellers experience significant decreases in demand. Farmers have difficulty paying their bills, and home and car buyers dramatically reduce their purchases. Although these actions do help reduce aggregate demand, these interest-sensitive businesses absorb a greater share of the burden of reducing inflation than do other types of businesses. Some economists believe that it is unfair to place the burden of reducing inflation on such a small proportion of the economy.

Second, high interest rates tend to hurt competitive businesses more than those businesses with market power. If businesses are competitive, an increase in the rate of interest is an increase in cost that will tend to affect competitive firms evenly. But what about the companies that have market power? Some of these companies have earned economic profits as a result of their market power. These companies can use their economic profits instead of borrowed money to finance their investments. As a result, these firms are less influenced by the prevailing interest rates. If some firms in an industry have market power while others do not, the impact of a tight-money policy will be uneven and less effective than might be anticipated.

Third, monetary policy attempts to control demand-pull inflation. What happens when cost-push inflation exists? When inflation occurs because of an unexpected shortage of a critical commodity, such as agricultural goods or energy, the general level of prices tends to rise because the economy's ability to produce has fallen. Aggregate demand exceeds aggregate supply because the economy is producing less, not because aggregate demand has expanded. If we institute a tight-money policy, investment and economic expansion will tend to fall at the very time we should be trying to expand production. Thus, a tight-money policy tends to increase unemployment significantly before it starts to reduce inflationary pressures.

Fourth, a tight-money policy causes a conflict with the United States Treasury, which is responsible for paying the interest on the federal debt. When the FRS takes steps to reduce inflation, the interest on government securities rises because the supply of money declines relative to the demand for money. The higher interest rates tend to reduce aggregate demand and demand-pull inflation, but the high interest rates also increase the costs of financing the national debt. As a result, government must either increase its spending to pay this interest or divert money from some other government program to pay the higher interests costs. If government increases its spending, the economy will be increasing its aggregate demand at the same time the FRS is attempting to decrease aggregate demand through a tight-money policy. If the government diverts money from some programs to pay the interest on the debt, the government is taking a political action without going through the usual political process. Either way a tight-money policy creates some problems that are not immediately apparent as the FRS attempts to reduce the money supply.

Some economists argue that these problems seriously weaken

the effectiveness of monetary policy. As a result they offer an alternative approach to managing the economy. They state that we should emphasize changes in production rather than demand. That is, they encourage the use of supply-side economics.

SELF-TEST

4. Evaluate the following statement: If the economy is experiencing inflation, then monetary authorities should reduce the supply of money. If the economy experiences unemployment, then they should increase the money supply.
5. Do you agree with the following statement? Why? A major advantage of monetary policy in comparison with fiscal policy is that monetary policy is neutral. Political authorities do not decide who should gain or lose as a result of a policy decision. Once the money is loosened or tightened, all businesses must still compete for the excess reserves by paying the existing interest rates.
6. Is monetary policy equally effective at reducing demand-pull and cost-push inflation? Explain

SUPPLY-SIDE ECONOMICS

Monetary policy as we have discussed it has emphasized changes in the supply of money to cause changes in aggregate demand. Similarly, the fiscal policy we discussed in Chapter 18 altered taxes and government spending with the intent of modifying aggregate demand to reach full employment or to achieve price stability. These approaches have had limited success and were particularly unsuccessful in the 1970s. As a result some economists claim that we can remedy this mediocre record by implementing *supply-side economics.*

Supply-Side Economics Economic policies designed to stimulate aggregate supply to achieve full employment with price stability

Supply-side economists argue that altering aggregate demand provides only a temporary solution to economic problems. Supply-side economists accept the tenet of the classical economists that supply creates its own demand. They believe that it is necessary to expand aggregate supply to generate the income necessary to achieve full employment. If the economy's capacity to produce grows, national income will increase. Aggregate demand will then rise to the level where the economy can experience full employment without inflation.

The basic logic of supply-side economics is as follows:

1. Increase incentives to work by reducing personal income taxes. If personal income taxes are cut, workers will react as if their pay has been increased. Because they then have higher take-home pay, many workers will find it advantageous to work longer hours. This incentive should be especially effective for spouses and teenagers who might not enter the work force if taxes stay high.
2. Alter the tax laws to stimulate savings. If members of the economy do not save a significant portion of their income, there will be insufficient funds for businesses to borrow so that they can expand their productive capabilities. By decreasing certain type of business taxes, savings will increase. Banks will experience an increase in the supply of loanable funds, causing interest rates to fall. When interest rates fall, businesses will increase their borrowing and expand their productive capacities.
3. Monetary policy should emphasize a steady growth of the money supply. Because supply-side economics primarily emphasizes an increase in productive capacity, the supply of money must grow at a rate sufficient to keep pace with the expanding production. If the money supply does not grow fast enough, high interest rates will choke off the economic expansion. If the money supply grows too rapidly, inflationary pressures will tend to divert savings away from productive uses to the purchase of items, such as paintings and jewelry, that provide some protection from losses caused by inflation. These items, however, do not add to the productive capacity of the economy.

   Supply-side economists have designed their policy to have a long-term effect on the economy. They are not interested in quick adjustments in the supply of money. They argue that the economy will function much more effectively if the business sector knows that the money supply will expand at a rate to accommodate the increases in production over the long run.
4. Government involvement in economic activity must decline. Supply-side economists argue that the private sector is more productive than the public sector. Thus, if economic resources are transferred from the public sector to the private sector, efficiency will increase, causing the general level of production to increase. Also, governmental regulations of business should be decreased. The supply-side economists argue that overregulation reduces the incentive to be creative and increases the cost of production. If regulations are reduced, costs will fall and inflationary pressure should decline.

Criticism of Supply-Side Economics

The basic tenets of supply-side economics assume that the economy is essentially competitive and that private markets will effectively allocate economic resources. Yet in Chapters 8 and 11 we studied markets with considerable inflexibility. In Chapters 9, 12, 13, and 14 we examined situations in which governmental activities play a significant role in economic activity. This information suggests that supply-side economics will not function as smoothly as predicted. But we should not be surprised by this observation, because it is unlikely that any theory functions perfectly. The more important issue is whether the market imperfections and the need for governmental involvement will negate the basic forces of the supply-side approach.

Market Imperfections Market power and labor immobility hinder the allocative mechanism of markets. In those industries where oligopolistic firms dominate, prices tend to be inflexible in the downward direction. Even if policies are successfully implemented to increase productivity, oligopolistic firms may not decrease their prices. If the oligopolistic influence is strong enough, increased productivity will become profits to the firms rather than provide irresistible pressure to decrease inflation.

In a similar vein labor immobility may hinder the adjustments of labor markets. When markets function competitively, some businesses succeed and others fail. Laborers who had jobs in the businesses that failed are expected to search for and find jobs in the businesses that are successful. Realistically this movement of labor from one industry to another takes place slowly or, in some cases, not at all.

For example, a new job may require new skills that take time and money to learn. If unemployed workers cannot afford the training, they are unlikely to get the new job. Even if unemployed workers have the appropriate skills, they may not get the new jobs because the jobs are located in a different part of the country. Unemployed workers may not be able to afford the move. Finally, workers may not want to move, because their family and culture exist in their current community. A move to a new job and location may involve a major cultural change that some workers are not willing to accept.

Governmental Involvement It may be accurate to claim that the private sector is more efficient than the public sector, but it is also accurate to claim that the public sector is assigned the responsibility of providing social goods and services to the economy. That is, government is given the responsibility of providing those goods and services that do not generate a profit but are necessary components of a modern economy. For example, we expect the public sector to ensure our safety in the air, provide an excellent highway system, maintain an effective educational system, and protect the quality of our air and water. If we reduce the level of governmental involvement in these areas, we are likely to see a decrease in their quality.

Thus, when advocates of supply-side economics argue that we need to reduce the level of governmental activity in the economy, we must first ask whether the government service is desired and whether the private sector will provide it if government does not. If we desire the service and it is truly a social good, then government must be involved. Reduction of these social goods and services will cause a decrease in the economy's capacity to expand production.

These criticisms do not prove that the supply-side approach is ineffective, but they do indicate that there are some serious concerns that must be addressed. For instance, will any significant market power in the economy dissipate over time? Will the labor force learn to adjust to an increasingly technological society and reduce the problems associated with labor immobility? Can we identify areas where reductions in governmental spending will actually cause an improvement of the overall effectiveness of the economy? If we can answer these questions in the positive, then the long-term prospects of the supply-side approach have considerable appeal. If, however, these questions are answered negatively, the effectiveness of the supply-side approach must be seriously questioned.

SELF-TEST

7. Supply-side economics emphasizes long-term effects on the economy. Explain why supply-siders believe that their policy will have long-term effects.
8. Explain why market imperfections hinder the effectiveness of supply-side economics.
9. Evaluate the following statement: If we examine the size of governmental spending over time, we see a rather pronounced increase in governmental activity. As government becomes more and more involved in economic activity, private production gets a relatively smaller supply of the resources. As the role of the private sector declines, the overall success of our economy will fail.

ASSESSMENT OF THE 1970s AND 1980s

Throughout the 1950s and 1960s inflationary pressure was relatively mild. The average rate of inflation between 1950 and 1970 was on 2.4 percent. During those two decades economic policy appeared to be functioning very well. But when we examine the period from 1971 to 1984, we find that the average rate of inflation jumped to 7.3 percent. What happened to cause the rate of inflation to triple? Do these inflationary data mean that monetary and fiscal policy suddenly lost their potency?

In responding to this question it is important to realize that choosing 1970 as the pivotal year is arbitrary. The data in Table 21–1 show that the inflationary rates were higher in the 1970s. By examining the data before and after 1970 we might be able to determine what happened to alter so dramatically the economy's success in achieving price stability. We will examine the two periods to determine whether there were any events after 1970 that were significantly different from the events between 1950 and 1970.

1950–70

During the early 1950s the United States economy endured the burden of the Korean War, and in the late 1960s we experienced a significant increase in spending on the Vietnam War. The rate of increase of M-1 averaged about 2 percent between 1950 and 1960. This figure suggests that even though the Korean War helped expand aggregate

Table 21–1
Average Annual Change in the Consumer Price Index

Year	Annual Change in Consumer Prices	Year	Annual Change in Consumer Prices	Year	Annual Change in Consumer Prices
1950	1.0%	1962	1.1%	1974	11.0%
1951	7.9	1963	1.2	1975	9.1
1952	2.2	1964	1.3	1976	5.8
1953	0.8	1965	1.7	1977	6.5
1954	0.5	1966	2.9	1978	7.7
1955	−0.4	1967	2.9	1979	11.3
1956	1.5	1968	4.2	1980	13.5
1957	3.6	1969	5.4	1981	10.4
1958	2.7	1970	5.9	1982	6.1
1959	0.8	1971	4.3	1983	3.2
1960	1.6	1972	3.3	1984	4.2
1961	1.0	1973	6.2	1985	3.7

Source: U.S. Bureau of Labor Statistics, *Monthly Labor Review* (Washington, D.C.: GPO, 1986).

demand, the rather moderate increase in the money supply apparently kept inflation under control.

During the latter years of the 1960s, a different pattern emerged. Aggregate demand began increasing in 1967 and 1968 as a result of the Vietnam War. The federal government decided to finance the military effort through deficit spending, which increased the level of government spending without decreasing consumption and investment. The government was able to increase its spending without negatively influencing consumption and investment because the Federal Reserve System dramatically expanded the supply of money.

This rapid growth in the money supply proved to be the basis for the demand-pull inflation that occurred in the late sixties and early seventies. For example, from 1950 to 1967 consumer prices rose at a rate of less than 2 percent per year. Between 1968 and 1972 prices rose at the rate of 5 percent per year. Many analysts believe that this demand-pull inflation set the stage for the inflationary pressures that occurred in the 1970s.

1970s and 1980s

The 1970s were complicated by many unusual forces. In 1971 President Nixon imposed price and wage controls and then removed them in 1974. Inflation weakened during the early stage of the controls but rose rapidly after the controls were removed in 1974. Oil prices soared in 1973 and beyond as a result of an oil embargo imposed by the Organization of Petroleum Exporting Countries (OPEC). During the same period many major industrial nations experienced poor harvests that resulted in significantly higher agricultural prices. In 1979 we experienced another dramatic increase in the price of oil as a result of the Iranian revolution.

A major difference between these forces and the ones that accompanied the inflation associated with the Vietnam War is that these forces reduced supply rather than expanded demand. If we examine the history of inflation, we will find the majority of inflationary periods can be explained by aggregate demand's expanding more rapidly than aggregate supply. In the 1970s, however, our production capabilities fell relative to our demand. The end result is the same in that aggregate demand exceeded aggregate supply, but this imbalance was caused by a relative reduction in supply rather than by a too rapid expansion of demand. In other words, we experienced significant cost-push inflation.

In 1974 the FRS adopted a tight-money policy in an attempt to control the inflation that had resulted from the removal of the price-wage controls, the OPEC oil boycott, and the poor agricultural harvests. The tight-money policy did manage to reduce aggregate demand. The consequences of this action were a dramatic increase in the rate of unemployment and very little effect on the inflation that was caused by reduction in supply.

When the second oil shock occurred in 1979, restrictive money policies were imposed again in conjunction with cuts in federal spending. By 1982 the unemployment rate climbed to over 10 percent, creating the worst recession since the 1930s. The inflationary rate, however, did fall to 3.2 percent by 1983. Yet we need to be cautious about assigning the credit for the increased price stability to monetary policy alone. During the early 1980s the prices of oil began to moderate because there was a surplus of oil at the price set by OPEC. Agricultural production increased during this period, causing farm prices to fall.

By mid-1985 the unemployment rate had fallen to 7 percent, and the inflationary rate appeared relatively stable around 3 to 4 percent. Although this performance is much better than that in the 1970s, both these rates are relatively high compared with the averages between 1950 and 1970. Unemployment during that period averaged 4.7 percent, while inflation averged only 2.4 percent. These data illustrate that the period from 1971 to 1985 contained economic forces that were considerably different from those between 1950 and 1970. The data also indicate that we need to consider different economic policies to deal with these new economic forces.

SELF-TEST

10. Prior to 1970 the United States had been relatively successful in controlling inflation by controlling aggregate demand. Can you explain why that type of policy seemed to fail in the 1970s?

INTERNATIONAL COMPARISONS OF BANKING SYSTEMS AND PRICE STABILITY

The basic structure of modern banking is relatively similar throughout the world. Typically, countries will have some form of a central bank that controls the money supply and regulates the financial institutions within the economy. The banking systems differ in how they organize these activities. Some countries may have a tightly controlled financial system, and others may permit the forces of competition to function somewhat more freely.

To give a quick glance into the banking systems of other countries, we will present a brief look at the banking systems of West Germany and Japan. Both countries have modern and productive economies, but they operate their banking system differently.

West Germany

The banking system in West Germany has a large number of institutions and a high degree of diversity among them. Like the United States with its Federal Reserve System, the banking system in West Germany is regulated by an autonomous central bank called the Bundesbank. Principally, the Bundesbank is the banker for the federal government, issues bank notes, is an intermediary for interbank transactions, controls the money supply, lends money to banks, and maintains the value of the Deutsche mark. The Bundesbank influences the money supply by changing the reserve ratio and the discount rate. Basically these functions are the same as those possessed by the Federal Reserve System in the United States.

The Bundesbank differs from the FRS in that the Bundesbank generally identifies with the outlook and interests of the German banking community and often represents the needs of those institutions to the appropriate authorities in the federal government. In the United States the FRS is also independent of the federal government, but the FRS does exert very significant influence over the financial institutions within the economy. The FRS is a regulatory agency, whereas the Bundesbank is a bank for banks. The primary responsibility for regulating the activities of German banks rests with the Banking Supervisory Office of the federal government. As a result of this arrangement the banking sector in West Germany enjoys a degree of freedom in its actions that is higher than that of the banks in most other countries.

The German banking system is characterized by universal banks. In many countries, banks tend to specialize in certain kinds of activities. In Germany, universal banks conduct every type of banking business. They make short-term and long-term loans, conduct business in securities, direct investment in other domestic and foreign businesses, and gain their resources from time deposits, saving certificates, and bank bonds.

The major advantage of universal banks is that they can meet all the financial needs of their customers. As a result strong ties tend to develop between banks and their customers. But just as this convenience is an advantage to customers, universal banks may cause some problems in that they may develop an undue influence over their customers and federal government. This type of arrangement is also conducive to a reduction in the degree of competition in the banking sector.

Japan

The Japanese banking system is very different from that of West Germany. The highly centralized government of Japan uses the banking system to pursue many national objectives. The federal government oversees the operations of the Japanese banking system and closely controls the number and distribution of banks within the banking system. As a result the banks steer Japan's corporate and industrial growth in the direction desired by the federal government.

Japanese banks are more highly concentrated and specialized than United States banks. In 1982 the largest Japanese banks averaged $46.4 billion in domestic assets, whereas the largest banks in the United States averaged $37.9 billion, even though the financial market in the United States is approximately 70 times larger than that in Japan. This high degree of concentration permits the federal government to influence the level of economic activity through the use of the banking system.

The Japanese Ministry of Finance has authority similar to that of the combined authority of the United States Treasury, Internal Revenue Service, Securities and Exchange Commission, and state banking commissions. In addition, the Ministry of Finance has the policymaking responsibility similar to that of the Federal Reserve System. The consequence of this authority is that the banking system and the political powers are tightly intertwined. The strong central government uses the banking system to achieve its economic and political goals.

This type of control works in the Japanese economy because there is a well-defined set of values that is shared by the government and the private sector. The Japanese society tends to analyze issues in terms of their impact on the group rather than on the individual. They emphasize the values of cooperation and conciliation to achieve harmony, and national interests rather than personal welfare. Given this strong cultural influence, the government is free to lead and interfere when necessary to achieve national objectives.

Inflationary Performance in Selected Countries

Although the structure of the banking system and monetary policy are by no means the only factors that may influence the rate of inflation in an economy, a comparative examination of inflationary rates may give us some clues about the effectiveness of different types of banking systems in controlling inflation. In Table 21–2 we examine the average annual inflationary rate of five countries from 1951 to 1982, as measured by the Organization for Economic Co-operation and Development. Over the 32-year period we find that West Germany and United States appear to be the most successful in controlling inflation. West Germany experienced an averge inflation of 4.2 percent, while the United States averaged 5.3 percent.

We need to be cautious in our interpretation of these statistics. We know that price stability is an economic goal of virtually every economy. Yet we also know that there are several other economic goals, some of which may conflict with the goal of price stability. Thus, if we examine just the average annual inflationary rate for different economies, we may misinterpret the data. For example, there is a strong tendency for us to conclude, as we did above, that West Germany and United States have been more successful at controlling inflation than have France, Japan, and the United Kingdom.

When we look at the data in a different way, it is possible to argue that Japan and France have been more successful in controlling fluctuations in the rate of inflation. By dividing the data into two separate periods we can examine inflationary pressures prior to 1970 and those after 1970, when the world experienced significant supply shocks from the disruption in the flow of oil and a significant decline in worldwide agricultural production. In every case we find that the inflationary pressures were greater after 1970 than before that date.

We suspect that you would not be surprised by that observation. You may be surprised, however, that prices rose less rapidly in Japan

Table 21–2
Average Annual Inflationary Rate (%), 1951–82

Years	France	West Germany	Japan	United Kingdom	United States
1951–82	9.0	4.2	8.0	9.7	5.3
1951–70	7.8	3.4	7.4	7.6	3.3
1971–82	10.6	5.4	9.0	13.7	8.4
Change between 1951–70 and 1971–82	+36	+59	+22	+80	+154

Source: Organization for Economic Co-operation and Development, *Main Economic Indicators* (Paris, 1984).

and France than they did in the other three countries, because all of these countries felt the pressures from the oil embargo. By looking at inflation in this manner, we see that United States performed especially poorly. Its inflation rose by 154 percent during the two periods.

From our very brief description of the Japanese banking system, can you hypothesize why Japan controlled the increases more effectively than did the United States? One potential answer is that the Japanese financial system is tightly controlled by the Ministry of Finance. That structural arrangement and the strong cultural pressure to cooperate probably assisted the Japanese in taking concerted monetary and fiscal actions to resist inflation.

In this particular case the achievement of the lower increase in the rate of inflation is rather remarkable because Japan must import most of its raw materials, including oil. Because a significant part of the inflationary pressure during the 1971 to 1982 period was caused by the reduced supply of oil, we would ordinarily expect Japanese prices to have increased substantially. The fact that it did not suggests that Japan has better control of its monetary system than does the United States.

SELF-TEST

11. Since the United States and West Germany had significantly lower inflationary rates from 1951 to 1982 than France, Japan, and United Kingdom, the United States and West Germany must have the most effective monetary systems. What do you think?

RELATIONSHIPS BETWEEN MONETARY AND FISCAL POLICIES

Up to this point our discussions of monetary and fiscal policies have been separate. We now need to emphasize that the two policies do interact. For example, if the federal government increases deficit spending in an attempt to stimulate the economy, the Federal Reserve System will often expand the money supply to accommodate governmental borrowing. If the federal government increases taxes to decrease inflationary pressures, the monetary authorities may reduce or stabilize the supply of money to complement the efforts of fiscal policy.

It is also important to know that monetary and fiscal policy do not always work in complementary directions. We noted earlier that the Federal Reserve System operates independent of the federal government; unlike Japan, the United States does not have a Ministry of Finance. The FRS has goals similar to those of the federal government, but the FRS is free to pursue those goals in whatever manner it believes appropriate. If the FRS believes that the federal government is expanding the level of aggregate demand too rapidly, then the FRS is likely to decrease the supply of money in an attempt to reduce inflationary pressures. When fiscal and monetary actions are working in opposite directions, it becomes very difficult to predict economic performance.

Why then does the United States keep monetary and fiscal policy decisions separate? If we wished a more consistent economic policy, would it not make sense for the two policies to work together rather than independently? In some economies, such as Japan, the direct coordination of monetary and fiscal policies apparently does make sense. But the United States has a cultural system that emphasizes individualism and competition instead of harmony and cooperation. Our political process encourages advocacy in which competing groups challenge one another to gain access to economic resources.

Political leaders who make the decisions about the implementation of fiscal policy must get reelected. As a consequence they may advocate a full-employment policy even though the probability for inflation is very high. Because these diverse interests exist within our political system, we are cautious about economic and political decisions becoming unduly influenced by some faction of the voting public. To avoid the potential for undesirable political influence, the Federal Reserve System has been established as an independent agency whose primary function is to oversee the money supply and to control the economic fluctuations within the economy. With an independent Federal Reserve System, our economic policy has a built-in checks and balances mechanism.

Influence of the National Debt on Monetary Policy

When the federal government engages in deficit spending, there is a strong tendency for the money supply to increase. This increase occurs because the United States Treasury often borrows excess reserves from banks to pay the deficit spending. This borrowing activity increases the money supply in the same manner as increased borrowing by businesses.

When the economy is in a recession, deficit spending and increases in the money supply can have a positive effect on the economy. In recessions, businesses typically reduce their investment activities, causing aggregate demand to fall. As deficit spending and the money supply increase, aggregate demand will tend to rise. If government uses its deficit spending for productive purposes, economic expansion will occur.

If the economy is operating at or close to full employment when the government engages in deficit financing, the economic consequences may be quite different. When the economy is prospering, private businesses are borrowing to expand their productive capacities. Banks have very limited excess reserves, which results in competition between private businesses and government for these loanable funds. Because government tends to have a greater ability to borrow, governmental borrowing to finance deficit spending will tend to crowd-out private borrowing and investments. If private investment declines, there will be a switch from private borrowing to public borrowing. To the extent that private borrowing is more efficient than public borrowing, the level of economic activity may decline.

Crowding-Out Effect An increase in interest rates caused by an expansion of borrowing by government. This increase tends to decrease private investment.

The Federal Reserve System often attempts to avoid the *crowding-out effect* by creating more money. With more money in the economy the banks will have more excess reserves. When government increases its borrowing, there will be less pressure for interest rates to rise and for private businesses to be squeezed out. On the other hand, the increase in government borrowing will cause an increase in aggregate demand that will cause inflationary pressure in a fully employed economy. Under these conditions it is clear that deficit spending complicates the role of monetary policy.

Timing of Monetary Policy

The timing of monetary policy is critical. To be effective policymakers must be able to predict economic conditions for as much as two years into the future. This predictability is necessary because there is an 18- to 24-month lag between an action by the FRS to alter the supply of money and the achievement of the desired effects on the economy. Thus, if the authorities of the FRS wish to control inflation, they must consider reducing the supply of money when the economy is still expanding. If the FRS waits until actual inflation is recorded by one or more of the inflation indices, then the actual decline in the money supply may not occur until after the inflation pressure has been in existence for many months.

Because of this timing problem some people argue that fiscal policy, especially a reduction in government spending, is more effective because aggregate demand will begin falling as soon as governmental spending is decreased. There is a significant flaw in this reasoning, however. Although a reduction in governmental spending does have a more direct effect on aggregate demand, there may be some difficulty in agreeing on the specific types of governmental spending that should be decreased. This decision requires political debate and compromise that may take considerable time to work its way through Congress. Thus, even if we can predict inflationary conditions, fiscal policy may be no more effective than money policy because they both have significant lags in their effectiveness.

The major distinction between monetary and fiscal policies is that monetary policy must run its course through the money multiplier to contract the money supply. The amount of time that it will take to enact fiscal policy depends on many factors that vary according to political and economic conditions. With the proper political leadership, fiscal policy could become effective quite rapidly. (The conditions necessary for rapid implementation of fiscal policy have not occurred frequently in the United States.)

SELF-TEST

12. Evaluate the following statement: Monetary and fiscal policies are separate policies that are used to control fluctuations in the economy. Changes in the level of governmental spending have no effect on the money supply, and changes in the money supply have no effect on the level of governmental spending.
13. Do you agree or disagree with the following statement? Since the FRS does not have to receive political approval for the changes it wishes to make in the money supply, the FRS can implement its policies much more quickly than government can implement fiscal policy. Because monetary policy is easier to use, it should be the preferred policy.

RECAP OF MONETARY POLICY

The purpose of Chapters 19 through 21 was to explain the significance of price stability as a goal and how the Federal Reserve System can manipulate the supply of money to help us achieve that goal. These chapters emphasized the importance of an expanding and contracting money supply. If the money supply tends to exceed the level of production in the economy, we tend to experience inflation. If the money supply is less than the productive capability of the economy, we tend to experience recession.

It is important to remember, however, that monetary policy can also be used to influence the level of employment. For ease of exposition we have chosen to demonstrate the capabilities of monetary policy by focusing our attention on controlling inflation. We recognize that the emphasis on price stability is an oversimplification, but we found that approach to be a convenient way to demonstrate the way monetary policy works. If we wished to study the way monetary policy attempts to reduce unemployment, we would find that the Federal Reserve System takes action to increase the money supply. There are some flaws in this approach to reducing unemployment.

Monetary policy works through the Federal Reserve Banks, which are independent of the federal government. The FRS uses its powers to control the size of excess reserves, which determine the amount of money that banks are permitted to lend. If the FRS believes that inflationary pressures are too strong, it will take action to reduce the level of excess reserves that are held in financial institutions. The smaller amount of excess reserves will reduce the amount of money available for loans and, as a result, cause interest rates to rise. Businesses will tend to borrow less money and thereby reduce investment and aggregate demand. Monetary policy will be implemented until the excess aggregate demand disappears.

Monetary policy can be implemented rapidly because the FRS does not have to consult with political authorities to seek approval for its actions. On the other hand, changes in the money supply take 18 to 24 months to achieve their full effect on aggregate demand. Thus, we find that monetary policy is a relatively potent tool for influencing the level of economic activity, but the policy is imprecise because it takes so long for the change in money supply to achieve its full impact.

ACTIVE REVIEW

1. John Cunningham and Mary Swartz are banking officials who are discussing the current economic conditions and are attempting to formulate an economic policy that will return the economy to a higher level of price stability.
   a. John argues that the money supply has been growing too rapidly and that the FRS needs to take some action such as selling securities on the open market. What does John expect from this action?
   b. Mary complains that John's policy suggestion would be inadequate because the major cause of the inflation was a significant reduction in aggregate supply approximately one year before. Explain why Mary believes that selling securities will not be effective. Can you predict what alternative policy Mary might suggest?

c. John counters by arguing that production is the most important component of policy. He contends that the FRS should adjust the money supply to increase at the same rate as the average rate of production increases. He also recommends that the federal government reduce taxes. These two changes would cause the economy to experience an increase in production that would reduce the inflationary pressure in the economy. Why does John think this policy will work?

d. Mary agrees with John that increases in production are important to achieve price stability, but she argues that inflation caused by supply shocks does not get corrected by a reduction in taxes. Give an example of the type of supply problem that Mary has in mind, and explain why she believes that a cut in taxes is an insufficient way to deal with the problems.

2. Identify the primary strengths and primary weaknesses of monetary policy. Under what conditions do you believe that monetary policy should be emphasized? Can you identify any conditions when monetary policy would be inappropriate? Explain why.

ANSWERS TO ACTIVE REVIEW

1a. John probably believes that the economy is experiencing a case of demand-pull inflation in which aggregate demand is greater than aggregate supply. When the Federal Reserve System sells securities on the open market, the excess reserves within the banking system fall. When excess reserves decline, the supply of funds available for lending decreases and the interest rate on these loans rise. Businesses tend to reduce their investment activities because of the higher cost caused by the interest rate. The reduction in investment spending reduces aggregate demand, bringing it to an equilibrium with aggregate supply at a noninflationary level of output.

1b. If the economy experienced a serious reduction in the supply of critical products such as oil or agricultural output, aggregate supply would decline. As a result aggregate demand would exceed aggregate supply and cause inflation. In this instance the inflation is caused by a reduction of output rather than by an expansion of spending. If the FRS decreases the supply of money, there will be a reduction in the demand that will not be confined to just the products in short supply. The general reduction in demand will cause unemployment, but it will not increase the production of oil and agriculture. Consequently, a reduction in aggregate demand is likely to cause unemployment without substantially reducing inflation.

Mary is likely to argue that the reduction in oil and agricultural production causes a reduction in real output. Our real standard of living has fallen because our productive capabilities have shrunk.

Reducing aggregate demand does not deal directly with the cause of inflation. Mary would argue that we should attempt to reduce the demand for oil and agricultural productions and take steps to increase production of these products. In either case Mary would remind us that our standard of living has fallen. Until we are able to increase production of these products, we will experience a lower standard of living either because of inflation or because of a reduction in output.

1c. John believes that money will not stimulate production and that the money supply must be allowed to expand as production expands. He argues that tax cuts will lower costs to businesses and will encourage an expansion of production. He also believes that tax cuts will motivate people to work harder and for longer hours because they want to earn higher take-home pay. If production does expand for these two reasons, and if the money supply expands at the same rate as production, gross national product will increase without inflationary pressure.

1d. Mary is concerned about reductions in output that are caused by supply shocks such as the oil embargoes in the 1970s. Under this type of condition production is low because a critical natural resource has become less available. This type of reduction is different from reduced output in the general economy because of poor demand conditions or poor business motivations. Tax cuts do not have a direct impact on the production of oil. If an oil shock was the major reason for the inflationary pressures, then specific incentives should be directed toward the production of energy, and toward all production.

ANSWERS TO SELF-TEST

1. The demand for goods and service defines the desire and ability to consume certain types of goods and services. The demand for money defines the desire to hold money to make future purchases. As the demand for money increases, the demand for goods and services must decrease, *ceteris paribus*. Money is an asset with a high degree of flexibility. We can convert money into goods and services whenever we wish. There is no other asset that has this same degree of flexibility. For example, if we hold gold or famous paintings, we would have to convert these items to money before we could make a purchase.
2. There is a cost to holding money—the opportunity cost of earning interest or dividends from assets you could have purchased with your money. When interest rates increase, the potential income that you could earn from other assets, such as stocks and bonds, rises. If you continue to hold the same amount of money, you will lose this income

that you could have earned from the other assets. In many cases people will decrease the amount of money they are willing to hold when interest rates increase, and expand their purchases of interest-earning assets.

3. This statement is accurate only when certain conditions exist. If monetary policy is able to reduce aggregate demand from AD_1 to AD_2 in Figure 21a, then the economy should experience a decline in inflation without an increase in unemployment. We can achieve this result because at AD_1 the economy is experiencing demand-pull inflation. There are too many dollars chasing too few goods. At AD_2 aggregate demand equates aggregate supply at its full employment level of output.

   If, however, aggregate demand is reduced still further, say to AD_3, the economy will not have sufficient spending power to purchase all the output the economy is capable of producing. If aggregate demand is insufficient, production will decrease and unemployment will increase. Under these conditions monetary policy can create considerable unemployment.

Figure 21a

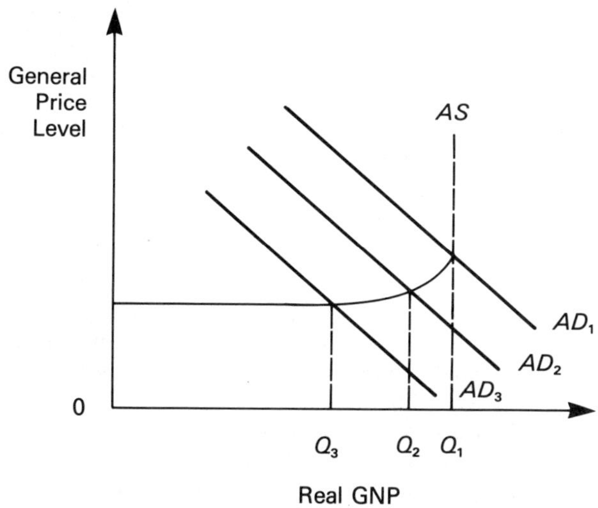

4. If you do not subscribe to the monetarist theory of economy, then increasing the money supply during periods of unemployment and decreasing it during periods of inflation are generally ways of moving the economy toward a goal of full employment with price stability. If, however, you believe that the monetarists have a more accurate view of the economy, then you will not accept the described policy.

   According to the monetarist, the supply of money should increase as production increases. Changes in the money supply do not have a direct effect on production. For example, according to the monetarists an increase in the supply of money will cause an immediate increase in aggregate demand. The increase in money will cause an imbalance in the amount of money people wish to hold and the amount they actually are holding. When people reduce these balances, their spending will increase, but there will not be a comparable increase in production. Since aggregate demand will increase more rapidly than aggregate supply, the monetarists argue, the increase in the money supply will cause inflation.

5. It is accurate to argue that the implementation of monetary policy does not require any political decisions about who should gain or lose as a result of the monetary action. When fiscal policy is enacted, governmental officials must decide who should feel the impact of changes in tax rates and governmental spending. Fiscal policy has both economic and political consequences. Yet monetary policy is not really neutral. Some businesses such as farming, residential construction, and auto sales are highly sensitive to interest rates. A relatively small increase in the rate of interest significantly increases the expenses associated with farming, because most farmers borrow in the spring to plant their crops and repay the loan in the fall after the harvest. A small increase in the interest rates can eliminate profits and cause losses. In a similar way potential home and auto buyers will postpone purchases when the interest rate increases. These products are typically purchased with borrowed money. An increase in the interest rate has the impact of significantly raising prices. In these cases we find that monetary policy designed to reduce inflation does have a greater impact on some specific segments of the economy that it does on others.

6. Monetary policy is more effective in reducing demand-pull inflation than it is in reducing cost-push inflation. Monetary policy decreases the money supply, increases the interest rates, and causes a decline in aggregate demand. Since demand-pull inflation results from aggregate demands being greater than aggregate supply, a reduction in aggregate demand should help move the economy toward an equilibrium with price stability.

   If inflation is caused by cost-push factors such as market power, a reduction in aggregate demand caused by monetary policy is more likely to increase unemployment than reduce inflation. The primary reason for this result is that the source of inflation is not directly related to demand. Cost-push inflation results from factors that drive up costs. If we wish to control this type of inflation, we need to alter the forces that increase costs; for example, we would have to make the economy more competitive and reduce market power.

7. We can explain virtually all inflation by pointing out that society's desire and ability to consume grows faster than its ability to produce. Monetary and fiscal policies operate on the principle of reducing demand and, thereby, creating a new equilibrium at a lower level of *money* gross national product. Supply-side economics puts its em-

phasis upon increasing *real* GNP. Supply-siders argue that an economic policy that increases *real* output will generate the income needed to consume that production. If we can increase production first, output should always be sufficient to meet demand. By emphasizing supply, income can rise only as fast as production, thus reducing any real threat of inflation.

8. Supply-side economics assumes a competitive economy. Resources are expected to move from less profitable production to those areas that are more profitable. Then, because of the pressure of competition, prices will be no higher than the costs of production. If market power or labor immobility exists, resources will not move as smoothly as the theory predicts. If resources do not move smoothly, production will not expand as expected. Without the expected increases in output, supply-side economics cannot achieve its goal. When production fails to respond as expected, the economy will most likely experience unemployment. If the money supply happens to increase in expectation of economic growth, the economy could also experience some inflation.

9. It is true that governmental activity has expanded over time, and it is also true that these governmental activities command an increasing share of the economic resources. But these two facts do not necessarily lead to the conclusion that this governmental activity will reduce the overall productivity of the economy. To determine whether or not governmental spending is relatively productive, we need to examine the nature of governmental activity more closely.

   A primary role of government is to provide public goods and services; that is, government has the responsibility of supplying society with those goods and services that society desires but will not produce in the private sector. Government must provide those goods and services that will not generate a profit, for example, education for the masses, city police and fire protection, and air and highway safety. If government did not provide these goods and services, the economy could not function effectively.

   Thus, if we wish to determine whether increasing governmental activity causes a drag on or a boost to the economy, we need to decide whether the governmental activity complements private production or whether it competes with private production. If governmental spending competes with the private sector, then we would probably improve our economic performance by reducing governmental spending. If, however, governmental spending is complementary to private spending, then government spending must grow as the economy grows.

10. During the 1970s the economy experienced several significant supply shocks. Productive capability decreased because of two reductions in OPEC's supply of oil and because of a world wide crop failure in the early 1970s. When economic tools are applied to reduce aggregate demand, the reduction in spending tends to affect all areas of pro-

duction, not just that of oil and agricultural products. Consequently, the general level of production tends to fall, but the demand for oil and agricultural products remains relatively strong. Under these conditions, the economy tends to experience unemployment and inflation simultaneously.

11. From 1951 to 1982 West Germany averaged 4.2 percent inflation, and the United States averaged 5.3 percent. These rates are considerably below the 8 and 9 percent rates of the other three countries. To the extent that monetary policy influenced these performances, the United States and West Germany appear to have done very well.

    If we examine the data differently, we see that the degree to which prices fluctuated differed over the two periods. If we divide the data into pre-1970 and post-1970, we discover that price changes appeared more stable over time in Japan and France than in the other three countries. In fact, the United States recorded the most pronounced change in prices from pre-1970 to post-1970. By looking at the data in this manner the United States performance in terms of price stability does not look as great. To determine which of these ways is more appropriate to assess the country's success in terms of price stability, we would need to know whether businesses react more to inflationary rates or to changes in those rates.

12. It is true that fiscal policy is controlled by governmental agencies and that monetary policy is controlled by the Federal Reserve System. It is also true that the governmental agencies have no control over the FRS and vice versa. It is not true, however, that changes in the level of government spending have no effect on the money supply and vice versa. If government increases spending without increasing taxes (that is, deficit spends), government must compete with private businesses for money that banks are willing to lend. This competition for loanable funds causes interest rates to rise, discouraging investment. A decrease in investment will counteract some of the expected results of the increase in governmental spending.

    To prevent this contradictory effect from occurring, the FRS may permit the supply of money to increase. As the supply of money increases, businesses are encouraged to increase investment, especially if government spending is successful in stimulating aggregate demand. Once again, however, we have created a complication. Fiscal authorities expanded government spending in expectation of certain results. If the FRS increases the supply of money, there will be an increased stimulus to aggregate demand that may cause aggregate demand to expand more strongly than fiscal authorities expected and lead to demand-pull inflation.

    Fiscal policy and monetary policy are also related with respect to the national debt. If the FRS keeps the interest rate relatively low, the cost (interest payments) of the national debt will remain relatively low. When these payments remain low, the government has more flexibility to spend its revenue on social goods and services.

13. Monetary policy is easier to use, but it is not necessarily more effective. Even though the FRS does not need governmental approval for its actions, monetary policy does not take effect immediately. There is an 18- to 24-month lag time between the implementation of the monetary tools and the desired economic consequences. Because of this relatively long time lag, monetary policy loses some of its effectiveness. It is very difficult to predict economic conditions 18 to 24 months from now. Because fiscal policy also has some complications, it would be inappropriate to pick one economic policy over another simply because it is easier to implement.

PART III TRADE-OFFS BETWEEN ECONOMIC GOALS

22 The Tension Between Economic Goals

When someone proposes an economic policy, the policy is justified in terms of its contribution to a particular economic goal. For instance, taxes on steel companies should be reduced because reducing the costs of operation may encourage them to employ more workers. When looked at superficially, all policies sound great because their proponents are very careful to word them in terms of their positive contributions to our economic performance. They are selling their ideas, so they emphasize the economic goals that will be advanced by their proposal.

Part II enabled you to better understand and evaluate economic policy proposals. You know, for example, that someone who sees no merit in govermental regulations on toxic-waste dump sites is ignoring the significance of *externalities*. Proponents of tax cuts for the purpose of economic growth should be required to explain the *tax incidence* of the cuts. Defenders of government antitrust cases in the interests of more efficiency must pay attention to the possiblity that mergers may enable us to take advantage of the cost savings from *economies of scale*. The economic principles you have learned equip you for a mental dialogue with normative economic analysis. When someone says X will further economic goal Y, you will be able to examine whether the causal link is likely.

Unfortunately, economic analysis is not simply a matter of deciding whether an economic change will have a particular effect. Part

II has, in one sense, protected you from an equally important and troublesome aspect of economic policy selection: *Even if X does move us toward goal Y, what price do we pay in terms of movement away from goal Z?* The very policies that advance us toward Y often propel us backward, away from one or more of the other economic goals. *Economic trade-offs* are the result of dilemmas created when a policy has a positive effect on reaching one economic goal and *at the same time* a negative effect on our ability to reach other economic goals. Thus, the first step in evaluating an economic proposal is to ask, Will it actually have the positive effect on reaching goal X? A second, and equally important, question provides the subject matter for Part III. What trade-offs will arise even if the proposal accomplishes what it promises?

Economic Trade-off The negative impact on one economic goal caused by improved performance in reaching a different economic goal

THE SEARCH FOR THE PERFECT ECONOMIC POLICY

A worthwhile purpose of studying economics is to improve our ability to reach our economic goals. Part II of this text emphasized the economic principles that fulfill that purpose. However, the desire to move toward *better* economic policy has limits. You recall from Chapter 3 that values are an important assumption of normative economic analysis. The choice among economic policies requires you to decide who you want to benefit most and *who you least mind harming.* Notice that the last part of the decision-making process can be reworded to say: Which trade-offs bother you least?

The search for better economic policy is thus limited by the trade-offs that occur while pursuing particular goals. In simple terms, the trade-offs are the disadvantages of policy proposals. They are usually the unspoken part of normative economic analysis. They are the impacts that proponents of policies would prefer to ignore.

Part III urges you to be aware that the search for a perfect economic policy is an illusion. There is no doubt that the illusion is attractive. It is that attractiveness that compels opponents of a policy to denounce a proposal on the grounds that it has *some* negative impact on our economic performance. It would indeed be hard to imagine any economic policy that did not have trade-offs associated with it.

Why must there be trade-offs? Why should you suspect their presence even though you cannot identify them in a particular instance? The concepts of scarcity and opportunity cost from Chapter 1 hold the key to the answer. Any allocative or distributional choices moving us toward an economic goal will have opportunity costs associated with them. The costs occur because of the limited resources available to meet our material desires. Using resources for one purpose prevents their being used for others. Even more important, their use for one purpose *denies* their use to those who had used the resources before.

Thus, there is a tension surrounding the pursuit of economic goals. More is involved than just a technical understanding about whether a proposed policy helps us attain an economic goal. Value judgments about the priority we should give each goal are also involved.

SELF-TEST

1. What is inadequate about this statement: I tend to agree with those economic policies that have the most advantages.
2. Explain the link between the concept of scarcity and the idea of economic trade-offs.
3. Why are economic policies acceptable even though they may have some disadvantages?

TYPICAL TRADE-OFFS

There are many trade-offs among the economic goals you have studied. For instance, almost any form of governmental regulatory, distributional, or allocational activity will reduce certain economic freedoms. Thus, when governmental behavior is intending to pursue equity, full employment, or some other economic goal, it is also threatening economic freedom.

We will focus on four specific trade-offs because they are frequent and significant. Part III includes one chapter each on the following trade-offs:

1. Full employment versus price stability
2. Growth versus environmental protection
3. Equity versus efficiency
4. Economic freedom versus equity

Each of these trade-offs results from an interaction between market and governmental decision making. Some group with power senses a problem with current market behavior in that such behavior is preventing us from attaining an economic goal. They pressure government for change, since government is the device we use to correct bothersome results from market decisions. If successful, the pressure results in a solution that has a cost associated with it. The cost is a movement away from another economic goal.

Full Employment Versus Price Stability

The trade-off between full employment and price stability arises when government engages in a particular kind of stabilization policy. When aggregate demand levels are changed to fight cyclical unemployment or demand-pull inflation, there is usually (especially in the short run) a trade-off between price stability and full employment. An upward adjustment in aggregate demand may create job opportunities, but it also creates upward pressure on prices. Reductions in aggregate demand may reduce a tendency toward inflation, but reduced spending also creates less demand for labor.

Growth Versus Environmental Protection

The protector in environmental protection efforts is some level of government. The inevitable effect of such efforts, as you learned in Chapter 13, is an increase in the short-run costs of doing business. Entrepreneurs may have reduced enthusiasm for new investments as they watch the cost of doing business escalate. Investment decisions necessary for economic growth are a matter of comparing expected rate of profit with the cost of making the investment. By increasing the costs of operation through environmental protection laws we reduce the expected rate of profit.

An alternative way to view this trade-off is by thinking about the impact of growth on the environment. The drive to expand output per person threatens certain parts of our resource base. From a short-run perspective, growth may accelerate by reducing concern for air and water quality. Our typical measures of growth are not sensitive to the magnitude of garbage we generate as a result of increased production. Certainly some kinds of growth cause less environmental damage than do other kinds. However, any economic growth carries with it a threat that the environment will be seen as a means for acquiring short-run profit, instead of as the basis for meeting the needs of future generations.

Equity Versus Efficiency

To achieve efficient use of resources there must be pressures or incentives that encourage optimal use of resources. Any incentive system contains those who for some reason do not respond to the incentives. Perhaps they are unable to perform, not given an opportunity to perform, or just choose not to participate in productive activities. The more vigorous the incentive system, the more an equity problem exists. When the market process results in sharply unequal incomes (all in the name of greater efficiency), society will begin to question whether the resulting income distribution is legitimate.

Another illustration of this trade-off involves the impact of governmental redistribution on efficiency. Greater equity requires expenditures and taxes that are progressive. Yet these expenditures and taxes threaten the incentive system that encourages personal achievement. Thus, distributional policy almost inevitably has an impact on our ability to achieve efficiency.

Economic Freedom Versus Equity

When government changes the market distribution of income, it alters the property rights possessed by those whose taxes were changed. You will remember from Chapter 13 that property rights represent the extent of the control various people have over specific resources. Tax increases reduce the freedom possessed by resource owners. If the community takes money from you and transfers it to others, the freedom you possess suffers. Certain opportunities that would have been available are no longer possible, because your ability to spend your market earnings has been reduced.

SELF-TEST

4. What trade-off would you expect to occur if the Environmental Protection Agency decided to require all United States businesses to provide an annual report documenting the environmental impact of their production activities?
5. Explain what is inadequate about the following statement: Since economic trade-offs are usually stimulated by some governmental action, the key to reducing economic problems would seem to be keeping government actions to a minimum.

THE MESSAGE FROM PART III

When you complete this Part, you will have increased your ability to understand and evaluate economic analysis. You will become more aware of four particular economic trade-offs. You will be better able to answer the following questions:

1. What trade-offs may result from the economic policy being suggested?
2. What causes a specific trade-off?
3. How can particular trade-offs be avoided?

Even more important you will be better prepared for a life of reading, discussing, and reacting reasonably to economic policy proposals.

ACTIVE REVIEW

1. An economic program of any president should represent a set of plans that will solve our economic problems. Many such programs are overly gloomy. They focus on what we cannot do rather than on what we can do. There is no reason why we cannot have a president with the vision to increase all our economic accomplishments.
   a. What is confused about the reasoning in the paragraph above?
   b. What economic idea would any president soon encounter if he or she believed that all economic goals can be achieved in unison?
2. The number of homeless in our large cities is a disgrace. How can the rest of us be comfortable while some roam the streets looking for shelter? I do not feel competent to decide whether we need weapons in space, but I do know that shelter is a basic need that should be met for everyone regardless of their income.

   While I wish that an appeal to voluntary contributions to the homeless would solve their need, I don't think voluntarism is the answer. It's too easy to imagine that your neighbor will take care of the problem. Therefore, I am suggesting that we increase the sales tax on all items over $500 and that we earmark these funds to provide shelter for the homeless.
   a. What economic goal is the argument explicitly designed to advance?
   b. What trade-offs would the proposal encounter?
   c. How would the "solution" create a new problem?

ANSWERS TO ACTIVE REVIEW

1a. The writer of the statement is confused because he or she appears to believe in the illusion of the perfect solution. Costs are gloomy. However, they do not disappear just because a presidential program fails to mention them. Whereas ignoring costs may be a popular thing to do, the costs will make their existence known later. Scarcity guarantees that we will pay opportunity costs when we improve our performance with respect to an economic goal.

1b. A president who believes that a perfect set of economic policies is a reality would run head-on into economic trade-offs. These trade-offs are the price we pay when we try to solve specific economic problems.

ANSWERS TO SELF-TEST

1. It is certainly a good idea to look at the advantages of a proposed economic policy. However, counting the advantages is hardly an adequate model for evaluation. First, you should ask, Will the advantages actually occur? Will an economic goal be furthered by adopting the suggestion? Part II of this text can help answer that question.

   In addition, the concept of economic trade-offs makes us aware that there are also negative impacts from economic policies. Evaluation is not complete until you have thought about whether it is worth the cost to achieve the projected advantages.

2. Trade-offs are present in economic decision making only because scarcity exists. If there were no scarcity, then using resources for one purpose would not require us to cut back on production or some other output. There would be no economic trade-off.

3. The existence of disadvantages is not by itself a basis for rejecting a policy proposal. Since all economic policies have costs, any policy option has disadvantages. There are no perfect (cost-free) solutions. Thus, it is the weighing of the accuracy and importance of the projected advantages and disadvantages that characterizes careful economic decision making.

4. The effect of requiring environmental reports from all United States firms would be an increase in the cost of doing business. While such reports might better enable the government to protect our natural resources, the increase in business costs will reduce interest in investment. The opportunity cost of the reports may well be reduced economic growth.

5. The statement falsely assumes that economic problems can be avoided. Particular problems can be solved, but the solutions almost always

create new problems. There will, thus, be economic problems whether or not government plays an active role in the economy. Government can resolve certain problems caused by market exchanges; however, economic trade-offs prevent the governmental policy from being cost-free.

23
Full Employment Versus Price Stability

During the 1970s inflation soared to over 13 percent. Businesses were reluctant to invest, because they were uncertain about earning enough revenue to pay their rapidly rising costs. Consumers were frustrated because prices seemed to rise every time they went shopping. Inflation made them feel poorer. There was a general consensus among businesses, consumers, and political leaders that inflation was our number one enemy and that action had to be taken to reduce inflation as soon as possible.

During the early 1980s the rate of unemployment soared to over 10 percent. The rate of unemployment for black teenagers approached 50 percent. Idle manufacturing capacity rose to almost 30 percent. The economy was losing billions of dollars worth of production because of the economic slowdown. Clearly the economic loss from this high level of unemployment extended far beyond those unfortunate workers who lost their jobs. Returning the economy to full employment became a primary objective for the economy. Nobody wanted to endure the lower standard of living imposed by an unacceptably high level of unemployment.

These two preceding paragraphs should be a reminder of the importance of price stability and full employment as goals. Economies are harmed by both inflation and unemployment. Thus we might anticipate that economic and political leaders work hard to keep the rates of inflation and unemployment low.

Yet when we examine our economic history, we find that success in achieving these goals has been cyclical. Sometimes we have achieved price stability, and at other times we have achieved acceptably low rates of unemployment. Rarely, however, has the United States economy achieved price stability and full employment simultaneously.

During the 34-year period from 1950 to 1984 the rate of inflation and the rate of unemployment fell simultaneously seven times, in the years 1952, 1953, 1955, 1959, 1972, 1976, and 1983. These declines might indicate that economic policies were achieving their desired goals. Yet a closer examination of the rates of inflation and unemployment in those years reveal that inflation or unemployment or both were above acceptable targets in at least as many as three of those years and maybe as many as 5 of the years.* Thus, the data seem clear in supporting the claim the United States has rarely achieved full employment and price stability simultaneously.

EXPLANATION OF THE TRADE-OFF

The data in Table 23–1 illustrate the trade-off between price stability and full employment. When the economy was successful in achieving price stability, we generally experienced unemployment, and when we were successful in achieving our full employment goal, we were likely to experience an undesirable rate of inflation. This trade-off between inflation and unemployment was especially apparent during the 1950s and 1960s when the relationship came to be known as the Phillips Curve, after A. W. Phillips, who first documented the trade-off with empirical data.

Figure 23–1 plots the data from Table 23–1 to illustrate the trade-off between inflation and unemployment for the period from 1950 to 1969. It appears that when the United States economy maintained a 4 percent level of unemployment, the economy experienced a 2 to 3 percent rate of inflation.

By the 1960s, monetary and fiscal authorities appeared to understand this trade-off so well that some economists predicted that we knew how to control the fluctuations in the economy and that we might not have to experience recessions again. This prediction was based on a successful tax cut in 1964 that stimulated demand and caused a continuous decline in unemployment from 1960 through 1969. Inflation hovered around the goal for price stability until 1969,

*Target rates of inflation and unemployment are slippery concepts, as we indicated in the chapters discussing these goals. For the purpose of discussion in this chapter we have chosen 2 percent inflation and 5 percent unemployment as legitimate policy goals.

Table 23–1
Annual Inflation and Unemployment Rates, 1950–1983

Year	Annual Rate of Inflation	Annual Rate of Unemployment	Year	Annual Rate of Inflation	Annual Rate of Unemployment	Year	Annual Rate of Inflation	Annual Rate of Unemployment
1950	1.0%	5.3%	1962	1.1%	5.5%	1974	11.0%	5.6%
1951	7.9	3.3	1963	1.2	5.7	1975	9.1	8.5
1952	2.2	3.0	1964	1.3	5.2	1976	5.8	7.7
1953	0.8	2.9	1965	1.7	4.5	1977	6.5	7.1
1954	0.5	5.5	1966	2.9	3.8	1978	7.7	6.1
1955	−0.4	4.4	1967	2.9	3.8	1979	11.3	5.8
1956	1.5	4.1	1968	4.2	3.6	1980	13.5	7.1
1957	3.6	4.3	1969	5.4	3.5	1981	10.4	7.6
1958	2.7	6.8	1970	5.9	4.9	1982	6.1	9.7
1959	0.8	5.5	1971	4.3	5.9	1983	3.2	9.6
1960	1.6	5.5	1972	3.3	5.6	1984	4.2	7.5
1961	1.0	6.7	1973	6.2	4.9	1985	3.7	7.2

Source: U.S. Bureau of Labor Statistics, *Monthly Labor Review* (Washington, D.C.: GPO, 1986).

when we began to experience an increase in inflation. Because of the success of controlling inflation and unemployment during the 1960s, policymakers became confident that they could use the Phillips Curve relationship to reduce unemployment to 4 percent without igniting inflation.

According to the Phillips Curve analysis we could expect inflation to rise to 2 or 3 percent when unemployment falls to 4 percent. Since

Figure 23–1
Phillips Curve for the United States, 1950–69

This diagram illustrates that low rates of inflation are generally accompanied by high rates of unemployment and vice versa.

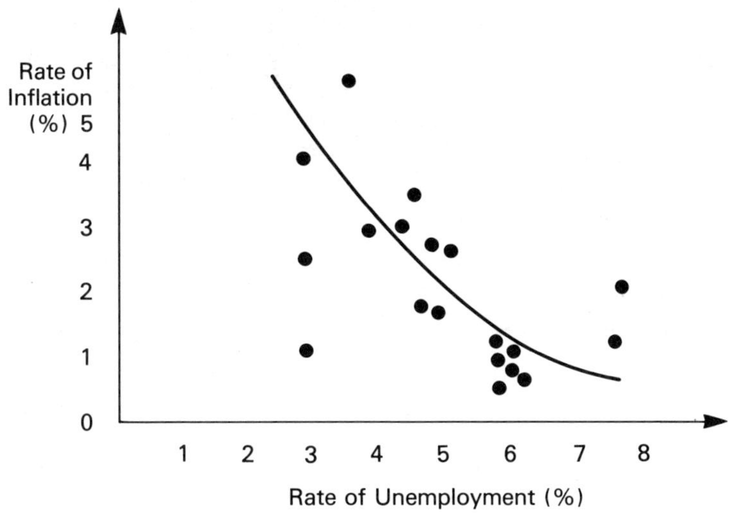

Figure 23–2
Phillips Curve for the United States, 1970–83

This figure illustrates how the trade-off between inflation and unemployment appeared to change between 1950–69 and 1970–83. The 1970–83 data are represented by the points above the 1950–69 Phillips Curve.

this rate of inflation corresponded with the goal for price stability, economic and political leaders felt comfortable in pursuing a full-employment goal of 4 percent unemployment.

This confidence in the Phillips Curve relationship proved to be somewhat hasty, however. Beginning in 1969 and continuing throughout the early 1980s the relationship between inflation and unemployment appeared to change (see Figure 23–2). During this period inflation and unemployment often rose simultaneously. In addition, the annual rates of inflation and unemployment no longer fell close to the Phillips Curve that represented the trade-off from 1950 through 1969. At times we experienced undesirable levels of both unemployment and inflation.

WHAT CAUSES THE TRADE-OFF?

In a mythical economy where the factors of production move easily from one type of production to another, full employment with price stability can be achieved. Through the forces of a market economy the factors of production (labor, capital, and natural resources) would

Figure 23–3
Price-Output Relationship for a Mythical Economy
This diagram shows that prices will not increase until we reach full employment, because the factors of production are moved from product to product as the real GNP expands.

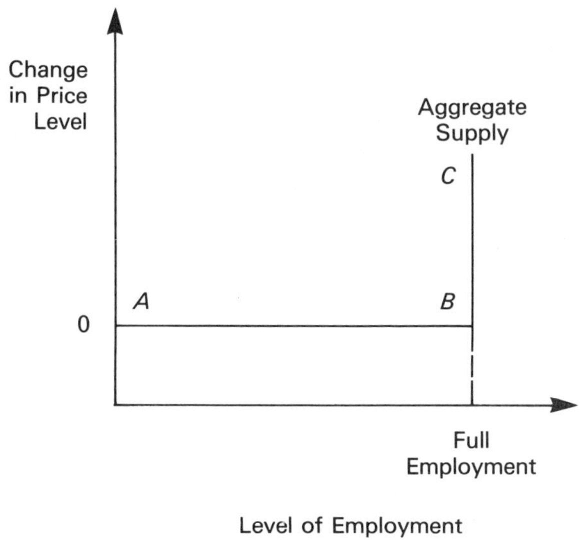

be combined in the most efficient manner to produce the goods and services that were the most profitable. If a particular good or service became unprofitable, the factors of production would switch from that production to something else that was earning profit. The mythical economy would not experience any transitional costs as these factors of production were switched from one type of production to another. Thus, real output would expand until the economy reached the level of full employment output (points *A* to *B*). Any further attempts to increase output would result in inflation (*B* to *C*). A diagram showing the relationship between prices and real output for this mythical economy would be shaped like a right angle (Figure 23–3). Once the level of full employment is reached, real output cannot expand. Any attempt to purchase more output will cause an increase in prices.

SELF-TEST

1. The Phillips Curve relationship says that as unemployment decreases there is likely to be an increase in inflation, and when inflation decreases, there is likely to be an increase in unemployment. Can you explain why?

Price Stability and Full Employment Trade-off Prior to 1970

The economy illustrated in Figure 23–3 is mythical because the factors of production are simply not that flexible. When unemployment is greater than 5 percent, production can increase with little pressure on inflation, because unemployed labor and other resources can be employed at the existing wage rate and level of production. (Do you remember the concept of opportunity cost in Chapter 2? When we use unemployed resources to increase production, the opportunity cost of the increased production in terms of lost output tends to be zero or minimal. We do not have to sacrifice the production of any other products to increase production.) Labor skills, necessary plant and equipment, and natural resources are available for production. Thus, inflationary pressure should be minimal.

When the rate of unemployment is 5 percent or less, the economy will experience difficulty in expanding production. For example, increased production may require labor with specific skills that are not possessed by those who remain unemployed. If production is to increase, employers must hire workers with the appropriate skills away from other companies, or the employers must train the workers. In either case the cost of production will tend to increase. Thus, as the rate of unemployment falls, the rate of production will increase more slowly, and the costs of production will tend to rise more rapidly. The increasing costs of production will cause the prices of final products to rise.

Figure 23–4 illustrates the trade-off between price stability and

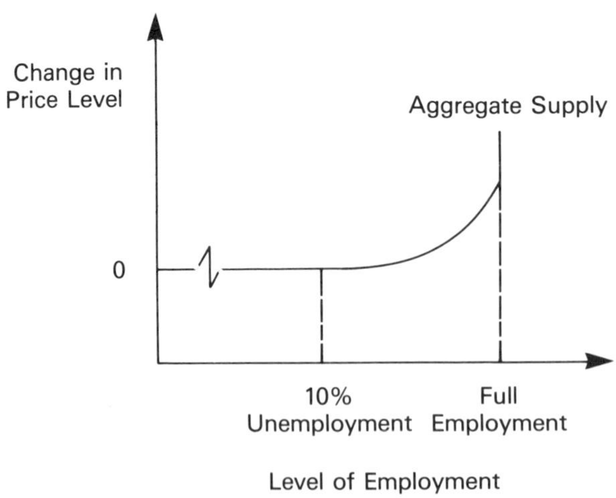

Figure 23–4 Price-Output Relationship for a Typical Economy

This diagram illustrates that a typical economy will begin to experience inflationary pressures prior to full employment.

full employment in a typical economy. If we attempted to employ 100 percent of the work force, we would experience very high rates of inflation. The achievement of 100 percent employment is an untenable goal because of the existence of frictional employment. (Do you remember its definition? Check Chapter 15.) If we experienced a relatively high rate of unemployment, say 10 percent, we would most likely experience price stability. Thus, we encounter a trade-off.

Price Stability and Full Employment Trade-off Subsequent to 1970

As we have indicated in previous chapters, especially 15 and 21, in approximately 1970 the United States economy experienced some significant changes in the relationship between price stability and full employment. Most notably the economy encountered an increased amount of pressure from structural unemployment and cost-push inflation. Concurrently, the economy incurred an increase in inflationary expectations. In other words, because there were higher than normal rates of inflation, people began to expect more inflation. As a result, consumers tended to increase their spending, laborers demanded higher wages, and businesses increased their prices in anticipation of higher costs. In all cases these actions fanned the fires of inflation.

Stagflation Situation in which an economy experiences unacceptably high rates of inflation and unemployment simultaneously

Stagflation occurred during the post-1970 period. In effect, the trade-off between price stability and full employment worsened. It appeared as if any attempts to reduce unemployment below 7 percent would cause inflation to rise above 10 percent. If we attempt to demonstrate the changing nature of the trade-off, we find that three Phillips curves appear to have existed between 1950 and 1982 (Figure 23–5).

One explanation for these three Phillips Curves was offered in Chapter 21. At the end of the 1960s the government attempted to finance the Vietnam War through deficit spending even though the economy was already operating very close to its potential full employment level of output. The annual rate of unemployment was 3.8 percent in 1966 and fell to 3.5 percent in 1969. This increased governmental spending stimulated aggregate demand and began to pull prices upward. The demand-pull inflation that followed this increased spending on the Vietnam War sparked inflationary expectations. As a result, attempts to reduce inflation by cutting aggregate demand were only partially successful, as illustrated by curve II in Figure 23–5.

Between 1974 and 1982 the economy experienced three signifi-

Figure 23–5
Shifting Phillips Curves

This diagram shows three potential Phillips Curves existing between the years 1950 and 1984, indicating that inflation was existing with higher and higher rates of employment.

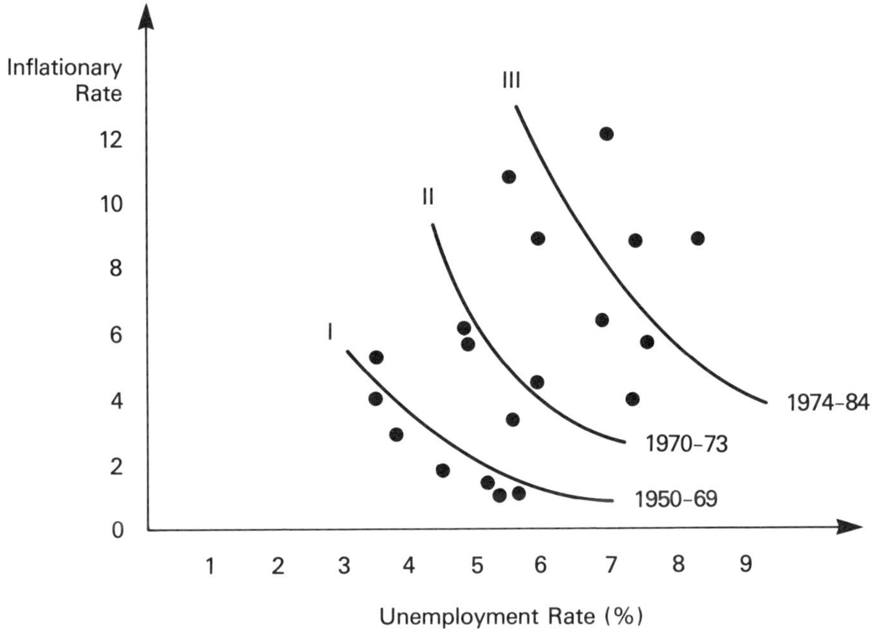

cant shortages of critical products. First, in 1972 and 1973 there was a dramatic reduction in the worldwide production of grain. By the end of 1973 the prices of food had risen significantly. Second, in 1973 and 1974 the Organization of Petroleum Exporting Countries (OPEC) dramatically reduced their sales of crude oil, causing the price of oil to increase by 400 percent. Third, the Iranian revolution occurred in 1979. Once again the supply of oil was reduced and the price of energy shot up. The combination of these three supply shocks and inflationary expectations significantly altered the relationship between inflation and unemployment, as illustrated by curve III in Figure 13–5.

SELF-TEST

2. In what way is stagflation different from inflation?
3. Inflation is defined as an increase in the general level of prices. When the price of any one commodity increases, we generally do not refer to that price increase as inflation. Why then do we claim that the increase in the price of oil during the 1970s was inflationary?

POLICY AND THE TRADE-OFF

Impact of Fiscal and Monetary Policy on Employment and Prices

The chapters on fiscal and monetary policy emphasized that these policies are usually used to increase aggregate demand for the purpose of stimulating production during periods of cyclical unemployment and to reduce spending during periods of demand-pull inflation. The previous sections in this chapter demonstrated that this approach appears to have been relatively successful, especially during the 1960s. Beginning in 1960 President Kennedy pledged to get the country moving again by increasing governmental spending and by decreasing taxes. This pledge followed a decade that experienced relatively low unemployment rates during the Korean War but higher than normal unemployment rates during the latter part of that decade. Inflation during that period stayed near 3 percent except in two years.

During the 1960s the Kennedy and Johnson administration based their economic actions on the Phillips Curve relationship. Government officials began to use government spending as a tool to increase economic activity. In 1964 a significant tax cut was passed. The combination of increased governmental spending and decreased taxes initially caused deficit spending. The size of deficit spending in relation to GNP did not change appreciably, because the expansion in output increased national income. This type of fiscal stimulus along with a complementary monetary policy appeared to reduce unemployment without causing unacceptable levels in inflation.

The trade-off began to worsen when President Johnson increased government spending without raising taxes to finance the Vietnam War. This action was taken for political rather than economic reasons. The Vietnam War was unpopular, and President Johnson did not want to risk making the war effort more unpopular by forcing people to pay higher taxes. He reasoned that the economy would be able to continue expanding and that the revenues from this increased production would pay the costs of the war effort.

By 1969 it was clear that the economy was producing at a level that was very close to its full employment limit. Unemployment had fallen to 3.5 percent, but inflation reached 5.4 percent, an 18-year high. In terms of the Phillips Curve the economy was performing at the leftward edge of curve I in Figure 23–5.

By deciding to use deficit financing to pay for the war effort when the economy was already close to full employment, we essentially agreed to accept significantly higher inflation as the price for maintaining full employment. The average rate of inflation jumped from 1.7 percent from 1960 to 1967 to an average of 4.8 percent for 1968 and 1969.

During the early years of the Vietnam War it would have been better if the fiscal and monetary authorities had taken steps to decrease aggregate demand to reduce the inflationary pressure. Since the economy was experiencing 3.8 percent unemployment and 2.9 percent inflation in 1967, we would expect a cut in aggregate demand to reduce inflation toward 2 percent without any significant increase in unemployment. Those results did not occur. Inflation varied between 5.9 percent and 3.3 percent during 1968 and 1972, but unemployment grew to 5.9 percent. The trade-off between inflation and unemployment appeared to have worsened.

Throughout the 1970s and early 1980s the trade-off appeared to change again. The average rate of unemployment during this period was 6.9 percent, and it grew to over 10 percent by 1982. If the Phillips Curve of the 1950s and 1960s were operable, we would expect price stability with these high rates of unemployment. In actuality we endured strong inflationary pressures. Inflation rose to 13.5 percent in 1980 and averaged 7.5 percent for the period.

What happened? Were monetary and fiscal policies that ineffective? Did we experience some fundamental changes in economic conditions?

Stagflation

The combined problems of inflation and unemployment presented a new challenge for the United States. It appeared as if the relatively simple trade-off between inflation and unemployment had disappeared. Was the stagflation caused by the earlier exercise of fiscal and monetary policy, or had some significant changes occurred in the economy, causing stagflation to be inevitable?

As you might suspect, the answer to this question is not clear, and economists disagree about the importance of the different forces. We do know that the economy experienced three major and unexpected supply shocks during the 1970s. These shocks contributed significantly to inflation and unemployment by reducing aggregate supply and increasing the costs of production. More specifically, the supply shocks increased inflation, and attempts to reduce inflation by decreasing aggregate demand caused unemployment. Inflation did not fall because of inflexible prices and wages and low productivity.

Decreases in Aggregate Demand In Figure 23–6 the shift from AS_1 to AS_2 represents the reduction in productive capacity resulting from the OPEC oil embargo, the reduction in the supply of oil caused by the Iranian revolution, and the dramatic decline in agricultural products in the early 1970s. The initial impact of the reduction in aggregate supply caused the equilibrium to switch from point *A* to point *B*. At this new equilibrium, the economy produced a lower level of output (Q_2), at a higher price (P_2).

As inflation increased from P_1 to P_2, the monetary and fiscal authorities took steps to reduce aggregate demand. This decline in spending caused aggregate demand to fall from AD_1 to AD_2. This action was expected to decrease inflation.

The decrease in aggregate demand did achieve a reduction in the general level of prices from P_2 to P_3, but it also caused a significant increase in the level of unemployment as a result of a decline in real output (see equilibrium *C*).

Why didn't the reduction in aggregate demand just decrease inflationary pressures? The answer lies in distinguishing between demand-pull and cost-push inflation.

When the economy suffered the reductions in the supply of oil, the costs of producing anything that contained oil or used oil for energy increased. In some cases production ceased because sufficient energy supplies were unavailable. In essence, the economy faced a reduction in its ability to produce. Since aggregate demand did not

Figure 23–6
Impact of Supply Shocks on Aggregate Demand and Aggregate Supply
This diagram illustrates how decreases in aggregate supply combined with policies to decrease aggregate demand may lead to inflation and unemployment.

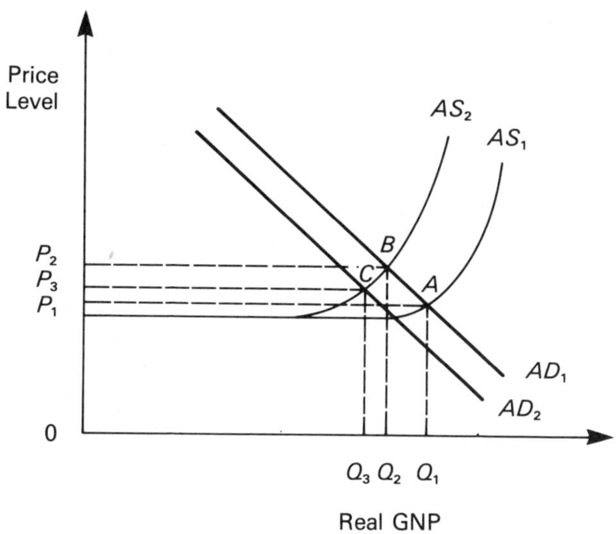

change immediately after the reduction in aggregate supply, the economy encountered a situation of too many dollars chasing too few goods, because the economy's ability to produce declined. The inflation was not caused by an expansion in aggregate demand. It was caused by a reduction in supply.

Under this circumstance a reduction in aggregate demand does not focus on just oil-related products. Sales of virtually all products decreased. Consequently, businesses found it necessary to reduce their costs by cutting back on production and laying off workers.

In the meantime not much had happened to influence the output and price of oil, since they were controlled by the oil cartel, OPEC. Because the supply of oil did not increase appreciably and the demand for oil did not decrease as much as supply decreased, the inflationary pressure from the reduction in the supply of oil remained relatively strong. Consequently, the monetary and fiscal policies that reduced aggregate demand when the economy was experiencing cost-pull inflation caused a significant increase in unemployment without significantly reducing the rate of inflation.

Inflationary Expectations Inflationary expectations also contributed to stagflation. Following the 1960s and the Vietnam War, workers and businesses began to expect the government to continue its emphasis on a fully employed economy. This expectation permitted workers and businesses to pursue contracts that maintained their purchasing power. Labor unions negotiated cost of living agreements (COLAs) that automatically adjusted their wages as inflation occurred. Businesses tended to increase their prices every time their costs increased, because they were attempting to maintain their real income. This behavior of labor and business led to wage-price spirals without compensating increases in production. As long as everyone expected inflation to continue and government to pursue policies designed to avoid recessions, continued inflationary pressure was inevitable.

Throughout the 1950s and most of the 1960s inflationary expectations were not a problem, because the rate of inflation was kept under control, averaging about 2 percent for the entire period. The rate of inflation began to show signs of continually rising in 1967. Between 1967 and 1983 prices rose at an average rate of 6.9 percent. Following the 1967–70 inflationary spiral, people began to anticipate more inflation and altered their economic behavior accordingly. This change in behavior contributed to an inflationary bias in the economy.

SELF-TEST

4. Evaluate the following statement: Inflation is always caused by an economy's having a supply of money that is greater than its supply of goods and services. Consequently, the only way to cure inflation is to bring the supply of money and the supply of goods and services back into equilibrium.
5. How do inflationary expectations reduce the effectiveness of policies designed to decrease inflation?

Inflexible Prices and Wages In a competitive world all prices, including wages, are supposed to be flexible. If the demand for labor falls, then we would expect wage rates to fall so that the economy could maintain a full employment equilibrium. Similarly, prices of goods and services will fall when demand for them falls. Under these theoretical conditions unemployment would be only a temporary problem resulting from adjustments by workers as they relocate from one job to another and away from high-wage toward low-wage job slots.

In the current United States economy, prices and wages do not appear to fluctuate that smoothly. When unemployment occurs, the wage rates rarely fall. When inflationary conditions exist, the workers who remain on the job may bargain for a wage increase because they wish to protect their standard of living. When prices and wages do not fall, cuts in aggregate demand will not reduce inflation as quickly as expected.

Similar types of counterpressures may exist among sellers. In oligopolistic industries there is evidence that some sellers have increased rather than decreased their prices during recessions. If the oligopolistic sector exerts sufficient influence over the economy, a reduction in aggregate demand for the purpose of reducing inflation will not have the desired impact. Reductions in aggregate demand will tend to increase unemployment significantly prior to creating pressure that will force prices of firms in concentrated industries downward.

Low Productivity A fourth cause of stagflation may be low productivity caused by high taxation and governmental regulations of businesses. Some economists, especially those who advocate supply-side economics, argue that governmental intervention in the economy has stifled the productivity of private enterprise so that businesses have not increased their production fast enough to prevent inflation. If taxes are reduced so that businesses will find it less costly to invest and expand productive capacity, inflation is expected to be moderate because production is expanding rather than because demand is contracting. With this approach, employment would also increase.

This solution to stagflation is appealing because it permits a market to function effectively. If businesses respond to a tax reduction, the increased production will generate sufficient income with which to purchase the additional goods and services. The major questions about this approach are whether businesses are willing to take the risk of expanding productive capacity if the economy is not stable and whether the monetary authorities are willing to cooperate with a monetary policy that will complement the tax cuts. The answer to both of these concerns is uncertain.

Supply-side economists argue that in addition to tax reductions, much of our social legislation has caused a decline in productivity. According to this argument the regulations designed to improve product safety, protect the environment, ensure worker safety, and promote equal opportunity have increased costs and made it difficult for companies to compete, especially internationally. Supply-side economists advocate that if we decrease the number and scope of these regulations or find better ways to implement them, we can reduce costs significantly. With lower costs of production, companies will have greater incentives to invest in new capital equipment and expand their productive capacity.

This argument also appears attractive. There is no debate about the fact that regulations raise costs. There is debate, however, about whether the benefits overwhelm the costs of regulation.

Many regulations influence the production of goods and services that cause significant externalities. For example, without regulations, textile workers become more likely to contract brown-lung disease. Without regulations, acid rain may cause significant damage to our wildlife in the northeast sector of our country and in Canada.

If markets are left unregulated, textile producers will take action to reduce the problem of brown-lung disease only if they face a shortage of textile workers. Even then the producers are more likely to increase wages than to reduce long-term health hazards.

In the case of acid rain, a regulation-free market is unlikely to reduce any of its emissions, because acid rain does not directly affect the cost of production on sales of the final product. Acid rain is truly a negative externality whose costs fall upon third parties and not upon the actual producers. If we desire a reduction in acid rain, then government must impose some type of regulation.

The question of whether regulations contribute to higher costs, lower productivity, and inflation involves two separate issues. First, if we must regulate, are we imposing regulations in the most effective manner? Could we achieve the desired effects by altering the way we regulate? If we agree that certain types of regulations are necessary for the well-being of the economy, then we should constantly reexamine our methods of regulation to determine if there are more effective ways to accomplish the objectives.

Second, the debate over regulation involves a clash of economic goals. If we reduce regulation, we can increase the efficiency of producing private goods and services and also increase the economic freedom of the sellers to decide what to sell and how to produce the product. On the other hand, if we reduce regulations we are likely to experience a reduction in environmental protection and equity. For instance, problems such as acid rain and job discrimination are likely to increase.

Thus, as we examine the problem of stagflation, we find that stagflation has occurred as a result of several factors, including decreased aggregate demand and aggregate supply, increased inflationary expectations, inflexible prices and wages, and low productivity. Because of the existence of these many factors, simple policy actions such as changing the money supply or altering the level of governmental spending are not likely to correct stagflation. A combination of approaches or new policies is necessary.

Income Policies

The existence of stagflation creates dilemmas for policymakers. Manipulation of aggregate demand through monetary and fiscal policy appears to increase unemployment dramatically without reducing inflation. Attempts to increase productivity are long-run policies. Their impact will not be felt for a year or more. In the meantime stagflation continues, and policymakers do not know if their long-term policies will work. To deal with this dilemma some economists argue that we need to suffer the consequences of protracted unemployment to burn the inflationary expectations out of the economy. Others, however, argue that we should impose some *incomes policies.*

Incomes Policies Direct intervention by government in the setting of prices and wages for the purpose of controlling inflation

Advocates of policies claim that concentrated sectors or business and labor are able to circumvent the forces of demand and supply. These concentrated sectors tend to operate with long-term contracts that are designed to minimize fluctuations and increase profit opportunities. Moreover, inflationary expectations add to the desire of these concentrated markets to set prices and wages in a manner that will maximize the gain and minimize the losses associated with inflation.

Oligopolistic sectors reduce employment instead of dropping prices and wages when aggregate demand falls. Both business and labor prefer to maintain their prices and wages in anticipation of future profits and inflation. The oligopolistic sectors will tend to let prices and wages fall only after unemployment has increased substantially. To avoid this unfavorable trade-off, some economists advocate incomes policies.

Incomes policies range from the relatively weak approach of jawboning, in which presidents use their powers of persuasion, to the implementation of price and wage freezes. Jawboning is used with the assumption that if a president can convince a few relatively visible businesses and labor organizations to restrain their price and wage increases, other companies and labor organizations will behave in a similar manner. Generally speaking, however, jawboning tends to have only limited success and, even then, only in the short run.

A more common form of incomes policy is wage and price controls. Advocates of this approach argue that monetary and fiscal policy cannot function effectively when inflationary expectations exist. They claim that controls are necessary to break an inflationary cycle caused by price-wage spiral. The controls do not need to be rigid. For example, companies could be permitted to increase their prices when they demonstrate a legitimate increase in demand, and laborers could receive wage increases when they demonstrate that their productivity has increased. To be effective, however, controls must convince the public that the general level of prices will not continue to rise once the controls are lifted.

Controls are unlikely to be effective when inflation is caused by demand-pull forces. At best, controls in this case would postpone the actual inflation. When inflation is caused by demand-pull forces, controls seriously distort the signals sent by market forces. Production will not expand in those areas where it is needed the most, and black markets will begin to replace legal markets.

When inflation is caused by cost-push forces or has gained a life of its own because of inflationary expectations, then price-wage controls may have some effect. When the economy experiences inflation that is essentially caused by a cost-push forces such as a commodity shortage, price-wage controls can provide some time for the economy to correct the shortage. Controls can be effective in keeping inflation in check if other action is taken to stimulate production of the commodities in short supply. If such stimulus is not provided, then inflationary pressures might actually get worse because producers will not have the incentive of higher prices to seek out alternative means of production. If controls are successful, then inflation can be reduced without negatively affecting the level of employment.

In general, advocates of a free enterprise economy do not like incomes policies at all. Controls are seen as interventions that distort market forces. Free enterprise advocates claim that we need to set the supply of money equal to the level of production. When stagflation exists, this approach will allegedly cause a significant increase in the rate of unemployment. Although the free enterprise advocates do not like the increased unemployment that results, they believe it is a consequence necessary to rid the economy of its inflationary expectations. Once inflationary expectations are eliminated, the natural forces of markets will function to expand and increase employment. These economists believe that price stability is a more important goal than that of full employment.

Advocates of incomes policies believe that there are significant imperfections in a free enterprise economy. A restrictive monetary and fiscal policy will cause undue hardship for the vast number of people who must suffer unemployment, and the economy as a whole will lose significant amounts of output because of the unemployment. Advocates of incomes policy believe that it is better to maintain high levels of employment and attempt to correct the causes of inflation while prices and wages are controlled.

SELF-TEST

6. In modern economies there appears to be a great reluctance of laborers to accept lower wages and for businesses to accept lower prices when unemployment increases and aggregate demand falls. Will these inflexible wages and prices influence attempts to achieve full employment with price stability?
7. How do regulations contribute to inflationary pressure? Will the removal of regulations automatically increase productivity?
8. Evaluate the following statement: Incomes policies attack only the symptoms of inflation and therefore cannot help solve the problem of stagflation.

International Experience

During the 1950s and 1960s the United States could establish its economic policies according to its domestic goals. The influence of other economies on the goals of the United States was minimal. But as the other economies recovered from World War II, they gained increasing ability to compete with businesses in the United States. As the level of international trade grew, the success or failure of one country to control inflation began to influence the level of inflation and unemployment in other countries.

After OPEC decreased the supply of oil in 1973 and 1974, the price of oil quadrupled. This dramatic increase in the price of oil caused significant inflationary pressure in most economies. Most major countries tightened their money supplies in an attempt to reduce this inflation. Because the inflation was substantially caused by cost-push factors, the decline in the supply of money caused a significant increase in unemployment and plunged the world economy into a deep recession.

Many countries responded to the recession by using monetary and fiscal policies to expand aggregate demand. These expansionary policies had little effect on the rate of unemployment, because OPEC was still restricting the supply of oil, and as a result, production could not increase very easily. This situation presented the world economy with expanding aggregate demand and a relatively stable aggregate supply, resulting in rapidly rising inflation in those countries that pursued the policies of demand stimulus. The inflation also caused a decline in the *exchange rates* of the inflating countries' currencies.

Exchange Rates The price of one currency in terms of another

We suspect that you are now wondering what difference it makes whether one British pound costs 2 United States dollars or 1.5 United States dollars. How could that difference influence the level of inflation and unemployment in the United States? The exchange rates have a direct influence on prices of products that are bought and sold internationally. For instance, if $2.00 exchanges for 1 British pound, then a suit that is made of British wool may cost 80 British pounds, or $160.00. If the value of the British pound falls to $1.50 per British pound, then that British wool suit will cost only $120.00.

Can you predict what would happen to the level of production and employment in the United States textile industry if the value of the pound falls? At the price of $160.00 a British wool suit may not be very appealing to you. But what happens when the price falls to $120.00? It is highly likely that consumers will stop purchasing domestically produced textiles and begin purchasing British textiles. As domestic textile production falls, unemployment in that industry will increase. This same switch will occur for every product that we wish to purchase from Britain or any other country whose currency has fallen in value relative to the United States dollar.

During the 1970s, Germany and Japan did a much better job of controlling their inflation than did most other major economies. (See Chapter 21, p. 357). Consequently, the value of the German mark and Japanese yen rose relative to the currencies of other countries. As the values of the German and Japanese currencies rose, it became more difficult for these countries to export products and easier for the Germans and Japanese to purchase goods from countries that, like the United States, were not as successful in controlling their inflation.

One negative consequence of Germany's and Japan's success in controlling inflation was an increase in unemployment. To keep inflation low, the countries had to maintain tight-money policies, which contributed to an increase in unemployment. In addition, their rising exchange rates made their domestic products relatively expensive and foreign imports relatively cheap. This change led the Germans and Japanese to purchase more foreign products and decrease domestic production, causing their unemployment to increase even more.

In the mid-1980s, United States found itself in a similar position. As a result of its recession (the worst recession since the Great Depression of the 1930s), the United States was able to reduce its rate of inflation relative to that of many other nations. With lower inflation the exchange rate for the dollar rose, causing the United States dollar price of Japanese Toyotas, French wines, and German steel to fall. Although these lower prices have assisted attempts to keep the United States inflation under control, the unemployment rates have stayed above 7 percent, which is significantly above the target rate of 5 percent.

These experiences of Germany, Japan, and the United States illustrate the increasingly important role of international trade in an economy's attempt to achieve price stability and full employment. The increased trade between nations has reduced the range and effectiveness of domestic economic policies.

It appears that in the United States during the period of 1980–85 the monetary and fiscal authorities decided that price stability was a more important goal than full employment. Throughout this period unemployment expanded to over 10 percent and then fell to approximately 7 percent. With the unemployment rate hovering around 7 percent for several years, some economists began to declare that 7 percent unemployment may actually be the full employment target. By making this type of decision these economists felt free to direct their efforts toward keeping inflation at or below its 3 percent rate in 1985.

SELF-TEST

9. Explain how a change in the exchange rate may help keep the inflationary rate low but have a negative effect on the unemployment rate.

CAN THE TRADE-OFF BE ALTERED?

Between 1969 and 1985 the trade-off between price stability and full employment appeared to worsen. During several of those years the United States economy experienced periods of high inflation and high unemployment. In other years we achieved some success in attaining one of the goals, but the price we paid was exceedingly poor performance in terms of the other goal. For instance, the rate of inflation fell from a high of 13.5 percent in 1980 to 3.2 percent in 1983, but the unemployment climbed from 7.1 percent in 1980 to 9.6 percent in 1983.

It also appears that even when the economy was successful in reducing either inflation or unemployment, the lower rates of 1969–85 did not reach the lower rates of 1950–68. For instance, ever since the first oil shock in the early 1970s, we have had difficulty in reducing unemployment below 7 percent.

The experience with inflation has been similar. We achieved 3.3 percent in 1972 and 3.2 in 1983, but the rates in each of the other years were considerably higher. The average rate of inflation since 1969 has been 7.3 percent.

Does the performance since the early 1970s indicate that we must accept higher levels of inflation and unemployment? Have we instituted policies that have created a permanent inflationary bias? Has structural unemployment become such an overriding force that we may have to accept 7 percent unemployment as the full-employment target rate?

The answers to these questions are neither easy nor clear. It is true that the United States, and most other industrial nations, established social policies that are designed to reduce hardship associated with problems such as unemployment, disability, death of the primary income earner, health problems, and old age. It is also true that the economy is pressured to keep expanding to provide consumers with higher standards of living. At the same time, however, we have become increasingly aware of environmental problems, safety and health conditions in the workplace, and potential depletion of natural resources.

The attempt to address these issues has required an increase in governmental activity, that is, an increase in governmental spending. Unfortunately, this increased governmental spending has occurred at the same time that the United States was experiencing a form of tax revolt. Political pressure to reduce taxes became so strong that President Reagan was able to achieve a major tax cut in the early 1980s. He was not successful, however, in significantly reducing the level of governmental spending. As a consequence, the federal deficit rose to over $200 billion in 1985. The existence of a growing federal deficit places an inherent inflationary pressure on the economy.

If we wish to improve the trade-off between price stability and full employment, we need to remove this inherent inflationary bias. There are three general ways to accomplish this objective:

1. Reduce governmental spending.
2. Increase tax rates.
3. Achieve a higher rate of economic growth while increasing governmental spending at a slower rate.

Reduce Governmental Spending

Decreasing governmental spending has a great deal of intuitive appeal. No one enjoys paying taxes, and we all want to reduce the waste in governmental spending. Yet the experience of the early 1980s has demonstrated that cutting governmental spending is a very difficult task. Governmental spending rose from $577 billion in 1980 to $946 billion in 1985. This increase occurred when the president and a substantial number of men and women in Congress were committed to the idea of reducing the role of government in the economy.

In 1986 Congress attempted to deal with this dilemma of wanting to reduce the deficit but not being able to reduce spending by passing the Gramm-Rudman bill. This legislation mandates that congress balance the budget by 1991. To achieve this goal the deficit is to be reduced each year until 1991. If the President and Congress fail to achieve the targeted reduction, automatic cuts in domestic and military spending would go into effect. As this text goes to press, we know that Congress has submitted a budget to the president that meets the 1986–87 targets. This budget was achieved by a great deal of compromise.

Apparently there are sufficiently strong economic and political reasons for continuing and possibly expanding governmental activities. Even a president and Congress that were predisposed to reducing that spending were unsuccessful in significantly reducing the role of government in the economy.

Those reasons include a legitimate concern for adequate provision of public goods and services. If governmental spending is to be decreased, a serious examination of current spending must be made, and decisions must be made about which budget items really are public goods and which are not. (This decision will be influenced by the different political and economic perspectives.)

Budget items that are determined to be private goods and services can be eliminated from the governmental budget because the private sector can provide them. The remaining items that are determined to be public goods and services must be provided by some form of governmental activity. Political leaders must determine whether the public goods and services are needed. If they decide yes, then political representatives must further determine the most effective way to provide them to the public.

Thus, governmental spending can be reduced by eliminating spending that can be provided by the private sector, determining whether all the public goods and services are really necessary, and finally, providing the public goods and services in the most effective manner.

Recent history indicates that reducing governmental spending may not be the most effective way of attacking stagflation. There is strong disagreement about the amount of social spending on items as varied as food stamps and the Strategic Defense Initiative (Star Wars). The opposing sides have articulate advocates. We are unlikely to see a significant change in the level of governmental spending. The existence of vocal constituencies on both sides of this issue tends to neutralize any attempts to make significant changes. Consequently, we are likely to see adjustments in certain types of spending, but the overall rate of governmental spending probably will not change dramatically.

Increase Taxes

Reducing governmental spending is a much more attractive policy alternative than increasing taxes. The circular-flow-of-income analysis in Chapter 16 illustrated that taxes reduce consumer spending. In a free enterprise economy such as that of the United States, it is evident that people prefer to spend their money themselves and not let government spend that money. In fact, supply-side economists argue that high taxes actually deter hard work and contribute to declines in productivity.

With these attitudes about taxes how could an increase in taxes help improve the trade-off between inflation and unemployment? The most basic answer to this question is that all forms of spending are generated from the income earned from production. If we determine that a certain level of governmental spending is essential for the well-being of the society, then we must collect taxes to pay for that governmental spending.

Won't increased taxes cause the economy to falter? High taxes could very possibly have a negative influence on the level of economic activity. This possibility is especially likely if the governmental activity is determined to be unproductive or undesirable. Then either aggregate spending will be greater than aggregate supply, causing inflationary pressures, or the undesirable governmental spending will cause people to become disgruntled and to seek ways to avoid paying their taxes. When people become upset with what they consider unnecessarily high taxes, their productivity may fall, causing gross national product to fall or to rise more slowly.

Governmental spending, however, is not necessarily unproductive. If governmental spending is directed to public goods and services, then governmental agencies are providing goods and services that are needed by the public. In Chapter 9 we emphasized that public goods and services are not profitable because these goods and services are nonexclusive. One person cannot use the good exclusively. For instance, if you purchase a street light for the street in front of your house, everyone who walks or drives past your house benefits. You cannot exclude them from using the light. Yet you have no way to charge those people for the benefits. Consequently, you are unlikely to install the light. We ask government to install the light.

In most cases this principle of nonexclusion will discourage people from purchasing public goods and services. Yet people want such public goods and services as street lights, streets, highways, public education, medicine, and national defense. In many of these cases public goods and services complement private goods and services. Good highways allow businesses to ship their products more effectively. Public education improves the quality of the work force. National defense provides us the security necessary to live and work without fear of aggression.

We determine the public goods and services we desire through the ballot box. Once we vote for a certain combination of public goods and services, we must pay for those purchases through taxes. But payment of these taxes is not a drag upon the economy, because they are paying for goods and services that society desires. The payment of taxes becomes a burden on the economy when we pay the taxes and get very little, if anything, in return.

SELF-TEST

10. In recent years government has been spending significantly more money than it receives in tax revenues. This spending creates an inflationary bias in the economy. What principle can we use to decide what types of governmental spending we should reduce?

11. Is it possible to increase taxes and increase productivity at the same time?

Increase the Growth of GNP

How can the increase in the production of goods and services improve the trade-off between unemployment and price stability? Won't attempts to increase production cause a strain on the factors of production and increase inflationary pressure? At first glance it may seem that attempts to grow more rapidly will create additional inflationary pressure because output will push against the full employment capacity of the economy. The Phillips Curve relationship illustrates that the closer the actual level of output gets to the full employment level of output, the greater the inflationary pressure.

If we want to use growth to reduce the inflationary bias in the economy, we must improve the ways we combine the factor of production. Businesses would have to increase their use of capital and technology. The labor force has to gain the skills necessary to pursue new, more technological jobs. The primary objective is to expand the production-possibility of the economy at the same rate as the demand for goods and services increases. If the economy can maintain this balance between production and demand, the basic relationship between price stability and full employment should stabilize, and the inflationary bias should disappear.

Capital expansion and an increased use of technology are critical if businesses wish to achieve this economic growth. To achieve capital expansion and acquisition of new technology, businesses need to earn economic profit and have easy access to loanable funds. When businesses earn economic profits, they are motivated to expand their productive capacities. Their profits become an excellent source of money to pay for this expansion. When businesses are profitable, they generally find that they can borrow money more easily (that is, at lower interest rates).

Yet pursuit of more capital and technology is an insufficient approach to solving stagflation. To achieve a full employment goal of 5 percent without significant increases in inflation, steps must be taken to improve the efficiency of labor markets. As the economy expands the use of new technology, the role of labor shifts from a blue-collar labor force engaged in production to a white-collar labor force that provides services.

As the labor force becomes more service-oriented, it requires more and different skills to gain employment. When the labor force consisted of production workers, there was an abundance of jobs that were semi-skilled. These jobs required very little training, and in most cases, the necessary training was provided on the job. Service jobs often require training that is not easily learned on the job. Classroom and technical school training for a year or two may be necessary.

In many cases today's unemployed workers are individuals who have worked and want to work again, but they do not possess the skills that are needed in our modern, high-tech society. These workers are structurally unemployed. Specific steps need to be taken to assist these workers in their quest for gainful employment. By improving their skills and, thus, their ability to work with new and sophisticated technology, we expand the production-possibility of the economy. In this way employment increases without significantly creating significant inflationary pressures.

National Job Location Centers One way to assist unemployed workers to find new jobs is to establish a national system of job-location centers. The purpose of these centers would be to provide unemployed workers easy access to job information. In today's society this information is not readily available, especially outside one's local area. The Bureaus of Employment Services are state agencies that help workers find work within their community.

But in today's economy this service is inadequate. Whole areas are often afflicted with high rates of unemployment. For instance, the Ohio Valley has suffered because of a decline in steel production. Michigan has not fully recovered from the significant decline in automobile production in the early 1980s. Neither of these areas is likely to regain its high level of employment because of aggressive competition from foreign steel and autos. Consequently, workers could use assistance in locating jobs in other parts of the country. When jobs are located, relocation assistance should be provided to improve the probability that unemployed workers can get to the jobs. The relocation allowance will help the workers afford the move and possibly adjust to a new cultural environment.

Job Training A system of job-location centers cannot improve the trade-off by itself. In many cases the unemployed steelworkers and auto workers will never find jobs in those industries again. These workers need to look for new jobs and new skills. Yet gaining new jobs and skills is more complex today because these workers cannot simply look for other manufacturing jobs. Most likely, they will find job openings in the service sector, and the workers will have to learn new skills before they can apply for these jobs. Many of these jobs cannot be learned by on-the-job training.

If government or private business would establish an effective job-training program, the structurally unemployed, the young, the unskilled, and minorities would have a better chance of gaining productive employment. If workers could learn skills that would permit them to compete for jobs that have a future, jobs with upward mobility, the incentive to endure the training should improve. If unemployed workers learn new skills that permit them to work productively with new technology, unemployment would fall without a noticeable increase in inflation.

Many European countries devote more resources to job retraining than does the United States. Historically, these countries have had lower rates of unemployment than United States. It would be wrong to conclude that they have achieved these lower rates solely by instituting job-training programs. It is proper, however, to point out that government-assisted training programs can help unemployed workers to gain new skills and to become productive members of the economy.

Government Incentive Programs In addition to providing assistance for worker relocation and job training, government can also provide incentives to businesses to increase their employment in areas that are economically depressed. This approach brings the jobs to the workers instead of the workers to the jobs. This type of subsidy has the advantage of using the economic, political, and social institutions that already exist. Communities can be revitalized.

European countries have used these incentives since the 1950s. Low-interest loans and subsidies for wages and salaries are given to companies that build plants in areas with high unemployment. When this approach is used in conjunction with job training, there is a good probability that geographically based structural unemployment can be reduced without significantly increasing inflation.

SELF-TEST

12. Would it be easier to stimulate economic growth if the unemployment within the economy were caused by cyclical forces instead of structural ones? (If you need a refresher, check Chapter 15 for definitions of cyclical and structural unemployment.)

ACTIVE REVIEW

1. Historically the United States experienced a trade-off between unemployment and inflation that appeared to be acceptable. A 2 to 3 percent inflationary rate did not seem to be an inordinate price to pay for 4 percent unemployment. But during the 1970s and early 1980s this trade-off appeared to worsen. Four percent unemployment seemed unattainable. Both inflation and unemployment soared.
   a. Identify two significant causes for the worsening of the trade-off, and explain why these causes influenced the trade-off.
   b. Given the above causes would a decrease in the money supply help improve the trade-off? Why?
   c. What steps, if any, should we take to increase employment without significantly increasing inflation?
   d. Does it make any difference what action other countries take to attempt to achieve full employment with price stability?
2. What would happen to inflation and unemployment if the world suddenly experienced a decline in the supply of iron ore? If banking officials decreased the supply of money after the supply of iron ore fell, what would you expect to happen? Why? Would a cut in taxes have been a better way to deal with the problem? Why? Would it make any difference if the government decreased the taxes of steel companies that explored for new sources of iron ore?

ANSWERS TO ACTIVE REVIEW

1a. During the late 1960s the United States government attempted to finance the Vietnam War without raising taxes. This action caused inflationary pressures because the economy was already producing a level of output that was close to the full-employment capacity. As the rate of inflation increased, inflationary expectations also increased. Businesses and consumers were unaccustomed to sustained inflation. As a result businesses began to raise prices in anticipation of future price increases, and workers negotiated cost of living allowances (COLAs) that adjusted their wages to the rate of inflation.

Second, the economy experienced three significant supply shocks during the 1970s. First, there was a worldwide shortage of grains that significantly increased the price of agricultural products. Then the Organization of Petroleum Exporting Countries (OPEC) placed an embargo upon the supply of oil. The impact of this embargo was a significant increase in the price of oil and virtually all products that used oil as energy or as a significant raw material. Finally, the

Iranian revolution reduced the supply of oil, and prices were forced upward once again.

Inflationary expectations worsened the trade-off because people did not believe that inflation was going to decline even after monetary and fiscal policies were used to reduce aggregate demand. Thus, as aggregate demand fell and unemployment increased, prices did not fall as much as expected.

When agricultural production and the supply of oil declined, the productive capacity of the economy decreased. We found ourselves in a position where we were unable to achieve the same standard of living as previously. When we spent the money we had earned from previous production, we found that there were fewer goods and services available. Thus, prices increased. When we tried to increase production to meet the demand, we could not, because of the reduced supply of oil for energy. As a result, unemployment increased at the same time prices were rising.

1b. A decrease in the supply of money tends to reduce the general level of spending in the economy. Yet a major portion of the inflationary pressure resulted from the inadequate supply of oil. Thus, the demand for oil would not fall at the same rate as the supply of oil. Therefore, the price for oil would continue to rise. In the meantime, the demand for all other goods and services would tend to fall because the Federal Reserve System is reducing the supply of money. As aggregate demand falls, unemployment increases. The trade-off worsens instead of improving.

1c. Commensurate with these three supply shocks the economy was also experiencing a transition from an economy that employed workers primarily for production to an economy that employed most workers to perform services. This transition led to a change in the type of worker employers wished to hire. They now needed workers with specific skills instead of laborers to work on a production line.

If we want to reduce unemployment that results from this structural change, a specific program should be established to assist workers in gaining new skills and finding new jobs by subsidizing training and moving workers from one location to another.

1d. We must be concerned about the actions other countries take to deal with their problems associated with inflation and price stability. If some of them are more successful than we in moving toward price stability, the exchange rates will change, and their currencies will increase in value. These countries will then be able to import United States products more cheaply.

If these countries do, in fact, increase their imports, their purchase of United States goods will increase the demand for United States products. As the demand for these products rises, the United States will experience renewed inflationary pressure.

ANSWERS TO SELF-TEST

1. As the economy expands production toward its potential full-employment level of output, it becomes increasingly difficult to match the unemployed resources with the needs of the expanding businesses. When the economy is stagnant and there is considerable unemployment, businesses have no difficulty in hiring workers who possess the skills required by businesses. Workers are immediately productive. But when the unemployment rate falls, the pool of unemployed, skilled workers shrinks. Employers have greater difficulty in hiring workers with the required skills. Consequently, production will increase more slowly, and costs of production will rise more rapidly. Businesses will then increase their prices to pay the rising costs of production. These increased prices contribute to inflationary pressures that appear as the rate of unemployment falls toward zero.
2. An economy generally experiences inflation when production approaches its full-employment capacity to produce. Under this condition, increases in production cannot keep pace with increases in income. Typically inflation is described as the condition of too many dollars chasing too few goods. When stagflation exists, the economy experiences inflation and unemployment at the same time. In this situation the inflation cannot be caused by aggregate demand's growing more rapidly than aggregate supply. Other factors, such as decreases in the supply of critical products, must have contributed to the inflationary pressure.
3. It is true that price increases in products such as textiles, appliances, or houses do not constitute inflation, because these increases are only a small fraction of the total prices within the economy. It is likely that as the prices of textiles increase, prices of other products fall. Thus, increase of prices for any one product cannot be used as an indicator of the inflationary pressure. Oil prices, however, create a different dimension. Not only is oil a major source of energy that is used in the production of a vast number of products but oil is also a major component in the production of a wide variety of goods ranging from food to records to plastic. Oil has a pervasive influence on an economy. So an increase in the price of oil will tend to have a significant influence over the general level of prices.
4. Inflation is a monetary phenomenon that occurs because an economy has more dollars to spend than it has goods and services to sell. It is correct to argue that if the supply of money increased at the same rate as aggregate supply, there would be no inflationary pressure. But these statements avoid more critical issues. We need to study the different ways to equate the supply of money with aggregate supply, and we should examine the consequences of these different methods. Because there is a trade-off between inflation and unem-

ployment, we need to search for an anti-inflationary policy that will reduce inflation without significantly increasing unemployment. When inflation is essentially demand-pull, we can correct the problem by using monetary and fiscal policy to reduce aggregate demand. When inflation is caused by supply forces (cost-push inflation), reductions in aggregate demand are more likely to increase unemployment than to decrease inflation. Under this condition inflation is a much more complex problem to solve.

5. When members of an economy expect inflation to continue, they increase their purchases because they want to buy items prior to their prices increasing again. Although this activity is very rational from the perspective of an individual, it is very irrational behavior for the entire economy. The increased buying stimulates aggregate demand and increases inflationary pressure. Once members of the society expect prices to continue to rise, their purchasing pattern works against attempts to reduce aggregate demand, because workers will bargain for higher wages (COLAs), and businesses will continue to increase their prices in anticipation of continued inflation. Then actions force monetary and fiscal authorities to consider decreasing the money supply, increasing taxes, and decreasing governmental spending by greater percentages than would be necessary if inflationary expectations did not exist.

6. Monetary and fiscal policies are usually based on the assumption that the forces of competition work effectively. If demand for product or a factor of production declines, the price of that product or factor will also decline. When these forces function effectively, policy action to reduce aggregate demand reduces the income not only through taxation, fewer governmental programs and a smaller supply of money, but also because wages will fall as pressures on unemployment rise. These combined pressures work to reduce prices.

   If, however, some wages and prices are inflexible, the process of reducing aggregate demand has a flaw in it. If wages do not fall when the demand for labor decreases, employers will tend to increase the number of workers they must lay off to decrease their labor costs. If some businesses fail to reduce their prices when the demand for their product falls, then aggregate demand must fall by greater amounts to achieve the desired reduction in inflation. If price and wages are inflexible in a significantly large sector of the economy, they will become a major reason why the economy may endure inflation and unemployment simultaneously.

7. Regulations contribute to inflation by reducing productivity. If businesses must conform to regulations by installing safety devices and reducing pollutants, then productivity falls and the costs of production rise. If production cannot expand as fast as aggregate demand, inflation will result. It follows, therefore, that a reduction in regulations will cause a reduction in the general level of prices.

This line of reasoning may be deceptive, however. Many regulations are imposed to control negative externalities. If the regulations are removed, the costs associated with the regulations may decline, but the negative externalities will remain. Businesses may be able to reduce the costs of installing safety devices, but injuries to workers may increase. The cost of installing antipollution devices will fall, but acid rain, smog, and other pollutants may increase. If we want to reduce the costs associated with regulations, we need to make sure that the regulations are not providing a useful service. Under these circumstances the regulations cause businesses to charge a price that covers *all* the costs of productions, including those that relate to negative externalities. These price increases are not inflationary.

8. Incomes policies can play a role in reducing inflation without causing significant increases in unemployment if they are used in conjunction with other policies. We should consider using incomes policies when there are significant imperfections in the market economy, for example, oligopolistic industries and strong labor organizations. When these market imperfections exist, monetary and fiscal policies do not work effectively. Oligopolistic industries and strong labor organizations contribute to the downward inflexibility of prices and wages. These conditions also contribute to inflationary expectations.

   An imposition of an incomes policy helps break inflationary expectations and provides some time to search for solutions to the underlying causes of inflation. If, for example, the inflation is caused by a serious supply shock, incomes policies can be used to keep price increases under control while specific action is taken to stimulate production in those areas where supply has been curtailed.

9. The exchange rate is the price of one currency in terms of another. When one country is more successful at controlling its rate of inflation than other countries, the currency of the country with the low inflation will rise in value relative to the currencies in other countries. This increase in value will permit the low-inflation country to import products more cheaply than before the change in value. As the low-inflation country increases its imports, the cheaper-priced imports help keep the rate of inflation low.

   The negative aspect of the increased imports is that as buyers purchase more foreign products, there is less demand for domestic production. With less demand for domestic production, businesses will not increase their employment. If the imports increase, unemployment in the importing country may increase.

10. A primary reason why governments spend money is to provide their economies with public goods and services. If we decide that a reduction in governmental spending is necessary to improve the tradeoff between inflation and unemployment, we first need to decide what types of governmental spending can be considered as spending on

public goods and what spending could be provided by the private sector. Government can cut its spending on items or activities that are considered private goods.

If we need to cut more governmental spending, we need to develop a set of priorities. We need to examine how the public goods and services provide important contributions to the economy and how they complement the production of private goods and services. Governmental spending that is least important in meeting these needs may be cut.

11. Some forms of governmental spending definitely contribute to the overall level of productivity in the economy. For example, private businesses depend upon a good highway system to transport their goods. Port authorities that operate airports and waterways also provide critical services to the private sector. Improved educational facilities enhance the quality of the work force. Spending on medical and scientific research increases the probability of major technological advances. Governmental expenditures on these and other activities either directly add to productivity or serve as important complements to the private sector so that businesses can increase their productivity. Increased taxes for this type of spending can increase productivity, just as increased spending by a private business for a computer can increase productivity.

12. Cyclical unemployment is caused by an insufficient demand for labor. Workers who become unemployed as a consequence of an economic recession expect to get their jobs back as soon as the economy starts moving toward its full-employment level of output. Structural unemployment is caused by a mismatch of the skills required by employers and those possessed by the unemployed. This type of unemployment can exist when the economy is expanding.

    If unemployment were caused by cyclical factors, no special action would be necessary to increase the productivity of the labor force. As steps are taken to expand the level of output, laborers would find jobs as production increased. Policymakers would place their emphasis upon expanding their capital because they are confident that laborers will get jobs as soon as the economy begins expanding.

    If a significant proportion of the labor force is unemployed for structural reasons, then the problem is very different. As the economy expands, there is no guarantee that the structurally unemployed workers will find jobs. As businesses increase the amount of capital equipment, the more routine jobs tend to disappear, and jobs that require specialized skills appear. The skills associated with a previous job are often not applicable to new jobs. Consequently, if a significant proportion of the unemployed workers are structurally unemployed, then attempts to stimulate the economy will require some action to assist workers to learn new skills and locate new jobs.

24
The Trade-off Between Growth and Environmental Protection

Times Beach, Missouri, has earned the dubious distinction of being the object of the first federal purchase of a polluted city. The one-square-mile town situated along the banks of the Merrimac River is a victim of chemical contamination whose potential for harm is so great that $33 million was allocated by the United States Environmental Protection Agency to buy the homes of the town's 2,000 residents and to relocate these residents to a safe environment.

The contamination of Times Beach occurred when waste oil polluted with an extremely toxic chemical, dioxin, was sprayed along the town's unpaved roads in the 1970s in an effort to control dust. A chemical waste transporter had been paid to dispose of the dangerous substance, but he then used it when hired to spray a dust-controlling oil in Times Beach, claiming to be unaware of its toxicity, yet undoubtedly cutting costs considerably. A 1983 flood exacerbated the situation; experts claim that the rising waters may have eroded the tainted soil and spread it all over town.

Though its precise effects on human health are not yet known, this form of dioxin, (2,3,7,8, TCDD), has been linked to the occurrence of cancer and birth defects in animals. Even more frightening is that while the Centers for Disease Control advises that humans not be exposed to more than one part per billion (ppb) of the toxic substance, soil samples taken at Times Beach reveal levels of up to 100 ppb in certain areas.

Times Beach is not alone in its plight. As many as 50 other sites in Missouri are contaminated by extremely high levels of dioxin. This finding suggests that many more Americans may soon face the same uncertainties as the residents of Times Beach: Will their health be endangered? Will their neighborhoods be safe again? It appears that we have only begun to realize the extent of the hazardous chemical waste problem in the United States.

THE NATURE OF THE TRADE-OFF

How could such a problem occur? Is it just a natural human error or the result of a more complex process of making economic decisions in a world of scarcity? The thrust of this chapter is to help you appreciate how incidents like Times Beach can be prevented as well as how costly it would be to limit the drive for economic growth that caused the problem in the first place.

This chapter is a synthesis of Chapters 13 and 14. Chapter 13 presented the economic goal of environmental protection. This goal consists of preserving the natural environment so that it can be used and enjoyed by future, as well as current, generations.

Two economic concepts play a special role in defining and reaching the goal of environmental protection—externalities and property rights. The natural operation of the profit motive in a market system ignores the negative and positive effects of market exchanges on third parties. Hence, typical market prices ignore these effects. Third parties lack a voice in market decisions. The consumption or production of a good or service affects them, but they are excluded from the market negotiations concerning how much will be bought.

Property rights interact with externalities in at least two ways. These rights refer to the reasonable expectations of individuals concerning their power to use, benefit from, and exclude others from using particular resources. The effects of externalities on the community occur in part because no one possesses any specific property rights in the air, health, water, peace and quiet, security, and safety that are threatened by the production of more and more goods and services in a market economy. If someone possessed such a set of property rights, he or she could refer to *my* air or *my* water and would aggressively protect against damage to that personal property.

The fact that such property rights do not exist means that a protected environment is in everybody's interest. Things that are in everybody's interest often have a way of becoming no one's concern. Each of us waits for someone else to protect our environment.

In one additional way the concept of property rights interacts with externalities. Those who produce goods and services do have property rights associated with their production facilities. They are understandably outraged when someone attempts to restrict their rights by imposing on them the costs of either clean-up efforts or environmentally sound production techniques. The existence of property rights on the supply side of the marketplace and their absence in the area of third-party effects makes it clear that the struggle for environmental protection will be intense and lengthy.

How is the material in Chapter 14 related to the goal of environmental protection? While the efforts of individual sellers to cut costs and grow is not itself what we mean by economic growth, these activities are prerequisites for economic growth. The efforts of workers to be more productive so that employers will want to hire them and the struggle of firms to reduce costs stimulate expanded output from limited resources.

One result is economic growth—an expanded capacity to provide more goods and services. Unfortunately, one of the by-products of profit-seeking behavior is the existence of negative externalities. No one wanted to cause contamination at Times Beach. The chemical waste transporter probably had little technical knowledge about the social effects of the form of dioxin found in the oil he sprayed on local roads.

One thing the transporter did know, however, is that finding a safer spray would have increased costs. Every producer is intensely aware of the need to find lower-cost methods of production. The profit motive itself thereby encourages economic growth *and* the environmental problems associated with production techniques that shift as many costs as possible onto the general public in the form of indiscriminate delivery of output—in other words, externalities.

The remainder of this chapter will present the reasons for the trade-off, the policy choices that affect the trade-off, the link between the trade-off and distribution, and an international perspective on the trade-off. As you should predict by now, given your current understanding of economics, even if we could put our finger on some technique for achieving both goals at once, the cost in terms of lost opportunities to achieve another of the economic goals will be high.

SELF-TEST

1. Evaluate this solution to environmental hazards: Urge all firms now engaged in behavior that harms the environment to become more sensitive to environmental damage.

2. Explain a relationship between property rights and externalities by using the Times Beach incident.
3. Distinguish between the growth of a firm and economic growth. Does this distinction matter in terms of the content of this chapter?

CAUSES OF THE TRADE-OFF

The fundamental explanation for every trade-off in economics is the same: the existence of scarcity forces us to make choices among alternative uses for resources. Many of those choices are unpleasant because of their high opportunity costs, but we are required to make them anyway.

Each of the causes of the trade-off between economic growth and environmental protection is derived from the existence of scarcity. Although we will discuss them individually, they are unified by their common ancestry. Scarcity is responsible for each cause.

Economic Growth Requires Consumption of Resources

Professor Bruce Hannon of the University of Illinois has estimated that it requires more than 630 square miles of forest to provide the McDonald's chain with a single year's supply of paper packaging. While hamburgers are a very small part of the output of our economy, they still use up a substantial amount of forest products. While there is no necessary reason a wise seller of wood products would not replace denuded forests with new plantings, our history of deforestation demonstrates that such long-term investments in productive capacity are rarely made. In the short term, it makes more sense to use existing forests than to plant new ones.

The point is that our capacity to produce output now can often be expanded by using resources that could enhance both production and our environment in the long run. Users of resources rarely calculate environmental harm when they consume resources. Instead, they rush to meet consumers' desires for current output.

While some resources such as the sun, wind, and hydroelectric power are renewable in the sense that my consumption of them does not make them less available for your use, most resources are gone after they have been used to produce output. To the extent that forests, land, and basic minerals are used as a means to achieve economic growth, they often cannot later be used for productive purposes. Supplies of these resources are not automatically regenerated even when, as in the case of forests, regeneration is possible. Humans have to *choose* to replace resources.

Allocation Decisions Tend to Be Short-Run

The role of the present is much more significant in our calculations than is the role of an uncertain future. When we decide what to do with resources, we are typically absorbed with the effect particular uses will have on our lives now and in the immediate future. None of us is sure what we will want in the future, what we will be like later, or whether we will even have a distant future. We do, however, know what we want right now.

Combined with this orientation to the present is the natural difficulty we have in thinking about the needs of future generations. As both Chapters 13 and 14 pointed out, allocation decisions rarely consider the interests of future generations. We do not see their faces or hear their wishes. Those alive today, however, are vociferous and clear about the desires they wish the economy to fulfill.

Most environmental problems will beset us at some later date. Thus the combined effect of our present orientation and tendency to ignore the interests of future generations is to overlook many of the negative social effects of current efforts to achieve economic growth. Environmental problems are primarily a transfer of resources from future generations to our own. We enlarge our capacity to produce goods and services, though many of the costs from that endeavor are paid by others.

Let's look at an illustration to see the effect of short-run allocation decisions on the trade-off. While studying the illustration, notice that if we conceptualized both economic growth and environmental protection in a future-oriented manner, the trade-off would not be as troublesome. Each decision about what to produce and how much to produce would require careful estimates of the long-term effect on both our capacity to produce as well as on the quality of our environment.

Every year farmers use 2.5 billion pounds of pesticides. Why? They are trying to enhance the productive impact of the resources they use to produce food. They are engaging in normal business behavior, expanding output per dollar of cost in the interests of higher profits. In 1985 more than one million watermelons in California had to be destroyed because farmers, according to the Environmental Protection Agency, chose cost-cutting efforts that eventually resulted in 1,400 reported cases of diarrhea, nausea and blurred vision. No one believes farmers intended that result; they were just trying to squeeze more output from their plants and fields.

A few cases of nausea are highly uncomfortable, but suppose the pesticides used in this instance had caused cancer of the colon. The short-run focus of allocation choices prevents farmers from adequately considering future health risks in their cost calculations. Similarly that same focus causes consumers to urge and enjoy higher levels of watermelon output. We can taste that juicy, red fruit now; its eventual effects on us and future generations is speculative and imprecise.

The Urge to Grow Feeds on Itself

A society that experiences economic growth succeeds in satisfying some wants, but the marketing activities that precede the satisfaction tend to create even more wants than existed before. The idea of economic growth has definite advantages in its conflict with environmental protection. Above all else, economic growth expands our ability to have whatever goods and services we want. It is highly satisfying in that respect.

Growth has two other advantages relative to environmental protection. Both cause the process of growth to be popular and ongoing. Growth is dynamic; it holds out the promise of great happiness in an amount never before experienced. Environmental protection, in contrast, is static, nostalgic, and even stodgy-sounding.

Second, economic growth is expressed in a measurable form, gross national product per person. Thus, we can watch it rise or fall; it is visible. Of course, *you* realize from Chapter 14 that this apparent precision is an illusion that is highly controversial. Environmental protection, on the other hand, is not operationally defined; it is vague, broad, and not reducible to a single number.

While each of these relative advantages benefits advocates of greater growth in their conflict with environmentalists, growth gains impetus from its very existence. Many people watch on television or in person while others eat sumptuous buffets, relax at plush resorts, lounge on exquisite furniture, or entertain at lavish parties accompanied by thousands of dollars worth of sound equipment. Their vantage point does not reveal any befouled air, polluted water, congestion, or anxiety associated with the productive efforts that created the feast of consumption.

The reaction of most is to want and maybe even expect similar consumption possibilities during our lives. Will we be satisfied if those wants are satisfied? Probably not!

Status Good or Service A good or service that instead of satisfying either a biological or economic need elevates the social status of the consumer

Several concepts from economics and psychology explain why the growth process feeds on itself. Many goods and services are status goods or services. Such goods or services do not fulfill a biological or economic need; rather they enhance the status of the consumer in the eyes of his or her neighbors. Protein or a home are biological requirements; we need them. A fur coat, a yacht, or a second home are not needed. They are status goods. Having them gives us a jump on other consumers.

Status goods by their essence can never be possessed in adequate numbers. Economic growth is limited in its ability to ever satisfy us, for it increases the number of people who can have the same number and type of status goods. The result is a mad rush to acquire even more status goods to regain the position of dominance we held formerly. The pursuit of status goods is inflamed by economic growth, making future economic growth even more popular.

Law of Hedonic Contrast The greater the discomfort that is being relieved, the more intense the pleasure. Too much comfort prevents pleasure.

Does the pursuit of economic growth make us even happier? There is little evidence that greater happiness exists, but our efforts to grow proceed as though we need just one more dose of goods and services to achieve ultimate pleasure. The Law of Hedonic Contrast helps us understand why growth does not leave us satisfied. The Law of Hedonic Contrast reveals the futility of economic growth as a means for reaching higher and higher levels of satisfaction.

The more we have, the less joy we get from additional goods and services. As Figure 24–1, the Wundt Curve, indicates, pleasure is felt

Figure 24–1 Wundt Curve

This graph suggests a psychological process that provides insight into why growth feeds on itself.

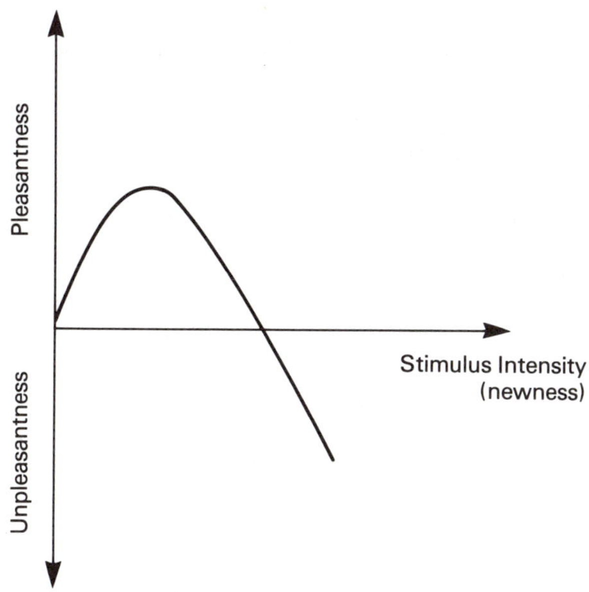

most intensely when we are miserable and acquire goods and services that relieve the misery. In most industrialized countries we have far surpassed the point where goods and services provide happiness, intensely felt.

The first units of a good or service provide so much joy because they remove us from a state in which we had none. Additional units, however, do not provide the same excitement; we have experienced that good or service already. However, we continue to strive for greater economic growth in a vain attempt to match the pleasure of those first surges of consumption.

The implication of the self-generating nature of economic growth for environmental protection is grim. Advocates of environmental protection, in the absence of some disaster, must fight an uphill battle. The next section discusses the policy tools governments and markets can use to achieve a particular trade-off between these two important economic goals.

SELF-TEST

4. Explain why someone would claim that just because certain resources can be reconstructed, restored, or recreated does not mean they will be.
5. What is a relationship between the Law of Hedonic Contrast and the short-run nature of allocation decisions?
6. Why can't we grow until our wants are satisfied and then worry about protecting the environment?

MARKETS, GOVERNMENT, AND THE TRADE-OFF

All decisions in economics are mixtures in the sense that they are influenced by market forces and governmental policies. You may recall from both Chapters 13 and 14 that markets and government have the capacity to stimulate each goal.

To achieve environmental protection, the role of the government is more noticeable than that played by markets. Yet both can encourage improved environmental quality. Governments, you will recall, can use taxes, subsidies, or direct restrictions to regulate treatment of the environment.

The first two attempt to alter the incentives that direct the profit motive. By altering the profitability of particular business activities, taxes and subsidies can be used to protect the environment. Direct restrictions are different only in that they are more coercive and thus more effective (assuming they are enforced). They interfere more with economic freedom, but they do not permit the firm to opt for an environmentally harmful business decision.

How can markets encourage environmental protection? Is it not the profit motive that directs market behavior and explains the cost-cutting behavior that creates so many environmental hazards? The answer to the second question is certainly yes, however there are market forces that encourage concern for environmental quality. Although these forces are often overwhelmed by short-term profit considerations, they do exist and play a role in enhancing our environment.

Specifically, there is an enormous incentive to develop new resources or techniques that will improve environmental quality. As the negative effects of economic growth become more noticeable, profit-making opportunities arise in the area of environmental protection. Those who can create a new resource that fulfills that objective can make lots of money. Thus, the market can accelerate discovery of innovative ways to improve our environment.

One other market force works toward environmental protection. As we use up more and more of a resource, its supply is reduced. The consequence of that shortage is an increased price for the resource in question. Increased prices, as you know, tend, *ceteris paribus*, to reduce the quantity of the resource that is demanded. Thus, markets tend to reduce consumption of a resource as it becomes less available. This tendency works against the destruction of resource supplies.

Just as governments and markets have an impact on environmental protection, they also have a role to play in stimulating economic growth. Governmental expenditures and taxes can affect the quality of resources, both physical and human. For example, governmental subsidies for students can enhance the future productivity of human resources. Another important effect of governmental taxes and expenditures on economic growth is their impact on levels of aggregate demand. High levels of aggregate demand are one of the prerequisites for economic growth.

Market forces create even more of a stimulus for economic growth than they do for environmental protection. Virtually no decision a business makes is based explicitly on its effect on economic growth. However, these same decisions do affect economic growth nevertheless. The acquisitive urge of businesspeople encourages them to seek higher levels of productivity so that they personally can make more money. These productivity-enhancing efforts enlarge our capacity to produce goods and services. They stimulate economic growth.

The impression that this section should give you is that policy tools are available to direct our energies and attention to either economic growth or environmental protection. The choice between the two goals is a matter of value preferences. We know how to accomplish each. The trade-off is technical; our response to it is moral.

DISTRIBUTION AND THE TRADE-OFF

One of the moral issues that affects the trade-off between economic growth and environmental protection is the effects of both goals on the distribution of income and wealth. As Chapter 14 pointed out, most people on the planet lack basic necessities. Can we realistically talk about limiting growth in such a context?

Advocates of greater economic growth criticize environmentalists for being insensitive to the needs of people who desperately need more goods and services. Economic growth promises an increased ability to provide more drinking water, schooling, transportation, housing, and health care to those who now lack these necessities. By stimulating growth we can provide life and comfort where death and disease now reign. Growth makes sharing less painful because it permits expanding goods and services for the poor without extracting them from the affluent. These advocates argue that growth enhances equity.

Environmentalists are often attacked as elitists. They are already comfortable in terms of having an abundant supply of goods and services. What about the living conditions of everyone else?

The response of environmentalists to the charge of elitism is to point out that it is not especially relevant to say that growth can lead to equity when it almost never does. Income distribution patterns do not become more equal as countries experience economic growth. Instead, the urge to grow feeds on itself. Those who are rich get even richer, relative to the poor, when growth occurs. The condition of the poor is made worse, not better, because the difference between their capacity to consume and that of the typical person has grown. They are relatively worse off as a result.

In addition, environmentalists argue that more-affluent members of an economy have the money to flee dirty air, polluted streams, and congested living conditions. The relatively poor are forced to pay the bulk of the costs of economic growth because they lack the financial ability to avoid them. Hence, it is the advocate of growth who is being insensitive to the needs of the poor.

This section points out the interrelatedness of the various economic goals. These trade-off chapters are merely suggestive. The trade-offs are much more complicated than these five chapters suggest.

INTERNATIONAL RESPONSES TO THE TRADE-OFF

The trade-off between economic growth and environmental protection rarely becomes a policy issue in those countries with very low levels of gross national product per capita. A country whose citizens are struggling to survive devotes its energies to producing food, providing shelter, and fulfilling other needs. Consequently, they do not have the luxury of thinking about the interests of future generations and how environmental protection would advance those interests.

Our search for international responses to the trade-off must, therefore, focus on the more affluent economies in Western Europe. As you might expect their environmental problems are at least as serious as ours. Crowded living conditions increase awareness of externalities. A firm's efforts to become more efficient by discarding some of its by-products into the community naturally has a larger social impact in a context where third parties are more numerous and reside in closer proximity to the firm.

Germany, for instance, is often cited as an industrialized country with an expanding awareness of the negative impact of economic growth on the environment. The reasons for this new self-consciousness about the environment are complex, but two stand out. First, West Germany has a very high standard of living, as you learned in Chapter 14. That relative affluence means that Germans can afford to ask, "Now that our basic needs are met, should we focus on even more goods and services or on preserving our environment?"

The second basic cause of Germany's heightened awareness of environmental problems is its high density of population. Approximately 60 million people in Germany live in an area the size of Idaho. Germany's population density is more than 700 percent greater than that of the United States. Translated into economic language, third party effects from market transactions are numerous and highly visible. Only two national parks offer refuge from crowded conditions, and there are small cities and farming even in both of these.

Pollution levels in Germany reflect the concentrations of people and industry. For instance, sulfur emissions per acre are 400 percent greater in Germany than in the United States. Air quality in general is at least as poor as in the United States. Noise levels and vibration effects from industrial activity are both so severe that governmental environmental agencies have separate branches to monitor each.

While Germany may be the most noticeable instance of an economy alarmed by environmental threats, other European countries have also perceived a conflict between expanded growth and environmental protection. While no European country has announced a freeze on economic growth, European economies have relied on a much sharper degree of governmental regulation of market activities that endanger the environment. They have apparently chosen to grow more slowly if necessary to avoid accelerated environmental damage.

European governments have not been hesitant to modify market decisions so that they would be more consistent with environmental protection. Yet they have been careful to preserve large degrees of discretion and the incentive of higher profits in the hope that market forces will continue to stimulate growth.

Denmark, for example, offers firms as much as a 15 percent subsidy on production processes that reduce pollution at the source. Management can still pollute if its business objectives encourage that action. The governmental policy though makes it more financially attractive to comply with an environmentally safe course of action. Market decision making has been retained, but in a modified form. The modification represents an attempt to balance environmental protection and the economic growth–enhancing investment behavior of the typical firm. It demonstrates the partnership that *can* exist between these two forms of economic decision making.

SELF-TEST

7. Evaluate this statement: Markets encourage environmental damage. The incentives for firms to cut costs create our environmental problems.
8. Does one's commitment to equity as the most important economic goal determine his or her attitude toward the trade-off between economic growth and environmental protection?
9. Why is environmental damage a common problem in any economy?

ACTIVE REVIEW

1. Chesapeake Bay, the United States' richest, most productive body of water—besides the two oceans—is sick and dying. Estimates of the bill to clean it range from $1 billion to $3 billion. Even in its current condition it is an incredible national resource. In 1982 it provided one-third of the oysters and one-half of the blue crabs harvested in the United States. Until recently, it yielded 50 percent of all striped bass caught in the United States, almost 6 million pounds a year.

   Oil refineries, housing developments, and urban sprawl from Richmond, Washington, and Baltimore have transformed the shoreline. What were formerly forests and pastures are now suburbs and factories. More than 50 polluted rivers empty into the Chesapeake. The by-products of farming, steel mills, chemical plants, and refineries all drain into the fragile ecosystem of the shallow bay. Must progress be so destructive?

How would you answer the question that concludes the description of Chesapeake Bay?

2. Are there any economic policies that could create harmony between economic growth and environmental protection? What other economic goals would be threatened by such policies? What economic lesson is contained in your answer?

ANSWERS TO ACTIVE REVIEW

1. In an important sense, certain kinds of progress must create specific kinds of destruction. As long as we wish to have rapidly expanding capacity to have more goods and services, we must use resources and build productive facilities.

The materialistic value structure highlighted in Chapter 14 as an essential for growth pushes us to have greater numbers of status goods and services. Since no one has property rights that cover Chesapeake Bay, the marinas, second homes, and factories that line its shores do not have to contend with an identifiable interest group when some of their costs are depositied in the bay. Everybody possesses the bay, so no one feels any special harm when it is dirtied.

Another type of progress, not defined as advances in gross national product per capita, might prevent environmental damage. But as long as we define progress in material terms, environmental problems will be an ongoing part of our future. The only question is the extent of the problems.

ANSWERS TO SELF-TEST

1. This "solution" to environmental hazards demonstrates a lack of understanding of the origins of environmental hazards. The people who operate firms are not especially insensitive to environmental damage. What they focus on, however, is the extent to which their firms make money. An important part of that process is discovery of methods to reduce costs.

You recall from Chapter 13 that pollution (or any other type of environmental hazard) is a cost. The firm would certainly prefer to shift that cost onto other people, either consumers or third parties. Third parties are a more attractive target because they lack voice or input into the exchange process. In other words, when decisions about price and quantity sold are made, they are nowhere to be found.

To expect firms to ignore opportunities to shift costs is to misunderstand their objectives as an institution. If managers become more sensitive to environmental damage from their behavior and cease certain cost-cutting strategies, what would be the *direct* and *personal* payoff to them? Their careers are judged by their ability to enhance profits, not environmental protection. Thus, it is unlikely that firms will voluntarily protect the environment. Generally, if we want to reduce environmental hazards, we must enforce some type of regulation.

2. One relationship between externalities and property rights is the extent to which the latter are disrupted by attempts to reduce the former. The businessman who sprayed the dangerous oil onto the roads was certainly creating negative effects on third parties, regardless of his lack of knowledge about those effects. Imagine, however, how he would react were his future business activities restricted by a statute that made him pay $10,000 to any community when his normal business behavior threatened their health in an unreasonable manner.

   This businessman began a business under one set of expectations, with one set of property rights, but the community has changed the rules on him. Now his expectations have been reduced. His "property" has lost some of its previous meaning. He is disappointed and angry.

3. When a particular firm grows, economic growth may or may not be affected. Suppose, for instance, that a firm grows by merging with another firm. This financial transaction does not improve the number or quality of existing resources. Capacity to produce has not been expanded.

   On the other hand, if a firm grows because of an innovation that results in greater output from a particular group of resources, the economy's capacity to produce has grown. Economic growth has occurred.

   This distinction is important for this chapter because a firm's antagonism to environmental protection efforts is often expressed in terms that ignore the distinction. The regulatory role of government is resisted on the grounds that hurting firm X necessarily harms the growth of the economy. As the distinction makes clear, the contention may or may not be true. To find out the worth of that claim we would have to examine the specific regulations and the business behavior actually restricted.

4. Forests can be replanted, top soil can be returned, and air quality can be restored. Yet the incentives to restore resources are not as strong as those responsible for the original consumption of those resources. The profit motive encourages producers to use resources; resources can be transformed into revenue through production activities. The restoration of resources, however, depends on a long-term perspective, one that weights highly the interests of future generations.

5. Both the Law of Hedonic Contrast and the short-run nature of allocation decisions make the trade-off between economic growth and

environmental protection unceasing or never-ending. Both accelerate environmental damage.

The Law of Hedonic Contrast provides that pleasure that is greatest when the discomfort it relieves is sharpest. Growth is sought because it enables us to have more goods and services. Possessing these goods and services is presumed to make us happier. The Law of Hedonic Contrast predicts that additional units of goods and services will give us less and less pleasure the richer we are. Hence our desire for more may heighten as we have more goods and services, because we are struggling to find greater happiness in a context where growth has a diminishing effect on our pleasure.

The short-run perspective of allocation decisions results in our downplaying the negative effects of growth on envionmental quality. Consequently, those hazards are made worse, and efforts to encourage growth are accelerated. In other words, the complete costs of growth are ignored when deciding current allocation issues.

6. The logic of this question is tempting. It ignores, however, the definition of scarcity. An important aspect of that definition is the concept of unlimited wants. For instance, there could never be enough status goods. The more of those that exist, the more are demanded. Consequently, whatever energies we are going to devote to environmental protection cannot wait for the urge to have more goods and services to relax. It won't.

7. This statement is true as far as it goes, but it exaggerates the negative impact of markets on the environment. Certainly the profit motive is responsible for much environmental damage. However, the profit motive can also be harnessed to solve environmental problems. With governmental adjustment of normal market behavior, profit incentives can be redirected toward environmentally sound policies.

8. No, a commitment to equity as the most important economic goal does not predetermine one's attitude toward the trade-off between economic growth and environmental protection. A strong argument can be made that growth is a prerequisite for providing basic necessities to the poor in both our country and the rest of the world. We are much more willing to share output that was made possible by economic growth. New output does not have to be extracted from the affluent. It is new; it belongs to no one yet. In a world with little growth, the only way we can aid the poor is for the relatively comfortable to give up some output to which they have grown accustomed.

   A powerful counterargument, however, can be offered by environmentalists. Growth permits, but has not historically led to, greater equity. Instead it elevates absolute conditions of the poor, while enlarging the relative gap between rich and poor. Growth, thus, accelerates inequality.

   Finally, growth often creates environmental damage in precisely those areas where the poor reside. The minerals from poor countries are extracted; the negative externalities from growth are deposited disproportionately on the poor. Hence, equity would be aided, from this perspective, by less attention to growth.

9. Environmental damage is a natural effect of accelerated production. Economies try to accelerate production of goods and services to meet the material desires of their population. The search for cheap production techniques often leads to the dumping of by-products into the community. Thus, the firm avoids the costs associated with cleaning up the by-products. Even in countries that limit the functioning of the profit motive, production uses resources. That use is selected in part on the basis of short-term cost considerations.

25
The Trade-off Between Equity and Efficiency

As Chapter 4 discussed, efficiency is an economic goal of all economies. There you learned the distinction between technical efficiency and economic efficiency. The objective of efficiency is to increase the gross national product. This goal is popular because it promises to get more output from the resources we have. Efficiency permits an increase in the size of the economic pie. Hence reaching that particular economic goal permits us to make someone better off without hurting anyone.

Remember the production-possibilities curve from Chapter 2? Figure 25–1 is a production-possibilities curve that provides a set of allocative options available to a society. All the points on the curve and below the curve can be attained. Points below the curve represent allocative choices that are inefficient relative to the options lying on the curve. Thus a movement from any point inside the curve to the curve enables the society to have more of one type of good or service without sacrificing any of the good or service on the other axis. Efficient decisions appear to provide something for nothing. However there are costs involved in achieving efficiency. One of these costs is a *possible* decline in equity.* To motivate resources to become more

*Notice that throughout this chapter equity is defined in terms of a movement toward equality. We share this habit with most who discuss equity. However, it would be perfectly consistent with some people's value assumptions to identify equity with more *in*equality. Pursuing that definition of equity would also have potential opportunity costs in terms of lost efficiency.

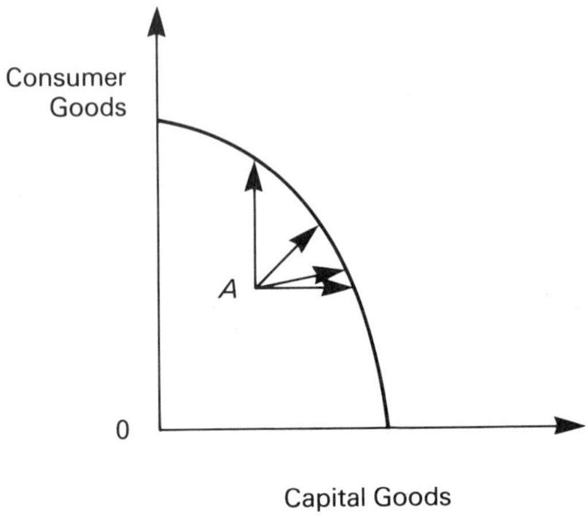

Figure 25–1 Production Possibilities Curve

This graph demonstrates the gains from more efficiency. The gains are indicated by the magnitudes of the lines from inefficient choice *A*.

efficient it may be necessary to create greater incentives and, thus, inequality.

Chapter 12 discussed equity. There you learned that an examination of equity requires knowledge about who will get the output that is produced. You know from that chapter that equity plays a role in the policy decisions of many economies. As is true for efficiency, the promotion of equity is not without cost. One thing we may have to give up to get more equity is efficiency. The total amount of income available in our economy is affected by how we distribute that income.

SELF-TEST

Each of these questions may require you to review earlier chapters on equity and efficiency.

1. How can inefficiency be measured?
2. Is efficiency just another name for full employment?
3. Evaluate the statement: Equity has so many meanings that we should not worry about it.

THE NATURE OF THE TRADE-OFF

Before we look at a detailed example of how the trade-off between equity and efficiency might occur, we will explain why the trade-off occurs. Efficiency can best be achieved when economic incentives are available to direct the use of resources. An equity problem arises when these incentives provide large incomes to certain individuals while other individuals receive small incomes.

To illustrate how the trade-off might occur, we will study two examples. The first example involves social security and the second examines the impact of taxes on work effort.

Social Security

Social security is a program designed and administered by the federal government. Employers and employees contribute a portion of their income to the social security fund. The government then takes the money that current employees and employers have paid into the fund and pays it out to currently retired workers. Initially the program aimed to provide support to the elderly who might not have had much income at retirement. Now the program also includes support for disabled workers and a medical care component so that some of the health care needs of the elderly can be met.

It is clear that a primary motivation for social security is equity. Social security reshuffles the amount of money individuals possess. The market provides one distribution of income. Government revises that distribution in an attempt to help some Americans finance their retirement. Through social security government *re*distributes income.

What possible efficiency issue could result from the social security program? To answer that question, we need to look at an alternative to social security. We could cancel the social security program and thus require each individual to satisfy his or her retirement through personal saving or by negotiating a retirement plan with a private firm. If this alternative response to the needs of the elderly were adopted, retirement incomes might rise on the average. The reason for the potentially larger retirement income is that if the money an individual contributes to the social security system were invested, the person would accumulate both the social security contributions and the resulting interest. The interest earnings would cause the retirement fund to exceed what is now available from the social security fund. Efficiency is thereby improved, in the sense that the same financial resources have produced larger retirement benefits. Is this move in the best interests of the society? It is surely in one sense more efficient.

Those who advocate an expanded private role for the provision of pensions for American workers are basing their arguments on enhanced efficiency. To see this efficiency argument more clearly, think of two possible retirement income systems and compare what happens to the retired under each system. Suppose we consider two individuals, one rich and one poor. Under existing social security provisions, the amount that either person gets back during retirement depends only partially on the amount the person contributes to the system. Thus, rich and poor retirees may well receive remarkably similar payments under social security. Over their lifetimes, poor persons, who contributed little to social security, will probably get back far more than they paid in.

Contrast this transfer system with a private pension system. The amount that each retiree gets back will depend only on his or her contribution. Thus poor persons who have little income during their lifetime will probably be at least as poor when they retire; the wealthy person could generate a very large pension to maintain his or her lifestyle. Under the private pension system, if you are poor while working, then you'll probably be even more poor between the time of retirement and death. But under social security some amount of redistribution of income occurs to help alleviate the poverty of the elderly.

If a more efficient private pension system is preferred, the primary cost of that efficiency may well be paid by the poor. Clearly there is an equity question here. This equity question is one that the society has perpetually faced. Note that we have not always "solved" the problem of poverty for the aged as we do currently. Social security did not come into existence until 1935, and the coverage has been extended on numerous occasions. Health care is now a prominent portion of the cost of social security, and social security recipients now receive cost-of-living adjustments that were not always available.

Other countries have generally been more willing than we to pay the cost of inefficiency in return for the greater equity provided by governmental pensions plans. To illustrate this willingness, expenditures on social security–type programs in several European countries over several years are reported in Table 25–1. The data are rough estimates because the programs are not strictly comparable from one country to another. Some effort has been made to adjust each country's numbers so that the extent of the redistribution can be seen. The health care component of social security is not included in this table.

Table 25–1 shows that the social security expenditures in the United States have been going up (as a percentage of GNP) over time. That experience is similar for the other countries surveyed. This increased expenditure is caused to a large extent by the fact that the proportion of the population that is retired is growing. In addition, from time to time the coverage of the programs is broadened.

Table 25–1 Expenditures on Benefits for Old Age, Survivors, and Disability Insurance (U.S. definition) as a Percentage of Gross National Product, Selected Countries 1957–77

Country	1957	1960	1963	1966	1971	1974	1977
Austria	4.0	5.0	5.3	6.0	7.0	7.0	8.0
Belgium[a]	3.0	3.1	4.0	4.0	4.2	5.1	6.0
France[a]	3.0	2.2	3.0	3.2	(n.a.)	5.1	6.2
Germany (FDR)	6.0	6.0	6.0	6.2	6.4	7.4	9.0
Netherlands	3.0	4.0	5.0	6.3	7.4	8.3	10.2
Sweden	3.4	3.3	4.0	5.0	6.0	7.1	9.2
Switzerland	2.0	2.2	2.3	3.0	4.0	5.3	7.1
United Kingdom[b]	4.0	3.2	4.0	4.0	4.0	5.0	6.0
United States[b]	1.5	2.2	2.6	3.4	3.4	4.0	4.3

From *Social Security in Europe: the Impact of an Aging Population*, prepared for use by the Special Committee on Aging, United States Senate, December 1981 (Washington D.C.: GPO, 1981), Table 1, p. 7.

Note: These statistics are based on data kindly provided by the International Labor Office, adjusted to include cash OASDI benefits. Gross National Product figures of the International Monetary Fund were used.

[a]Disability insurance is administered together with sickness insurance and is not included.

[b]Adjusted to fiscal year.

Table 25–2 shows the dates that various countries extended basic social security provisions to other areas besides retirement. Again the remarkable thing about the table is how recently the United States has added programs, especially compared with Western European countries. Some questions you should ask as you study the table are, What do we gain by having smaller payments for the elderly? What do the Europeans give up by having larger payments for the retired? One lesson you should learn from this table is that these European countries have implemented social security–type programs much

Table 25–2 Dates of First Statutory Programs

	Program			
Country	Occupational Hazard	Old Age and Survivors	Sickness or Maternity	Unemployment
Denmark	1898	1891	1892	1907
France	1898	1905	1928	1905
Germany	1884	1889	1883	1927
Italy	1898	1923	1910	1919
Netherlands	1901	1913	1913	1916
Sweden	1901	1913	1910	1934
United Kingdom	1897	1908	1911	1911
United States	1908	1935	1965	1935

From *Comparative Public Policy*, First Edition, by Arnold J. Heidenheimer, Hugh Heclo, and Carolyn Teich Adams, p. 189. Copyright © 1975 by St. Martin's Press, Inc., and used with publisher's permission.

sooner than the United States. A second lesson that is equally clear is that these countries paid some opportunity cost for the extended coverage. A major question we must resolve involves the consequences that result from these differences.

Income Taxes and Work Effort

The second example of the efficiency-equity trade-off focuses on the impact of income taxes on work effort. This example highlights the idea that the imposition of taxes has both efficiency and equity effects. In the social security example, the question revolved around two issues: who would receive retirement benefits and what would be the options for financing retirement benefits. The income tax example will stress the efficiency impact of a tax compared with the equity that could be generated from the proceeds of the tax.

When income taxes are raised, the increase may create incentives for people to work less than they did before the taxes were raised. The reason for this reduction in work effort might have a negative impact on efficiency. The same amount of labor is available, but less output is produced because taxpayers may not work as hard.

What impact do taxes have on equity? One way to categorize the equity impact of a tax is by who pays the tax. Of course, it is not enough to know who pays the tax, but we must also know the rate of taxation paid by each taxpayer. Then we can see the direct distributional effect of the tax.

There are three ways to describe the equity effects of a tax. As you learned in Chapter 12, a tax may be progressive, proportional, or regressive. Progressive taxes mean that the rich will pay a greater share of their income in taxes than will be paid by a person with less income. Regressive taxes occur when the poor pay a larger part of their income in taxes than do those who are less poor. Under a regressive tax program, a rich person could still pay more actual tax than a poor person. But a rich person would be paying a smaller proportion of income as taxes than the typical poor person would pay.

In the United States, the federal income tax is designed to be progressive. That means that individuals with higher income are scheduled to pay a larger portion of their income in taxes. The tax schedules tell the amount of tax you owe at various levels of taxable income.

Another independent variable that affects our distribution of income is the type and distribution of expenditures made by governments. You will remember from Chapter 12 that these expenditures are just as important as taxes in revising the market distribution of income. Thus, to identify the total equity effect of government we must look at both government taxes and expenditures.

One way to summarize the equity effects from governmental activities is to look at a Lorenz Curve (see Chapter 12), which plots percentage of total income generated on the horizontal axis and percentage of family income *after* income taxes and transfers on the vertical axis. Of course, one problem is that income taxes are only one form of taxes that we pay. We also pay sales and property taxes, and the question of who pays those taxes is more complicated. For instance, it is not easy to determine how much of sales taxes are paid by a particular income class.

Let's return to the social security example to see whether the tax supporting social security is regressive, progressive, or proportional. By examining the social security tax, we can get a better idea of what is meant by a regressive tax. The social security tax is based on earnings. This tax is a flat 6.65 percent of the first $39,600 earned. The tax falls to zero on any income over $39,600. The person with an income of less than $39,600 would pay 6.65 percent of his or her income in social security taxes. On the other hand, a person with $100,000 in income would pay 6.65 percent on the $39,600 and zero percent on the remaining $60,400, resulting in an actual tax rate significantly below 6.65 percent. The effective rate of social security tax for someone earning $100,000 is 2.6 percent. Consequently, this tax is a regressive tax.

Should the rich always pay more of their income in taxes? There are two divergent views on this issue. Some feel that those who have the income to afford taxes should pay them. People having this point of view believe that taxes should be imposed on those with the ability to pay the tax. A second point of view is one that says the taxes should be paid by those who will benefit from what the taxes buy. For example, if the taxes are used to build roads, those taxes should be paid by those who use the road.

For those who prefer the benefits-received approach, there is no question of whether you can reasonably afford the tax or not. We can see that those who favor taxing on the basis of benefits are more efficiency oriented. They are essentially arguing that you should not receive something without paying for it. Those who favor an ability-to-pay tax system are more concerned with equity. They are arguing that a lack of income should not be a barrier to the consumption of certain goods. Furthermore, they want the government to change what they see as unfair market incomes.

Let's evaluate social security from the two alternative views on the proper basis for paying taxes. The ability-to-pay principle directs higher-income earners to pay a higher percentage of the social security tax so that lower income earners would reap relatively larger benefits. The benefits-received approach not only directs us to look at who pays the costs of a project, as the ability-to-pay principle suggests, it also asks who benefits from the project. Clearly the social security tax is regressive. Those who have the ability to pay a larger share based upon the ability to pay principle actually pay a smaller percentage. Those who favor the benefits-received principle might be more content with the existing social security tax structure. Under the current system of social security, the poor pay a larger part of their income in taxes *and* are the relative beneficiary of the plan.

The social security system then impacts on equity in two ways. First, some receive relatively more income from the program than others. Second, some pay more than others to support the program. What is the net impact of these two conflicting equity impacts?

The Lorenz Curve may help us answer that question. Suppose that we look first at the Lorenz Curve in the absence of social security and compare it with the Lorenz curve that would occur if there were social security. If the Lorenz Curve with social security is closer to the curve of absolute equality, we would know that social security moves us toward greater equality. What would cause the Lorenz Curve to be different in these two cases? The payment of a regressive tax associated with social security would cause the Lorenz Curve, *ceteris paribus*, to move farther from the line of absolute equality. The receipt of social security payments would shift the Lorenz Curve back toward absolute equality. Thus, the overall equity impact of the social security system requires a comparison of the effect of the social security taxes with the impact of the social security payments.

SELF-TEST

4. Before passage of the Social Security Act in 1935, retirement frequently meant that the retired worker and spouse were forced to live with their children and grandchildren. What are the equity and efficiency aspects of this arrangement compared with those made possible by social security?
5. Describe the probable effect on the efficiency-equity trade-off were social security to be financed by progressive income tax revenues rather than by employer and employee contributions.
6. Could rising real per capita social security payments be motivated by some economic goal besides equity?

CAUSES FOR THE TRADE-OFF

In the previous section you learned that there is a trade-off between equity and efficiency. In this section you will learn more about *why* this trade-off occurs and how to recognize its existence. You can use certain clues to discover when to look for the trade-off between equity and efficiency in someone's proposal. A related question is what causes this trade-off? We will begin by explaining how to know when the trade-off is occurring, because the answer to the first question will lead us to an answer for the second question.

What clues can you use to know when to look for this trade-off? The answer comes largely from observing what role the government is asked to take in a policy proposal. One of the primary roles the government can play is in redistributing resources on the grounds of equity. Any anticipated redistribution by the government is likely to have an efficiency component. So, if you hear someone advocating that the government step in and act, think about the probable impact on efficiency. Or, if you see someone arguing that the market would more efficiently do certain tasks, look for the equity argument that should be considered as well.

Now let's turn to the causes underlying the trade-off. To generate efficiency, to get the most from our resources, we can use incentives or rewards. One of the incentives in any market is the income you could earn in alternative occupations. Notice though that everyone doesn't choose the high-paying professions. Not everyone is able to choose to be a doctor. Why not? First, not everyone has the intellectual interest or ability. But just as important, many who do have the interest and ability do not have enough money to pay for the training. The point is that because of the initial distribution of income, not everyone has an opportunity to improve his or her economic status. Thus, if we compare the income distribution of market incomes of one generation with those of another, we would be surprised to see dramatic changes in the income distribution. The level of your parents' income will be a significant influence on your level of income. Children of rich families tend to become rich; children of poor families tend to stay poor.

Although a market may generate efficiency, its behavior and results reflect the distribution of income that existed prior to any market decisions that encouraged efficiency. We have considered equity in terms of income; we could have measured it in terms of wealth, including property. Had we defined equity in terms of wealth, the basic observation would be the same. Those who have income or wealth have opportunities that others less well endowed do not have.

The wealthy will have opportunities to respond to incentives that the less wealthy will not have. Thus the initial distribution of wealth or income will shape in a major way who will get the wealth or income from the production activities of the economy. In summary, the incentives necessary to promote efficiency will largely attract those who already have wealth. Thus the existence of incentives that generate efficiency may detract from the equity dimension of the economy.

Now shift directions and suppose that equity were the only goal. One definition of equity would require that all workers be paid the same regardless of their jobs. Wouldn't such a payment scheme reduce incentives to work? What difference would it make if you were a doctor or a mechanic? You would earn the same pay either way. Surely in this case resources would not be used efficiently, yet equity in one sense would prevail.

Let's think again about the trade-off resulting from the provision of social security. If there is mandatory social security, the incentives to provide for one's own retirement are reduced because each worker is required to participate in social security. Individuals have lost the right to take the money they pay for social security and use it as they see fit. Yet, some people who could not have been cared for otherwise will receive benefits under mandatory social security.

If a purely private system of retirement is used, individuals have a strong incentive to provide for themselves. But the existing distribution of income may prevent some people from providing for their old age in an adequate manner. Hence a different degree of equity results when social security is provided than would exist if individuals were required to finance their own pensions. Yet the monetary incentives that encourage an efficient use of resources for retirement are thereby reduced.

SELF-TEST

7. Explain how prices acting as incentives promote efficiency.
8. What incentives are associated with a policy that would reduce the size of the federally sponsored school lunch program?
9. In the calculation of taxable income, the government allows individuals to deduct some contributions to charity. What efficiency impacts can you see in this incentive?

HOW DOES GOVERNMENT POLICY AFFECT THE TRADE-OFF?

For measuring equity, the usual method is to examine the impact on the income distribution of some activity, such as altering taxes. The income distribution can also change by methods other than governmental intervention. Market actions frequently alter the income distribution. The market starts with an initial distribution of income, demands and supplies are calculated, and new prices are determined. These new prices also establish a new distribution of income. The new distribution of income will no doubt be different from the initial distribution of income. Thus the action of the market itself alters the income distribution.

In a market economy the distribution of income that occurs after the market transactions depends to a large degree on the distribution of income before transactions. The market does not alter the equity of the initial distribution of dollar votes. Hence government often becomes the focus of struggles to create greater equity. The government is the logical agency for altering the income distribution. A change in distribution may be done in several ways. The government can impose taxes and give the proceeds to those with less income. Social security is an example of this kind of activity. The government may also require that the hiring of minorities be given special emphasis. When this happens, certain workers may get jobs that they would not have otherwise acquired. This result means someone else will not have that same job. Hence the distribution of income is changed.

In Chapter 12 you learned how equity can be enhanced. Chapters 6 and 7 suggested how to improve efficiency. One question you may want to ask is, What happens to efficiency when the government acts to change equity (or, What happens to equity when the government tries to change efficiency)? In this section we will discuss how efforts to alter either equity or efficiency may trade off with efficiency or equity. Most of the efforts to alter the mix of equity and efficiency are initiated by the government.

There are two obvious ways the government can interfere directly in economic activity. One is for the government to set prices, the other is for quantities of firms or output to be established by law. What are the impacts of these activities on efficiency and equity?

Suppose you were required to have a license to undertake some activity, say operate a cab. If the number of licenses is limited, or if they are sold only at a high price, there would be a restriction on the number who could enter that occupation and reap the rewards. Further, the society could have more cab service for the same expenditure on cabs if the license fee were reduced. Thus the license perpetuates inefficiency. This kind of restriction would increase the rewards to the existing cab driver above what they would have been without the restriction. Hence the income of individuals with licenses is protected by this device. Government is acting here to protect the income of a group of workers who would have had less income under market conditions.

Government may redistribute incomes toward greater equality or toward greater inequality. You should not get the impression that government always benefits those who are weak in our economy. It often aids those who are earning substantial market incomes, for example, corporate farmers.

The government may act directly to improve efficiency. When government acts to improve efficiency, what are the equity impacts of these efforts to improve efficiency? The emphasis of the Carter and Reagan administrations on deregulation of transport sectors in our economy ultimately favors efficiency over equity. Allowing airlines to price fares more competitively and allowing them to drop unprofitable routes was a move toward greater efficiency. Yet not everyone is receiving the transportation service that they once enjoyed. Thus, access to air travel has become less equitable.

Not every governmental action can be easily categorized as "good for equity, bad for efficiency" or "good for efficiency, bad for equity." For example, when the government decided to break up AT&T, there may have been both efficiency and equity grounds for doing so. The breakup was alleged to be efficient in that the improved competition allowed people to get more service for the same cost, and although AT&T lost, many firms and consumers gained. The equity aspects of government action depend on who gains and who loses.

Clearly the importance of equity relative to efficiency is reflected in the economic system. Economic systems that stress reduced roles for government are ordinarily more efficiency oriented than economic systems where the government plays a more active role.

SELF-TEST

10. Suppose government decides to permit the price of natural gas to be determined by market forces. What are the equity and efficiency impacts?
11. How does a competitive market redistribute income?

12. What are the equity and efficiency impacts of laws that require employers to pay minimum wages?

This chapter has discussed a possible trade-off between equity and efficiency. The main points are that the trade-off cannot be avoided and that when someone suggests an economic policy change, there is often both an equity and an efficiency issue. Note that if the government acts, there are bound to be gains and losses so that the outcome of the equity issue depends on who gains and who loses. Too, if the government ends up producing a good or regulating a market, there is a presumption that a negative impact on efficiency has occurred. This will be true only if the provision of the good by the government leads to less competitive conditions.

ACTIVE REVIEW

1. In recent years the smoke from the smokestacks of the industrial heartland of the Unites States has been falling on New England and Canada. The impact of this pollution has been to make the lakes and rivers in these remote areas more acid than they were. The increased acid has killed off fish populations and destroyed forests. This problem is surely serious and not one that can be ignored. The problem occurs not only in the United States and Canada; it has been claimed that pollution from British fumes has caused similar problems in Norway and Sweden. What should be done? What can be done?

    There are several aspects of interest in the problem. First is that while there are surely damages, much of the damage occurs in relatively uninhabited places. There is no clear reason to believe that enormous costs fall directly to humans. Second, there is no legal remedy. The residents of New Hampshire may not take the state of Ohio to court. Certainly there is no United States court that would hear the Canadian claim. Thus, if anything is to be done, the Canadian government must somehow prevail on the United States government. Of course, there are some tools in the hands of the Canadians; for example, they could erect certain trade barriers until pollution abatement occurs.

    If pressure to reduce pollution is put on the United States firms, the main impact will be to raise production costs. The producer has the choice of changing fuels or cleaning up the pollution before it leaves the plant. The first may require burning a higher-priced fuel with smaller amounts of the pollutant. A second alternative would be to put in cleaning devices to remove the pollution as the firm produces it. In either case, the firm would have higher costs, and the consumers would have to pay the bill.

The choices are not easy. Either we put up with the pollution and have lower prices or we cut back the pollution and charge higher prices for some basic goods.

a. In what way does equity enter this argument?

b. How does efficiency conflict with equity?

c. We could view the air pollution issue as largely one of who pays for the pollution. Is there an efficiency aspect to this argument?

2. One of the impressive aspects of foreign travel is the transportation system. In most foreign countries, cars are not as heavily relied upon as trains. In general, the trains are cheap, fast, and go almost everywhere. Moreover, they go as scheduled. This experience is clearly different from the usual United States train trip. The American passenger train is expensive, generally dirty, goes infrequently, and is rarely on schedule. Why is there so much difference between these experiences? One main difference is that in foreign countries, the train system is owned and operated by the government.

There is little doubt that rail systems are more efficient than autos. We could save quite a bit of oil if train travel were promoted. Perhaps if the government took over and upgraded passenger service, trains would make a comeback. One of the reasons that the passenger rail system fell into disuse was that streets and roads were dramatically improved. We can easily get on a four-lane highway and go nearly anywhere we wish at nearly any time. The fact that we do not have to pay directly to use the highway means that we underestimate the cost of travel by car. Yet, when we buy a rail ticket from a private corporation, the corporation must charge us for the maintenance and upkeep of the rails, roadbed, and rail cars.

One way to allow both modes of transport to compete equally would be for the government to subsidize the railroads for upkeep of the track and roadbed just as the government now subsidizes the car driver. But if we really want to induce cost savings, the proper strategy is for the government to take over passenger rail service completely and operate the trains just as they are operated in foreign countries.

a. What is the equity-efficiency trade-off in this analysis?

b. What goals besides equity or efficiency could a society have that might be incompatible with government ownership?

c. How does the fact that the government subsidizes air travel affect the argument?

d. Suppose that railroads are entirely under governmental control. What are the equity issues associated with a tax on gasoline to be collected for the purposes of highway repair and maintenance?

e. How do the equity aspects of this issue depend on whether the tax revenues for the subsidy are generated by income taxes or special-purpose transport taxes that fall to the train users?

ANSWERS TO ACTIVE REVIEW

1a. The equity aspect of the problem is that the Canadians are required to clean up the mess made by the United States firms. Thus, the Canadian environment is hurt by the actions of the United States firms, and there is no compensation in terms of goods or money. The Americans gain in that they do not have to pay for the cleanup of the pollution.

1b. It is hard to identify the inefficiency in the argument. The main problem is that because firms may use the air as a dump without cost, the air is polluted. In that sense we can argue that air is not being used efficiently, because we have more pollution per volume of air than is desirable. Of course, the problem is that air cannot be bought and sold in a market. So the solution to the inefficiency is not to require greater competition in the market but to make sure that the pollution does not occur. This result can be accomplished by rules set by government (rules establish either allowable levels of pollution production by the firm or allowable levels of pollution in the air or both) or by having firms pay for the right to use the air.

1c. The remaining issue is who pays for the pollution. Will the costs fall mainly to those who receive the pollution or to those who generate the pollution? But there is an efficiency issue as well. One way to look at the efficiency issue is in terms of how much pollution each firm should be allowed to produce. Should we allow any firm to increase the pollution per volume of air? How much pollution can the air efficiently handle? A second aspect of efficiency asks how the firms can be brought into compliance with pollution rules for the least cost. This second issue assumes that pollution targets are established and that the only problem is to bring the firms into compliance. The point is that the problem of air pollution involves more than just equity.

ANSWERS TO SELF-TEST

1. Finding a measure for inefficiency is not easy. What we need is a comparison between how resources are actually used and how they could be used. Sometimes when discussing national income, we compare potential GNP with actual GNP to get a measure of the misallocation of resources. But the calculation of potential GNP requires an arbitrary definition of full employment.

Good measures of efficiency are hard to find. One alternative is the difference between the price of good or service and the marginal cost of producing that output as a measure of inefficiency. This measure is derived from the material on noncompetitive markets in Chapter 8. It measures inefficiency when the amount that people pay for the good is greater than the value of the resources that went into the production of the good. The extra payment above the resource cost is a form of waste.

Another measure is based on a production-possibilities curve. As was explained in the discussion of Figure 25–1, the vertical or horizontal distances between the current allocative choice and the production possibilities curve is a measure of inefficiency.

2. Unemployment is just one type of inefficiency. Another form occurs when human resources are not used in their best way. If we make a lawyer and a doctor exchange jobs, the employment level will not fall, but total output will fall. Such an exchange would be inefficient. So efficiency requires more than full employment.

3. Though it is true that there is no definition of equity with which we would all agree, a certain distribution of output and income now exists. The existing distribution is both affected by and affects the productivity of the economy. There are many alternative distributions of that same output and income. The essential point is that we have a choice about the correct distribution of income. To ignore the choice is actually to make the choice by leaving things as they are. *Especially* because we cannot all agree, we should think carefully about the design and impacts of both the current and future distributions.

4. Prior to the Social Security Act the cost of retirement fell largely on the retired worker and his or her family. If the retiree had managed to save only a little, the cost of the retirement fell more on the family than on the retiree. This solution to the financial problem of retirement is not a lot different in its impact from that created by relying on privately arranged pension plans. If you are poor while working, your children are likely to be poor too, hence your retirement may not be very comfortable.

   This plan is efficient in that the incentives of the market induce individuals to provide for themselves. Given the total amount people provide for themselves, a larger portion of the contribution will be available to them for retirement than if the same amount had been contributed to social security. Personal incentives would suggest that the total benefits available from private pension plans will be greater than the total available from social security because the private funds should accrue more interest payments. Following this approach, those who benefit from such a system will do so as a result of their relative success in the labor market. If you view the existing distribution as inequitable, this plan will be very unfair in your eyes.

5. The essential impact of this suggestion is to change the financing mechanism from a regressive payroll tax to a progressive income tax. The efficiency aspect is mixed. By replacing a regressive tax with a progressive tax, the poor will pay a smaller part of their income in taxes, and the rich will pay a larger part of their income. The poor will get to keep a larger part of their income and will have an incentive to work more. The rich have an incentive to work less. We cannot tell whether there will be more or less total work provided. On the equity side, since the rich would pay more of the social security bill under the income tax than would the poor, the equity of the system would be altered in favor of the poor.
6. To the extent that a concern about the freedom provided by income security is a goal, the pursuit of freedom would be compatible with rising real per capita social security payments. Under current conditions the typical retired worker is none too secure; larger real payments would be desirable for additional security. Without sufficient income, an individual is not free to live a decent life. Hence, increasing real per capita social security could be an attempt to provide economic freedom to those who are retired. This goal would be achieved by reducing the economic freedom of those who are not retired.
7. Perhaps the easiest way to answer the question is to look at the labor market and the price of labor, the wage. In competitive markets, individuals respond to monetary incentives. For example, one of the factors that determines an individual's job selection is the wage paid for doing various jobs. Jobs with higher wages generally attract more people. If some wages go up relative to others, the effect is to induce people to switch jobs. Thus, even though the total number employed may not change, the value of the output produced goes up, and a more efficient use of resources results.

   Another efficiency effect from higher wages is productivity. If productivity rises, the worker may produce more output. One way to induce higher productivity is to pay for it. Thus, wage increases can be used to induce higher productivity which promotes efficiency.
8. There are at least two incentives that would be important. First is a more efficient use of resources. The argument is that more output could be obtained if federal resources were spent elsewhere. For instance, some would claim that if investment in the textile industry were substituted for food stamps, efficiency would be enhanced. A second incentive would be for people who might otherwise benefit from the "free lunch" to support themselves. This is naturally an equity issue as well.
9. Before answering the efficiency question, note that in this case incentives are being used to promote equity. The idea of charitable deductions is that the rich will help the poor, so that income is voluntarily redistributed.

On the efficiency side, the argument is that money channeled through private agencies yields a greater volume of support than if the same number of tax dollars were given to the poor. Out of every tax dollar collected, there are the expenses of the tax collection as well as the cost of administrating the welfare program. Advocates of the deduction for charitable contributions claim that the more efficient private sector has smaller collection and administration costs, so a larger part of each dollar collected actually goes to the poor.

10. The problem here is on the efficiency side. The argument to allow these markets to be free of regulation is based on the belief that these markets would exhibit the same response to deregulation as would a competitive firm. Specifically, the claim is that an increase in the quantity of gas available would occur. This result is efficient because the firm would produce more natural gas from the same investment. There is an equity problem in that the poor may not be able to afford to heat their homes in the winter if the price of natural gas is allowed to rise.

    An interesting aspect of this question is whether these firms will respond as a competitive firm would respond. If the effect of the regulation has been to hold the price below equilibrium for a monopoly market, deregulation that allows the price to rise will cause a decrease in the quantity of natural gas. Thus not only is there an equity problem, but the efficiency claim could be suspect in this case.

11. Why does the question ask about redistribution, not distribution? The reason is that for a market to operate, there must be an initial distribution of property and resources. The market redistributes from that initial position.

    If markets reward on the basis of productivity, those who are productive will get large rewards. The difficulty occurs with the definition of productivity. Suppose a concert pianist was as skilled as a baseball player, each in their respective occupations. Do you think they would reap equal rewards? Probably not. The baseball player would earn considerably more, because our economy prefers baseball to piano concerts. Thus, productive means productive in satisfying the demand of the public

    Upon what does this productivity depend? To some extent, how productive you are depends on what you start with. Those who start with more are more likely to be successful than those who start with less. Of course, luck will be important too. Two equally talented people may compete for a job and only one will get it. The loser may have to be content with a less productive position. There is no doubt that hard work will improve your prospects.

    But you should be aware that other factors or causes enter the calculation as well.

12. The question revolves around the extent to which the minimum wage law has any impact on labor markets. If every wage were above the minimum, there would be little reason to ask this question. If there

are markets where the wage would be lower than the minimum wage if there were no minimum wage, we need to identify them. The most obvious markets are the markets for nonwhite, teenage, unskilled labor. The minimum wage law has the following impacts in those markets. Those who are employed in those markets gain because they get a higher wage. But because of the higher wage, employers may hire fewer workers. Some workers may lose their jobs and not find any other work. These workers lose. Thus the equity side is a mixed picture. Some gain and some lose. The law probably does not promote efficiency, since we get less work from the same population under the law than without the law.

26
Freedom Versus Equity

Economic freedom is an essential goal for any economy that emphasizes the concept of free enterprise. Businesses must have the freedom to pursue economic profits, because profits provide the stimulus that makes the system work. Economic freedom gives producers the opportunities to take risks in expectation of earning economic profits. If businesses are unduly restrained in their pursuit of profits, they may decide to minimize their risks and reduce their efforts to produce new products.

Equity is also a very important economic goal in that we want an economic system in which everyone has a fair opportunity to earn a decent income and to afford an acceptable standard of living. During the administration of President Johnson we committed ourselves to reducing the incidence of poverty from one out of every six persons to some more respectable ratio by implementing such antipoverty programs as food stamps and subsidized housing. We also want women and minorities to have more equitable access to jobs and income. In essence, we achieve the goal of equity when we eliminate poverty and discrimination.

Yet in Chapters 10 through 12 we studied some of the difficulties in achieving economic freedom and equity. In some cases it was hinted that if we attempted to improve economic freedom, we would have to sacrifice some equity and vice versa. Why might this trade-off occur? How might different policies affect the trade-off? Are there actions that we can take to moderate the trade-off? These questions are the focus of this chapter. By the time we finish the chapter, you should have a better idea of the consequences of emphasizing one goal over the other.

WHAT IS THE TRADE-OFF?

Economic freedom and equity are abstract terms that require more concrete definitions. In the abstract everyone is in favor of freedom. What does that support for freedom mean? Does it mean that consumers should have the final say on quantity and quality of goods and services that get produced? Or does it mean that producers should have the primary influence over what gets produced? Is there any difference in the answers to these two questions?

According to Chapter 10, there is a significant difference between producer freedom and consumer freedom. Freedom for sellers provides producers the opportunities to seek profits without intervention by governmental agencies. This freedom permits sellers to produce goods and services that will maximize their economic profits. Freedom for buyers provides all consumers the opportunity to influence the quantity and quality of goods and services that get produced. The end result of economic freedom for buyers is that consumers have an acceptable choice of products given their level of income.

These two forms of economic freedom are likely to clash with one another. Producer sovereignty emphasizes freedom from coercion in the producing and selling of products. Consumer sovereignty emphasizes freedom to choose the products consumers wish to purchase. If producer sovereignty increases relative to that of consumers, the freedom for buyers will decline. For example, existing companies prefer to be price-makers than to be price-takers. If companies succeed in gaining market power, they enjoy the ability to alter the price and quantity of their products. If these companies use this ability to gain more market power, buyers must lose some ability to influence the quantity and quality of goods and services.

Advocates of a free enterprise economy reconcile this problem by claiming that market power cannot become a problem. The forces of competition will prevent companies from gaining market power. If one company manages to earn economic profit as a result of providing consumers with the products they want, other companies will react to those profits and expand into profitable areas of production. As the supply of that product increases, consumers gain greater freedom because they have more sellers from which to choose.

As entry occurs, the original company will no longer control supply, output will increase, and prices will fall. Economic profits will decline toward zero, and consumers will enjoy the satisfaction of knowing that the price of the product is just high enough to ensure that an adequate quantity of the product is offered for sale. With additional companies producing the product, consumer freedom increases because consumers have greater choice of products to purchase.

Conceptually, this free enterprise model is very logical, but there are some problems with its implementation. As we indicated in Chapter 10, economic profits often lead to an accumulation of property. An accumulation of property increases the likelihood that the property owners have greater access to economic resources and higher incomes than those who have little or no property. As wealth and income of property owners increase, their economic freedom will grow relative to those who have less property. Thus, unless there is a progressive tax on wealth, those who own property will tend to accumulate more property and more freedom. Those who have little or no property will experience less freedom relative to the property owners.

This type of reasoning about economic freedom also applies to the goal of equity. In many respects the goal of equity suffers from a similar vagueness in its definition. No one is willing to argue that an unfair distribution of income is desirable, but we do have difficulty in deciding how equal the distribution of income should be to achieve equity.

The extreme positions are clear and undesirable. We do not want an economy in which one person or a very small group of people controls the sources of income. On the other hand, we do not want an economy in which everyone earns exactly the same income. We know that some diversity in the level of income must exist to provide incentives to individuals to strive to achieve higher standards of living by increasing our national output. But how much diversity do we need to provide these incentives? Does it make any difference which groups tend to earn high incomes and which groups tend to earn lower incomes?

In Chapter 11 we explained that a specific definition of equity requires a normative judgment. We exercised this judgment and stated that the goal of equity is achieved when no one in the economy is poor. Although others may define this goal differently, we contend that eradicating poverty is a legitimate but difficult goal to attain.

In pursuit of this goal we discovered that income inequity and poverty exist when some people have more economic resources than others and when some people have resources that are not in current demand. In the first case, it is highly probably that someone whose family encourages its children to get a good education, instills the values of hard work and responsibility, and provides its children with a taste for success is more likely to earn higher levels of income than someone who does not have access to these values and influences. Individuals who grow up under the latter influences are unlikely to develop any specific job skills and are unlikely to gain a decent-paying job.

In other cases, individuals may have job skills, but society may not have any current use for those skills. We studied this problem when we examined structural unemployment. For instance, there have been generations of families who have worked in coal mines, auto factories, and steel mills earning respectable wages. Today, we demand less coal and domestic steel and use more robots to produce autos. As a consequence, many workers find they do not have jobs, although they have previously proven themselves as very capable workers.

Given the goal of equity we need to investigate ways to allow individuals to gain access to a fair income. We also need to ask why this task seems so difficult. Even though President Johnson declared a "war on poverty" in the 1960s, approximately 15 percent of today's population still experience poverty.

Does More Freedom Imply More Equity?

When we first ask this question, there is a tendency to answer yes. If everyone has greater freedom to pursue economic rewards, does it not follow that everyone has the opportunity to earn whatever income is commensurate with his or her skills? It seems as if economic freedom is an essential component for achieving other goals, such as equity, efficiency, growth, and price stability.

Yet we know that we need to be very cautious about drawing such a conclusion. We saw in both Chapter 10 and the earlier section of this chapter that economic freedom is an abstraction that has very little meaning until we provide a more precise definition. For example, if we emphasize economic freedom for buyers, we tend to reduce the opportunities for sellers to earn economic profits. When profit opportunities decline, sellers have difficulty in acquiring additional property.

We examined this process when we studied the competitive market model in Chapter 7. We discussed the tendency for economic profits to fall toward zero as new companies entered the market and competed away the profits of the previously successful companies. As a result of this competitive pressure, companies know that they must become more efficient and develop new products if they want to earn economic profits in the future. Under this theoretical model, sellers have the freedom to respond to consumer demands, but they do not have the freedom to dominate any markets.

Unfortunately, this textbook model of competition is not very realistic. Some companies do dominate markets. Governmental agencies often help companies achieve dominance by granting patents and protecting companies from some forms of competition (for example, foreign trade). When this dominance occurs, the companies are more likely to earn economic profits, and consumers are left paying higher prices for limited quantities. Under these conditions, the economic freedom of the seller is increased, but the freedom of the buyer is reduced.

As the freedom of sellers increases, businesses are likely to earn more economic profit, accumulate more property, and increase the probability of earning more profits. This process would be great if everyone had an equitable chance to accumulate profits and income, but those opportunities are not equal. It is true that someone who is raised in a very poor environment can become very rich. A market economy allows this possibility. Realistically speaking, however, those people who come from a very poor environment are much more likely to remain in that environment, and those who grow up in middle- and upper-income environments are more likely to achieve success. Thus, economic freedom tends to help people in some segments of society and actually to hurt people in other segments. Pursuit of the goal of equity requires some activity that provides people living in poverty with an opportunity to accumulate property. Typically these opportunities are provided by a progressive tax that is designed to tax families with above average incomes at a higher rate of taxation than those with lower incomes. Government then uses this tax revenue to help the poor achieve an improved standard of living.

SELF-TEST

1. Why is it desirable to distinguish between economic freedom for sellers and economic freedom for buyers?
2. Since it is unlikely that many would advocate that poverty is desirable, why have we been unsuccessful in eradicating it?
3. Evaluate the following statement: Economic freedom should be emphasized as a goal instead of other goals because the freedom of businesses to participate in the economy will keep any one company or small groups of companies from dominating.

CAUSES OF THE TRADE-OFF

Scarcity of economic resources is the general causes of trade-offs. As we have stated throughout the text, if abundance existed, the conflict between economic freedom and equity would disappear. But since scarcity does exist, we must struggle with problems associated with who owns property rights. If we emphasize economic freedom, some people (those who are successful at earning income and accumulating wealth) will gain access to property and increase their likelihood of earning larger amounts of income. These individuals will use their economic freedom to gain even higher degrees of freedom.

As the economic freedom of successful individuals or businesses increase, does it follow that economic freedom of less successful individuals or businesses will also increase? It does follow that a successful business will produce more products and create more jobs. These jobs will increase the income of workers to purchase additional products. Thus, it *appears* that the increased freedom of successful businesses will also increase the freedom of the rest of the members of the economy.

We need to consider this line of reasoning very carefully. There are some problems in matching the abstractions of greater freedom and higher incomes with actual groups of people. For instance, successful businesses may increase production by expanding their use of technology. When production is increased in this manner, either employment of specifically skilled workers is increased or employment of workers may actually decrease.

If the first possibility actually occurs, people living in poverty are not likely to benefit from the new jobs, because the jobs require skills that unemployed workers typically do not possess. We identified this problem earlier when we indicated that structural unemployment is likely to become an increasing problem as businesses expand their use of technology.

We may find that in addition to increasing problems caused by structural unemployment, expanded use of technology may also cause the displacement of workers. This displacement will be most notable among less skilled workers who perform repetitive tasks, because computerized machines can perform those tasks with greater efficiency. If this displacement occurs, equity is not likely to improve, because these displaced workers will have great difficulty in finding new jobs.

The trade-off is also evident when we attempt to improve equity. Let us assume that we decide to improve family incomes of those below the poverty line by establishing free, high-quality day care centers for the children of these families. With the children receiving good care, the parents have the opportunity to pursue education and jobs.

This approach has two positive effects on reducing poverty. First, it allows the unemployed the chance to earn enough income to rise above poverty. Second, and potentially more important, the day care center can provide the children with an environment that can nurture the values of education, hard work, and success.

So far the plan sounds pretty good. If it has this potential, why has it not been tried? The answer to this question is that this plan to reduce poverty, and most others, decreases economic freedom. Can you explain why? Where is society going to get the money to provide free, high-quality day care centers, especially centers that are designed do do much more than just provide babysitting services?

Generally, programs to assist the poor require the use of tax money. If our purpose is to improve the conditions of those in poverty, then we must impose a progressive tax that requires those with higher levels of income to pay higher rates of taxes. When progressive taxes are levied, some individuals must sacrifice income they have earned to assist those who have failed to earn income. In other words, progressive taxation reduces economic freedom.

MARKETS, GOVERNMENT, AND THE TRADE-OFF

In today's economy very little economic activity is performed without some mixing of market and governmental forces. We may talk about an individual's freedom to choose his or her career, but that choice will be influenced by the quality of the public education that he or she receives. Businesses are free to choose the products they wish to produce, but government influences the wage rate with the minimum wage, the working conditions with rules about health and safety, and the environment with antipollution standards.

In a more specific illustration we can demonstrate the trade-off between economic freedom and equity by examining whether plant closings should be a private decision of individual companies or whether government should intervene to protect the income security of individuals and communities. This issue is important because businesses have grown from relatively small, neighborhood operations to huge corporations that employ hundreds and sometimes thousands of workers in plants all over the country. When businesses are small, employing a relatively small number of workers, their failure or their relocation from one part of the country to another does not create any serious problems of equity. But when large companies fail or relocate, there may be significant disruption in the communities they leave.

When a small business leaves town, the few workers who lose their jobs usually find new jobs without great difficulty because their unemployment has not significantly increased the ranks of the unemployed. When a large corporation leaves town, the problem changes considerably. Not only do the unemployed workers have great difficulty in finding new jobs but the entire community suffers from the decline in income caused by the significant increase in unemployment.

An example of the above problem occurred in Youngstown, Ohio, between 1977 and 1979, when the shut-down of several major steel mills resulted in the unemployment of about 10,000 steelworkers. As a result of this significant loss of income within the community, many other businesses and essential services, such as education and police and fire protection, also experienced significant declines. The entire community suffered an economic recession.

In response to the economic trauma of Youngstown, the National Employment Priorities Act of 1979 was introduced but not passed by Congress. This legislation would have required prenotification to employees and communities who may be affected by the closing or moving of a business. The concept of prenotification was advocated because it provided the community a chance to make adjustments and prepare for the closing. The act would have also provided retraining to employees who lost their jobs, and economic assistance to business and communities that were threatened by dislocation. If this or some similar legislation were to become law, what would be the effects on equity and economic freedom?

Government and Equity

By 1982 the unemployment in the Youngstown area reached 19.9 percent. Young people began to leave the area because the entire community had become stagnant. Many of the young people believed that they had no future in Youngstown. Public services were in disarray. School systems barely managed to stay open by offering a minimum of classes and by drastically reducing extracurricular activities.

If businesses were required to notify their workers of a pending closing up to one year in advance, workers and community would gain some important security that would allow them to work with the business to keep the plant open or to search for alternative sources of income. This cooperation between government and business is considered important because a plant closing will affect the entire community and not just a few isolated individuals.

If government does not require businesses to offer economic assistance to the affected workers and communities, these large corporations are free to leave th area and weaken the economic amd social fabric of a community. For instance, five years after the plant closings began, Youngstown was still functioning in depression-like conditions. Thousands of workers and their families who did not work at the mills, but who depended upon the mill workers' incomes, were thrust into poverty conditions.

With the income level of an entire community depressed, new businesses have little incentive to begin operations in cities like Youngstown. In addition to their lack of purchasing power, these cities cannot offer new businesses incentives such as excellent schools, good park systems, and other community services. Without some form of government intervention, the incidence of poverty increases, and we tend to move away from the goal of equity instead of toward it.

Government and Economic Freedom

If government does pass a law that requires businesses to give workers advance notice of pending layoffs and to provide economic assistance to displaced workers and communities, these businesses will experience a decrease in economic freedom. In other words, businesses must absorb new costs associated with their decisions to close a plant. These costs may alter their decisions to move and, as a result, reduce their profitability.

In more specific terms, plant-closing legislation may retard economic development in all areas of the country. If a business is hindered from moving from one part of the country to another, it is forced to accept higher costs of production. These higher costs will reduce the overall level of production and increase the price of the final product. As a result of these higher prices, economic freedom is reduced because everyone tends to absorb the costs of relocation.

Economic freedom for sellers is also reduced by the plant-closing rules because these rules alter property rights. Individuals have purchased stock in companies with the expectation that these companies will produce their products as efficiently as possible. The stockholders expect to receive dividends from this efficient production. If government introduces plant-closing rules, then profitability will most likely fall and stock holders will experience a decline in the value of their property. In essence, plant closing rules cause a redistribution of income from the owners of businesses to the workers and the community in which they live. For example, if the National Employment Priorities Act were to become law, the income of the owners of business would fall relative to that of the workers and the community. Of course, if the act or something similar to it does not become law, then the income transfer moves in the opposite direction. The workers and the community will lose income relative to that of the owners.

In the case of Youngstown, Ohio, several major steel mills did close, and unemployment increased dramatically. The steel companies reduced their capacity to produce but maintained their freedom to compete as effectively as they could in the domestic and world markets. On the other hand, the 10,000 steelworkers who lost their jobs and the thousands of others who depended upon the income of the steel workers suffered a decrease in equity. The employment and profit opportunities in Youngstown fell precipitously. What, if anything, can we do about this trade-off?

SELF-TEST

4. When companies exercise their economic freedom and introduce computers to their production process, what will happen to the economic freedom of buyers?
5. Explain how the events in Youngstown, Ohio, led to legislation designed to improve equity within the economy.
6. Evaluate the following statement: Laws to restrict the freedom of companies to close their plants are necessary if we wish to maintain or improve the level of equity within the economy.

INTERNATIONAL RESPONSE TO THE TRADE-OFF

In many European communities, the security of workers is a more important objective than it is in the United States. In most other industrial nations government agencies are directly involved in decisions about plant closing and workers' relocation. Sweden's rules on plant relocation provide us with one specific example.

Most production in Sweden occurs through private enterprise, just as in the United States. The major difference in production between the two countries is that business and government coordinate activities in Sweden, and in the United States government acts as a monitor of business. In the United States businesses see government as an intervenor or meddler. In Sweden, government is seen as doing things no other institution can do—good and necessary things.

When the Swedish steel industry encountered the problem of overcapacity and low profitability, the Swedish government and the major steel companies decided to protect the existing communities and to develop a plan that would permit the companies to modernize and the workers to ease into new jobs.

In return for keeping most of their production facilities open, the steel companies received assistance from government to facilitate modernization. Since modernization and relatively low demand for steel resulted in the need for fewer steel workers, the Swedish government and steel companies designed imaginative programs to assist workers in finding employment outside the steel industry. All Swedish employers were required to list all job openings, which were posted daily on computerized printouts within each mill. Any workers who wished to apply for any of those jobs were given subsidies to visit the communities in which the jobs were located. Every steel worker was guaranteed two years' pay during the period of transition. The primary objective of the Swedish plan was that no one should be compelled to leave a job unwillingly.

The Swedish plan clearly emphasized equity over economic freedom. In doing so the plan also required that government collect enough taxes to support the subsidies to the steel companies and the steelworkers. But one of the consequences of this plan was that government did not have to collect taxes to pay unemployment compensation and welfare. Workers either remained on the job or learned new skills and became productive in new jobs.

The consequence of the Swedish plan appears to be that workers and consumers had a greater opportunity to participate in the economic system. Fewer people received support because they could not find a source of income. On the other hand, businesses lost the freedom to make independent decisions, but they gained assistance in their attempts to modernize. From this example, can you choose which goal, economic freedom or equity, should have the greater emphasis?

SELF-TEST

7. What difficulties would we experience in trying to follow the Swedish plan in the United States?

ACTIVE REVIEW

1a. Two students of economics were discussing the poverty that seems to persist in the inner cities of many of our major cities. The first student, Stuart Jacobs, argues that a major problem is that businesses have left the areas and that workers in the inner city no longer have a source of income. To correct this problem he states that government should require some businesses to begin producing in the area. Explain why he is making that argument.

1b. Gloria Stein countered by saying that forcing businesses to accept costs that are not helpful in maximizing profits will just make the situation worse. She argued that businesses should expand in those areas that offer the greatest opportunities for profits. As these businesses succeed, they will create more jobs. Explain Gloria's argument.

1c. Overhearing this discussion John White claimed that Stuart and Gloria were both wrong. John argued that equity can be achieved only after those in poverty are given the necessary skills to compete within the economy. Do you find any of these three positions more convincing?

2. The freedom to acquire private property is an important right in a free enterprise economy. In what ways does this right influence the goal of equity?

ANSWERS TO ACTIVE REVIEW

1a. People who live in inner cities often are very poor because workers cannot find jobs. Businesses have moved elsewhere, often to the suburbs. The poor have no effective way of getting to work. Businesses are unlikely to move into the area because the people do not have enough money to buy the products and because the local labor force is generally improperly trained.

If government encourages businesses to move into these areas by giving the companies some form of subsidies, the businesses will have incentives to train workers in the skills needed to increase the productivity of the workers. Once workers acquire the necessary skills the company should be able to compete without government subsidies. The economy would grow and more people would get jobs. Eventually the ghettos would disappear.

1b. Gloria interjected that whenever you force a business to behave in a certain way, you encounter increased costs that will cause a decrease in the general level of production. With less production there will be less income taxes, and if we have less revenue from income taxes, governments cannot afford to establish the type of program described by Stuart.

According to Gloria, the only way to solve this problem of poverty is to let businesses behave like business. In other words, we should encourage businesses to seek out profit. In doing so they will create new jobs. As job opportunities expand, the unemployed workers will find new jobs that will increase their income, resulting in another expansion of production. The expansion will slow as we approach full employment.

1c. John would point out that Gloria's position lacked some realism. When high unemployment exists as it did throughout the late 1970s and early 1980s, an employer is unlikely to search for workers in a ghetto, especially when better-trained and more work-oriented people are also looking for work. Gloria's answer may make sense when the economy is close to full employment, but not when significant unemployment exists.

Stuart's argument is also weak, because businesses are going to do whatever they can to hire skilled workers rather than training new ones. Even if government supervises the training, businesses are more likely to hire the most trainable, not the least trainable. This approach looks at the problem from the tip of the iceberg instead of from the bottom.

John claims that we need to start with the most basic education, and eventually the workers will respond productively. Unfortunately, John's approach is very long-term and may take a generation or more to be effective. His program is also very costly.

Gloria's argument has merit in a free enterprise economy, but many sections of our economy possess various degrees of market power. When these conditions exist, it is almost impossible to prevent some companies from gaining more property and more economic freedom while other businesses keep doing worse.

Stuart's position suffers from the assumption that businesses will undertake the problem of training the unemployed and poor with some sense of enthusiasm. Most companies will not have this enthusiasm.

If we desire a society that possesses a higher degree of equity, then some form of John's answer makes sense, because he wishes to improve the workers' opportunity to work. If, however, we emphasize economic freedom for the sellers, then workers must accept the individual responsibility to locate jobs and learn the skills necessary to get jobs. When events like those in Youngstown occur, workers are at a significant disadvantage in finding work and learning new job skills.

ANSWERS TO SELF-TEST

1. Economic freedom is an abstract concept that does not have a great deal of meaning until we distinguish whose freedom we are discussing. A business wants to be free to earn profits and to find ways to protect

those profits. New companies want to be free to enter profitable markets but often find that entry difficult because of actions of existing companies. Buyers want freedom to choose from a wide range of products so that they can be confident that the products they purchase will be the best quality for a given price.

If all the characteristics of perfect competition existed, these freedoms would tend to balance one another. In other words, no one type of freedom would dominate another. But when *all* the competitive characteristics do not exist, imperfect competition exists. Under these conditions, people who exercise economic freedom for sellers are likely to acquire property, which will enhance their ability to earn more income. If property owners are successful in using their property to earn more income, then it is likely that some form of market power will evolve. As some firms gain market power, economic freedom for buyers will tend to decrease.

2. Eradicating poverty requires the use of scarce resources. If scarcity did not exist, we could achieve equity without hindering any of the other goals. But since resources are scarce, governments must tax income earners if it wishes to increase economic opportunities for the poor. The tax will be progressive and, thus, reduce the economic freedom of those who must pay taxes. In other words, those who have acquired property and earn more than the average level of income will share some of their income with the less fortunate.

3. As the answer to question 1 stated, this statement is meaningful if all the competitive characteristics are operable. Typically, some forms of imperfect competition are more likely to exist within our economy. Under imperfect competition, some businesses will gain market power that they will use to keep new companies from entering a market. When market power exists, some companies are likely to dominate some markets by decreasing output and increasing price.

4. When sellers use computers to increase the productivity of the business, the productivity and income of workers generally increases. The workers who receive increased incomes will experience an increase in economic freedom. Unfortunately, there is a negative side to this increase in productivity. When a company increases its use of computers, it is likely to need fewer workers, especially those workers who perform very repetitive tasks. If these workers lose their jobs, they lose their freedom to participate in economic activities. Economic freedom for these workers (buyers) is significantly reduced, especially if they cannot find alternative employment.

5. The events in Youngstown provide a dramatic example of how emphasis upon economic freedom can have a relatively devastating effect upon a community. When several major steel mills shut down, 10,000 steel workers lost their jobs, and thousands of others suffered economic losses because the steel workers had very little money to spend. These consequences occurred because steel companies were the dominant employers in the area. When they quit producing, the entire

community felt the impact. If smaller companies had gone bankrupt and a few hundred people has lost their jobs, the impact on the community would have been much less. The unemployed would most likely have been able to get jobs on their own. But because the impact was so great, individuals were much less likely to find jobs on their own. Government assistance seemed necessary.

6. Before we can begin to evaluate this statement we need to agree on the definition of economic freedom. Throughout the text we have defined freedom as the freedom of sellers to strive for economic profit. It is within this context that advocates of economic freedom argue that companies do have the freedom to close plants when those plants are no longer as efficient as other plants within the company. Yet advocates of equity argue that this freedom to close plants also causes a significant reduction in equity, because entire communities can lose their economic base. Restrictions on a company's ability to relocate provide opportunities for workers and other people in the community to help improve the efficiency of the company or to have some time to search for alternative sources of income if the plant closing is inevitable.

   Restricting the closing of plants is only one way to attempt to achieve equity. Companies could be free to close plants whenever the company officials thought it appropriate. Government may then provide assistance to workers to find new jobs, learn new skills, or relocate. Government may subsidize the local area to make it more economically attractive. The purpose of these subsidies would be to entice the old businesses to stay open and to attract new businesses to the area. The intent is to keep enough businesses in the area to provide workers with a decent opportunity to earn income.

7. The spirit of individualism is very high in the United States. Both sellers and buyers express a desire to make choices without governmental intervention. Although this desire often changes when a specific problem occurs (as in Youngstown, for example), government is often considered to be an intruder into our lives rather than an agency that can assist us. This attitude is one reason a cooperative venture like the one described in Sweden would be difficult to implement in the United States.

   Another difficulty is the size and diversity of the United States. Because of its size and diversity, planning and coordination within the United States is a more complex process than in a country such as Sweden. Yet that very size and diversity could be an asset in helping workers find new sources of income.

Index